הגדה של פסח

Published by

Mesorah Publications, ltd

FIRST EDITION
First Impression ... February, 1977
Second Impression ... March, 1977
Third Impression ... March, 1977
SECOND EDITION
First Impression ... January, 1978
Second Impression ... January, 1979
THIRD EDITION
First Impression ... January, 1980
Second Impression ... March, 1980
Third Impression ... January, 1981
Fourth Impression ... November, 1981
Fifth Impression ... December, 1982
Sixth Impression ... January, 1984
Seventh Impression ... January, 1985
Eighth Impression ... January, 1986
Ninth Impression ... October, 1986

Published and Distributed by
MESORAH PUBLICATIONS, Ltd.
Brooklyn, New York 11223

Distributed in Israel by
MESORAH MAFITZIM / J. GROSSMAN
Rechov Harav Uziel 117
Jerusalem, Israel

Distributed in Europe by
J. LEHMANN HEBREW BOOKSELLERS
20 Cambridge Terrace / Gateshead
Tyne and Wear / England NE8 1RP

THE ARTSCROLL MESORAH SERIES®
THE HAGGADAH
© *Copyright 1977, 1978, 1979, 1980, 1981, 1982, 1986*
by MESORAH PUBLICATIONS, Ltd.
1969 Coney Island Avenue / Brooklyn, N.Y. 11223 / (718) 339-1700
ALL RIGHTS RESERVED.

ISBN
0-89906-150-8 (hard cover)
0-89906-151-6 (paperback)

Typography by CompuScribe at ArtScroll Studios, Ltd.
1969 Coney Island Avenue / Brooklyn, N.Y. 11223 / (718) 339-1700

Printed in the USA by Moriah Offset
Bound by Sefercraft, Inc., Brooklyn, N.Y.

ישיבת
לב

"... אל תקרא חרות אלא חירות, שאין לך בן חורין
אלא מי שעוסק בתלמוד תורה." (אבות פ"ו מ"ב)

ברגשי כבוד, הוקרה והודיה
מגישה ישיבת ל"ב את ההגדה הזאת
לראש הישיבה ומנהלה המסור,
המחנך הדגול והמחונן בכשרונות

ה"ה הרב שמחה צבי פרידמן שליט"א

לרגל מלאת לו שלשים שנה
של פעילות פוריה בשדה החינוך התורני,
אשר כאוד מוצל מאש השואה האיומה,
בחר בחירות האמתית
להקדיש את ימי חייו במסירות נאמנה
לחנך ולהעמיד מאות תלמידים
על דרכי התורה ויראת שמים.

With reverence, affection, and gratitude,
this Haggadah is dedicated to

Rabbi Dr. Armin H. Friedman

*in celebration of thirty years of inspired leadership
of the*

HEBREW ACADEMY OF LONG BEACH

*Having witnessed the dark flames of enslavement and death,
he brought with his freedom a vision
to build a generation of Torah-proud children.
He leads by example, and inspires through Torah.
May his vision continue to shine brightly.*

RABBI J. KAMENETZKY

38 SADDLE RIVER RD.

MONSEY, NEW YORK 10952

יעקב קאמענצקי

מאנסי, נוא יארק

כבוד ידי״ע הרב הגדול בתורה ויראת ד׳ טהורה מוה״ר יוסף הלוי נ״י עליאש שלי׳ וברכת כ״ט.

ע״ד שאלתו אם כדאי להוציא הגדה לסדר לילי פסחים הן בדבר מנהגי הסדר ודיניו והן לעשות ביאור מחודש לדברי בעל ההגדה. הנה לפי דעתי ראוי ונכון הוא למי שביכלתו לעשות זה, כי מכיון שמצינו שהתורה סידרה נוסחת ההגדה לכל בן ובן בפני עצמו כדי שדברי אב יפעלו על הבן א״כ ודאי הוא שבכל דור ודור אנו חייבין לפרש ולבאר דברי בעל ההגדה לפי רוח הדור והשגתו. ולפי דעתי כ״י הוא הנהו המוכשר והמתאים לעשות זה. שהרי מי כמוהו הנושא והנותן עם בני הנעורים והיודע ומכיר הלך רוחם. ומה שנוגע למנהגי הלילה הזה, ישנה נחיצות גדלה להתעסק בזה, כי בזמננו שחלק גדול מעמנו, בעוה״ר, אין לו מסורת אבות, גם מסורת מנהגי ישראל של כל מדינה ומדינה בטלו אחרי שבעוה״ר רוב יישובי אחב״י באירופה נעקרו ממקומותיהם ובטלו קהלות הקודש. ובחסדי השי״ת נתיסדו פה קהלות חדשות ע״י הנפזרים שנתקבצו וצריכים אנו מחדש ליסד מנהגינו, מנהגי בית ישראל שהן הן שעמדו לנו בגלותנו ולהתקיים כגוי מיוחד ומצוין. והנה מנהגי בתי כנסיות, ב״ה שהשאיר לנו לפליטה בני תורה, והם הם הקובעים סדרי ביהכ״נ והצבור נשמע לדבריהם, ובכן נקבעו ונתחזקו סדרי בתי כנסיות. אבל מנהגים לילי פסח שכל יחיד ויחיד צריך להתנהג בביתו, מה נחוץ מאד לסדרם ע״י הגדה כזו. ומה טוב יעשה בעמיו אם ע״י ,,הגדתו״ ימצא דרך סלולה בזה. וד׳ יהיה בעזרו.

הכותב וחותם בידידות נאמנה ביום ה׳ ב׳ טבת תשל״ז.

[signature]

הערה: אחרי רואי את ההגדה בשלמותה עברתי על כל הדברים התלויים בהלכה ובדרך כלל נסתדר הכל ע״פ הכרעת הפוסקים האחרונים, ובמקום שישנם חילוקי דעות קבע בפנים כהרוב, ומ״מ לא השמיט לגמרי דעת המיעוט והביאם באותיות זעירות או מתחת לקו, ומי שימצא בדעה זו מנהג אבותיו יתנהג כפי קבלת אבותיו.

[signature]

Letter of Approbation

מאת הגאון מהור״ר שמעון שוואב שליט״א

רב דקהילתנו קהל עדת ישורון, נוא יארק

ב״ה

RABBI SIMON SCHWAB
736 WEST 186TH STREET
NEW YORK, N. Y. 10033
—
STUDY: 923-5936
RES: 927-0498

שמעון שוואב

רב דק״ק

קהל עדת ישרון

נוא־יארק, נ. י.

The new Haggodo is a masterful compilation of old and new פירושים and דינים ומנהגים, beautifully executed by the Principal of our Rika Breuer Seminary and Samson Raphael Hirsch Beth Jacob School for Girls, Rabbi Joseph Elias.

It is a veritable treasure house of lofty ideas and in-depth research skillfully assembled with scholarly reverence and erudition from which many may draw inspiration and an enhancement of their knowledge and understanding of the very essentials of our אמונה which is based on יציאת מצרים.

The author has spared no effort to present us not only with a comprehensive and informative companion for the nights of the Seder, but with a valuable Sefer which should be a resourceful addition to any Torah library for all-year-round study and enjoyment.

Simon Schwab

מכתב ברכה וחזוק
מאת הגאון מהור"ר מרדכי גיפטר שליט"א
ראש ישיבת טלז

מרדכי גיפטער
ישיבת טלז
RABBI MORDECAI GIFTER
28570 NUTWOOD LANE
WICKLIFFE, OHIO 44092

בע"ה — ב' יתרו, תשל"ז

מע"כ ידידי, מגדולי החינוך התורני באמריקא, הרב יוסף עליאש, שליט"א

שלום וברכה נצח!

אחדשה"ט באהבה ויקר,

קבלתי עלי ההגהה מהגדת פסח בתרגום לשפה המדוברת בצירוף ביאורו של ידידי. לדאבוני מכיון שהנהו אץ עלי מפאת דוחק הזמן לא אוכל להפנות ולעיין בדברים אף מקופיא, אבל הרי חזקה על חבר שאינו מוציא מתחת ידו דבר שאינו מתוקן. ובהיות שיסוד מצות ההגדה ללמד בישראל יסודות הדת והאמונה במציאות הבורא ית' אדון כל והשגחתו הפרטית על עמו הנבחר. וידוע הוא ידידי כאומן מומחה בשטח החנוך התורני בטח השקיע מיטב כחותיו בביאור ותרגום ההגדה למשוך לב אלה הרחוקים משפת המקור להגיעם לאותה רוממות רוח ונפש של סדר של פסח.

תשמש עבודתו זו עוד טבעת בשלשלת הזהב של המפעל הקדוש של ארטסקרול להביא מקורות האמת לנבוכי הדור השוגים ומושפעים מהשקר, למען הגיע לאותו היעוד של ,,ומלאה הארץ דעה את ה' כמים לים מכסים.''

מצרף אני הערות אחדות, שאולי יהיו לו לתועלת בעבודתו.

ידידו, דושה"ט באהבה

Approbation   [x]

Preface

The Haggadah is one of the most treasured possessions of our people. Uncounted commentaries have been written through the generations. The present volume does not seek to offer novel interpretations; nor does it seek to provide an exhaustive sampling of what has been written on the Haggadah up to now. Yet neither is it meant to be a random collection of explanations on the Haggadah. It aims to present the Seder as a central experience in the life of the Jew, and to aid the reader in sharing this experience.

It goes without saying that this volume represents a very imperfect effort in the direction of its objective. I am deeply conscious of my inadequacy in pursuing such a lofty goal. I pray to הקב״ה that nothing that I have written shall be a source of error or misunderstanding, whether in connection with the interpretation of the Haggadah or the halachic directions included. The readers of this volume are urged to bring to my attention any corrections or suggestions that they may have.

In undertaking such an ambitious project as this Haggadah at all, I have been moved by the hope that — rather than provide a definitive work — this volume will suggest to the reader how to approach the observance of the Seder, and encourage him to strike out on his own, seek out his own sources, and find his own way to unlock the treasures of the spirit that the night of Pesach holds in store.

ACKNOWLEDGEMENTS

That I was able at all to undertake the writing of this Haggadah is, of course, due to all those who have guided and inspired me on my way through life. First and foremost I must pay humble tribute to my dear father אאמו״ר החבר ר׳ מרדכי בר׳ מאיר הלוי שליט״א, whose love of Torah and perseverance in its pursuit were an inspiration to me from my very earliest years. May we be privileged to have him and his cherished עזר כנגדו שת׳ at the head of our family for many, many more years, עמו״ש.

There pass before my mind's eye all those from whom I was privileged to learn Torah; my debt to them is of course infinite, and I pray that what they have given me shall bear fruit as they wanted it. At the writing of this

Haggadah, as in every aspect of my life for the last decades, I had the privilege of the inestimable encouragement and guidance of the Rosh Yeshiva of Torah Vodaas, מרן הגאון מהור״ר יעקב קאמענצקי שליט״א. Of him it can truly be said in the fullest sense that עיני כל ישראל נשואות אליו, our generation needs his leadership, and it is our fervent prayer that we shall be able to look to it for many years to come, עמו״ש.

I am deeply grateful to Khal Adas Jeshurun and its educational institutions, under the inspired leadership of הרבנים הגאונים RABBI DR. JOSEPH BREUER, שליט״א and RABBI SIMON SCHWAB שליט״א: may they continue their blessed work for Klall Yisroel for many years indeed. They have built a true center of Torah; with their warm encouragement and guidance, it has been a privilege for me to work there with my students and, in the process, to be profoundly enriched myself. Next to the Sedarim in the circle of my family, it was my annual Haggadah class in the Rika Breuer Teachers Seminary that led to the writing of this Haggadah.

Even so, it would not have taken form if not for the pioneering work of RABBI MEIR ZLOTOWITZ, and his inspired and dedicated undertaking in creating the ArtScroll series of publications להגדיל תורה ולהאדירה. His work has already acquired a firm place in the minds and hearts of the Jewish community, and its immense value need not be belabored. However, my deep gratitude is due to him for his invaluable advice in the preparation of this Haggadah; his resolute determination to make it the very best that his efforts could produce; and for his infinite patience in the face of an unduly long drawn out undertaking.

The team at ArtScroll put me in their debt by their devoted efforts to turn his vision into concrete form. Above all, tribute is due to REB SHEAH BRANDER, who so faithfully and totally dedicates his great artistry to the service of Torah.

In producing this volume, I was aided immeasurably at every step by RABBI DAVID COHEN, RABBI NOSSON SCHERMAN, and RABBI NISSON WOLPIN. I owe them profound gratitude. Their advice and assistance, most generously given, are in large measure responsible for the best features of the present undertaking. For its imperfections, needless to say, I must take full responsibility.

Many others, members of my family, devoted friends and students, have helped in the making of this Haggadah. Thus, MRS. REVA JUNI assisted in the verification of sources. Others read parts of the manuscript and greatly helped me by their comments and suggestions. To all of them, I am deeply grateful.

THE PATTERN OF THE HAGGADAH

The design of this Haggadah involved, in the first place, the preparation of an accurate Hebrew text (with major text variants indicated, at least in the commentary) and a readable English translation (for which I drew on a number of earlier English renderings).

Detailed directions for conducting the Seder have been included; where the commentary provides additional halachic background for any particular directive, an asterisk (*) has been inserted in the directions at the appropriate place. There is also a special chapter, 'Preparing for Pesach', which deals with the removal of Chametz and the preparation of the Seder.

There exist many differences in Seder custom and observance. Such differences are indicated in the directions or the commentary. Wherever general usage favors one particular practice, this has been made clear; in a few instances, however, no such definite direction could be given. In any case, it is important for anybody conducting a Seder to follow the tradition of his family, or place of origin, if he is familiar with it.

Like the other volumes in the Artscroll series, the Haggadah starts with an Overview. It aims to introduce the basic structure and central ideas of the Seder, as interpreted by the Talmudic and Rabbinic sources. The commentary traces these ideas through the text of the Haggadah and elaborates on them. Certain parts of the commentary that were deemed of more technical complexity and specialized interest were printed in smaller type, to set them off from the main body of the commentary.

It was extremely difficult to decide what to include in this Haggadah of the extraordinary wealth of material available; occasionally it was necessary to choose between contradictory views on a certain point. I have done so with the greatest diffidence, guided by the overall objective of this Haggadah to provide a unified continuous interpretation of the Seder.

Of course, in quoting material from a very large number of works, ideas inevitably were condensed, highlights emphasized, and nuances missed. I have tried to do justice to the material quoted; it is my sincere hope that I have not altogether failed in this respect. I was also faced with the difficulty that many explanations are quoted in many different works, often with slight differences of emphasis; to trace the original source (if indeed there was one) would have been an impossible undertaking.

This factor, alone, made a meticulous detailed citing of sources very difficult; it would also have involved more details than the ordinary user requires.Except for the Biblical and Talmudic sources, where the exact references are given I have therefore limited myself to giving the name of the authority, or the work, in whose name material is cited. A bibliographical list at the end of the volume will help the interested reader in further pursuing the source of the material (where ideas have their source in word-of-mouth transmission, a box (□) was put next to the name of the person quoted).

A final word about transliteration. The Haggadah follows the general ArtScroll practice of rendering consonants according to the Ashkenazic pronunciation, and vowels according to the modern Sefardic pronunciation; the only exception were words rendered differently in general usage (for instance, Shabbos rather than Shabbas). The ineffable name of God, in four letters, is always rendered as 'HASHEM'; in other places, the term used is 'God.'

I would like to conclude with thanks to הקב״ה that He granted me the privilege to dwell in the tents of Torah. It is my fervent prayer that I should be able to continue to devote myself to the learning and teaching of Torah; that, together with my dear wife שת׳, who has stood by my side as a true עקרת הבית, I should continue to have the joy of seeing my own children and grandchildren follow in this path; and, together with all of Klall Yisrael, we should be vouchsafed to see the coming of Mashiach, speedily in our days.

Joseph Elias

יום ב׳ לפ׳ משפטים
כ״ו שבט תשל״ז

Preface to Second Edition

This new edition of this Artscroll Haggadah is marked by a large number of changes. However, except for the inclusion of an Index of Topics, the changes are generally minor in nature, such as the correction of typographical errors, clarification of language or ideas, and the addition of further source references. Thus the basic content of this volume has remained unchanged.

Needless to say, for this basic content I am totally indebted to all those who have written on the Haggadah heretofore — from our earliest giants of Torah to the latest commentators — those whose names are mentioned in this Haggadah as well as those who are not specifically quoted. At the same time I am most thankful to all the users of the Haggadah who have sent me their comments and suggestions. They have inspired many of the changes that have been made, and have thereby helped to make it a better and more useful work.

Above all, I am deeply grateful to הקב״ה for letting me see the appearance of a second edition so soon after the initial publication of this Haggadah. Apparently it has met a need that existed — and it is my hope and prayer that it will continue to prove of service and, in some measure, contribute to a better understanding and observance of Pesach.

Joseph Elias

ה׳ לפ׳ חיי שרה
כ״ב חשון תשל״ח

לזכר נשמות
אמי מורתי מרת בריינדל בת ר׳ משה יצחק הכהן הי״ד
אחותי היקרה מרת מרים ע״ה
בת אאמו״ר החבר ר׳ מרדכי הלוי שליט״א

Index of Topics

Page numbers referring the reader to the text of the Haggadah are in bold.

Abraham 36, 47, 51, 68, 69, 92-100, 117, 139, 162, 202, 206;

Afikoman eating of 162; hiding, 64; in place of *Pesach* sacrifice, 23, 163; symbol of liberation, 34; see also *Pesach sacrifice;*

Anti-semitism 100, 107, 178;

Birchas Hamazon 164; explanation; 166-174;

Bondage, Egyptian foreshadowed all later exiles, 20 (see also *Exiles*); 97, 148; physical and spiritual, 31-32; duty to talk about and appreciate it, 30, 73 91, 94-5; cleansed us from human weaknesses 31, 91-5, 146; by its severity led to our growth and liberation, 73, 95,107-8, 113, 118, 143; made us appreciate our liberation and God's power, 30, 73, 91; had its roots in earliest human history, 91-95; had to be in Egypt, 94 (see also *Egypt*);role of Laban, 103; of Joseph, 104; limited in time, 95-97; stages, 36, 96-97, 106-107, 110-114, 118; Jews preserved identity, 105-106, but declined spiritually, 106-107, 124-5; were kind to each other, 106; finally merited liberation, 115-116, 117, 118; ended by God Himself, 74-75, 119-122 (see also *Exodus*); Levites exempted, 77, 108, 110-111, 113;

Candle-lighting 52;

Chametz symbol of evil inclination, 23, 38, 43; unusual stringency in removal, 29; removal before Pesach, 38-40; search and disposal, 42-45; see also *Matzah;*

Charoses preparation, 49, dipping of *Maror*, 159, of *Korech*, 161;

Children Egyptians tried to destroy them, 82, 117, 118; basis of national continuity, 29, 82; father-child relationship reflects liberation, 27, is basis of *Maggid*, 27, 29, 78; should be kept awake, 46, 56, 64, 70, 76; should ask 70-71, get answer, 73, according to their nature, 80-88, 140;

Circumcision 23, 109, 110, 141, 167, 177, 216;

Commandments *Seder* built around *Pesach, Matzah, Maror*, 22, 84; must be explained, (*Pesach, Matzah, Maror*) 140-141; duty of talking about Exodus fulfilled by talking about them, 77, 84; Exodus was in merit of commandments, 23, 86, 90; reformers object to them, 85, 88;

Counting of Omer 212;

Creation paralleled by Exodus, 28, 68, 131;

Egypt corrupt civilization, 94, 106; punishment, 73, 98-99, 128-131; not to rejoice over punishment, 127, 144; Jacob's fear to go to Egypt, 103-104; caused Revelation of God, 121;

Elijah's Cup 36, 149, 174, 177;

Erev Pesach fast of firstborn, *Siyum*, prohibition of work and *Matzah*, baking of *Matzah*, 44-45; preparation of *Seder*, 46-52; on *Shabbos*, 44, 46, 48, 49, 60-61, 155;

Eruv Chatzeros, 45; *Tavshilin*, 45-46;

Exiles,later 149; all rooted in Egyptian exile, 20, 97, 148; follow Egyptian pattern, 98, 167; none equal to Egypt, 75; causes, 68, 93-94, 202; physical and spiritual dangers, 69, 101, 106; assimilation, oppression, and survival, 100, 107-108;

Exodus revelation of God's power, 25-27, 73, 120; birth of Jewish people, 27-30, 73; source of special Jewish obligations, 30; grew out of bondage, 73, 94-98, 107-8, 116-8(see also *Bondage, Egyptian*); physical and spiritual, 31-32, 99, 137, 155; by God Himself, 74-5, 119-122; no preparation by Jews, 74, 121, 144; permanent effect, 74-75; but not complete, 33-4, 97, 146; root of all later redemptions, 20, 34, 75, 84-

5, 125, 146, 177 (see also *Redemptions*), and mentioned in Messianic times, 80; beyond human comprehension, 76; kindness to Jews, punishment for Egyptians, 73, 99, 135; length , 96-97, 109, 116; stages and goals, 36, 123-5, 128, 137, 139; made possible by Jews keeping identity, unity, 106; due to merit of Patriachs, prayer, circumcision and *Pesach* sacrifice, Divine mercy 23, 109, 116-7; for sake of Divine plan, 116, to assure Jewish survival, 97, 118; because of *Pesach, Matzah, Maror*, 86, 88, 216; not experienced by sinners, 86, 88; to be our own personal experience, 146-148;

Family Pharaoh sought to disrupt it, 27, 82, 117; Exodus and *Seder* celebrated in family circle, 27, 29, 78, 82, 117; see also *Children;*

Festivals dependent on Jews, 56; cycle starts in Nissan, 28; significance, 19, 58-60, 154; to be reliving of historical experience, 19-20; see also *Pesach festival;*

Four Cups reflect Egyptian and Messianic redemption, 25; other explanations, 35-36, 50, 57, 71, 83, 149, 176; amount, 51, 199; red wine, 51; pouring for each other, 57; blessings over cups, 61-62; why not included in child's questions, 72; 1st cup is drunk, 60; 2nd cup is poured, 70, drunk, 154; 3rd cup is poured, 164, drunk, 174; 4th cup is poured, 174, drunk, 198, 210; spilling from cup, 127;

God known through fathers, 115; revealed through Exodus, 25-27, 74-5, 120, 123-5, 131, 152; had to redeem us, 74-5, 119-121; praise, 76, 81, 149, 179, 211;

Haggadah see *Maggid;*

Hallel recited **150, 178;** explanation, 149-152, 178-188; divided, 33-34, 151, 176, 178; said at night, 72, 151; no blessing, 151; introduction, 176; expression of our personal experience, 75, 148, 151; was recited in Egypt, 150-1; and future redemption, 178;

Jewish People need for a chosen people, 91-2; its task, 116; prepared by Patriachs, 92-93, 96, and through Egyptian bondage, 93-98; created through Exodus, 27-30, 131; had no hand in Exodus, 74; supernatural origin, 28, 30, 92, 100; indestructible, 29, 100; compared to stars, 105; started as 70 souls, 104-5; united by bond with God, 38, 105; anti-semitism, 100, 178;

Joseph and Exodus, 32, 51, 94, 104, 111; and Pharaoh, 112-113;

Karaites 102;

Karpas dipped and eaten, **62;** explanation, blessings, 63; which vegetables, 50; preparation of salt water, 50;

Kiddush 56; no blessing שֶׁעֲשָׂה נִסִים, 154: *Havdalah,* 60-61;

Kittel worn at *Seder,* 51-52;

Korech *Matzah* and *Maror* together, **160;**

Laban 101, 103;

Maggid 64-154; central to *Seder,* 24; because *Pesach* is birthday of Jewish people, 28; structure and history, 65-66, 69, 95, 151, 198; to be told over *Matzah,* when *Pesach, Matzah, Maror* before us, 24, 66-7, 88-90, 140; question and answer, 27, 70; starts with bondage, 30, 73, 91; ends with praise, 92, 151; and blessing, 153-4; requires discussion of commandments, 140-141 (see also *Commandments);* describes spiritual and physical liberation, 32, 90-1, 155; obligation, 64, 76, 78-9, 89; different from daily recall of Exodus, 65; duty to go beyond it, 76-8; even for great men, 76-77; improves person, 77; blessing, 65, 81; central place of *Midrash,* 102;

Mah Nishtanah 70; selection of questions, 72; asks about bondage and freedom, 31, 72;

Maror eating **158;** dipped in Charoses, 49, 159; horseradish and lettuce, 48; amount, 48; eating with *Matzah (Korech),* **160;** blessing, 63, 158-9; obligation dependent on Pesach sacrifice, 23, 142; expression of suffering 23, 142, 146; and liberation, 143;

Matzah eating **156;** amount, 47, 158; blessing, 156; dipping in salt?, 159; breaking *Yachatz,*

62, and its explanation, 47, 63-4; eating with *Maror (Korech),* **160;** three needed, 47, 64; forbidden on *Erev Pesach,* 44; baking on *Erev Pesach,* 45; symbol of purity, 23, 39, 142, 145-6; minutely different from *Chametz,* 38 (see *Chametz);* making up for Adam's sin, 91; food of slavery as well as liberation, 23, 64, 67, 95, 144-5; 'get *Matzah* in hurry,' 46, 64, 70, 76;

'**Money for Wheat'** 68;

Moses not mentioned, 74; his birth, 112; role at Exodus, 121, 124, 126, 133; and Joseph's coffin, 99; his reward, 74;

Nissan special month, 88; time of renewal, 20; birthdate of Jewish people, 28; future redemption, 177;

Nirtzah 200;

Patriarchs and Matriarchs 47, 68, 71, 92-107, 109, 110, 116, 117, 120, 122, 202, 216; see also *Abraham;*

Pesach festival recurrent time of redemption, 19-20, 176(see *Redemptions);* as personal experience, 18-20, 77, 146-8; meaning of names, 24, 59; dedicated to *Chesed,* 68; centered on family, 27, 29, 78; marks birthday of Jewish people, is source of laws of conversion, 29; preparation for, 38-9; eight days, 127-128;

Pesach sacrifice 23, 124; account of offering recited on *Erev Pesach,* 45; must be eaten last, 84, 163; to test Jews, 109; central role, 141-3; different from Gentile sacrifices, 89; non-Jew excluded from it, 28;

Preparation for Pesach 37-52, 88, 90, 201; reading *Haggadah* on *Shabbos Hagadol,* 90;

Reclining reason, 51; when, 51, 63, 161; exemptions, 65, 72; on left side only, 61; during Haggadah recitation? 66;

Redemptions, later all rooted in Exodus, 20, 34, 75, 84-5, 125, 148, 176-7; compared to Exodus, 97-8 204; physical and spiritual, 69; predicted in Covenant between the Portions, 100; how brought about, 68, 94, 97, 117, 177, 178; *Seder* night set aside for them, 20, 176-7, 201, 205, 220; second part of *Seder* devoted to them, 34, 151, 176; faith in future redemption, 78-79, 87, 176-7;

Revelation at Sinai 19, 24, 30, 32, 37, 75, 99, 100, 125, 136, 138, 189, 216;

Seder meaning of name, 21, 200; definite pattern, 21, 53, 140; key words, 22, 53-5; preparation for future redemption, 22, 33, 68, 148; *Seder* night set aside for redemption, 20, 176-7, 201, 220; stay up all night, 220; reenactment and experiencing of Exodus, 21, 64, 77, 146-8; symbolizes bondage and freedom, 30, 72-3; *Haggadah* central to *Seder,* 24, 140; and commandments, 22-3, 84, 90, 140, 146; invite guests, 68, 166; start promptly after nightfall, 36, 56-7; meal has sanctity, 151, 162; eat egg, 162, no roast, 161;

Seder plate preparation, 46-50; order of items on plate, 50;

Shabbos independent of Jewish people, 56; significance, 58-9; every day is preparation for *Shabbos,* 37; *Seder* on, 50, 51, 57-58; see also *Erev Pesach;*

Shemurah Matzah 38, 47, 163;

Splitting of Sea 99, 119, 120, 124, 127, 128, 133-6, 138, 190;

Temple 45, 92, 99, 136, 137, 139, 149, 211-2;

Ten Commandments and Exodus, 125; and ten plagues, 131;

Ten Plagues 98, 122-136, 149;

Tisha B'Av 68, 70-71, 97, 162;

Washing hands before *Karpas,* **62;** before *Matzah,* **156;**

Women role in Exodus, 71, 114; obligations at *Seder,* 51, 65, 178;

Yachatz see *Matzah*

An Overview
The Meaning of the Seder

Amidst the unspeakable horrors of Nazi death camps, Jews risked all chance of survival for a brief and pitiful *Seder*. In homes far adrift from traditional Jewish life, families still gather on *Pesach* night in response to some deep inarticulate yearning. *The observance of Pesach* — and, in particular, of the *Seder* — is rooted in the uttermost depths of the Jewish heart.

The Seder is rooted in the uttermost depths of the Jewish heart.

Why? What is the meaning of the *Seder*? Can it be meant merely to commemorate events from the dawn of our history, through a burdensome array of prayers and Biblical texts, rituals and customs? That is how the *Seder* is usually understood, even while its *Haggadah* is recited and its wine drunk. Yet this is a gross misconception.

To Experience Redemption

בכל דור ודור חייב אדם לראות את עצמו כאילו
הוא יצא ממצרים (הגדה)

'In every generation one is obliged to see himself as though he himself had actually gone forth from Egypt.' (Haggadah)

Far from a commemoration of ancient events, *Pesach* night is meant to be a profound personal experience. It invites and, indeed, requires us to become part of an event of the utmost significance

for us, for our people, and for mankind as a whole, and by so doing to help shape the very destiny of the world we live in. But how is it possible for us tonight to participate in an event that took place 3,000 years ago?

How is it possible for us tonight to participate in an event that took place 3,000 years ago?

The Torah calls our sacred days מוֹעֲדִים, days of encounter with God. Each of our holy days carries a Divine message, based on its historical significance; thus *Pesach* conveys the message of our liberation from Egypt (*Rabbi S.R. Hirsch*). But these messages do not come to us from the distant past — rather, we are brought face to face with the historic event that gave rise to the holiday.

This is difficult for us to understand, for we are used to considering time as stretching out in a long line from a dim past, gone forever, to an unforseeable future that we cannot anticipate; therefore the events of יְצִיאַת מִצְרַיִם, the Exodus from Egypt, seem to us to lie far back in our history. In reality, however, as the days and seasons pass us by, we are not moving ahead in a straight line, leaving the past behind us. We are moving in a circle or, better, a spiral — and thus, year after year, we always again pass through the same seasons, past the same historical moments of encounter with God that our fathers experienced (*Michtav M'Eliyahu*). So it is that when we thank God for the miracles that shaped our history, we do not speak of great events of *those* days, but בַּיָּמִים הָהֵם בַּזְּמַן הַזֶּה, in those days but *at this time* — we are still participants today.

Year after year, we always again pass through the same seasons, past the same historical moments of encounter with God that our fathers experienced.

Thus, when Jews study the entire night of *Shavuos*, they do not merely commemorate God's giving of the law at Sinai; they prepare for an annual קַבָּלַת הַתּוֹרָה, receiving of God's revelation. When they sit on the floor on *Tisha b'Av*, they become part of a relived tragedy. And when they kindle the *Chanukah menorah*, they usher in a season of sacred light. As Rabbi Moshe Chayim Luzatto puts it,

> 'Any achievement that was attained, any great light that radiated at a certain time — when that time comes around again, the radiance of that light will

shine again and the fruits of that achievement will be received, for whoever is there to receive them.'

(Derech Hashem)

Through the cycle of the year we can seek to relive the great happenings of our history and — entering into their spirit — draw from them strength.

Each season of our year thus contains its unique emanations of holiness; through the cycle of the year we can seek to relive the great happenings of our history and — entering into their spirit — draw from them strength and inspiration for the future (*Sfas Emes;* see Overview to ArtScroll edition of *Megillas Eichah*.)

First and foremost, however, in this yearly cycle is *Pesach,* זְמַן חֵרוּתֵנוּ, the season of our freedom. The Brisker Rav used to say that *Nissan* did not become the season of freedom because the events of *Pesach* fell into it, but these events happened in *Nissan* because it was the time Divinely ordained for the manifestation of freedom. This phenomenon extends beyond the spiritual: during *Nissan,* nature undergoes renewal, throwing off the chains of winter and bursting out in new bloom. This is the time of our liberation. *'My Beloved called out and said to me: "Arise My love, My fair one, and go forth. For the winter of bondage has passed ..."'* (*Shir Hashirim* 2:10-11).

In Nissan the wellsprings of freedom from slavery, freedom to serve God, opened up long ago in Egypt, and they still run strong every Nissan.

Thus in *Nissan* the wellsprings of freedom from slavery, freedom to serve God, opened up long ago in Egypt, and they still run strong every *Nissan.* The history of Jewish bondage and redemption in Egypt is still very much a part of our living national existence — as our Sages point out, every period of גָּלוּת, exile, in the history of our people was foreshadowed in the Egyptian bondage, and every act of liberation down to the coming of *Mashiach,* has its roots in the ancient redemption that occurred during the perennial season of our freedom.

So we are asked to see ourselves on *Pesach* night as actually partaking in that cataclysmic event by which God took one people from amidst another, demonstrating His mastery of the world and adopting the rescued people as His own. By entering into this experience, and absorbing its lessons, we

help prepare the world for the coming of *Mashiach*, the ultimate revelation of God's glory and His liberation of His people. To achieve this aim, and to relive the past, we sit down — as they did — to the special meal that marks the night of redemption, the *Seder*.

How little we do justice to the challenge of *Pesach* if we merely sit at the *Seder* table perfunctorily reciting the *Haggadah*! The goal of this night is not the recitation of the *Haggadah*, nor is it a scholarly or inspirational comment on this word or that passage. The goal is nothing less than a grasp and a sense of participation in the *Haggadah's* awesome ideas. No wonder the *Shulchan Aruch* stresses that even after completing the *Haggadah*, one should study the laws of *Pesach* and retell the miracles done for our forefathers, until sleep overtakes him.

The goal of this night is not the recitation of the Haggadah ... the goal is nothing less than a grasp and a sense of participation in the Haggadah's awesome ideas.

The Structure of the Seder

יהא כל אדם חרד באימה לקיים מאמר חכמים
שתקנו מצות סדר והגדה; ולא יהא הדבר קל
בעיניו, אף אם כמה דברים יש בסדר שנראה
בעיני האדם שאין קפידה בהם, ... שאין דבר
ריק בהם (מהר״ל)

'Everyone should seek in awe to fulfill the directions of the Sages who arranged the observances of the Seder and the Haggadah. Let nothing appear petty in one's eyes, even if there are many things at the Seder which would appear not to matter ... for there is nothing insignificant among them.'

(Maharal)

The *Seder's* observances and texts down to the last detail — far from having been put together at random — form a very definite pattern, designed to help us re-experience the redemption from Egypt. He the name סֵדֶר שֶׁל פֶּסַח, the *'order'* of Pesach, for the minutiae of the night are part of a definite

Hence, too, a series of keywords, סִמָּנִים (p. 53), marks every stage of the evening, as we are led from the experience of bondage to the joy of freedom. In following this pattern, the *Maharal* stresses, we are actually preparing the design of the coming redemption for, as we have seen, each *Pesach* repeats the experience of the first one and foreshadows each succeeding one until the final, climactic redemption. What, then, are the main elements that make up the structure of the *Seder*?

Pesach, Matzah and Maror

בעבור זה עשה ה' לי — בעבור זה לא אמרתי
אלא בשעה שיש מצה ומרור מונחים לפניך
(הגדה)

'Because of this, HASHEM did for me' —
'Because of this' can only be said when
Matzoh and Maror lie before you.

(Haggadah)

The *Seder* is built around the commandments which marked that first *Pesach* night in Egypt — the *Pesach* sacrifice, *Matzos* and *Maror*.

Now as then, these מִצְוֹת מַעֲשִׂיּוֹת, practical commandments, form the center of *Pesach* observance. It would have been possible to envision a celebration based on only a recital of events; however, הָאָדָם *'A man is molded by his actions,'* rather than by ideas, philosophical נִפְעָל כְּפִי פְּעוּלוֹתָיו, 'a man is molded by his actions,' rather than by ideas, philosophical speculation, and *speculation, and ideology.* ideology *(Sefer Hachinuch)*. For *Pesach* to be a meaningful, impact-laden experience, rather than a mere memorial, it demands concrete action. In turn, it is through his readiness to act that the Jew 'earns' his liberation.

The Sages indeed stressed that our forefathers were redeemed from Egypt in the merit of their faith in God; but they did not mean a faith limited to intellectual knowledge and noble verbalization; faith does not evince a real commitment unless it leads to action

(*Chever Ma'amarim*). In Egypt, the Jews proved their faith by taking a lamb, the deity of their Egyptian masters, and slaughtering it as their *Pesach* offering. They entered into the covenant of circumcision to demonstrate their acceptance of God's overlordship. We, too, must express our faith in action — to prove its authenticity, and to be molded and uplifted by it. Hence, by definition a *Seder* must include the observance of practical commandments.

We, too, must express our faith in action — to prove its authenticity.

Sorrowfully (and this sorrow is expressed in various ways, even on *Pesach* night) we cannot offer a *Pesach* sacrifice, as the symbol of our liberation from our Egyptian masters; but it is represented by the *Afikoman* instead. We do have the *Maror*, which symbolizes the bitterness of our suffering in Egypt — though our eating of the *Maror*, in the absence of a *Pesach* sacrifice, is only a Rabbinic injunction. The fact that the Torah makes the *Mitzvah* of *Maror* dependent on the קָרְבַּן פֶּסַח, the *Pesach* sacrifice, is perhaps meant to teach us that suffering must always be seen in its proper context, as ultimately bringing deliverance.

Finally, we have the *Matzah*, which links exile and redemption. On one hand, it is לֶחֶם עוֹנִי, the bread of poverty, which was eaten in Egypt by slaves who could not aspire to tastier food; and, on the other hand, it became the mark of freedom, because — when the hour of liberation finally struck — the Jews could not even wait long enough to let the dough rise. The characteristic feature of *Matzah* is the absence of שְׂאוֹר, yeast or leaven, which makes the dough rise and taste good, and, therefore, is the symbol of self-assertion and indulgence, the manifestations of the יֵצֶר הָרַע, man's evil inclination itself. As slaves of Pharaoh, the Jews in Egypt had no choice but to do without, and to subordinate themselves; when freedom came, they became worthy of it by accepting God's overlordship in the same spirit of self-abnegation: '*Thus says HASHEM, I remember for you the kindness of your youth, the love of your*

Leaven is the symbol of self-assertion and indulgence.

*bridehood, how you followed me into the desert, a
land that was not sown' (Jeremiah 2:2).*

Telling of the Exodus

ולמען תספר באזני בנך ובן בנך את אשר
התעללתי במצרים . . . וידעתם כי אני ה׳ (שמות
י:ב)

*'So that you will tell in the ears of your son
and your grandson what I wrought in
Egypt . . . and you shall know that I am
HASHEM.'*   *(Shemos 10:2)*

Pesach, Matzah, and Maror, the practical
commandments of the *Seder* are the basis for the
recitation of the *Haggadah*. Our Rabbis point out
that the Biblical description of *Matzah* as לֶחֶם עוֹנִי,
bread of affliction, can also be understood as לֶחֶם
שֶׁעוֹנִין עָלָיו דְּבָרִים הַרְבֵּה, *'the bread over which many
things are said.'* *Matzah* and *Maror* are in front of
us, but before we partake of them, we are called upon
to 'talk' about יְצִיאַת מִצְרַיִם, the Exodus from Egypt.
The very word *Pesach* has been interpreted as פֶּה סָח
'the mouth talks,' to stress the importance of putting
the meaning of this event into words. Just as mere
contemplation of the awesome event is woefully
deficient, action alone will not do; only a combination of deeds with a clear articulation of their meaning will lend majesty to the *Seder* night — if words
without action are not sufficient, as we stressed, action without spelling out its meaning is not good
enough either.

*Only a combination
of deeds with a clear
articulation of their
meaning will lend
majesty to the Seder
night.*

The commandment to tell about the liberation
from Egypt involves the narration of the happenings
in all their miraculous uniqueness. But there have
been other extraordinary happenings in our history,
such as the revelation on Mount Sinai; why have we
not been commanded to talk about them? Very obviously, the Exodus conveys very special lessons that
were overwhelmingly clear to those who witnessed it,
and which, through the *Haggadah*, we must impress

upon ourselves as strongly as though we ourselves had marched triumphantly out of Egypt: the revelation of *God's Kingship*, and our emergence as *God's people*.

The Kingship of God

בגאולה ההיא נגלה לכל ישראל וגלוי לכל
העמים כי לו לבדו הממשלה בשמים ובארץ
(רבנו מנוח)

'Through this redemption it was revealed to all Israel — and became clear to all nations — that to Him alone belongs the kingship over heaven and earth.'

(Rabbeinu Manoach)

Pharaoh, ruler of a highly civilized empire at the height of its power, posed a question which, in various forms, has echoed throughout history: *'Who is HASHEM that I should listen to Him?'* (Shemos 5:2). There have always been men who felt themselves masters of their world. They might tolerate deities whom they created in their own image and manipulated at whim; but they were unable to accept the existence and sovereignty of a Supreme Being, all-knowing and all-powerful, who not only created this world but still directs it in all its aspects. Pharaoh was such a man. The response to his arrogance was the extraordinary miracles that shook his empire to its deepest foundations.

The events of the Exodus were designed to make clear beyond possibility of a doubt, 'I am HASHEM in the "midst" of the earth.' The events and circumstances of the Exodus were designed to make clear beyond possibility of a doubt, to Pharaoh, and to all mankind, that *'I am HASHEM in the "midst" of the earth (Shemos 8:18) — not an abstract Deity in a distant heaven — and 'the earth belongs to me'* (Vayikrah 25:23), to do with it as My Divine will dictates (*Ramban*). Therefore, when giving the Torah at Mount Sinai, God described Himself as the Supreme Being whom the world had come to know through the traumatic events in Egypt

(*Shemos* 20:2). Small wonder, then, that we are commanded to discuss to the fullest the events of the Exodus, to enter into their spirit, and indeed actually to experience them, so to speak. By introducing the world to the knowledge of God, these events became the foundation and prelude to all worthwhile human endeavor.

Many, many generations later, in his famous classic *Kuzari*, Rabbi Yehudah Halevi has the king of the Khazars ask the Rabbi about his beliefs. Paraphrasing the First Commandment, the Rabbi answers that he believes in '*the God of Abraham, Isaac, and Jacob, who led the Jews out of Egypt with signs and miracles ...*' The king reproaches him for ignoring something far greater — that he believes in God Who created heaven and earth, to which the Rabbi replies that such statements would have been nothing more than unprovable speculative assertions; instead, he spoke out of a firm knowledge of God, based on the actual historical experience of the huge multitudes of the Jewish people. This knowledge — that there is one God, master of nature which He created, and of history which He directs — was gained at long last even by Pharaoh and his people, from the גִּלּוּי שְׁכִינָה, the self-revelation of God in Egypt; and it is spelled out for us every *Seder* night by the *Haggadah*.

The idols of olden times are gone; but substitute deities are not lacking in our days. Frederick the Great gave voice to the arrogance of the modern believers in their own power and might when he argued that 'God is always with the strongest armies.' Virchow, the turn-of-the-century pathologist, spoke for all those who believe that science can unravel all the secrets and solve all the problems of existence when he ludicrously announced that 'I have dissected thousands of corpses and never found a soul.' As long as people refuse to acknowledge the fragility of man's power and the limits of his intellectual insight, the *Haggadah* reminds us forcefully that we are like clay in the hands of the Creator, and that our life depends upon our response to His moral

By introducing the world to the knowledge of God, these events became the foundation and prelude to all worthwhile human endeavor.

As long as people refuse to acknolwedge the fragility of man's power and the limits of his intellectual insight, the Haggadah reminds us forcefully that we are like clay in the hands of the Creator.

imperatives. This lesson is so fundamental that we can appreciate the *Haggadah*'s insistence that 'the more one talks about the Exodus from Egypt, the more he is praiseworthy.'

God's People

אני ה' והוצאתי אתכם מתחת סבלות מצרים . . .
ולקחתי אתכם לי לעם והייתי לכם לאלקים
(שמות ו:ו-ז)

'... I am HASHEM and I will take you out from beneath the burdens of Egypt ... and I will take you for Me for a people, and I will be God for you ...'

(Shemos 6:6-7)

Our attention is drawn to yet another unique feature of the *Seder:* the duty to narrate about the Exodus must follow the form of question and answer, wherever feasible between child and father (*'If your son will ask you tomorrow, "What is this?", you shall say to him ... ' [Shemos* 13:14]). We can well understand the requirement that questions be formulated: after all, only he who is truly bothered by a question will be interested in the answer. But why within the family, rather than in a public forum? And why between father and son?

Celebrating the Seder in the family circle is itself a reliving of the Egyptian experience when the Jews gathered in their homes. Of course, celebrating the *Seder* in the family circle is itself a reliving of the Egyptian experience when the Jews gathered in their homes, around *'a lamb for each family, a lamb for each house' (Shemos* 12:3). In this very mode of celebration lay a demonstration of their new freedom. As slaves they had been unable to live a normal family life — what a change, then, when they were able to congregate in their homes whilst, outside, judgment was done on the Egyptians! Even more, the father-son relationship does not exist in slavery — a slave's children legally are not his own. Thus, families sitting together, and fathers passing on to sons the heritage

of their people, is in itself a proud demonstration of freedom *(Chochmah Im Nachalah).*

But there is more than this. That the Jew is charged to tell his children about the redemption is because the Exodus has a meaning for the Jewish people, beyond its message to the rest of the world. (That may be why a non-Jew is forbidden to partake of the *Pesach* sacrifice.) The deliverance from Egypt marks our miraculous emergence as a nation, linked by a special bond to God, charged by Him with special duties, and blessed by Him with indestructibility. Just as God created a fully formed world at the beginning of days, so He created His people: not through natural evolutionary processes in the normal manner of nations, but in defiance of all rules of nature and principles of history *(Maharal).*

The deliverance from Egypt marks our miraculous emergence as a nation, linked by a special bond to God, charged by Him with special duties.

'One nation was to be introduced into the ranks of the nations which, in its life and fate, should demonstrate that God is the entire foundation of life; that the fulfillment of His will is the only goal of life; and that the expression of His will, the *Torah*, is the only unifying bond of this nation. Therefore a nation was needed that lacked everything upon which the rest of mankind built its greatness ...' Everything was taken from Jacob's family that makes a people into a people or even man into a man — land, dignity, freedom — in order to receive it all through the Exodus newly from His hands Himself *(Rabbi S.R. Hirsch).*

Pesach marks our national birthday.

Pesach marks our national birthday. This helps explain why the Jewish people is instructed to count its months and begin its festival cycle from *Nissan*. It also explains the difference between the observance of *Pesach* and of later crucial and miraculous happenings in Jewish history. On no other occasion are we specifically commanded to recount miracles. No other day in our calendar, no other law in the Torah, brings with it provisions as stringent as *Pesach*, when forbidden items, such as *Chametz*, may not even remain in our possession. *Pesach* represents the actual birth and creation of our people; therefore, ac-

cording to *Rambam*, we derive the laws of conversion to Judaism from the events of *Pesach* for it was then that we became Jews. Such initiation, requires that the meaning of events must be made absolutely clear, and that not even the slightest impurity (represented by *Chametz)* can be tolerated.

With the Exodus marking the creation of the Jewish people, and *Pesach* its birthday, the *Seder* night is the national night of Judaism, an affirmation of national continuity — which has its natural roots in the family. Hence the gathering of each family in Egypt; hence the fact that Jews were always counted in family groups, and hence, too, the gathering by families on *Seder* night when, every year anew, a father has to speak to his children, to make them fully aware of their beginnings and to add them as new links to the unbroken chain of our national tradition. The child is made to experience the happenings of *Pesach* in stark immediacy — for in retelling what has been passed down through the generations, the father is no purveyor of a legend, but the witness to historical truth and national experience. 'He does not speak to his children as an individual, weak and mortal, but as a representative of the nation, demanding from them the loyalty to be expected ...' *(Isaac Breuer).*

He is called upon to make them sense the special nature of the Jewish people as a Divine creation and as a nation with characteristics peculiarly its own. Like all that God has directly created, we enjoy indestructibility. From the moment we came into existence we have defied the forces of 'normalcy,' represented by the nations of the world; thereby we provoke their hostility — but we forever outlast them: *'In every generation a man must see himself as if he himself had gone out of Egypt'* and therefore *'in every generation they rise against us to destroy us — but God saves us from their hand'* (Rabbi Avrohom Wolf).

As God's people, however, we also carry a special obligation to demonstrate that 'normalcy' is a

The Seder night is the national night of Judaism, an affirmation of national continuity.

The father is no purveyor of a legend, but the witness to historical truth and national experience.

smoke-screen, an illusion — that *'man does not live by bread alone, but by the pronouncement of HASHEM' (Devarim 8:3).* Because our very being was a miraculous gift of God, we must conduct our lives by His word—this obligation is a direct outgrowth of the Exodus; indeed, it was not only to identify Himself to the entire nation but also to establish the authority of His Law that at Mount Sinai God began with the words, *'I am HASHEM, your God, who took you out from Egypt.'* Many individual commandments, particularly those demanding that we share with others, carry a special reminder of the Exodus when we received everything — existence, freedom, and nationhood — from the hands of God Himself.

To establish the authority of His Law at Mount Sinai God began with the words 'I am HASHEM, your God, who took you out from Egypt.'

From Bondage to Freedom

ונודה לך על גאולתנו ועל פדות נפשנו (הגדה)

'... and we will thank you for our redemption and the deliverance of our soul.'

(Haggadah)

אל תקרי חרות אלא חרות — אין בן חורין אלא מי שעוסק בתורה (אבות ו' ב')

'Do not read that the Tablets were "engraved", but that they were "freedom" — a man is only free if he occupies himself with Torah.' (Avos 6:2)

In conveying the message of *Pesach* to his children, the father is given yet another directive — מַתְחִיל בִּגְנוּת וּמְסַיֵּם בְּשֶׁבַח — *'begin with the shameful part of our history and conclude with the glorious' (Pesachim 116a).* This, too, helps us experience the liberation from Egypt: we must feel bondage and slavery in all their starkness, so that we should be able truly to appreciate our deliverance and take to heart it lessons. The commandments of the *Seder* symbolize both slavery and freedom; they force upon our consciousness both extremes of this night, and indeed of all our history. The perceptive child is aroused by this twin symbolism to ask מַה נִּשְׁתַּנָּה, why is this night different from all other nights? Why does it re-

The commandments of the Seder symbolize both slavery and freedom.

quire us to demonstrate both bondage (*Maror* and *Matzah*, the bread of affliction) and freedom (repeated dipping of our food, and reclining)? It is this very question of the child which the father answers by stressing that in this night we experienced both extremes — bondage and freedom (*Abarbanel*).

But what was the meaning of this bondage and freedom — was it simply slavery and emancipation, or was there some deeper significance? Two opinions are expressed by our Sages, Rav and Shemuel. One holds that we begin with the physical slavery of Egypt (based on the passage in *Devarim* 6:21); the other goes back to the pagan beginnings of our history, when our earliest ancestors were enslaved to idolatry (based on the passage in *Joshua* 24:2). We follow both opinions — we first answer our children עֲבָדִים הָיִינוּ, we were slaves in Egypt; then we go back and tell them מִתְּחִלָּה עוֹבְדֵי עֲבוֹדָה זָרָה הָיוּ אֲבוֹתֵינוּ, that our forefathers were idol-worshippers at the dawn of our history. It is unusual for us to follow both of two opposing opinions; the *Ritva* therefore suggests that Rav and Shemuel disagreed only on which of the two passages should be recited first, but they agreed that both should be recited.

Very obviously, Rav and Shemuel emphasize two aspects of our historical experience. From a purely *socio-political* perspective, we will recall the physical enslavement and emancipation, but then will wonder why we should be grateful for God's liberating hand when it was He Who thrust us into slavery. But this *The Egyptian* question disappears when we look at our Egyptian *bondage must be* bondage from a wider *spiritual* perspective. From our *seen as part of a* *much larger* earliest origins in a pagan society we carried a burden *development.* of spiritual imperfection, the most profound and destructive form of bondage, one which would not have permitted us to become God's people and to carry His message. Only by being cast into the כּוּר הַבַּרְזֶל, the iron melting pot of Egypt, and then being miraculously withdrawn from it, were we able to achieve insights and to scale spiritual heights that

freed us once and for all from our ancient bondage of the spirit (*Maggid of Dubno*).

Thus we can speak of a dual slavery and a dual deliverance, clearly described by *Rambam*:

> '*He should start by telling that, at first, in the times of Terach and before him, our forefathers were unbelievers who pursued vanities and strayed after idols; and he should end with the true faith, that God brought us close to Him, separated us from the nations, and brought us to acknowledge His oneness. Likewise he should start by explaining that we were slaves to Pharaoh in Egypt, and all the evil he did us, and end with the miracles and marvels that were done for us, and our liberation. ...*'

Rambam meant to emphasize the primary importance of the spiritual redemption achieved through the Exodus. Apparently, *Rambam* meant to emphasize the primary importance of the spiritual redemption achieved through the Exodus. The Sages say that Joseph gave his brethren a sign by which to recognize the ultimate redeemer — he would twice use the term פְּקִידָה, *redemption*. This would seem to be a poor sign, because it was public knowledge that any impostor could use. Moreover, at the Burning Bush Moses was told, '*This shall be the sign for you that I have sent you: when you take the people out from Egypt, you shall serve God on this mountain*' (*Shemos* 3:12); and *Rabbi Meir Shapiro*, the Lubliner Rav, pointed out that this, too, could hardly be an acceptable proof of the redeemer's identity: after all, it could only be verified *after* the Jews agreed to obey Moses and he actually led them out of Egypt.

The promise of a twofold redemption — physical and spiritual. In reality, the Lubliner Rav explained, Joseph hardly meant to prophesy the future redeemer's choice of words. Instead he referred to the promise of a twofold redemption — physical and spiritual. That was what God told Moses at the Burning Bush: do not promise the Jews only physical redemption from the slave labor of Egypt; tell them also that at Mount Sinai they will be given the Torah, to complete their spiritual redemption.

The Redemption To Come

כימי צאתך מארץ מצרים אראנו נפלאות (מיכה
ז' ט''ו)

*'Just as in the days of your going out from
Egypt will I show wonders to them.'*

(Michah 7:15)

בליל פסח מתחדש ומתעורר כל מה שנעשה
במצרים וזה עצמו סיוע לגאולה האחרונה
(רמ''ח לוצאטו)

*'In the night of Pesach all that happened in
Egypt renews and bestirs itself; and this
itself helps to bring the ultimate redemption.'* *(Rabbi Moshe Chaim Luzzatto)*

As we finish retracing the road from bondage to freedom we naturally want to offer praise and homage to God for all that He did for us. We raise our cups to recite *Hallel*, echoing the songs of praise which the Jews sang at the Exodus. But can we really do so with all the fibers of our heart? Has the process of redemption that started at the Burning Bush really run its course? Very clearly it has not — and so on *Seder* night, even as we rejoice with the dawn of freedom in Egypt, we look ahead to the full unfolding of the ultimate redemption. In fact, we hope and pray with all our heart that our celebration — nay, our reliving of the momentous events of the Exodus — and our renewed dedication to God who revealed Himself then as the source of all freedom, will help reopen the wellsprings of freedom that are meant to flow in this night, bringing about our speedy final deliverance.

Even as we rejoice with the dawn of freedom in Egypt, we look ahead to the full unfolding of the ultimate redemption.

There is, thus, a duality about *Pesach:* the liberation from Egypt and the redemption to come; occurring at the two extremes of our history, they are inextricably linked at this moment in our lives. At the Burning Bush Moses was told by God, *'I will be He who I shall be'* (*Shemos* 3:14). Our Sages explain this

as an assurance that *'I will be with them in this time of suffering as I will be with them when they are in bondage to other powers.'* In the same vein, the Prophet Michah assures the Jewish people that *'just as in the days of your going out from Egypt, I will show wonders ...'* (7:15). This — it has been suggested — does not tell us that the future redemption will merely be an aftermath of our deliverance from *The Exodus must be* Egypt; rather, that the Exodus must be viewed as the *viewed as the* prelude to the Messianic redemption *(Rabbi Isaac* *prelude to the* Hutner).
Messianic Hutner).
redemption.

In the deliverance from Egypt on that *Pesach* night long ago, lay the seeds of all future salvation: *'It is for Hashem a night of keeping watch, to take them out from Egypt — this night remains for Hashem to keep watch for the children of Israel for their generations'* (Shemos 12:42). It is up to us, through our עֲבוֹדָה, our self-dedication to *Hashem* on *Pesach* night, to actualize its potential — to bring about that this dark night of exile should be turned into day by the light of redemption — as happened in Egypt and as it will, please God, happen again very speedily in *We stand as* our days. Meanwhile, we stand as travelers on the *travelers on the* road from the Egyptian deliverance to the glorious *road from* goals of the Messianic age.
the Egyptian goals of the Messianic age.
deliverance to the
glorious goals of the To this duality of *Pesach* we give expression
Messianic age. through an unusual procedure: we divide the *Hallel* into two parts. The first two psalms, which refer directly to *Yetzias Mitzrayim*, are recited before the meal, as the fitting conclusion of the recounting of the Exodus; the remaining psalms, with additional praise to God, are said after the *Pesach* meal, as we look ahead to the future redemption to come — with the taste of the *Afikoman*, symbol of liberation, in our mouths. The *Seder*, thus understood, falls logically into two parts: from the *Kiddush* to the meal it belongs to the past, from the meal to the end it looks to the future.

The Four Cups

כוס ישועות אשא ובשם ה' אקרא (תהלים קט"ז
י"ג)

*'I will lift up the cup of salvations and call
upon the name of HASHEM.'*

(Tehillim 116:13)

This structure of the *Seder* is underlined by the
arrangement of the אַרְבַּע כּוֹסוֹת, the four cups of
wine, which according to the *Halachah* must be
drunk at specific points of the evening. Two cups
clearly underline the past redemption and the future
deliverance, as they are drunk after מַגִּיד, the narration of the Exodus, and the last part of הַלֵּל, the
praise in anticipation of the future redemption
(*Avudraham*).

Two cups clearly underline the past redemption and the future deliverance.

The other two cups are not unique to *Pesach* — the
cup of *Kiddush* and that of *Birchas Hamazon* which
concludes the meal, have their counterparts
throughout the year. Nevertheless, it is only on
Pesach night that everyone at the table must drink a
cup after *Kiddush*, and, again, only on *Pesach* is the
cup after *Birchas Hamazon* a fixed requirement. Our
Sages ordained a specific rule that we must drink
four cups on *Seder* night, as testimony of our
deliverance and newly bestowed freedom: *'I will lift
the cup of salvations'* (Tehillim 116:13). They based
the requirement of four cups on the passage in the
Torah describing the four stages by which the Jews
were delivered from bondage: *'Therefore say to the
Children of Israel: "I am Hashem, and I will take you
out from beneath the burdens of Egypt, and I will
save you from their servitude, and I will redeem you
with an outstretched arm and great judgments; and I
will take you for Me for a people and I will be God
for you ..." '* (Shemos 6:6-7).

In another illustration of the parallel between past
and future, we also find four expressions of

deliverance in connection with the Messianic redemption: *'And I will take them out from the nations, and I will gather them from the countries, and I will bring them to their land, and I will tend them the mountains of Yisrael ...' (Ezekiel 34:13).*

Rabbi Samson Raphael Hirsch points out that the four expressions of deliverance found in *Shemos* correspond to the deliverance from the three stages of Egyptian bondage, announced to Abraham at the בְּרִית בֵּין הַבְּתָרִים, the Covenant Between the Portions (exile, slavery, and affliction), and to the final attainment of freedom as God's people. But the passage in *Shemos* contains yet a *fifth* expression of deliverance, *'And I will bring you to the land ...'* We do not drink a fifth cup to correspond to this expression; but in its honor we place a filled cup called the Cup of Elijah on the *Seder* table. The Rabbis disagree whether *'I will bring you'* should be considered a fifth expression of deliverance, requiring that a fifth cup be drunk at the *Seder*. The question remaining undecided, we put aside a cup until Elijah, who will come preparatory to the coming of *Mashiach*, answers all such *halachic* questions *(Vilna Gaon).* We are meant to understand thereby that the fifth cup belongs to the realm of the future coming of *Mashiach* and the ultimate redemption, when we shall finally be brought to our land never to depart: the fifth cup points ahead to the final fulfillment of the promise of *Pesach.*

The passage in Shemos contains yet a fifth expression of deliverance ... the fifth cup belongs to the realm of the future coming of Mashiach and the ultimate redemption.

We have outlined here, in brief — and in the Commentary we will trace in detail — the *Seder* night pattern that makes us relive *Yetzias Mitzrayim* and prepare for the redemption to come. But is it realistic to aspire to such spiritual height? Is it not very possible that we may go through the motions of the ritual without being caught up in its spirit? This is indeed a real danger whenever a person is called upon to rise above his petty daily concerns. The *Torah* has an antidote for it: הַכָנָה, preparation — not merely a matter of getting ready in a practical sense, but of thoughtful inner concentration on the goals lying ahead.

Preparation For Pesach

כשם שאני מבער חמץ מביתי ומרשותי, כך ה'
אלקינו... את רוח הטומאה תבער מן הארץ
ואת יצרנו הרע תבערנו מאתנו (ע"פ אר"י
הקדוש)

*'Just as I remove Chametz from my house
and possession, so You, HASHEM, ...
remove the spirit of impurity from the
earth, and our evil instinct from within us.'*
(According to *Ari Hakadosh*)

Alll of human life is a preparation. For mankind as
a whole, all events prepare the world for the rule
of the Almighty — the time of *Mashiach* and Resurrection of the Dead. For each individual, all of life
represents preparation for *Olam Habah*, the World
to Come. Even within our this-worldly existence,
every worthwhile step that we take on the road to
our ultimate goal demands careful preparation.
Before the departure from Egypt and, again, before
the giving of the Torah, the Jews were told to prepare
for these great events (*Shemos*, 12 and 19). And, ever
since, the *Mitzvos*, the signposts on our way through
life, have demanded from us preparation: study of
their laws, and proper dedication to their punctilious
execution.

*The Jew goes
through life passing
from the pursuit
of one Mitzvah to
the preparation for
the next.*

As a result, the Jew goes through life passing from
the pursuit of one *Mitzvah* to the preparation for the
next. He gets up in the morning, washes, and
prepares for his daily prayers — enjoined by the
words of the Prophet, *'Prepare to meet your God,
Israel'* (*Amos* 4:12). Every day is a preparation for
Shabbos — *'whoever labored before Shabbos, will
have something to eat on Shabbos.'* Rising for
Selichos gives way to the frantic rush to obtain *Lulav*
and *Esrog* and to build a *Sukkah* ... and so the Jewish
year goes by.

Above all, however, we find the need for proper

preparation stressed by the Torah in connection with *Pesach* — and the duty to 'guard the *Mitzvos*' carefully is actually derived by our Sages from the injunction of the Torah to *'guard the Matzos'* (*Shemos* 12:17) and prepare for a *Pesach* totally free of any *Chametz*.

Pesach has barely passed when the first steps must be taken to secure wheat suitable for the next year's *Matzos* and, in particular, for the מַצָּה שְׁמוּרָה, the specially guarded *Seder Matzah* which must be made from wheat protected from the moment it is harvested in the field against any possibility of becoming *Chametz*. The preparation of other *Pesach* foods also starts long before *Pesach*. But even the Jew who receives *Matzos* and *Pesach* provisions delivered to his doorstep, is concerned with the *Yom Tov* long in advance. He may avoid putting books near food all year long so that no *Chametz* should get into them. Many weeks before *Pesach* the thorough cleaning of every nook and cranny starts. Slowly the area where *Chametz* is kept and eaten contracts to a few square yards; finally, on the night before *Pesach*, all rooms are searched by candle-light, for any last vestiges of *Chametz*. On the next morning, we burn any remaining *Chametz*. How are we to understand these extraordinary preparations and precautions?

The Jew is concerned with the Yom Tov long in advance.

It has been pointed out that the difference between the letters of חָמֵץ, and מַצָּה, *Chametz* and *Matzah*, is the difference between the letters 'ה and 'ח — a minute point. And in fact, because the slightest amount of yeast or leaven can cause food to become *Chametz*, the most extreme caution is indicated. Leaven is the symbol of man's evil instinct, the יֵצֶר הָרַע; as explained before, our avoidance of any trace of *Chametz* on *Pesach* is a warning that on this day of our national birth, there is no room for even such slight manifestations of *spiritual* impurity as might be tolerated at other times. We must remember that only the minutest difference separated the Jews from the impurity of Egyptian life, and only by not tolerating even the slightest further spiritual decline

There is no room for even such slight manifestations of spiritual impurity, as might be tolerated at other times.

could they be redeemed to become God's people (Ari Hakadosh). Similarly, if we are to draw on the well-springs of spiritual liberation that flow every Pesach, and relive that momentous period of initiation, we too must avoid even the smallest concessions to evil and imperfection.

Before we can sit down to the Seder table and try to enter into the spirit of Pesach, we must first prepare for it by strenuously removing every speck of Chametz.

Now we perceive a further truth: before we can sit down to the Seder table and try to enter into the spirit of Pesach, we must first prepare for it by strenuously removing every speck of Chametz from our homes and, in the same way, remove the characteristics symbolized by Chametz from within ourselves.

'The Talmud derives the obligation to search for Chametz with a light, from the verse, "The soul of man is like a Divine light, searching all chambers of the body" (Mishley 20:27). Apparently there is a deeper connection between the search for Chametz and the searching of one's inner self' (Chever Ma'amarim).

Caution in avoiding the smallest concession to the Yetzer Harah, the evil instinct, and zeal in unrelentingly doing right — characterize the preparation for Pesach.

An extraordinary degree of caution is needed to remove all Chametz, and an equal degree of zeal to hurry the baking process of Matzos without their rising. Caution and zeal, זְהִירוּת and זְרִיזוּת, however, are presented by Rabbi Pinchas ben Ya'ir as the beginning steps to the attainment of the highest sanctity possible to a human being. Caution in avoiding the smallest concession to the Yetzer Harah, the evil instinct, and zeal in unrelentingly doing right — characterize the preparation for Pesach. Some may regret that we approach the Seder night so very exhausted from the work done before Pesach; in reality, however, this very work, done with utter devotion and disregard for personal comfort, raises us to the heights of single-minded spirituality, eager and ready to enter into the experience of the Seder night.

Rabbi Pinchas of Koretz explained the statement in Melachim (2, 23:22) that 'no Pesach was held like this one [in the time of King Josiah] since the time of

the Judges …' by pointing out that *Josiah* first destroyed all pagan altars and places of worship; in other words, he truly removed all *'Chametz.'*

This, then, is the secret of proper preparation for that great moment when we sit down to experience the redemption from Egypt and, hopefully, thereby to prepare the way for the coming of *Mashiach.*

✑§Preparing for Pesach

Preparing for Pesach

Erev Pesach begins on the evening before *Pesach*. It is easily the busiest day in the Jewish calendar, taken up by the removal of all *Chametz* and the preparation for *Yom Tov* and, in particular, for the *Seder*.

As soon as night has fallen, the search for *Chametz* begins,* involving every part of the house where *Chametz* might have been brought during the year. During the days before the time of the search the house should have been thoroughly cleansed; any *Chametz* which will be sold to a non-Jew should be put in a secure, secluded place, and *Chametz* for the next morning's breakfast must be kept carefully set aside.* Before starting the search, the following *Brachah** is recited:

בָּרוּךְ אַתָּה יהוה אֱלֹהֵינוּ מֶלֶךְ הָעוֹלָם אֲשֶׁר קִדְּשָׁנוּ בְּמִצְוֹתָיו וְצִוָּנוּ עַל בְּעוּר חָמֵץ:

Blessed are You, HASHEM our God, King of the universe, who has made us holy by His commandments and has commanded us about removing the Chametz.

---

* *The search for Chametz begins* — The Torah requires that we should not have *Chametz* in our possession. We could fulfill this requirement by בִּטוּל, declaring our *Chametz* to be ownerless, like the dust of the earth; it would then no longer matter that this *Chametz* is on our property. However, our Sages feared that such a sweeping declaration would be insincere and therefore null and void, in which case any *Chametz* in one's property would remain his possession. They were also concerned that if we can keep *Chametz* in our house, we might come to eat it by mistake, since we are used to eating the *Chametz* in our home during the rest of the year. They therefore required us to search for it (בְּדִיקָה), and dispose of it, by sale or destruction (בְּעוּר). However, since we may have overlooked some *Chametz*, after the search we declare any *Chametz*

not found by us to be masterless; and in the morning, after disposing of the *Chametz* which we had found or saved for the morning, we repeat this declaration for any *Chametz* which accidentally might still be in our possession.

* *Carefully set aside* — There is a widespread custom to put ten pieces of bread (which should be well-wrapped) in different places, to be found during the search. The reason for this custom is that otherwise one might not search properly, or might forget to recite the required declaration in the morning if he has nothing to burn. Even if one does not follow this custom, and finds nothing during the search, the search (or the *Brachah* we recite before it) is not considered in vain.

* *The following Brachah* — Although it is said before the search, it does not

For the search, a candle must be used. However, a flashlight is recommended for places that cannot be reached safely or effectively with a candle. When the search is concluded, the master of the house makes the following declaration (if he does not understand its meaning, he should recite it in English):

כָּל חֲמִירָא וַחֲמִיעָא דְּאִכָּא בִרְשׁוּתִי דְּלָא חֲמִיתֵּהּ וּדְלָא בְעַרְתֵּהּ וּדְלָא יָדַעְנָא לֵיהּ לִבְטֵל וְלֶהֱוֵי הֶפְקֵר כְּעַפְרָא דְאַרְעָא:

All Chametz, leaven and leavened bread, in my possession which I have neither seen nor removed nor know about, should be annulled and considered masterless, like dust of the earth.

All bread or other *Chametz* that was found during the search has to be carefully preserved till the morning, when it is burned, together with any *Chametz* left over from breakfast. If there was too much *Chametz* to be easily burned, part of it may be flushed down or otherwise destroyed prior to the burning. *Chametz* can usually be eaten till about 2½ hours before noon, although the time varies according to location and time of year. For the exact time, a reliable calendar should be consulted, or a Rabbi should be asked. Within the hour that follows, the sale of *Chametz* to a non-Jew must be concluded, and the burning of the *Chametz* must take place. After the burning, the following declaration* is made (here, too, it is necessary to understand the meaning of the words, in order for them to take effect):

refer to a "commandment to search" but to the "commandment to remove the *Chametz*", for the entire purpose of the search is the removal (*Levush*).

Usually, when we do a *Mitzvah* that only occurs from time to time, we pronounce the *Brachah* שֶׁהֶחֱיָנוּ, thanking God for letting us reach this time. We do not recite it on this occasion because the removal of the *Chametz* is only a means to an end, to keep us from having *Chametz* in our possession, and also because it entails an expense (*Meiri*); moreover the שֶׁהֶחֱיָנוּ which we recite at

the *Kiddush* includes all the *Mitzvos* connected with *Pesach* (Rosh).

* *The following declaration* — This declaration is meant to bring about the total removal of *Chametz* from our possession. Many recite after the burning of the *Chametz* a prayer (from the *Siddur* of the *Ari Hakadosh*), asking that 'just as I remove *Chametz* from my house and possession, you, HASHEM, will remove the spirit of impurity from the earth, and our *Yetzer Hora* from within us ...'

כָּל חֲמִירָא וַחֲמִיעָא דְּאִכָּא בִּרְשׁוּתִי דַּחֲזִתֵּהּ וּדְלָא חֲזִתֵּהּ דַּחֲמִתֵּהּ וּדְלָא חֲמִתֵּהּ דְּבַעֲרָתֵּהּ וּדְלָא בַעֲרָתֵּהּ לִבְטֵל וְלֶהֱוֵי הֶפְקֵר כְּעַפְרָא דְּאַרְעָא:

A ll Chametz, leaven and leavened bread, in my possession, whether I have seen it or not, whether I have removed it or not, should be annulled and considered masterless, like dust of the earth.

If the day before *Pesach* is a *Shabbos*, then the search is made on Thursday night, *Nissan* 13, and the *Chametz* is burnt on Friday morning, except for any *Chametz* that is kept for the Friday evening or *Shabbos* morning meals. The declaration, however, is made on *Shabbos* morning, at the same time as if it were an ordinary *Erev Pesach*, after any traces of *Chametz* left from the *Shabbos* meals have been rinsed down the drain.*

Erev Pesach is a fast day for first-born males. It is, however, customary for them to participate in the celebration of a סִיּוּם, completion of the study of a tractate of the *Talmud*; after partaking of the food served in celebration of this event, they may eat during the rest of the day.If the day before *Pesach* is a *Shabbos*, the fast of the firstborn (or the celebration of the סִיּוּם in its place) is observed on the Thursday before *Pesach*.

From the middle of the afternoon on, no meal may be eaten, so that the *Seder* meal can be eaten with a hearty appetite. The eating of *Matzah*,* however, is forbidden all day, although many have the custom to abstain already from *Purim* or from the beginning of *Nissan*.

* *Rinsed down the drain* — Many people eat *Pesach* food from *Pesach* dishes for the *Shabbos* meals, and use only two small loaves of bread for the start of the meal. They must take great care to keep these loaves away from the *Pesach* table and dishes, and to eat them over a napkin in order to collect the crumbs and wash them down the drain. Others prefer to prepare the Friday evening and *Shabbos* morning meals in *Chametz* pots and eat them from *Chametz* dishes. (It is, however, recommended that the food contain no actual *Chametz* since the *Chametz* utensils cannot be cleaned properly on a *Shabbos* and, also, the kitchen is already fully prepared for *Pesach*). After eating, the pots, plates, and eating utensils, must be wiped clean with paper tissues (which are then flushed down the toilet bowl), and are put away where all the other *Chametz* dishes are kept.

* *The eating of Matzah* — The *Rokeach* finds a Biblical allusion to this prohibi-

The afternoon before Pesach has a festive character, for it was the time when the *Pesach* sacrifice was offered in the Temple.* (Some Rabbinic authorities hold that the *Seder Matzos* should preferably be baked on *Erev Pesach* after noon — and many people therefore do so, in a spirit of rejoicing and while chanting chapters from *Hallel*.)In fact, the afternoon has the halachic status of the Intermediate Days of *Pesach*, which are not full *Yomim Tovim*, but during which many everyday activities are forbidden, to preserve the festive spirit. For that reason, haircuts — for instance — should be taken before noon.

Erev Pesach is the day when it is customary to renew עֵרוּבֵי חֲצֵרוֹת, *Eruvey Chatzeros*, by means of which it becomes permissible for all the residents of a building, a courtyard, or an otherwise enclosed area, to carry on *Shabbos* in the entire area. Normally, a person may only carry in his own apartment or house; however, if an *Eruv* is made (by depositing some *Matzah* with one of the residents of the whole building or area in behalf of all the families living there), all the residences are, so to speak, merged into one, and carrying is permitted throughout the area. It is customary to dispose of the old *Eruv* before *Pesach*, and to make a new one.

If *Erev Pesach* falls on a Wednesday, it is moreover necessary to make עֵרוּב תַּבְשִׁילִין, *Eruv Tavshilin*, making it permissible to prepare for *Shabbos* during *Yom Tov*. It is forbidden to prepare on *Yom Tov* for the next day; however, if the next day is *Shabbos*, and preparations began before *Yom Tov*, they may be continued on *Yom Tov*. Therefore, we prepare a *Matzah* and some cooked food (such as an egg, meat, or fish) before *Yom Tov*, and put them aside to be eaten on *Shabbos*, after making the following declaration:

tion in the verse specifying that *"in the evening you shall eat Matzos"* (*Shemos* 12:18). Various reasons have been given for abstaining from *Matzah* before *Pesach*: we should be able to eat *Matzah* at the Seder with proper appetite; we also want to make a distinction between eating *Matzah* by choice all year round, and eating it as a *Mitzvah* on *Pesach*; and we want to show that, at the *Seder*, we eat it because we are com-

manded to do so, rather than for our pleasure (*Avudraham, Vilna Gaon, Remah*).

* *In the Temple* — It is therefore a common custom to recite at this time the account of the *Pesach* sacrifice found in the *Mishnah* or in later works, just as we read every day the account of the daily sacrifices. Sadly, it is only in this form that we can offer sacrifices today.

בָּרוּךְ אַתָּה יהוה אֱלֹהֵינוּ מֶלֶךְ הָעוֹלָם אֲשֶׁר
קִדְּשָׁנוּ בְּמִצְוֹתָיו וְצִוָּנוּ עַל־מִצְוַת עֵרוּב:

בְּהָדֵין עֵרוּבָא יְהֵא שָׁרֵא לָנָא לַאֲפוּיֵי וּלְבַשּׁוּלֵי
וּלְאַצְלוּיֵי וּלְאַטְמוּנֵי וּלְאַדְלוּקֵי שְׁרָגָא
וּלְתַקָּנָא וּלְמֶעְבַּד כָּל צָרְכָנָא מִיּוֹמָא טָבָא לְשַׁבַּתָּא
לָנוּ וּלְכָל יִשְׂרָאֵל הַדָּרִים בָּעִיר הַזֹּאת:

Blessed are You, HASHEM our God, King of the
universe, who has made us holy by His commandments and has given us the commandment of Eruv.

Through this Eruv, we should be permitted to
bake, cook, fry, keep warm, kindle lights and do
anything necessary on the festival in preparation for
the Shabbos, we and all Jews who live in this city.

All that is needed for the Seder should be prepared in advance on *Erev Pesach*. If *Erev Pesach* is on *Shabbos*, the necessary preparations should be made on Friday. Otherwise the
beginning of the *Seder* will be delayed and the children may fall
asleep.* (The Talmudic rule, חוֹטְפִין אֶת הַמַּצָּה *'to get the Matzah
in a hurry, so that the children should not fall asleep,'* is understood by *Rashi* as a warning to hurry the *Seder* as much as possible; for other interpretations, see pp. 64,70.) The *Seder* centers on
Matzah and *Maror* (and, in the time of the Temple, the *Pesach*
sacrifice), as explained in the Overview. Therefore, the Master
of the *Seder* — usually the father of the family — needs to have
before him *Matzah* and *Maror*, together with several other
items, each having its own symbolic significance.

Three *Matzos** are required by the Master of the *Seder*, in

---

* *May fall asleep* — Moreover, we do
not want to delay the start of the *Seder*,
since the *Afikoman* should be eaten
before midnight. It has also been suggested that preparing the meal in advance is one of the many ways we use
on *Pesach* to show that we are free men

— the poor and the enslaved grab their
food and devour it at once.

* *Three Matzos* — The three *Matzos*
have been seen as a symbol of the
Jewish people (composed of כֹּהֲנִים
Priests, Levites, and — לְוִיִּם וְיִשְׂרְאֵלִים

contrast to an ordinary *Shabbos* or *Yom Tov* when only two loaves, לֶחֶם מִשְׁנֶה, are required. The reason is that the *Matzah* over which we are to tell the *Haggadah* should be לֶחֶם עוֹנִי, *bread of poverty*, and we therefore have to break it before the start of the *Haggadah* — poor people do not feast on whole loaves. For לֶחֶם מִשְׁנֶה, however, we need two whole loaves and therefore we need two *Matzos* in addition to the one that is broken (the *Rif*, however, is of the opinion that, on *Seder* night the broken *Matzah* can be counted as one of the two *Matzos* required for *Lechem Mishneh* and only one other *Matzah* is needed). The three *Matzos* should be on top of each other, separated by napkins or inserted into the compartments of a *Seder* plate *(Ari Hakadosh)*. All the *Matzah* used for the *Seder* must be מַצָה שְׁמוּרָה, *Matzah* made specifically for this purpose, from grain that was specially guarded against any conditions that could cause it to become *Chametz* — wetness, for example — from the moment it was cut.

Additional *Matzos* should be prepared, as the three *Matzos* of the Master of the *Seder* will usually not suffice for the whole company. It must be realized that on three occasions during the *Seder* each participant must eat a quantity of *Matzah* that, when ground up, will equal at least the volume of an olive (on two of these three occasions he should ideally eat the equivalent of two olives). Moreover, this refers to olives as grown in ancient times, which are believed to have been twice the size of our olives. How big a piece of *Matzah* corresponds to an olive? The exact answer will, of course depend on the thickness of the *Matzos*; however, the *Chazon Ish* considered a piece the size of half a machine baked *Matzah* generally sufficient, while others have required as much as a whole machine *Matzah (Moadim Uzmanim)*. According to Rabbi Moshe Feinstein a piece of about 4″ by 7″ (roughly two-thirds of a machine *Matzah)* is needed; however, when a double portion is

Israelites); or of our three Patriarchs whose merit helped bring about our redemption from Egypt; or of the three measures of flour from which Abraham baked *Matzos* for the three angels. Also three types of *Matzah* are part of the thanks offering *(Vayikrah 7:12)* that the Torah requires of people that were released from prison, recovered from sickness, or crossed an ocean or a desert. The Jews who were freed from Egypt were in every one of these categories and our three *Matzos* represent the thanks-offering which we owe *(Orchos Chayim; Maharal; Rav Sherira Gaon; Mordechai)*.

called for, he considers a piece of about 6¼" by 7" sufficient.

On top of the *Seder* plate is *Maror*. The Talmud mentions several kinds of vegetables suitable for *Maror*, among them תַּמְכָא, horseradish, and חֲזֶרֶת, which is commonly identified as Romaine Lettuce. *Chazeres* has the advantage* over horseradish that the required quantity can be eaten more easily; however, it is extremely difficult to cleanse it because of the tiny insects that infest it. Some opinions instead accept Iceberg Lettuce or Endives for *Chazeres*; if, however, Romaine Lettuce is taken, it is urged that only the white center ribs of each leaf be used, as they are much easier to check and clean. During the *Seder*, *Maror* is eaten twice — once by itself and once with *Matzah*. Some will use *Chazeres* both times; others will use horseradish once or even twice, or mix it with *Chazeres*.

If horseradish is used, it may not be cooked or prepared with vinegar; it should be grated, but only reasonably fine, and should be kept well-wrapped or in a tightly sealed container lest it lose its sharpness before the *Seder*. For this reason the grating of the horseradish is one procedure that is best not done on Friday if *Erev Pesach* is on *Shabbos*; instead the horseradish should be grated just before the beginning of the *Seder*, with a small change from the normal way of grating (*Mishnah Berurah*). The same procedure should be followed in preparing *Maror* for the second *Seder*, since day-old horseradish very likely will have lost its sharpness.

The quantity of *Maror* to be eaten on each occasion also has to be equal to an olive. In the case of Romaine Lettuce this requires, according to Rabbi Moshe Feinstein, enough center ribs to cover an area 3" by 5" (if whole leaves are used, they should be 8" by 10" in area). In the case of pure grated horseradish we require the amount that can be packed into a vessel measuring 1.1 fluid ounces. (It is suggested that, for measuring purposes, one prepare before the *Seder* a small glass or jigger of known volume, and also a piece of cardboard on which he has marked off the area to be covered with Romaine Lettuce and *Matzah*.) Again, the *Seder* plate will not hold enough *Maror* for all par-

---

* *Chazeres has the advantage* — We also like to use *Chazeres* because it initially tastes sweet and then bitter, like the life of our forefathers in Egypt — first paid workers and then oppressed slaves (*Rashi, Pesachim* 39a).

Moreover, its Aramaic name, חַסָא, *mercy*, can be taken as an allusion to the

ticipants and an additional amount should therefore be prepared.

On the *Seder* plate there should also be a roasted bone with some meat on it, and a hardboiled egg, representing פֶּסַח, the *Pesach* sacrifice, and חֲגִיגָה, the festival sacrifice, that had to be offered in the times of the Temple. For the *Chagigah* we use an egg, even though some boiled meat would also serve; the egg is a sign of mourning for the destruction of the Temple — its round shape symbolizes the turning of the wheel of destiny and holds out the hope for a speedy rebuilding. The *Pesach* sacrifice is preferably represented by a roast piece of the shoulder-bone of a lamb,* and, according to *Rabbeinu Manoach*, it should be broiled on the afternoon before *Pesach*, the time when the *Pesach* sacrifice was offered, unless *Erev Pesach* is on *Shabbos*. It should not, however, be called *Pesach* for this would make it appear as if we actually dedicated it as a sacrifice — something strictly forbidden outside the Temple.*

Another object needed on the *Seder* plate is the חֲרוֹסֶת. *Charoses* is a mixture of grated apples, nuts, and other fruits, mixed with red wine and spiced with cinnamon and other spices. We dip the *Maror* into it before eating it, in order to counter any possible harmful effects of the *Maror's* sharpness; but at the same time we are commanded to use *Charoses* because it has a symbolic message* to convey by its similarity to the mortar used in ancient Egypt.

end of our bondage: out of the bitterness of Exile grew the miracle of our redemption (see p.146).

* *Shoulder-bone of a lamb* — The shoulder-bone is a reminder of the זְרוֹעַ נְטוּיָה, the outstretched arm with which God brought punishment upon the Egyptians; and the egg has been interpreted as a sign of God's kindness to the Jews (the Aramaic term for "egg" בֵּיעָה, suggests that it *should please* God to redeem us, בָּעָא רַחֲמָנָא לְמִפְרַק יָתָנָא; *Kolbo*). *Rav Sherira Gaon* suggests that the bone and egg symbolize Moshe and Aaron, the great leaders of the Jewish people who, in their own lives, embodied strict judgment and overflowing kindness respec-

tively. In line with this interpretation there used to exist a custom to add a piece of fish, in memory of Miriam (the embodiment of צְנִיעוּת, *modesty*, symbolized by fish dwelling in the water's depths).

* *Outside the Temple* — For this reason, some prefer not to roast the bone, and others (for instance, *Chabad*) do not even use the bone of an animal but the neck of a chicken. For the same reason, we do not lift up or even point to the bone when we speak of the *Pesach* sacrifice during the *Seder*.

* *Symbolic message* — The entire mixture has the color and consistency of the clay with which the Jews had to work in

Finally, the *Seder* plate contains *Karpas* (celery, parsley, radishes or, according to some, boiled potatoes — but no vegetable that can be used for *Maror*). *Karpas* is eaten right after the Kiddush, after it has been dipped into saltwater. For that reason a bowl with saltwater should also be prepared in advance (especially if *Seder* night is on a *Shabbos*, as it is not permitted on *Shabbos* to prepare saltwater in quantity or in very strong concentration).

It is customary to arrange the various objects on top of the *Seder* plate according to the directions of the *Ari Hakadosh*, Rabbi Yitzchak Luria. Closest to the seat of the Master of the *Seder*, the vegetable for *Karpas* should be to his left, and the dish with *Charoses* to his right; in the front center we put *Chazeres*, the green leafy vegetable used for *Maror*. In the back, behind the *Karpas*, is the egg; behind the *Charoses*, the bone; and, behind the *Chazeres*, in the rear center of the plate, horseradish for *Maror* [see diagram on page 52.] Thus, the proximity of each food is determined according to the order of its use, making it unnecessary for the Master of the *Seder* to bypass any object in reaching for what is needed next. However, there are some other opinions on how to arrange the *Seder* plate — notably that of the Gaon of Vilna who put on it only *Maror* and *Charoses* (on the further side) and egg and bone (on the nearer side); also, he put only two *Matzos* underneath, in accordance with the above-quoted view of the *Rif*.

We also prepare sufficient wine for each participant's four cups.* The cups must hold a *Revi'is* of wine; according to the

Egypt, and the cinnamon sticks represent the straw that they put into the bricks. In ꜰact, חַרְסִית means "brick" (*Mordechai*).

The red wine represents the spilled blood of the Jews (*Yerushalmi Pesachim* 10:3).

The apple is a reminder of the fact that (*Shir Hashirim* 8:5) תַּחַת הַתַּפּוּחַ עוֹרַרְתִּיךָ, "I bestirred you under the apple tree" — the pious Jewish women went into the apple orchards, to give birth without the knowledge of the Egyptians, and God cared for them (*Yalkut*).

The various fruits used are a tribute to the Jewish people — they are all fruits to which the Jews are compared in the Bible (*Gaonim*).

The almonds also symbolize the speediness of the redemption, for their Hebrew name שְׁקֵדִים is an allusion to שְׁקִידָה, diligent action (in keeping with *Jeremiah* 1:11-12).

* *The Four Cups* — Several explanations for the Rabbinic injunction to drink four cups have been given in the *Overview* (p. 35); several others will be mentioned in connection with the com-

Chazon Ish this is 5.3 fluid ounces, and according to Rabbi Moshe Feinstein 3.3 fluid ounces (however, he rules that when the *Seder* is on a *Shabbos*, the first cup should hold at least 4.42 fluid ounces). Ideally, the cups should be drunk completely each of the four times that we drink at the *Seder*; however, at least the greater part of the wine *must* be drunk. Red wine should be used preferably — it is considered of better quality *(Mishley* 23:31), and it also serves as a reminder of the blood of the Jewish children killed by Pharaoh *(Pri Megadim);* of the blood of *Pesach* and *Milah,* through which the Jews gained their freedom *(Or Zorua);* and of the plague of the blood. Grape juice should be used only for children who cannot yet drink wine, or if health reasons prevent the use of wine. Generally, in the case of any difficulty in eating or drinking the required amounts of *Matzah, Maror* or wine, a competent Rabbi should be consulted.

As a sign of our freedom, we are required to recline on our left side when we drink the four cups, and while we eat *Matzah, Korech, Afikomen* and, according to some, *Karpas.* (The practice is referred to in *Shir Hashirim* 1:12: עַד שֶׁהַמֶּלֶךְ בִּמְסִבּוֹ, *the king reclining at his feast).* It is therefore customary to provide pillows so that we should be able to recline properly. (Women are not required to recline but may do so; see p. 65.) A widespread and ancient custom also calls for the Master of the Seder to wear a white *Kittel* — a sign of his special dignity on this solemn night when he, so to speak, functions like the High Priest on *Yom Kippur,* performing the Divine service and

mentary to the *Haggadah* (pp. 57,71,83, 149, 176). Here are some further explanations:

According to the *Talmud Yerushalmi (Pesachim* 10:1), the four cups correspond to the four times that Pharaoh's cup is mentioned in the dream interpreted by Joseph while he was in jail *(Bereishis* 40:11-13); this dream was the beginning of the development which ultimately led to the Exodus.

According to the *Midrash,* the four cups symbolize the four edicts Pharaoh issued against the Jews in connection with their slave labor and the killing of their children; and the four ways in which the Jews kept themselves separate from the Egyptians, thereby assuring their survival (see p.106).

The *Abarbanel* explains that the four cups are an expression of praise and thanks to God for choosing us in the days of Abraham *(Kiddush),* for redeeming us from Egypt *(Haggadah),* for protecting us in this exile *(Birchas Hamazon),* and for sending *Mashiach (Hallel).*

It has also been pointed out that we owe thanks to God if we were sick or in prison, or crossed the sea or the desert; as pointed out above, the Jews who were freed from Egypt were in every one of these categories and therefore should offer fourfold praise.

thereby obtaining forgiveness and redemption for the Jewish people.*

The table itself should be laid with the finest linen and silver we own, as yet another sign of the freedom and dignity which we enjoy this night *(Maharil)*, and in memory of the gold and silver that the Jews took from Egypt. Finally, the *Yom Tov* candles are lit in preparation for the beginning of the festival:

בָּרוּךְ אַתָּה יהוה אֱלֹהֵינוּ מֶלֶךְ הָעוֹלָם אֲשֶׁר קִדְּשָׁנוּ בְּמִצְוֹתָיו וְצִוָּנוּ לְהַדְלִיק נֵר שֶׁל (שַׁבָּת וְשֶׁל) יוֹם טוֹב:

Blessed are You, HASHEM our God, King of the universe, who has made us holy through His commandments, and has commanded us to light the (Shabbos *and*) Yom Tov *light.*

In many communities the women add:

בָּרוּךְ אַתָּה יהוה אֱלֹהֵינוּ מֶלֶךְ הָעוֹלָם שֶׁהֶחֱיָנוּ וְקִיְּמָנוּ וְהִגִּיעָנוּ לַזְּמַן הַזֶּה:

Blessed are You, HASHEM our God, King of the universe, who has kept us alive and sustained us, and brought us to this festive season.

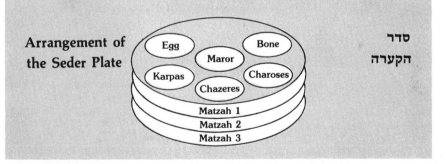

Arrangement of the Seder Plate

Egg
Bone
Maror
Karpas
Charoses
Chazeres
Matzah 1
Matzah 2
Matzah 3

סדר הקערה

---

* *For the Jewish people* — This explanation is given by the *Maharal* who also emphasizes that a white garment reflects the joyousness of the *Yom Tov* and the purity attained on this evening. At the same time, the *"Kittel"* (also worn by the dead) is worn to evoke a certain humility and to prevent excessive exuberance on this joyous evening *(Taz)*.

It has also been suggested that we want to show that we wear distinctively Jewish garb like our forefathers in Egypt who did not change their attire *(B'nei Yisoschor)*.

The Order of the Seder

קַדֵּשׁ וּרְחַץ, כַּרְפַּס יַחַץ

מַגִּיד רָחְצָה, מוֹצִיא מַצָּה.

מָרוֹר כּוֹרֵךְ, שֻׁלְחָן עוֹרֵךְ.

צָפוּן בָּרֵךְ. הַלֵּל נִרְצָה

The order of the Seder — A number of סִמָנִים, brief poems summarizing the *Seder*, have been composed through the ages. We are told to announce aloud each step of the *Seder* as we proceed through the evening, as a reminder of the proper sequence in which the various parts of the *Seder* are performed, and to keep us from making mistakes. This is not only a matter of convenience or *halachic* exactness. It also makes us aware of the profoundly significant pattern of the *Seder* observance and all its details. The structure of the *Seder* is meant to help us relive the experience of the Exodus; and every step, it has been said, contains deep lessons and esoteric allusions. At the same time, in following through this sequence, we help prepare the pattern of the future redemption [See Overview] (*Maharal*).

The סִימָן here given, which is the most widely accepted one, is ascribed to *Rashi* or to Rabbi Shmuel of Falaise, one of the *Baaley Tosfoth*. It sums up the *Seder* in fifteen stages, which correspond to the fifteen steps which the Levites ascended in the Temple and for which King David wrote the fifteen שִׁירֵי הַמַּעֲלוֹת, Songs of Steps (or: Ascents). On *Seder* night we are to seek to ascend to such heights of Divine service. To advance from the first level, starting with *Kiddush*, to the fifteenth, when we reach *Nirzah*, fourteen steps are taken. They correspond to the יָד הַגְּדוֹלָה, the great hand, that God showed in Egypt, and to which we pray tribute at the *Seder* (יָ"ד has the numerical value 14 — *Maharal*). As we do our part, we pray that in turn we should be privileged once again to see God's hand revealed in the world, with the coming of *Mashiach*.

To make the pattern of the *Seder* as clear as possible, we indicate here when the four cups are drunk, and list the various parts of מַגִּיד, the *Haggadah*, which form an ascending sequence within the overall progression of the *Seder*.

קַדֵּשׁ **Kaddesh** / Recite the *Kiddush*
over the Feast-day;

כּוֹס א׳

The first cup is drunk here;

וּרְחַץ **U'rechatz** / Wash hands
in preparation for ...

כַּרְפַּס **Karpas** / Eating of *Karpas*
(vegetable dipped in salt-water),
to arouse children's curiosity;

יַחַץ **Yachatz** / Break the middle *Matzah,*
the smaller half serving as
'bread of proverty' over which ...

מַגִּיד **Maggid** / *Haggadah* is recited:

הָא לַחְמָא עַנְיָא draws attention to the 'bread of poverty'
over which the *Haggadah* is to be told;

מַה נִּשְׁתַּנָּה are the child's questions to which the father replies:

עֲבָדִים הָיִינוּ we were enslaved, and God freed us, and therefore
we should recount the story at length;

מַעֲשֶׂה בְּרַבִּי אֱלִיעֶזֶר shows that our greatest Sages did so;

אָמַר רַבִּי אֶלְעָזָר
בֶּן עֲזַרְיָה shows the duty to do so at all times;

בָּרוּךְ הַמָּקוֹם shows how every type of child is to be
instructed at the *Seder;*

יָכוֹל מֵרֹאשׁ חֹדֶשׁ explains when this special duty applies;

מִתְּחִלָּה shows the deeper roots of the exile,
and the Exodus as the way to spiritual redemption;

צֵא וּלְמַד the Midrash presents the details of the *Pesach* story
to its triumphant end;

רַבָּן גַּמְלִיאֵל explains the concrete *Mitzvos* ordained for
the *Seder: Pesach, Matzah, Maror;*

בְּכָל דּוֹר וָדוֹר emphasizes that, in celebrating the *Seder, we must*
see ourselves as having gone out from Egypt,
and therefore...

הַלְלוּיָהּ we praise HASHEM for His kindness,
ending with a *Brachah* over the *Haggadah;*

כוס ב׳ — The second cup is drunk here;

רחצה **Rachtzah** / Wash hands, preparatory to . . .

מוציא **Motzi** / Customary *Brachah* over bread
(in this case *Matzah*) . . .

מצה **Matzah** / And special *Brachah* over *Matzos*,
from which we then eat;

מרור **Maror** / Special *Brachah* is said over *Maror*
and it is eaten after we dip it into *Charoses*;

כורך **Korech** / Combination of *Matzah* and *Maror*
is eaten, and then . . .

שלחן **Shulchan Orech** / Eat the festive meal,
עורך ending with

צפון **Tzafun** / Eating the *Afikoman*, and . . .

ברך **Barech** / *Birchas Hamazon*, the blessing
after a meal;

כוס ג׳ — The third cup is drunk here;

הלל **Hallel** / Psalms of praise and declarations
of our faith in HASHEM are recited;

כוס ד׳ — The fourth cup is drunk here;

נרצה **Nirtzah** / The *Seder* is completed
with our prayers that our service be accepted
by HASHEM, and *Mashiach* come speedily.

קַדֵּשׁ

יש להזדרז להתחיל הסדר תיכף לאחר צאת הכוכבים. אך יזהר שלא יתחיל
קודם הלילה. נוהגים באיזו קהילות לברך את הילדים.
ממלאים כוסות המסובים והאב מתחיל את הקדוּשׁ:

[בליל שבת קודש מתחילים **וַיְהִי עֶרֶב** ואומרים מה שמוקף בחצי
עיגולים; בשאר לילות מתחילים **סַבְרִי**]

°בראשית
א:לא–
ב:ג

בלחש: °וַיְהִי־עֶרֶב וַיְהִי־בֹקֶר

יוֹם הַשִּׁשִּׁי: וַיְכֻלּוּ הַשָּׁמַיִם וְהָאָרֶץ וְכָל־צְבָאָם:
וַיְכַל אֱלֹהִים בַּיּוֹם הַשְּׁבִיעִי מְלַאכְתּוֹ
אֲשֶׁר עָשָׂה וַיִּשְׁבֹּת בַּיּוֹם הַשְּׁבִיעִי מִכָּל־מְלַאכְתּוֹ אֲשֶׁר
עָשָׂה: וַיְבָרֶךְ אֱלֹהִים אֶת־יוֹם הַשְּׁבִיעִי וַיְקַדֵּשׁ אֹתוֹ כִּי
בוֹ שָׁבַת מִכָּל־מְלַאכְתּוֹ אֲשֶׁר־בָּרָא אֱלֹהִים לַעֲשׂוֹת:

סַבְרִי מָרָנָן וְרַבָּנָן וְרַבּוֹתַי:

בָּרוּךְ אַתָּה יהוה אֱלֹהֵינוּ מֶלֶךְ הָעוֹלָם בּוֹרֵא
פְּרִי הַגָּפֶן:

קַדֵּשׁ — *Make Kiddush.* Every *Shabbos* and *Yom Tov* is ushered in by *Kiddush.* Even though we already proclaimed the holiness of the day in our evening prayers, its proper celebration belongs in the home, where we usually pursue our weekday activities. As we gather for our festive meal, therefore, we begin by dedicating ourselves to the special message of the day *(Rabbi S.R. Hirsch).*

In keeping with the special character of the *Seder* night, the recitation of the *Kiddush* on this evening is of course fraught with a particular solemn significance. The Yemenite rite gives expression to it by including in the *Kiddush* a special addition already quoted in the *Siddur* of *Rav Saadiah Gaon:* '... *He sanctified His name before the entire world, for the sake of the Patriarchs who did His will ... He did miracles for us and redeemed us from our enemies.'*

The *Kiddush* recited on *Yom Tov*
blesses God who sanctifies the people of Israel and the festive seasons *(Yom Tov).* If the *Yom Tov* coincides with a *Shabbos,* we bless God who 'sanctifies the *Shabbos,* and Israel, and the festive seasons.' We mention the *Shabbos* before we mention Israel, for the seventh day of the week was sanctified at the creation of the world, long before the Jewish people. In the case of the festivals, however, although the Torah ordains the date on which they are to be celebrated, this date depends on the Jewish people, which, according to the Torah, has to regulate and fix the calendar through its Rabbinic Courts; we therefore mention the festive seasons only *after* first proclaiming the sanctity of the Jewish people itself *(Beitzah* 17a).

* *As soon as the father returns.* — The *Talmud* stresses that the *Seder* should start as early as possible, for the sake of

הגדה של פסח   [56]

Kaddesh / Make Kiddush*

As soon as the father returns* from the synagogue and night has fallen, the *Seder* begins. First, in many communities, parents bless their children, as on other *Shabbos* and *Yom Tov* evenings. Then, the company gathers around the festive table for קדוש, proclaiming the holiness of the day. The participants fill each other's cups,* and the father begins:

(On Friday night, start with וַיְהִי עֶרֶב and say all the passages in parentheses; on other evenings start with סָבְרִי and omit the words in parentheses.)

Quietly: And it was evening and it was morning,

The sixth day. And the heaven and the earth were completed, and all their host. And on the seventh day God completed His work which He had made; and He ceased on the seventh day, from all His work which He had made. And God blessed the seventh day and made it holy, because on it He ceased from all His work that He, God, had created to continue working on it.

By your leave, my masters and teachers:

B *lessed are You, HASHEM, our God, King of the universe, who creates the fruit of the vine.*

the children. However, it may not begin before nightfall. As a rule, *Kiddush* may be said on *Shabbos* or *Yom Tov* immediately upon return from the synagogue, even *before* nightfall. Not so on *Pesach*. In the first place, *Kiddush* marks the beginning of the *Seder* meal, which must be eaten at night (*Shemos* 12:8). Also, the cup of wine drunk at *Kiddush* is the first of the Four Cups — and like all other *Mitzvos* of the *Seder*, the drinking of all Four Cups must take place at night (*Trumas Hadeshen; Taz*).

* *The participants fill each other's cups.* — Thus, each participant is served by someone else. This is yet another demonstration of the freedom and dignity we enjoy on *Pesach*. In olden times, particularly, the nobility would not dream of filling their own cups. It is indeed possible that our Sages ordained the use of wine, as well as the requirement that it be drunk while comfortably reclining, to emphasize our status

as free men of substance both by the choice of beverage and by the manner of drinking. On *Pesach* even the poor should view themselves in this light, and the *Talmud* therefore emphasizes that they, too, are obliged to drink the Four Cups.

It has also been stressed that men will particularly want to celebrate with wine if they have newly attained their freedom: '*I will lift up the cup of salvation and call upon the name of HASHEM*' (*Tehillim* 116:13, *Mordechai*). In fact, the wine itself helps to change a person's disposition from sadness to happiness (*Ha'amek Davar*). For the significance of drinking *Four Cups*, see the Overview (p.35) and p.50.

וַיְהִי עֶרֶב — *And it was evening.* When *Yom Tov* falls on *Shabbos*, we preface the *Kiddush* with the same verses from *Bereishis* that we recite every Friday night, and which describe the *Shabbos* of the week of creation. These verses re-

בָּרוּךְ אַתָּה יהוה אֱלֹהֵינוּ מֶלֶךְ הָעוֹלָם
אֲשֶׁר בָּחַר בָּנוּ מִכָּל־עָם וְרוֹמְמָנוּ
מִכָּל־לָשׁוֹן וְקִדְּשָׁנוּ בְּמִצְוֹתָיו. וַתִּתֶּן לָנוּ יהוה
אֱלֹהֵינוּ בְּאַהֲבָה (שַׁבָּתוֹת לִמְנוּחָה וּ)מוֹעֲדִים
לְשִׂמְחָה חַגִּים וּזְמַנִּים לְשָׂשׂוֹן אֶת יוֹם (הַשַּׁבָּת
הַזֶּה, וְאֶת־יוֹם) חַג הַמַּצּוֹת הַזֶּה זְמַן חֵרוּתֵנוּ
(בְּאַהֲבָה) מִקְרָא קֹדֶשׁ זֵכֶר לִיצִיאַת מִצְרָיִם. כִּי
בָנוּ בָחַרְתָּ וְאוֹתָנוּ קִדַּשְׁתָּ מִכָּל־הָעַמִּים (וְשַׁבָּת)
וּמוֹעֲדֵי קָדְשֶׁךָ (בְּאַהֲבָה וּבְרָצוֹן) בְּשִׂמְחָה וּבְשָׂשׂוֹן
הִנְחַלְתָּנוּ. בָּרוּךְ אַתָּה יהוה מְקַדֵּשׁ (הַשַּׁבָּת וְ)
יִשְׂרָאֵל וְהַזְּמַנִּים:

mind us of the profound purpose of the *Shabbos*. The phrase, בַּיּוֹם הַשְּׁבִיעִי, is usually translated 'on the seventh day God completed His work'; but *Rabbi S.R. Hirsch* translates בְּ as 'with', not 'on': 'with the seventh day God completed His work' of creation. The *Shabbos* was not a respite from creation, but an essential part of it. It was instituted to serve as an eternal reminder that God is the sole Creator, and that our task in the world is only to do His will.

The Torah stresses that בָּרָא אֱלֹהִים לַעֲשׂוֹת, *God created the world in order to continue working on it*, to lead it towards the attainment of the ultimate goal that He set for it. The task of bringing about this further development of the universe was, however, assigned to man. He was to use his intelligence and freedom of choice in the service of God — and the *Shabbos* was to keep this duty alive in his mind, by reminding him of the Creator.

מוֹעֲדִים לְשִׂמְחָה חַגִּים וּזְמַנִּים לְשָׂשׂוֹן — *Appointed times for rejoicing, feasts and festive seasons for joy.* The term חַגִּים, *feasts*, is derived from חוּג, circle, and describes our festivals as times of national reunion; זְמַנִּים, *festive seasons*,

describes them in their seasonal role, marking God's self-revelation through the changing phases of nature; and מוֹעֲדִים, *appointed times*, characterizes them in their historical role, marking the great encounters between God and Israel, in Egypt and in the desert (*Rabbi S.R. Hirsch*).

The expression used here is מוֹעֲדִים לְשִׂמְחָה, *appointed times for rejoicing*, rather than מוֹעֲדֵי שִׂמְחָה, *appointed times of joy*. This tells us that *Yomim Tovim*, festivals, are not only days of rejoicing but sources of joy and inspiration for the remainder of the year. In the same way, שַׁבָּתוֹת לִמְנוּחָה, *Shabbos days for rest*: the *Shabbos* furnishes us with the blessing of restfulness for the entire week (*Sfas Emes*).

In the *Kiddush* — and in our prayers generally — the *Shabbos* is characterized as given בְּאַהֲבָה וּבְרָצוֹן, *in love and favor*, while *Yom Tov* is given בְּשִׂמְחָה וּבְשָׂשׂוֹן, *in joy and gladness. Rabbi S.R. Hirsch* explains that *Yom Tov* marks a joyful celebration of national experiences, which we are permitted to enhance by cooking and baking. On *Shabbos*, however, we celebrate solely our own devoted personal relationship to God, and we abstain from all self-

*B*lessed are You, HASHEM our God, King of the universe, who has chosen us from all peoples and lifted us up above all tongues and made us holy through His commandments. And You have given us, HASHEM our God, in love, (the Shabbos days for rest,) appointed times for rejoicing, feasts and festive seasons for joy; (this Shabbos and) this Feast of the Matzos, the season of our freedom, (in love,) a holy convocation, as a memorial of the departure from Egypt. For You have chosen us and sanctified us above all peoples, and You have given us as a heritage (the Shabbos and) Your holy festivals (in love and favor), in joy and gladness. Blessed are You, HASHEM, who sanctifies (the Shabbos and) Israel and the festive seasons.

seeking activity. Therefore the *Shabbos* mood is one of *love*, whereas that of *Yom Tov* is joy.

חַג הַמַּצּוֹת הַזֶּה — *This feast of the Matzos.* This is the name by which the Torah always calls the *Yom Tov* whilst we call it *Pesach*, the day when God 'passed over' our houses.

Rabbi Levi Yitzchak of Berditshev explained that the Torah uses a name that gives credit to the Jews for trusting God so much that they left Egypt with nothing but a few *Matzos*. We Jews use a name that gives credit to God for saving us. (Similarly we find that God commanded Moses to 'take revenge for the Jews from the Midianites', whilst Moses told the Jews 'to avenge HASHEM in Midian', *Bamidbar* 31:2-3). This relationship between God and Israel is epitomized in the verse, 'I belong to my Beloved, and my Beloved belongs to me' (*Shir Hashirim* 6:3).

The explanation has also been offered that the Torah uses the name 'Feast of Matzos' because the *Pesach* sacrifice marked only *Pesach* eve (when it was offered) and the first night (when it was eaten), unlike the *Matzos* which mark the entire *Yom Tov* (*Mayana Shel*

Torah). The Jews speak of *Pesach* as a reminder of the sacrifice that, unfortunately, we cannot offer at present (*Ateres Zekeinim*).

זֵכֶר לִיצִיאַת מִצְרָיִם — *As a memorial of the departure from Egypt.* This phrase occurs in every *Kiddush*, not only that of *Pesach* which specifically celebrates the Exodus. Not only *Pesach* but *Shabbos* and all the other *Yomim Tovim* serve as reminders of the Exodus from Egypt. This is quite obvious, for their observance only began with the birth of the Jewish people at that time (*Avudraham*). But there is also a deeper connection:

Every year calls on us to renew our service of God, and every day plays its role in this renewal. The key to it is our awareness of God, King of the universe, who revealed Himself to the world at the Exodus and made us His people. That is why our daily prayers recall our liberation from Egypt. Our *Shabbos* rest, in particular is a reminder that God freed us from our slave labors in Egypt, by means of miracles which revealed Him as the Creator and master of nature (*Ohr Hachayim, Ramban* to *Devarim* 5:15). Thus the verse in *Tehillim*, 'He

במוצאי שבת מוסיפים שתי ברכות אלו לפני ברכת **שהחיינו**
(כשמברך בורא מאורי האש ידקדק ליהנות מאור הנר)

בָּרוּךְ אַתָּה יהוה אֱלֹהֵינוּ מֶלֶךְ הָעוֹלָם בּוֹרֵא מְאוֹרֵי הָאֵשׁ:

בָּרוּךְ אַתָּה יהוה אֱלֹהֵינוּ מֶלֶךְ הָעוֹלָם הַמַּבְדִּיל בֵּין קֹדֶשׁ
לְחוֹל בֵּין אוֹר לְחשֶׁךְ בֵּין יִשְׂרָאֵל לָעַמִּים בֵּין יוֹם
הַשְּׁבִיעִי לְשֵׁשֶׁת יְמֵי הַמַּעֲשֶׂה. בֵּין קְדֻשַּׁת שַׁבָּת לִקְדֻשַּׁת יוֹם
טוֹב הִבְדַּלְתָּ וְאֶת יוֹם הַשְּׁבִיעִי מִשֵּׁשֶׁת יְמֵי הַמַּעֲשֶׂה קִדַּשְׁתָּ.
הִבְדַּלְתָּ וְקִדַּשְׁתָּ אֶת עַמְּךָ יִשְׂרָאֵל בִּקְדֻשָּׁתֶךָ. בָּרוּךְ אַתָּה יהוה
הַמַּבְדִּיל בֵּין קֹדֶשׁ לְקֹדֶשׁ:

בברכת **שהחיינו** יכוון על החג וגם על כל מצוות הלילה.

בָּרוּךְ אַתָּה יהוה אֱלֹהֵינוּ מֶלֶךְ הָעוֹלָם
שֶׁהֶחֱיָנוּ וְקִיְּמָנוּ וְהִגִּיעָנוּ לַזְּמַן הַזֶּה:

מסיבים על שמאלם ושותים כל הכוס ולכל הפחות רובו, ולא יפסיק
בשתייתו. יכוון לצאת בזה מצות כוס ראשון מארבע כוסות.

made a memorial to His wonders — kind and merciful is HASHEM' (111:4), is interpreted by Rashi in this manner: 'Because God is full of compassion and wishes His children to be pious, He granted them the Shabbos and holy days, to remind them of the bondage in Egypt.'

Above all, however, the holiday of Pesach itself is the wellspring and source of this message of the Exodus (see Overview, p.20). On this day we can re-experience the initial self-revelation of God, and the creation of the Jewish people as a free nation.

The other Yomim Tovim in the yearly cycle carry us further along this road that starts on Pesach. The freedom gained in Egypt is further unfolded on Shavuos, through the receiving of the Torah ('Only he who occupies himself with Torah is truly free'). It finds its final expression on Sukkos when the Jew leaves the temporal world, to take refuge in the Sukkah, which symbolizes the wings of the Shechinah, the Divine Presence (Maharal).

The Sfas Emes describes this festival cycle as the progression from קַבָּלַת

עוֹל מַלְכוּת שָׁמַיִם, the acceptance of God's kingship, to קַבָּלַת הַמִּצְוֹת, the acceptance of the Torah's laws on Shavuos, and finally, to entering the Sukkah in one's entirety, similar to wrapping oneself in the Tallis — three stages that reflect the three chapters of the Shema.

Pesach marks the inception of God's reign over Israel, and its observance is meant to bring about 'that you shall remember the day of your leaving the land of Egypt all the days of your life' (Devarim 16:3). The influence of Pesach must carry through the entire year, as a basis for all the commandments. This accounts for the special stringency of the laws of Pesach (Zohar, see Overview, pp. 28, 38).

בּוֹרֵא מְאוֹרֵי הָאֵשׁ — Who creates the lights of the fire. If the first or second day of Pesach falls on Sunday, it is insufficient to sanctify its beginning by reciting Kiddush — we must also mark the end of the Shabbos with הַבְדָּלָה, the ceremony by which we separate the rest of the week from the Shabbos.

We are permitted certain activities on

(If it is מוֹצָאֵי שַׁבָּת, Saturday night, say the following two *Brachos* as הַבְדָּלָה, to conclude the *Shabbos;* when reciting the first *Brachah* look at the candles. On other evenings, continue directly with the last *Brachah*, שֶׁהֶחֱיָנוּ).

Blessed are You, HASHEM our God, King of the universe, who creates the lights of the fire.

Blessed are You, HASHEM our God, King of the universe, who separates between the holy and the secular, between light and darkness, between Israel and the nations, between the seventh day and the six days of toil. You have made a distinction between the holiness of the Shabbos and the holiness of a festival, and You have sanctified the seventh day above the six days of toil. You set apart and made Your people Israel holy with Your own holiness. Blessed are You, HASHEM, who makes a distinction between holiness and holiness.

(The following *Brachah* is said over the *Yom Tov* as well as all the *Mitzvos* connected with it)

B*lessed are You, HASHEM our God, King of the universe, who has kept us alive and sustained us and brought us to this festive season.*

All lean on their left side* and drink the whole or at least most of the wine in their cup, which is the first of the four cups* required at the *Seder.* Each of these cups should be drunk promptly and without delay, in no more time than is normally required to drain the cup.

Yom Tov, such as baking or cooking, that are forbidden on *Shabbos;* therefore it is necessary to declare the *Shabbos* as ended. For this purpose, we pronounce this blessing over the *Yom Tov* lights, and also the blessing of הַבְדָּלָה, distinction between *Shabbos* and *Yom Tov.* This blessing alludes to seven distinctions that we should take to heart: between the sacred and the profane, between light and darkness, between Israel and the nations, between *Shabbos* and weekdays, between the holiness of *Shabbos, Yom Tov* and *Chol Hamoed* (the Intermediate Days of the *Yom Tov),* and — within the Jewish people — between *Kohanim,* priests, and Levites, and between Levites and Jews in general.

שֶׁהֶחֱיָנוּ — *Who has kept us alive.* This blessing is said on the first day of every *Yom Tov* and, outside *Eretz Yisrael,* on the second day as well.

* *All lean on their left side* — The *Talmud* stresses that to lean on the right is inconvenient and possibly dangerous, as it could cause a person to choke. (*Pesachim* 108a). For the amount of wine that the cup must contain, see p.50ff.

* *The first of the four cups* — Why is there no special blessing for the commandment of drinking Four Cups? Since they are not drunk at one time,

וּרְחַץ

נוֹטְלִים הַיָּדַיִם וְאֵין מְבָרְכִים **עַל נְטִילַת יָדָיִם**. נוֹהֲגִים לְהָבִיא הַכֵּלִים לִנְטִילָה לַמָּקוֹם הָאָב דֶּרֶךְ חֵירוּת. בְּהַרְבֵּה מְקוֹמוֹת נוֹהֲגִים כָּל הַמְּסֻבִּים לִיטוֹל יְדֵיהֶם, וְיֵשׁ שֶׁנּוֹהֲגִים שֶׁרַק הָאָב נוֹטֵל יָדָיו.

כַּרְפַּס

הַמְּסֻבִּים לוֹקְחִים כַּרְפַּס (אֵיזֶה יֶרֶק חוּץ מִמָּרוֹר) פָּחוֹת מִכַּזַּיִת וּמַטְבִּילִים בְּמֵי מֶלַח וּמְבָרְכִים:
כְּשֶׁמְּבָרְכִים מְכַוְּנִים לִפְטוֹר בִּבְרָכָה זוֹ גַם הַמָּרוֹר
(יֵשׁ שֶׁמְּסִבִּים בִּשְׁעַת אֲכִילַת כַּרְפַּס).

בָּרוּךְ אַתָּה יהוה אֱלֹהֵינוּ מֶלֶךְ הָעוֹלָם בּוֹרֵא פְּרִי הָאֲדָמָה:

יַחַץ

הָאָב חוֹלֵק מַצָּה הָאֶמְצָעִית לִשְׁתַּיִם, מַחֲזִיר הַפְּרוּסָה הַקְּטַנָּה בֵּין שְׁתֵּי מַצּוֹת הַשְּׁלֵמוֹת וְהַפְּרוּסָה הַגְּדוֹלָה מַצְנִיעַ בְּמִטְפַּחַת לְאוֹכְלָהּ בְּסוֹף הַסְּעוּדָה

but scattered through the *Seder*, it is inappropriate to recite a blessing for 'four cups' (*Rokeach*). Also, the first cup is used for *Kiddush*, as on other *Yomim Tovim*; therefore, we cannot refer to a special commandment to drink Four Cups (*Avudraham*).

As we pointed out in the Overview (p.35),however, on other *Yomim Tovim* only the father has to drink wine at the *Kiddush*; but this is not so on *Pesach* for everybody is required by our Sages to drink four cups. These four cups therefore, do belong together as a group, specifically mandated by the Rabbis. In consequence we do not make a בְּרָכָה אַחֲרוֹנָה, concluding blessing, after drinking each cup, since they are connected with each other. (*Rav Hai Gaon*).

In that case, however, why do we make a blessing before drinking each cup? One answer is that each cup has a significance of its own, as though each were a distinct experience. *Rabbi S.R. Hirsch* interprets it this way: each cup symbolizes a new and further stage of

redemption, but does not, by itself, represent complete redemption (see Overview, p.36). We therefore welcome each one with a blessing, but do not say a concluding blessing until after the fourth cup.

* *Washes his hands* — This washing is in preparation for eating the *Karpas* dipped in saltwater. In the times of the בֵּית הַמִּקְדָּשׁ, the Holy Temple, when people were able to observe the laws of ritual purity in full, they were required to wash their hands before eating any produce that had been dipped in water or certain other liquids.

According to many opinions this washing is not necessary nowadays, when we are unable to attain ritual purity. Nonetheless, on *Seder* night the Master of the *Seder* washes his hands before eating *Karpas*. This serves as a reminder of the procedure that was followed in the time of the Temple and expresses the hope that we will soon be required to follow it again, with the coming of *Mashiach*. It also represents a courtly custom in keeping with the

U'rechatz / Wash Hands*

The father washes his hands, without making a *Brachah*; as yet another sign of freedom and dignity, the washbasin is brought to his seat. (According to many opinions, the other *Seder* participants also wash their hands.)

Karpas / Eat Karpas*

All participants take a piece of *Karpas* (some vegetable other than *Maror*), smaller than the size of an olive, dip it into salt water and eat it, without having to recline, after reciting the following *Brachah*; when they say this *Brachah*, they should have in mind that it is also for the *Maror* that will be eaten later. (Some recline while eating *Karpas*.)

Blessed are You, HASHEM our God, King of the universe, who creates the fruit of the earth.

Yachatz / Break the Middle Matzah*

The father now takes the middle *Matzah* and breaks it into two. The smaller part he puts back between the two whole *Matzos* in front of him; the larger part

special dignity that the Master of the *Seder* enjoys tonight. Moreover, it serves to provoke questions by the children, like many other *Seder* night practices that help to keep them awake.

(Many rabbinic authorities, however, take the view that this ritual washing is required even nowadays, whenever one eats produce that was dipped in liquid. According to them, all the participants at the *Seder* must wash their hands before eating *Karpas*. Some Rabbis, finally, are of the opinion that the washing is not really required nowadays — but on *Seder* night we ought to be particularly punctilious in observing even practices that are not strictly necessary; therefore they agree that all participants should wash.)

כַּרְפַּס — *Karpas*. In olden days, banquets were started with such appetizers. The custom was preserved, in order to make the children ask questions, and also as a sign of freedom (for slaves obviously are not accustomed to such luxuries).

The dipping of the food is a further sign of comfort and indulgence. Yet we dip it into salt water, to remind us of the bitterness of the bondage *(Shloh)*.

Moreover, the very name of *Karpas*, when reversed, alludes to Egyptian slavery: ס׳ פֶּרֶךְ — *sixty* [myriads of Jews] *at hard labor*. The *Karpas* can thus be viewed either as primarily a symbol of bondage, or as a symbol of freedom. (That is why there are conflicting opinions on whether one should eat it whilst reclining like a free man.)

We do not recite a blessing that we were 'commanded to eat *Karpas*,' because it is a custom rather than a formal enactment of the Rabbis. But we do recite a blessing over *Karpas* as 'fruit of the earth,' and have in mind that this blessing should also refer to the *Maror* that we will eat later. For that reason we eat less than a כְּזַיִת (size of an olive) of the *Karpas*, so that we do not have to make a concluding blessing over the *Karpas* and, as a result, a new blessing before eating *Maror*.

יַחַץ — *Break the middle Matzah*. We are

למצות אפיקומן. יש נוהגים להשים הפרוסה במטפחת על שכמם ופוסעים
איזו פסיעות ואומרים ,,בבהילו יצאנו ממצרים".

מַגִּיד

now ready to begin the narrative of the Exodus. As explained in the Overview, however, this must be done when the *Matzah* lies before us (p.24), for the *Matzah* is called לֶחֶם עוֹנִי which is interpreted by our Sages as לֶחֶם שֶׁעוֹנִין עָלָיו דְּבָרִים הַרְבֵּה — *the bread over which many things are said*, namely the *Haggadah*. But the term לֶחֶם עוֹנִי also means 'bread of affliction and poverty' — and a poor man does not feast over a whole loaf because he is never certain that he will have food for the next meal. He takes a small piece, putting most of the bread away for later *(Rav Hai Gaon)*. Therefore we break the *Matzah* and put away the larger part for the *Afikoman*, keeping the smaller piece in front of us during the telling of the *Haggadah*.

Why not break the top *Matzah*? The first blessing said at the meal is הַמּוֹצִיא לֶחֶם מִן הָאָרֶץ, praising Him '*who brings forth bread from the earth*'. At *Shabbos* and *Yom Tov* meals this blessing must be said over unbroken loaves or, on *Pesach, Matzos*. Only afterwards will we say the blessing for the commandment of *Matzah*, which is recited over the broken piece, the 'bread of poverty.' We therefore arrange the *Matzos* in the order in which they are needed — leaving the top *Matzah* unbroken, ready for the first blessing.

Under his pillows — Many explanations have been offered for this custom: to protect the *Afikoman* (in keeping with the obligation '*to guard the Matzos', Shemos* 12:17); to insure that it will not be mixed up with other *Matzos* and inadvertently eaten; and not to 'shame' it, so to speak as it will be set aside and by-passed till the very end of the meal. Also, the hiding of the *Afikoman* stimulates the children's questions and keeps them awake by encouraging them to try and steal it. This custom reflects another interpretation of the Talmudic rule '*to get the Matzah quickly ...*' that was quoted previously, (p. 46, also p. 70).

According to the *Rokeach*, in wrapping up the *Afikoman*, we reenact the way in which the Jews carried their dough out of Egypt *(Shemos* 12:34). This is also the purpose of the custom, mentioned in the instructions, to put the *Afikoman* over one's shoulder. The *Mechilta* explains that the Jews cherished the *Mitzvah* of *Matzah* too much to let their animals carry the dough; instead, they carried it on their backs. Various similar customs exist, particularly among Sefardic Jews; they are all designed to help us 'live through the experience' of going out from Egypt.

In a deeper sense the hiding of the *Afikoman* symbolizes that the Exodus was only the beginning of the process of redemption, and part of it is still hidden (צָפוּן). That is why the eating of the *Afikoman* (which, as the substitute for the *Pesach* sacrifice, represents our liberation) begins the second part of the *Seder*, which is dedicated to the future redemption — and why the *Afikoman* is the last food of the evening, so that its taste remain in our mouths for the rest of the night *(Sfas Emes)*.

מַגִּיד — *Recite the Haggadah*. With the *Matzah* lying before us, we are ready to begin the central commandment of the night, סִפּוּר יְצִיאַת מִצְרַיִם, telling about the Exodus from Egypt: *Haggadah* (see Overview, p.24). We commonly use this word to describe the text that is used at the *Seder*; but in a wider sense it refers to all the discussion of our deliverance from Egypt which takes place in this night. It·is derived from the verse, וְהִגַּדְתָּ לְבִנְךָ, '*You shall tell your son*' *(Shemos*

הגדה של פסח [64]

he wraps into a napkin or bag and conceals under his pillows,* for use — later — as *Afikoman.* (First, however, some have the custom of putting the bag with the *Matzah* over their shoulder, taking a few steps, and saying בְּבְהִלוּ יָצָאנוּ מִמִּצְרַיִם 'in haste we went out from Egypt.')

Maggid / Recite the Haggadah*

13:8) and, literally, means 'telling' — but it can also be understood as 'showing', 'demonstrating', or as 'giving thanks' for our liberation (*Targum Jonathan to Devarim 26:3*).

We are obliged to remember the Exodus from Egypt every day; but this obligation differs from our duty on *Seder* night in several respects. It only requires remembering (according to some opinions) or, at most, mentioning the Exodus — whereas on *Seder* night we must tell the full story, from bondage to deliverance, in the form of question and answer, with as much elaboration as possible (*Besomim Rosh, Maaseh Nissim, Shaagas Aryeh, Rabbi Chayim Soloveitchik*). Moreover, according to most opinions, the daily remembrance of the Exodus is not reckoned among the 613 commandments (*Behag, et al*); but the narration on *Seder* night is one of the commandments.

Why, then, do we not recite a blessing for it? A number of reasons are given: according to some opinions we may already have fulfilled the commandment, at least minimally, by mentioning the Exodus in our evening prayers and *Kiddush*; we will say a blessing as we finish our narration; *Haggadah* is itself a form of Divine praise and therefore need not be introduced by a blessing; it has no defined dimensions; it is primarily a matter of thinking rather than doing; and it would be required by logic even if there were no Divine edict (*Besomim Rosh, Rashbo, Avudraham, Maharal, Sfas Emes*). The *Rosh* takes the view that no special blessing is called for because *Haggadah* is not a duty by itself, but an outgrowth of the practical commandments of *Seder* night; it is when we are asked the reason for them, that we must

respond by explaining about the Exodus.

Generally, women are exempt from מִצְוַת עֲשֵׂה שֶׁהַזְּמַן גְּרָמָא, a commandment which can be performed only at a specified time. However, they are required to eat *Matzah*, for the Torah links this commandment to the prohibition on eating Chametz, and this law, like all prohibitions, applies to women just as to men. When the Sages instituted the duty of drinking אַרְבַּע כּוֹסוֹת, the Four Cups, they included women because 'they, too, were involved in the miracle' of the Exodus (*Rashi*: they were instrumental in bringing it about through their virtue and piety; see p.71; *Yerushalmi*: they were in the same danger as the men). What about the obligation of *Maggid*, narrating the Exodus story? According to some, they are included in the Biblical commandment (*Sefer Hachinuch*), perhaps because it is linked with the duty of eating *Matzah* which they are charged with (see above, יַחַץ). Others hold the view that the obligation of women to tell the *Haggadah* was ordained by the Rabbis, because 'they, too, were involved in the miracle' (*Shulchan Aruch Harav*). Since the Four Cups, which are an obligation for women, were instituted to be drunk in connection with the various parts of the *Seder* observance, such as *Maggid* and *Hallel*, it is clear in any case that women are obliged to perform all these observances too. They are only exempt from the duty of reclining, since women ordinarily did not eat while reclining, even in olden days (however, they may recline if they so desire).

The duty of *Haggadah* has no definite delimitation. However, the Torah not only ordained the *Seder*, with *Pesach*, *Matzah* and *Maror*, and discussion of the Exodus, but also provided an actual outline for this discussion (*Devarim 6:20-25*):

¶ The verse, '*If your son asks you tomorrow saying: "what are the laws …"* ' — corresponds to the child's questions מַה נִּשְׁתַּנָּה (p.70 of this *Haggadah*);

¶ '*You shall say to your son: "We were*

מַגְבִּיהִים הַקְּעָרָה וּמְגַלִּים הַמַּצּוֹת (וְיֵשׁ שֶׁמַּקְפִּידִים לְהָסִיר הַזְּרוֹעַ וְהַבֵּיצָה)
וְאוֹמְרִים:

הָא לַחְמָא עַנְיָא דִּי אֲכָלוּ אַבְהָתָנָא בְּאַרְעָא דְמִצְרָיִם. כָּל דִּכְפִין יֵיתֵי וְיֵכוֹל. כָּל-

slaves to Pharaoh in Egypt and HASHEM took us out ...' ' — corresponds to the father's reply עֲבָדִים הָיִינוּ (p. 72);

¶ 'And HASHEM made signs and wonders ...' — corresponds to the Midrash צֵא וּלְמַד (p.100);

¶ 'And us He took out from there ...' — corresponds to the reminder לֹא אֶת אֲבוֹתֵינוּ בִּלְבַד (p.146).

¶ 'And HASHEM commanded us to do these statutes ...' — corresponds to Rabban Gamliel's statement about Pesach, Matzah, Maror (p. 140).

¶ 'And it will be a merit for us if we carefully do this entire commandment' — corresponds to our performance of the Mitzvos of Pesach and our prayer for the future redemption.

The Haggadah was undoubtedly given its basic form at the beginning of the Second Temple, by the אַנְשֵׁי כְּנֶסֶת הַגְּדוֹלָה, the Men of the Great Synod, who composed all our main prayers. Much of the Haggadah was included in the Mishnah and the oldest Midrashim (Mechilta, Sifri). However, some details were fixed as late as the time of the Amoraim, the Rabbis of the Talmud, well after the destruction of the Second Temple (note the controversy between Rav and Shemuel, quoted in the Overview, p.31). The final editing took place at the end of the Talmudic era, by the early Gaonim. A few passages were added still later, as will be noted in the Commentary. However, basically our Haggadah corresponds to the version that Rabbi Amram Gaon included when he compiled the first Siddur, about 1100 years ago.

The Zohar stresses that when a man recites the words of the Haggadah, paying tribute to the transcending miracles of Yetzias Mitzrayim, and rejoicing

with his Lord, God in turn rejoices with him and calls upon all the heavenly host to listen and to join in. Thus — so to speak — new heavenly glory and strength are generated. Therefore, one who truly rejoices in telling of Yetzias Mitzrayim is sure to rejoice with the Divine Presence in the World to Come. In keeping with this awe-inspiring significance of Haggadah, many authorities hold that we are not supposed to recline while reciting it (Shloh), just as we should not recline when saying a blessing (Birkey Yosef). However, some take the view that, in demonstration of our freedom, we should recline during the Haggadah (Meiri).

הָא לַחְמָא עַנְיָא — This is the bread of affliction that our forefathers ate in the land of Egypt. The Haggadah must be told 'at the time when Pesach, Matzah, and Maror lie before you,' and we are to discuss and explain all three (see p. 89). Yet we begin the Haggadah with a special reference to the Matzah alone. This can be explained by the fact that this passage does not appear in the earliest sources; it was composed after the destruction of the Second Temple, when the exile had already begun. Therefore it ends with a prayer for redemption (Hashir Vehashevach; see Rambam). In exile, we cannot fulfill the Biblical commandments of Pesach and Maror (in the absence of a Pesach sacrifice, Maror is a Rabbinic duty); so that Matzah is left as the preeminent obligation of the evening.

However, the Matzah probably occupied a special position even in the times of the Temple, for it is לֶחֶם עוֹנִי — לֶחֶם שֶׁעוֹנִין עָלָיו דְּבָרִים הַרְבֵּה, the bread over which many things are said (עוֹנִי has the same numerical value, 136, as קוֹל, voice or sound). But why this

The *Seder* plate is lifted up, with the *Matzos* uncovered (and, according to some, with bone and egg removed); and the father begins מַגִּיד by pointing out:

This is the bread of affliction that our fathers ate in the land of Egypt. Whoever is hungry, let him

emphasis that the *Haggadah* be narrated just over the *Matzah*? Perhaps because it applies in all generations, unlike the *Pesach* sacrifice; or because unlike *Pesach* and *Maror*, it symbolizes both bondage and freedom and therefore uniquely conveys the message of the *Seder*.

The Torah underlines the connection between *Matzah* and the remembering of the Exodus; it stresses that '... *you shall eat Matzos, the bread of affliction ... so that you will remember the day of your going out from Egypt all the days of your life'* (Devarim 16:3). Hence, we keep the *Matzah* uncovered when the *Haggadah* is recited, except for those occasions when we lift our cups; then it is covered in order, so to speak, not to shame it while it is ignored in favor of the wine.

[According to *Rabbeinu Chananel*, however, the duty to talk about the *Matzah*, as לְחֶם עוֹנִי, does not mean that the *Haggadah* has to be told over the *Matzah* in particular; it merely entails explaining the commandment to eat *Matzah* — just as we have to explain the commandments to eat *Pesach* and *Maror* with which the Torah equates it. According to this view, the role of the *Matzah* is no different from that of *Pesach* and *Maror*. Therefore, the *Rambam* (who apparently follows *Rabbeinu Chananel's* interpretation of the term לְחֶם עוֹנִי) does not even consider it necessary to have the *Seder* plate with the *Matzos* on the table while the *Haggadah* is told, except when *Rabban Gamliel* is quoted in explanation of *Pesach, Matzah* and *Maror* (p.140).

It has, however, been suggested that, in accordance with the view of *Rabbeinu Chananel*, the telling of the *Haggadah* was preceded in Temple times by a reference to *Pesach* and *Maror* as well as to *Matzah* (see *Shibolei Haleket*, quoted below, (p.69). The reason for this practice can be found in the Torah's directive to tell the *Haggadah* 'at the

time that *Pesach, Matzah,* and *Maror* lie before you.' Such a practice would explain the custom, mentioned in the Instructions, to remove bone and egg from the *Seder* plate before lifting it up for הָא לַחְמָא. This custom seems meaningless (and *Rashbam* therefore declares it to be an error); however, if *Pesach* and *Maror* were also referred to at this point in the Temple times, it would be logical to remove bone and egg nowadays, so that they should not be mistaken for the *Pesach* sacrifice itself. It is for this same reason that we do not point at the bone when we quote *Rabban Gamliel*.]

As pointed out, the *Matzah* has a dual character. With the hasty departure of our forefathers from Egypt, it became a symbol of freedom; originally, however, it was their food when they were slaves, and therefore a symbol of bondage *(Vilna Gaon,* contrary to *Maharal).* It is this one feature that we here emphasize: a broken piece 'that our forefathers ate in the land of Egypt' — hard to digest and very filling, a typical staple of slaves *(Ibn Ezra).*

Why do we stress this aspect of the *Matzah* here? Not given time to rise and, therefore, the very picture of unimpressive lowliness *(Abarbanel),* it is the perfect symbol of oppression. Thus, it triggers the recollection of the events in Egypt, and helps us project ourselves into the situation of our forefathers — so that we can better feel the relief and joy of the deliverance. This, after all, is the goal of the *Seder.*

But there is also another thought. הָא לַחְמָא עַנְיָא is a reflection of the feelings of the Jew in exile: happy as we are with the redemption from Egypt, the end of our long road — the final redemption — has not yet been reached. So we appreciate all too well the taste of bondage that lies in the *Matzah.*

כָּל דִכְפִין יֵיתֵי וְיֵכוֹל — *Whoever is hungry, let him come and eat.* It appears strange

דִּצְרִיךְ יֵיתֵי וְיִפְסַח. הָשַׁתָּא הָכָא לְשָׁנָה הַבָּאָה
בְּאַרְעָא דְיִשְׂרָאֵל. הָשַׁתָּא עַבְדֵי לְשָׁנָה הַבָּאָה
בְּנֵי חוֹרִין:

to invite guests at this point; were this an invitation, it should have been made earlier. Rather, this passage is an outgrowth of the discussion of the 'bread of poverty.' We are truly eating the bread of poverty today, for we are again in exile. As a result, we may invite anyone to join our meal because we have no *Pesach* sacrifice; in Temple times guests could not be invited while the *Seder* was in progress, because the *Pesach* could be shared only with prearranged participants. Our call to guests is to emphasize that we are in exile.

Moreover, we stress that we are eager to open our houses to the poor and to share our meal with them because it is through such generosity that we can aspire to redemption. גָּלְתָה יְהוּדָה מֵעֹנִי, *the Jewish people went into exile because of poverty (Eichah* 1:3); the word עֹנִי can be taken as a reference to poverty as well as to the *Matzah*, the לֶחֶם עֹנִי; therefore our Sages saw here an allusion that our exile was due to our neglect of *Matzah* as well as to our disregard of the needs of the poor. These transgressions highlighted the failure to do our duty both toward God and toward our fellow-beings. Therefore, as we lift up the *Matzah* and welcome the poor to our table, we pray that in consequence we may merit a speedy redemption — for *'Zion will be redeemed through righteousness and its penitents through charity' (Isaiah* 1:27) *(Chasam Sofer).*

Pesach is indeed not only a festival dedicated to the encounter between God and the Jewish people, but to חֶסֶד, loving kindness practiced between Jew and Jew *(Shloh).* Our Sages tell us that the Jews attained redemption from Egypt because even in the darkest times of bondage, when they had fallen to the lowest spiritual estate, no Jew ever denounced another to the Egyptians; in fact, they made a covenant among themselves to preserve whatever they had learned from the Patriarchs and to render kindness to each other *(Tanna D'Bey Eliyahu,* see p. 106). In turn, they merited that the wellsprings of divine kindness were opened to them, and they were redeemed.

Their redemption, as explained in the *Overview,* p. 28, parallelled the creation of the world. Interestingly, we see here a further similarity between these happenings, for in connection with the creation of the world, it is stated that *'the world has been built upon kindness' (Tehillim* 89:3). *Pesach,* marking this overflowing of kindness, has been called the festival of *Abraham* whom our Sages characterized as the ultimate exponent of kindness. By concluding this passage with the prayer that this be the last *Pesach* in exile, the *Haggadah* enjoins us to recognize charity and kindness as the foundations of the future redemption, which has its roots in this festival.

That may be the reason for the institution of מָעוֹת חִטִּים, 'money for wheat,' the custom to gather funds before *Pesach* for *Matzos* and other needs of the poor. And it also explains why such special emphasis is placed on inviting needy guests for *Pesach.* In fact, the *Malbim* suggests that the phrase, 'whoever is hungry, let him come and eat,' is addressed to the poor who are gathered around the table in response to an earlier public invitation, in order to make them feel welcome.

כָּל דִּצְרִיךְ יֵיתֵי וְיִפְסַח — *Whoever is in need, let him come and join in celebrating the Pesach festival.* We do not translate וְיִפְסַח literally, as an invitation to eat the *Pesach* sacrifice, for today

come and eat; whoever is in need, let him come and join in celebrating the Pesach festival. This year we are here, next year may we be in the land of Israel! This year, slaves, next year — free men!

we have no *Pesach* sacrifice, and in Temple times, as mentioned, only pre-arranged guests could partake of it. The term וְיִפְסַח may perhaps refer to the eating of the *Afikoman* which nowadays takes the place of the *Pesach* sacrifice *(Ravon)*. However, it can be taken simply as an invitation to celebrate the *Pesach* festival with us — duplicating the preceeding phrase, וְיֵכוֹל, 'let him come and eat.' Why this duplication? The *Shibolei Haleket* suggests that this alludes to Temple times, when the *Seder* began with a reference to *Pesach, Matzah* and *Maror*; nowadays, we specify only *Matzah*, since the Biblical commandments of *Pesach* and *Maror* do not apply today — however, we still do include an allusion to them: וְיֵכוֹל alludes to the eating of *Maror*, and וְיִפְסַח to the eating of the *Pesach* sacrifice.

The twin invitations can also be taken as offers of both physical and spiritual sustenance to the needy. Our exile today, like that in Egypt (see Overview, p. 31), is marked by both material deprivation and spiritual impoverishment. We therefore offer aid for both — providing first for material needs, and then for spiritual ones — as our father Abraham did for his guests *(Rabbi Myski)*. And we pray that we ourselves may thereby become worthy of redemption in both body and soul.

In the same vein, it has been suggested that the 'bread of poverty' before us should be a source of encouragement in our exile. We are threatened by physical extinction and by ideological assimilation. We, therefore, invite those who are fearful of these twin threats, to come and celebrate with us; they will realize that God saved us from these same dangers in Egypt, and we too will attain a twofold redemption, physical

and spiritual *(Hashir Vehashevach, see Overview p. 32)*.

הָשַׁתָּא הָכָא ... הָשַׁתָּא עַבְדֵי — *This year we are here ... this year we are slaves.* In these sentences the meaning of a twofold redemption is spelled out: not only do we yearn for our own Holy Land, we want to be free. And, as our Sages stress, 'Nobody is free until he occupies himself with Torah.' The implication is that one can be in the Holy Land and yet not be truly free — or that, even if we cannot have *Eretz Yisrael* as yet, we should at least want to attain some freedom of the spirit wherever we find ourselves *(Rabbi Elazar Fleckeles)*. At present we might have all civil rights, but spiritually we are slaves — in bondage to wrong ideas or, as has been suggested, serving God only out of fear and awe (like a servant) rather than out of love (like a son).

There exists a different version in an ancient *Haggadah* manuscript: 'Yesterday we were slaves and today we are free, today we are here and next year in Eretz Yisrael.' This version would seem to fit well with the view of *Rashbam* that this passage was recited by our forefathers in Egypt (see הַלֵּל, p. 151). Thus, our forefathers thanked God for the first stage of their redemption, the Exodus from slavery, and looked forward to the next stage, the entry into the Holy Land.

Generally, however, it is thought that this part of the *Haggadah* was composed either after the destruction of the First Temple or, more likely, after that of the Second. As it was not part of the official text, it was written in Aramaic, which was then the everyday language of the people. Only the phrase לְשָׁנָה הַבָּאָה, *next year*, expressing our hope to be free and in *Eretz Yisrael*, was written

מוזגים כוס שני (וְיֵשׁ שֶׁמְּסִירִים הַקְּעָרָה מִמְּקוֹמָהּ לְקְצֵה הַשֻּׁלְחָן, וְיֵשׁ שֶׁמְּסַלְקִים אוֹתָהּ לְגַמְרֵי) וְהַבֵּן שׁוֹאֵל:

מַה נִּשְׁתַּנָּה הַלַּיְלָה הַזֶּה מִכָּל־הַלֵּילוֹת. שֶׁבְּכָל הַלֵּילוֹת אָנוּ אוֹכְלִין חָמֵץ וּמַצָּה הַלַּיְלָה הַזֶּה כֻּלּוֹ מַצָּה. שֶׁבְּכָל הַלֵּילוֹת אָנוּ אוֹכְלִין שְׁאָר יְרָקוֹת הַלַּיְלָה הַזֶּה מָרוֹר. שֶׁבְּכָל הַלֵּילוֹת אֵין אָנוּ מַטְבִּילִין אֲפִילוּ פַּעַם אֶחָת הַלַּיְלָה הַזֶּה שְׁתֵּי פְעָמִים. שֶׁבְּכָל הַלֵּילוֹת אָנוּ אוֹכְלִין בֵּין יוֹשְׁבִין וּבֵין מְסֻבִּין הַלַּיְלָה הַזֶּה כֻּלָּנוּ מְסֻבִּין:

in Hebrew, in order not to give offense to the foreign overlords (Kolbo), or because this phrase was universally understood in all ages (Rashbatz); however, in the Haggados of Rav Saadia Gaon and the Rambam this phrase also is in Aramaic.

* The second cup — Pouring yet another cup of wine before the meal is a further step designed to surprise the children and to stimulate questions. So is the custom of removing the Seder plate (based on yet another interpretation of the Talmudic rule 'to get the Matzah in a hurry ...', namely to take it away). For the same reason, the Talmud also speaks of distributing nuts to children; some do so before מַה נִּשְׁתַּנָּה, the Four Questions, or on עֶרֶב פֶּסַח, the day before Pesach (Pesachim 109a).

* A child asks — Customarily the youngest asks; but, if he is not old enough to understand his own questions or to comprehend the answer, the questions should be repeated by an older child. If there are no children at the table, an adult asks — and if the Master of the Seder is alone, he poses the questions himself. In all circumstances the Haggadah is to be told in response to questions. (There is actually a view that we are not obliged to tell the Haggadah unless a question has been asked.)

Why the need for questions? In the Overview (p. 27) we pointed out that only he who is bothered by a question is really interested in the answer (Ksav Sofer). We are particularly eager to pass the message of Pesach on to our children because the assurance of our national continuity lies within the family unit. If fathers will awaken the interest of their children and teach them to turn to their elders for the inherited wisdom of our people ('Ask your father and he will tell you ...', Devarim 32:7; 'Hear, my son, the teaching of your father ...', Mishley 1:8), then we will attain a situation where 'in every generation a person will see himself as having gone out of Egypt' and will take to heart the lessons of that great event.

On the other hand, failure to train our youth must lead to national disaster. Tisha B'Av resulted from a situation 'when you bear children and children's children, and you grow old in the land' (Devarim 4:25, read on Tisha B'Av): no longer aspiring to a deeper Jewish consciousness, you forget — and let them forget — about your Divine mission. That may be why our Sages have pointed out an inner connection between Seder night and Tisha B'Av

The second cup* is now poured (and, according to the custom of some, the
Seder plate is moved to the end of the table or altogether removed); whereupon a
child asks:*

W hy is this night different from all other nights?
   For on all other nights we may eat Chametz and
Matzos, and on this night only Matzos.
   For on all other nights we eat any kind of
vegetables, and on this night Maror.
   For on all other nights we are not required to dip
our vegetables even once, and on this night we are re-
quired to do so twice.
   For on all other nights we eat sitting upright or
reclining, and on this night we all recline.

(which always falls on the same day of the week in any given year): in connection with the destruction of the Temple we have to grieve that *'He made me sated with Maror, He fed me with bitter roots' (Eichah* 3:15). This may indicate that, if we do not observe the *Pesach* properly, and are too comfortable to learn the lesson of its *Maror,* then we will be forced to suffer the bitterness of the destruction of the Temple (see pp. 68, 162).

It has also been suggested that the questions of a child find a special echo in Heaven, particularly as they are so suggestive of the close relationship between God and Israel at the Exodus: *'for Israel was a youth and I loved him' (Hoshea* 11:1) *(Lubavitch Haggadah).*

מַה נִּשְׁתַּנָּה — *Why is this night different from all other nights?* These words are the introduction to the four questions that follow. Many of the things done so far this evening were meant to prompt the children to follow the example of the wise son *(Devarim* 6:20), and to ask about the meaning of the observances that mark the *Seder.*

Our Sages outlined for them four particular questions. In the *Mishnah* these questions refer to *Matzah, Maror, Pesach* and dipping twice. After the destruction of the Temple, the question

about the *Pesach* sacrifice was replaced by one concerning reclining. (According to the *Vilna Gaon,* this custom was too common in earlier times to warrant questioning; *Rambam,* however, suggests that in the time of the Temple there was a question about reclining too.)

It has been noted that the number four plays a large role at the *Seder;* there are four questions, four sons, four cups, four commandments *(Pesach, Matzoh, Maror, Haggadah).* This has been interpreted as an allusion to the four wives of the Patriarchs; they set the pattern of pious modesty that was followed by the Jewish women in Egypt — and, according to our Sages, בִּזְכוּת נָשִׁים צִדְקָנִיּוֹת שֶׁבְּאוֹתוֹ דוֹר נִגְאֲלוּ אֲבוֹתֵינוּ, it was in their particular merit that we were redeemed*(Sotah* 11b).Even though their slave status made them particularly vulnerable, only one woman ever disgraced herself in Egypt (see *Vayikrah* 24:10); without the extraordinary sense of morality of all the other women and their dedicated ministrations to their husbands, the Jews would have disappeared in the depths of Egyptian corruption.

Why did our Sages single out just these four questions? It has been suggested that they show the equal validity

עֲבָדִים הָיִינוּ לְפַרְעֹה בְּמִצְרָיִם. וַיּוֹצִיאֵנוּ יהוה אֱלֹהֵינוּ מִשָּׁם בְּיָד חֲזָקָה

of Biblical commandments *(Matzah, Maror)* and Rabbinic ones (dipping, reclining) — although our version of the *Mah Nishtanah* lists the Biblical ones first (Sefardim have a different arrangement, based on the order in which the various commandments are done).

However, the *Abarbanel* explains that the Four Questions were chosen to highlight the paradox that we should sense on this evening *(Overview,* p. 30). Many of its practices reflect a sense of enslavement (the broken *Matzah,* the saltwater, and the *Maror* and *Charoses* that the child sees on the *Seder* plate); others (from the beautiful table-setting and white *kittel,* to the wine, the reclining, and the dipping of food) express the spirit of freedom; and the child asks: how can one night reflect simultaneously both bondage and freedom? The child gives two examples for each — so-to-speak like the two witnesses that Torah law always requires to establish a fact.

Why are the Four Cups not the subject of a question? There are various possible reasons. The child sees before him *Matzah, Maror,* as well as the saltwater and *Charoses* for dipping; also, he has watched everybody reclining whilst drinking the first cup; but there is nothing to indicate that *four* cups will be drunk. The child may be surprised that we already poured a second cup (see above); but the drinking of wine, in itself, is common at festive meals and not necessarily a special religious practice. For this reason, it would also be difficult to phrase a question that would show a contrast between *Seder* night and other nights in this respect. The *Maharal* suggests that the *Haggadah* only poses questions concerning Rabbinic observances (like dipping and reclining) that are at least con-

nected with Biblical commandments (the eating of *Maror* and *Matzah* respectively), while the Four Cups are purely Rabbinic in nature.

The questions are introduced by the phrase, 'Why is this *night* different?...', because the interplay of bondage and freedom has *made the night itself* different *(Sfas Emes).* Usually commandments are not assigned exclusively to nighttime; and we never say *Hallel* at night. This night, however was lit up like day when HASHEM revealed Himself in Egypt *(Tehillim* 139:12), and therefore it is actually called day *(Shemos* 13:8).

In some places it is customary for the father to repeat the *Mah Nishtanah* after the child has finished. The reason may be that perhaps the child did not ask with understanding (see above); or that the father poses the questions with a deeper understanding of undercurrents not perceived by a child. It has even been suggested that, in repeating the questions, we address them to the Father of all of us, in Heaven, Who alone can give us the fullest answer.

[Some comments on the text of the passage: *Rambam,* here as well as everywhere else in the *Haggadah,* uses for מָרוֹר the Biblical expression מְרוֹרִים. *Tosfos* stresses that we should not say כּוּלּוֹ מָרוֹר, *only Maror,* since we also eat other vegetables; and *Rav Saadiah Gaon* does not say that 'we *all* recline,' since some people are exempt from reclining (for instance students in the presence of their Rabbi).]

עֲבָדִים הָיִינוּ — *We were slaves.* The father's answer (based on *Devarim* 6:21) very briefly sums up the events of the Exodus from Egypt. Some parents, however, send their younger children to sleep as soon as they finished asking

We were once slaves of Pharaoh in Egypt, but HASHEM our God brought us out from there with a strong hand and an outstretched arm. If the

מַה נִּשְׁתַּנָּה. Obviously it does not make sense to prompt children to ask the Four Questions and then send them to bed; they should be given an answer, explained on their level. In fact the commentators emphasize that it is desirable that the entire *Haggadah* should be translated and explained for the benefit of all *Seder* participants — after all, the *Seder* is not meant to be an empty ritual but an effort to grasp and relive the experience of our ancestors. (At the very least, we are required to translate and explain מַה נִּשְׁתַּנָּה and הָא לַחְמָא עַנְיָא as well as עֲבָדִים הָיִינוּ and, later, רַבָּן גַּמְלִיאֵל, p. 140.)

The father's reply can be explained very simply in this manner: the observances questioned by the child must be performed by us, even if we do not know their meaning, for they were ordained by God — and He is our master, having freed us from Egyptian bondage (*Ma'aseh Nissim*). However, the father's words also provide an explanation of the observances questioned, and of the paradox posed by them: the practices of the *Seder* reflect both bondage and freedom because in this night we *were* slaves and *became* free. Both points are tellingly enlarged upon:

We were slaves to *Pharaoh*: a harsh tyrant, from whom we could hope for no mercy or consideration; in *Egypt*: a harsh country, from which no slave had ever escaped, so that we could have no hope of freeing ourselves (archaeologists have found records documenting the strict border controls in ancient Egypt). In fact, as slaves, we had been totally broken by our masters. They represented brutal might at its highest, and sought to rob us of the last shreds of our humanity. At that point,

God took us out of Egypt. In overthrowing Egypt and turning a horde of slaves into a nation, He demonstrated that the most powerful empire is impotent before Him, the true master of all human destinies: the will of God, rather than physical strength, determines the course of history. Moreover, the miraculous creation of our people established us once and for all as God's nation.

The words אֱלֹקֵינוּ, *our God*, and זְרֹעַ נְטוּיָה, *His outstretched arm*, do not occur in the verse, in *Devarim*, from which our passage is drawn; there, only the divine name יהו־ה is used, which refers to God as the master of mercy (מִדַּת הָרַחֲמִים), in contrast to אלהי־ם which refers to Him as the master of judgment (מִדַּת הַדִּין). Apparently the Torah wants us to tell our children about the kindness of God in redeeming us. We, however, use both names of God here, to show that we also appreciate His sternness in putting us into bondage: it was the very severity of our suffering that, in the end, caused our liberation and made it such a telling experience (*Sfas Emes*). In fact, that may be the deeper reason why our Sages instructed us that, in telling the *Haggadah*, מַתְחִיל בִּגְנוּת וּמְסַיֵּם בְּשֶׁבַח, *one starts with the shameful part and ends with the praise*; liberty has a sweeter taste when compared to earlier suffering, and the lesson of the liberation is brought home so much more forcefully.

[It has also been suggested that God is here referred to as God of Mercy because the Jews experienced Him this way at the Exodus — and we speak of Him as God of Judgment because that is the way the Egyptians experienced Him (*Rabbi J. Myski*).]

וּבִזְרוֹעַ נְטוּיָה. וְאִלּוּ לֹא הוֹצִיא הַקָּדוֹשׁ בָּרוּךְ
הוּא אֶת אֲבוֹתֵינוּ מִמִּצְרָיִם. הֲרֵי אָנוּ וּבָנֵינוּ
וּבְנֵי בָנֵינוּ. מְשֻׁעְבָּדִים הָיִינוּ לְפַרְעֹה בְּמִצְרָיִם.
וַאֲפִילוּ כֻּלָּנוּ חֲכָמִים. כֻּלָּנוּ נְבוֹנִים. כֻּלָּנוּ זְקֵנִים.

וְאִלּוּ לֹא הוֹצִיא — *And if the Holy One,
blessed be He, had not brought out our
fathers.* If our fathers had not been
liberated at that time, they could not
have counted on Pharaoh's mercies or
their own efforts. Thus, they would
have remained in slavery and, before
long, would have totally disappeared in
the morass of Egyptian society (they
would have fallen to the fiftieth stage of
impurity, from which there is no
return). That is why we, too, would still
be מְשֻׁעְבָּדִים, *enslaved,* to the things for
which Pharaoh and Egypt stood. (Note
that the word used here is *enslaved,* not
עֲבָדִים, actual slaves.)

But even if, somehow, our fathers
had been freed through some political or
social developments, we would still be
enslaved in a very real sense. We would
be grateful to Pharaoh or whoever else
had brought about our freedom; or we
would trust in כֹּחִי וְעוֹצֶם יָדִי, *my
strength and the power of my hand*
(*Devarim* 8:17); or put our confidence
in the workings of material and social
forces. Thus we would have remained
enslaved to dangerous illusions that
have misled mankind throughout
history. טוּמְאַת מִצְרַיִם, the spiritual
blindness in Egypt, was such that only
God's own direct and open intervention
could make us truly free, for it taught us
to see the truth — that He alone can help
us and deserves our adulation (*Michtav
M'Eliyahu*).

Hence the *Haggadah* (p. 120) emphasizes that God Himself redeemed us,
without the use of any intermediary or
agent. Thus, it does not mention the role

of Moses at all, since this could easily
lead to misinterpretation.[1] The Golden
Calf, for instance, was made because of
fear over the 'disappearance' of Moses
'who led us up from Egypt' (*Shemos*
32:1); in reality, Moses by himself
could do nothing — a fact underlined by
his difficulty in speaking — and he
merely served as God's messenger. The
Torah also makes it clear that the Jews
had no hand at all in their own liberation; on the crucial *Pesach* night they
were confined to their houses, and they
were not even given the opportunity to
prepare food for the way (*Rabbi S.R.
Hirsch*). Thus, it was made clear to all
that God was the sole cause of our new
freedom.

That is, ultimately, the real reason
why the Exodus, once and for all, freed
us from enslavement. God *'alone does
great wonders, for His kindness endures
forever'* (*Tehillim* 136:4); the *Sfas Emes*
interprets this verse to mean that God's
kindness endures forever when He, *by
Himself,* does wonders. Anything done
by human beings has a limited impact,
is transitory and passes with time.
Even Divine help, if sent through intermediaries, can be of limited duration,
miraculous though the deliverance
might have been. Thus, after having
been delivered from the hands of our
enemies on *Purim,* we still remained
subjects of Ahasverus and his succes-
sors, אֲכַתִּי עַבְדֵי אַחַשְׁוֵרוֹשׁ אֲנָן (*Megillah*
14a), for God saved us through the ef-
forts of His servants.

In contrast, when God Himself took
one nation out of the midst of another,

1. No human action is left without its due reward. Moses went to Pharaoh all alone, as the
elders of the Jews dropped behind; therefore, he alone was found worthy to ascend Mount
Sinai at the giving of the Torah, whilst the elders had to wait below.
Likewise, even though his role in the Exodus is omitted in the *Haggadah,* we find that he

Holy One, blessed be He, had not brought our fathers out from Egypt, then we, our children and our children's children would have remained enslaved to Pharaoh in Egypt. Therefore, even if we were all wise, all men of understanding and ex-

with signs and miracles, contrary to every rule of nature and history, He created a new phenomenon, a people belonging to Him — and this act can never be undone. In the same way, the fall of the Egyptians was a phenomenon of everlasting impact. At the Sea of Reeds Moses indeed told the Jews that *'never again will you see the Egyptians as you have seen them today' (Shemos* 14:13).

It is true that in the course of history mankind has turned its back on God time and again; and the Jewish people, too, has fallen short of its assigned task. That is why we have gone through exile after exile; even today we speak of ourselves as slaves (above, p. 68). But we have never returned to that abject state of slavery in which we found ourselves in Egypt, a band of slaves, lacking a national unity based on our knowledge of God and Torah. The redemption from Pharaoh's rule and the subsequent reception of the Torah have left their eternal mark on us, so that we have remained forever free in our פְּנִימִיּוּת, innermost self *(Maharal)*. This was emphasized by the Prophet Haggai (2:5): *'[Do] what I covenanted with you, when you went out from Egypt, and My spirit stays with you — do not be afraid!'* Thus it is still true for us today that ultimately *'the children of Israel are servants unto Me, they are My servants whom I took out from Egypt' (Vayikrah* 25:55).

As as result, such enslavement as we have had to endure in later exiles, up to our days, could never be permanent and everlasting — the redemption from

Egypt contained within itself the assurance of our survival and the seed of redemption from any future exile in which we would be found *(Rabbi A. Wolf)*. That is why, in the language of our prayers, the redemption from Egypt brought us חֵרוּת עוֹלָם, everlasting freedom. However, if God had not Himself taken us out from Egypt, but had sent us freedom in some other way, it might well not have lasted until our generation. Thus we are direct beneficiaries of the liberation from Egypt — just as we also share directly in קַבָּלַת הַתּוֹרָה, the giving of the Torah by HASHEM Himself at Sinai.

אָנוּ וּבָנֵינוּ וּבְנֵי בָנֵינוּ — *We, our children, and our children's children.* This expression is used because, in general, we are concerned with what happens to us, our children, and our grandchildren. Usually we are not as deeply involved with the fourth generation and its welfare. It has also been pointed out that three generations are needed to establish a solid foundation for the right life, as our Patriarchs did. Our Sages generalize from the verse in *Isaiah* 59:21 that, wherever there are three generations of Torah, the Torah will always return to that family (see also *Koheles* 4:12). Therefore, any delay in our deliverance would, for sure, have beclouded the destinies of at least three more generations.

וַאֲפִילוּ כֻּלָּנוּ חֲכָמִים — *Even if we were all wise. Abarbanel,* the *Vilna Gaon,* and many others do not include the word זְקֵנִים (elders, or men of experience), but only mention men of חָכְמָה, wisdom,

received due recognition for it — the entire Torah is called after him: *'Remember the Torah of my servant Moses' (Malachi* 3:22) *(Midrash).*

כֻּלָּנוּ יוֹדְעִים אֶת הַתּוֹרָה. מִצְוָה עָלֵינוּ לְסַפֵּר בִּיצִיאַת מִצְרָיִם. וְכָל הַמַּרְבֶּה לְסַפֵּר בִּיצִיאַת מִצְרַיִם הֲרֵי זֶה מְשֻׁבָּח:

מַעֲשֶׂה בְּרַבִּי אֱלִיעֶזֶר וְרַבִּי יְהוֹשֻׁעַ וְרַבִּי אֶלְעָזָר בֶּן־עֲזַרְיָה וְרַבִּי עֲקִיבָא

בִּינָה, understanding, and דַּעַת, knowledge. We find these three qualities grouped together in many instances. They characterize God's wisdom as shown in the creation of the world (Mishley 3:19), and at the same time they describe the ultimate heights to which a human being can aspire in the perception of God's ways (see Shemos 35:31). They occupy a crucial place in the teachings of Kabbalah, and are the object of our daily prayers for wisdom (particularly according to the Sephardic version).

We are told here that even men who have attained these qualities must ever anew dwell on the story of the Exodus. Since it deals with an act of God, we can never exhaust the depths of its meaning: God does נִפְלָאוֹת עַד אֵין מִסְפָּר miracles beyond count (Iyov 5:9).

With each new insight we discover new avenues of thought to pursue. There is no limit to how high a person can rise — and, therefore, there is no limit to how much he can gain by dwelling on the story of our redemption.

This may also be the reason why the Haggadah stresses that we must dwell on this story even if כֻּלָּנוּ, all of us are so very wise. If, as in today's situation, most Jews have only a limited understanding of Torah, it is obvious that the outstanding personalities have to talk at length about the Exodus, to enlighten their contemporaries. But one could think that there is no more need to elaborate once all Jews have achieved the deepest understanding of Torah and everybody fully grasps the significance of the redemption from Egypt.

Therefore, the Haggadah tells us that, even then, we must talk ever more about it because even for the greatest men there is no limit to what they will gain by it (Rabbi Myski).

וְכָל הַמַּרְבֶּה לְסַפֵּר — And whoever tells very much about it. This phrase implies that, after a person has done his duty, he is praised for going beyond it. At what point is one considered to have done his duty? During the time that 'Matzah and Maror are in front of you', it is obviously everybody's duty to talk about the Exodus. When that time has passed, however, what merit could there be in continuing to talk? A number of solutions have been suggested: a person deserves praise if he continues talking after he has recited the basic facts (as outlined in the Haggadah); or if he continues after the meal (this is the opinion of the Kolbo and, probably, also of the Rashbam, who holds that, on account of the children, one should not talk too much before the meal); or, if he talks after midnight, when there is no more duty to talk, according to some opinions (Netziv; see below, מַעֲשֶׂה בְּרַבִּי אֱלִיעֶזֶר; or, simply, if he goes particularly deeply into the subject (Vilna Gaon). Rambam stresses that the duty to elaborate applies particularly to the Midrash included in the Haggadah (צֵא וּלְמַד).

הֲרֵי זֶה מְשׁוּבָּח — Is praiseworthy. Our Sages stress that a person should not go to extraordinary lengths in praising God; otherwise it might appear that he presumptuously thinks that he exhausted God's praises (Megillah 18b). There is, however, an exception: a person who

perience, all fully versed in the Torah, we would still be obliged to tell about Yetzias Mitzrayim, the Exodus from Egypt; and whoever tells about it at length is praiseworthy.

I t once happened that Rabbi Eliezer, Rabbi Yoshua, Rabbi Elazar, son of Azaryah, Rabbi Akiva and

has experienced a miracle may praise God without constraint, for this is merely the proper way of showing his gratitude *(Sfas Emes)*. In fact, when a person does *not* give thanks to the fullest, it shows that he does not appreciate the benefits he received. Therefore, we should praise God in every possible way, from a full awareness that He redeemed us. The extent to which a person elaborates on the story of the Exodus shows how far he sees himself as having been involved in that event and as having benefitted from it.

The word מְשׁוּבָּח may also be translated (in keeping with *Mishnah* usage) as 'improved'. The more one talks about *Yetzias Mitzrayim* the better a person he becomes, for he impresses upon himself the eternal truths taught by the event: the Torah tells us to '*tell into the ear of your child and grandchild what I have worked in Egypt ... and you shall know that I am* HASHEM' (Shemos 7:2) *(Hashir Vehashevach)*. We pointed out before that there is no limit to the spiritual growth a person can attain. Moreover, we know that the ultimate goal of the Exodus has not yet been attained; by talking about it and delving into its deeper meaning, we help bring to the fore the potential still inherent in that happening — the universal recognition of God that will mark the ultimate redemption *(Sfas Emes)*.

מַעֲשֶׂה — *It once happened.* This story is inserted to illustrate the point just made: even the wisest of men are commanded to talk about the Exodus to the fullest. Here we find the greatest sages

of the age, among them the heads of the Sanhedrin, the supreme Rabbinical council, talking of the deliverance from Egypt through the entire night, until it became sufficiently light in the morning for the recitation of the *Shema*.

In fact, it has been pointed out that each of these Sages could have considered himself excused if he had taken the duty of *Haggadah* more lightly. For instance, Rabbi Akiva was a descendant of proselytes and therefore his ancestors were never in Egypt; Rabbi Elazar ben Azariah, Rabbi Eliezer, and Rabbi Tarfon were Kohanim and Rabbi Yoshua a Levite, and — according to most opinions — their ancestors were exempt from slave-labor. Despite this, they spent the entire night discussing the Exodus *(Simchas Haregel)*.

[There is another account, in the *Tosefta (Pesachim* 10b), of Rabban Gamliel and his associates staying up the entire *Pesach* night discussing 'the laws of Pesach'; this indicates that such a discussion would also fall under the commandment of סִפּוּר יְצִיאַת מִצְרַיִם, talking about the going out from Egypt. As mentioned in the Overview, the story of *Pesach* and its laws form a unity, each throwing light on the other. Therefore the *Shulchan Aruch* lists both the story of the Exodus and the Pesach laws as topics for discussion at the *Seder.*]

We are told that this *Pesach* celebration took place in *Bnei Brak*, a town where Rabbi Akiva served as the rabbi. This explains why Rabbi Akiva would recline at the *Seder* meal even though he was in the presence of his teachers; or-

וְרַבִּי טַרְפוֹן שֶׁהָיוּ מְסֻבִּין בִּבְנֵי־בְרַק וְהָיוּ מְסַפְּרִים בִּיצִיאַת מִצְרַיִם כָּל־אוֹתוֹ הַלַּיְלָה עַד שֶׁבָּאוּ תַלְמִידֵיהֶם וְאָמְרוּ לָהֶם. רַבּוֹתֵינוּ הִגִּיעַ זְמַן קְרִיאַת שְׁמַע שֶׁל שַׁחֲרִית:

אָמַר רַבִּי אֶלְעָזָר בֶּן־עֲזַרְיָה. הֲרֵי אֲנִי כְּבֶן שִׁבְעִים שָׁנָה. וְלֹא זָכִיתִי שֶׁתֵּאָמֵר יְצִיאַת מִצְרַיִם בַּלֵּילוֹת. עַד שֶׁדְּרָשָׁהּ בֶּן זוֹמָא.

dinarily, a student is not permitted to sit in such a position in front of his teachers (R'ma Mipanu).

It would also account for the fact that Rabbi Elazar ben Azariah participated in such a protracted Seder. The Talmud states his opinion that the Pesach lamb as well as Matzah and Maror had to be consumed by midnight (Pesachim 120b). Since the obligation of Haggadah applies when Pesach, Matzah, and Maror are in front of us, it would appear that, according to Rabbi Elazar ben Azariah, there is no obligation to continue telling of the going out from Egypt after midnight— however, in deference to Rabbi Akiva, whose authority ruled in Bnei Brak, he spent the entire night talking about the Exodus.

[The Meshech Chochmah, however, offers a different explanation. Rabbi Elazar ben Azariah is indeed of the opinion that the main time for reciting the Haggadah is before midnight (and so is Rabbi Eliezer too). But we are supposed to go beyond the limits of our bare duty in talking about the Exodus. It was because of this consideration, rather than Rabbi Akiva's authority, that everybody joined in extending the Seder past midnight. The Haggadah thus relates the story of this Seder at this point to reinforce the preceding statement that 'whoever tells very much is praiseworthy.']

The text appears to suggest that the disciples were absent during the night. If so, where were they during all this time? It has been suggested that they conducted the Seder for their own families, in keeping with the entire character of this Yom Tov; from the very beginning in Egypt its observance was centered in each home and each family group, שֶׂה לְבֵית אָבוֹת שֶׂה לַבָּיִת, a lamb for each family, a lamb for each house (Shemos 12:3; see Overview, p. 27).

הִגִּיעַ זְמַן קְרִיאַת שְׁמַע שֶׁל שַׁחֲרִית — The time has arrived for reading the morning Shema. This expression, chosen by the disciples to make their teachers aware that the morning had come, has caused the commentators to find an additional, deeper message in our story. It took place during the darkest stage of Roman oppression, after the destruction of the second Temple (several of the Sages mentioned here later died a martyr's death). Yet the Rabbis talked so fervently about the redemption from Egypt, with its implication that the Jews thenceforth would always be God's people, that the disciples were able to come and declare themselves ready to recite the Shema with total קַבָּלַת עוֹל מַלְכוּת שָׁמַיִם, utter acceptance of God's overlordship.

Others suggest that the disciples were so inspired by God's concern for us that they actually felt able to discern the dawn of the future redemption, as

Rabbi Tarphon, were celebrating the Seder in Bnei Berak. They were discussing the Exodus from Egypt the entire night, until their students came and said to them: Our teachers, the time has arrived for reading the morning Shema.

Rabbi Elazar, son of Azaryah, said: I am like a man of seventy, yet I was never able to convince my colleagues that one is obliged to mention the Exodus at night, until Ben Zoma explained it:

reflected in the morning prayers that are recited in connection with *Shema;* whereas in the darkness of night we follow up *Shema* by declaring אֱמֶת וֶאֱמוּנָה, that we have faith in God's help, in the light of morning we say אֱמֶת וְיַצִּיב, that God's help is clearly evident before our eyes. In fact, our story may want to make the point (in keeping with the ultimate significance of the *Seder*) that if, in the dark night of Exile, we dwell with full faith upon God's succour, we will actually bring about the coming of our redemption.

שֶׁתֵּאָמֵר יְצִיאַת מִצְרַיִם בַּלֵּילוֹת — *That one is obliged to mention the Exodus at night.* The obligation that Rabbi Elazar ben Azariah here discusses concerns the Biblical passages connected with the *Shema.* In the morning *Shema* we include three passages of which the third is פֶּרָשַׁת צִיצִית, the Torah passage commanding us to wear *Tzitzis.* Even though *Tzitzis* are not worn at night, Rabbi Elazar ben Azariah held the view (which we follow) that this passage should also be recited in the evening *Shema* because it makes reference to the Exodus.

His statement is quoted from *Mishnayis Brachos* 1:15 and does not directly refer to the duty of talking about the Exodus on *Seder* night; but it is included in the *Haggadah* because it underlines the importance of the subject of the redemption from Egypt. Moreover,

it also throws an indirect light on the commandment to talk about the Exodus on *Seder* night: if we are obliged to mention it every night, it follows that our special obligation at the *Seder* must go beyond mere mention and requires a full discussion of our deliverance from Egypt. This is, indeed, the view of most rabbinic authorities (see מַגִּיד, p. 65).

Rabbi Elazar ben Azariah was only כְּבֶן שִׁבְעִים, *like* a seventy year old; the Talmud tells us that when he was chosen to be נָשִׂיא, to head the supreme Rabbinical Council, and felt unworthy to accept the position on account of his youth, his hair turned white overnight, giving him the appearance of an old man *(Brachos* 27b). Even though he was deserving of the authority of an older man, as shown by this incident, he was not successful in convincing his colleagues of his opinion until Ben Zoma presented his argument (this is the interpretation most commentators give to the passage).

But did Ben Zoma convince the other Sages that the passage of *Tzitzis* should be said at night? At first glance it would seem that he did not, and that their controversy continued. However, the words of Rabbi Elazar ben Azariah ('I did not succeed ... until Ben Zoma came') indicate that the question of mentioning the Exodus at night was indeed settled with the coming of Ben Zoma. It has therefore been suggested that Ben Zoma and the Sages only con-

° דברים
טז:ג

שֶׁנֶּאֱמַר °לְמַעַן תִּזְכֹּר אֶת יוֹם צֵאתְךָ מֵאֶרֶץ מִצְרַיִם כֹּל יְמֵי חַיֶּיךָ. יְמֵי חַיֶּיךָ הַיָּמִים. כֹּל יְמֵי חַיֶּיךָ הַלֵּילוֹת. וַחֲכָמִים אוֹמְרִים. יְמֵי חַיֶּיךָ הָעוֹלָם הַזֶּה. כֹּל יְמֵי חַיֶּיךָ לְהָבִיא לִימוֹת הַמָּשִׁיחַ:

בָּרוּךְ הַמָּקוֹם. בָּרוּךְ הוּא. בָּרוּךְ שֶׁנָּתַן תּוֹרָה לְעַמּוֹ יִשְׂרָאֵל. בָּרוּךְ הוּא.

tinued to disagree on whether the third passage of Shema would be recited in the days of *Mashiach*. All agreed, however, that the Exodus has to be mentioned at night (*Aruch Hashulchan*).

Ben Zoma was of the opinion that in Messianic times there will be no duty to talk about the Exodus from Egypt; for in those days God will be praised for His new miracles rather than for those which He did in Egypt (*Jeremiah* 16:14-15 and 23:7-8). Therefore Ben Zoma felt that the commandment to remember the Exodus 'all the days of your life' cannot include Messianic times. Instead he suggested that 'all the days of your life' includes the nights. Without such a specific scriptural directive we might have thought that the Exodus need not be mentioned at night — either because there was no oppression at night, or because the main act of liberation was the departure from Egypt which took place in the daytime (hence the Torah's reference to 'the day of your going out from Egypt').

The Rabbis, however, felt that no special scriptural hint was needed to tell us that we should mention the Exodus at night; this was obvious to them — either because they held that the Jews were oppressed at night too, or because they saw the slaying of the firstborn and Pharaoh's capitulation, in the middle of the night, as the main event of the Exodus. In consequence, they took the phrase, 'all the days of your life' as a hint that the commandment to mention the Exodus included the Messianic age, despite Jeremiah's statements. According to them, Jeremiah did not mean to say that in those days the miracles of Egypt would be ignored, but merely that they

would be considered secondary to the newly experienced miracles (*Rashbatz*). It is only on this point that Ben Zoma and the Sages disagreed.

In fact, *Rambam* seems to hold that there was never, in the first place, any disagreement over the question of reciting *Parshas Tzitzis* at night; the phrase לֹא זָכִיתִי merely meant that Rabbi Elazar ben Azariah 'never found a Biblical basis for this obligation' until Ben Zoma presented his deduction.

Rabbi S.R. Hirsch suggests that the controversy over the remembrance of the Exodus reflects a deeper question. Everybody agrees that the redemption from Egypt has to be in our minds as the basis of our active endeavors in life (pursued during daytime). The question is whether we also have to pay heed to the lessons of the Exodus during the times of passive endurance and suffering in our life (the nights) — or even at the time when our ultimate goal will have been reached (the Messianic age).

בָּרוּךְ הַמָּקוֹם — *Praised be the Ever-Present.* The preceding passages illustrated the importance of talking about the Exodus. Now the *Haggadah* shows *how* this is to be done. For this purpose it draws on four Torah passages: they direct us to tell the Exodus story to our children, and they illustrate the various approaches to be used for different types of children.

Every morning, before we can under-

It is stated in the Torah: "That you may remember the day when you came out of the land of Egypt, all the days of your life." "The days of your life" merely refers to the days; "all the days of your life," on the other hand, includes the nights too. The Sages say: "The days of your life" indicates this life, but "all the days of your life" includes the times of Mashiach too.

Praised be the Ever-Present, praised be He! Praised be He who has given the Torah to His people

take Torah study, we must recite the blessing over the Torah. This blessing is also recited before we can read in the Torah scroll. There is no requirement to offer this blessing *every* time we study Torah — for instance when we now turn to the four Torah passages mentioned. Yet the *Haggadah* at least wants us to preface the recitation of the four passages with a fourfold expression of praise to God — in the spirit, albeit not in the form, of a regular blessing ('Blessed are you, HASHEM, ...').

In a similar vein, the *Shibolei Haleket* points out that we are not required to pronounce a blessing over the commandment to recite the *Haggadah* (see p. 65). However, since we are about to quote the four Torah passages that direct us to talk about the Exodus, we preface them with four expressions of בָּרוּךְ, *praise* for God; they, so to speak, take the place of a regular blessing.

We praise God as הַמָּקוֹם, which literally means *'The Place'*. The *Midrash* explains that we use this term for God because 'He is the place of the universe, and the universe is not His place.' God is not limited by space, or encompassed by it; rather, He encompasses everything, and therefore is present everywhere. We also praise Him as the Giver of the Torah. In it we find the guidance we need for dealing with the various kinds of children about whom we are about to speak.

The phrase בָּרוּךְ הוּא, *Blessed be He*,

has been explained as a response to the Master of the *Seder*. The custom in olden days was for him to intone, בָּרוּךְ הַמָּקוֹם, *'Blessed be the Ever-Present'*; the participants would respond in unison, בָּרוּךְ הוּא, *'Blessed be He.'* The master of the *Seder* would then declare, בָּרוּךְ שֶׁנָּתַן תּוֹרָה לְעַמּוֹ יִשְׂרָאֵל, *'Blessed be the Giver of the Torah'*, and again the response would be, בָּרוּךְ הוּא, *'Blessed be He'* (Malbim).

The first of the two blessings pronounced by the Master of the *Seder* has been interpreted as an expression of thanks for our material needs; for it refers to the merciful presence of God, wherever and whenever we require His assistance. The second blessing, addressed to God as the Giver of the Torah, refers to His care for our spiritual needs (*Vayagidu Lemordechai*).

Others suggest that the four expressions of praise (בָּרוּךְ) correspond to the four sons. We acknowledge God's kindness in giving us children, even though some of them may present problems (*Kolbo*); and we thank God for giving us the wisdom, through the Torah, to guide each of their different personalities. The two brief and in-specific phrases, בָּרוּךְ הוּא, *blessed be He*, may refer to the bad son, and to the son who does not know how to ask — their positive qualities have not yet emerged to be singled out for praise. Despite the evil of the first and the dis-interest of the second, however, we do

כְּנֶגֶד אַרְבָּעָה בָנִים דִּבְּרָה תוֹרָה. אֶחָד חָכָם.
וְאֶחָד רָשָׁע. וְאֶחָד תָּם. וְאֶחָד שֶׁאֵינוֹ יוֹדֵעַ
לִשְׁאוֹל:

חָכָם מָה הוּא אוֹמֵר. °מָה הָעֵדוֹת וְהַחֻקִּים
וְהַמִּשְׁפָּטִים אֲשֶׁר צִוָּה יהוה אֱלֹהֵינוּ

° דברים
ו:כ

not despair. Instead, we bless God for having given them to us, and go about the task of improving them. בָּרוּךְ הַמָּקוֹם *blessed be the Ever-Present*, may refer to the wise son, who perceives God everywhere, and בָּרוּךְ שֶׁנָּתַן תּוֹרָה, *blessed be the Giver of the Torah*, relates to the simple son who is only beginning to set out on his Torah study.

[A different suggestion is made on the basis of a *Mishnah* (*Midos* 5:4) which states that, when the Sanhedrin examined the qualifications of the priests and found them all worthy, it declared: '*Praised be the Ever-Present, praised be He, that no blemish was found among the children of Aaron, and praised be He who chose Aaron and his sons . . .*' It would, therefore, be appropriate to relate the '*praise to the Ever-Present, praised be He*' to the children whom we see growing up the right way; and the '*praise to the Giver of the Torah, praised be He*' would refer to the bad children, whose upbringing requires the specific help of the Torah.]

כְּנֶגֶד אַרְבָּעָה בָנִים — *The Torah speaks of four sons.* On the day marking the birth of our nation we are particularly concerned to safeguard our national continuity by passing our sacred legacy on to our children (*Rabbi S.R. Hirsch*; see pp. 29 and 70). This dedication to the education of the next generation is a direct answer to the schemes of Pharaoh, who made every effort to rob us of the children who are our future —through the murder of the newborn, and the immuring of the babies in the walls of Pisom and Ramses; through in-

terfering with the family life of the Jews; and, at the very end, through trying to keep the children from going with the adults to serve God (*Shemos* 10:8-11).

The upbringing of children can only be successful if it is '*according to each child's way*' (*Mishley* 22:6). Therefore the Torah tells us how to deal with four specific types of children. While it does not actually mention four sons, it instructs us in four passages on how to tell our children about the Exodus, and each of the passages is phrased differently. In the *Mechilta*, quoted here by the *Haggadah*, our Sages explain that the Torah refers to four different kinds of people. In three of the verses, children address questions to the father; in the fourth one, no question is asked. We infer from this fourth passage that we must even educate children who lack the understanding or interest to inquire about the happenings of the evening (*Malbim*).

Avudraham explains that the four sons are not mentioned here in the order in which they occur in the Torah, but in order of their growing up. The wise son and the evil son are first; then comes the תָּם, the simple one, who (according to most commentators) is growing up to become a חָכָם; and finally the אֵינוֹ יוֹדֵעַ לִשְׁאוֹל who remains silent, according to these commentators, not from immaturity but disinterest, and therefore threatens to grow up into a רָשָׁע.

It has also been suggested that the four sons are referred to in *Tehillim* (18:26-27): עִם חָסִיד תִּתְחַסָּד עִם גֶּבָר

Israel, praised be He! The Torah speaks of four sons: a wise son, a wicked one, a simple one, and one who does not know how to ask.

What does the wise son say? "What are the testimonies, statutes and laws that HASHEM our God has commanded you?"

תָּמִים תִּתַּמָּם עִם נָבָר תִּתְבָּרָר וְעִם עִקֵּשׁ תִּתְפַּתָּל, 'To the one who awaits kindness (the son who, not understanding enough to ask, merely passively waits for God's merciful guidance), show kindness; with the simple man, deal straightforwardly; to the enquiring mind, provide clarification; and with the crooked person, enter into contention' (Sfas Emes).[1]

חָכָם — The wise son. Both wisdom and interest are shown by the detailed question of this son, which differentiates between the various types of commandments: עֵדוֹת, laws which 'testify' to the historical happenings, such as Matzah, which is a reminder of the swiftness of the Exodus; חֻקִּים, statues whose reasons are neither given nor readily understood, such as the rule against breaking the bones of the Pesach sacrifice; and מִשְׁפָּטִים, ordinances that regulate our relations with our fellow men, such as the rule against letting an uncircumcised person eat of the Pesach sacrifice (Ritva). The differentiation made by the wise son is well taken; even though the various commandments connected with the observance of the Pesach holiday are primarily עֵדוֹת, the

Torah itself specifies that the Pesach sacrifice should be prepared 'according to all its חֻקִּים and מִשְׁפָּטִים' (Bamidbar 9:3; Shibolei Haleket).

The wise son's reference to laws that God 'commanded you' would indicate that he — like the evil son, later on — dissociates himself from them. However, because he speaks of 'our God', it can be assumed that he does not mean to exclude himself from the fulfillment of the commandments (Rashi). Perhaps he uses the expression 'commanded you' because he is still a minor, and the Pesach sacrifice must not be offered for minors alone (Shibolei Haleket); or because he addresses himself to the earlier generation that actually received the commandments.

To avoid a possible misunderstanding, the Mechilta and Yerushalmi change the text of the question and have the wise son say אוֹתָנוּ, commanded us. Actually, however, this may hardly be necessary. In contrast to the word לָכֶם, used by the evil son, the word אֶתְכֶם, you, can be understood to include the speaker, for it can be taken as a contraction of אוֹתִי וְאֶתְכֶם, me and you, like the word אוֹתְכֶם (Sota 34a; Yavetz).

The Torah replies to the question of the חָכָם by explaining that 'we were slaves to Pharaoh in Egypt, and

1. The Sfas Emes sees the four sons as concerned with four different aspects of the redemption from Egypt. The חָכָם inquires into God's purpose in instituting Pesach; he is told that it teaches a divine lesson that is to stay with us forever. The תָּם merely wants to know what happened, and is told the story of the redemption. The רָשָׁע questions what he stands to gain from the deliverance from Egypt; we tell him that, if that is his only concern, he really has no stake in it. The אֵינוֹ יוֹדֵעַ לִשְׁאוֹל, finally, is silent because the only thing that would impress him is if he could see the downfall of the forces of evil — and that is nowhere in evidence; to him we say that, through our observance of the laws of Pesach, the triumph of good over evil is sure to come about. These answers to the four sons can be seen reflected in the four cups: Kiddush (God's purpose in the world), Maggid (the story of the Exodus), Birchas Hamazon (the benefit we derive from this world if we use it in God's service), and Hallel (the final redemption).

אֶתְכֶם. וְאַף אַתָּה אֱמָר־לוֹ כְּהִלְכוֹת הַפֶּסַח.
אֵין מַפְטִירִין אַחַר הַפֶּסַח אֲפִיקוֹמָן:

°שמות
יב:כו
רָשָׁע מָה הוּא אוֹמֵר. °מָה הָעֲבוֹדָה הַזֹּאת
לָכֶם. לָכֶם וְלֹא לוֹ. וּלְפִי שֶׁהוֹצִיא
אֶת־עַצְמוֹ מִן הַכְּלָל כָּפַר בְּעִקָּר. וְאַף אַתָּה

HASHEM *took us out from there ... And He commanded us to do all these statutes ...' (Devarim 6:21-25).* The *Haggadah,* however, does not quote this passage in answer to the wise son; instead it talks about the statutes which are mentioned at its end. The explanation may be that the *Haggadah* already quoted most of the passage in response to מַה נִּשְׁתַּנָּה, in stating עֲבָדִים הָיִינוּ, *'We were slaves ...';* the basic question and answer of the חָכָם were given there, as the beginning and foundation of *Maggid.* Here the *Haggadah* goes further. After all, the Torah's reply to the wise son indicates that our talking about the Exodus should lead us to tell him about the statutes of *Pesach;* and his question shows that he does indeed want to know more about them *(Ritva).* Therefore the *Haggadah* tells us to instruct him about them all, down to the rule that he must not eat any dessert after the *Pesach* sacrifice. Normally, after the main course of a banquet, people used to call אַפִּיקוּ מָן, *bring on different kinds of sweets,'* to end the meal; at the *Seder,* however, this is not permitted.

Why is this rule singled out here? It is the last provision concerning the *Pesach* sacrifice mentioned by the *Mishnah;* thus we infer that we must teach the questioner all the laws, down to the last. Or, possibly, this rule is stressed because it shows the importance of the *Pesach* sacrifice: it must be eaten at the end of the meal, so that its taste will stay in our mouths. It has also been suggested that this rule has been singled out because it is of Rabbinic origin and appears easy to observe; the wise son is

told, in effect, that *all* laws must be kept with equal care.

According to our interpretation, the wise son is eager to know more about the laws, and we offer the information he seeks. The stress is on the laws, rather than on the rationale for them, the details of the Exodus and their lesson for us. This is in accordance with the point, made previously (p. 77), that the duty to tell about the Exodus can be discharged by talking about the laws of *Pesach.*

Some commentators, however, feel that the חָכָם, wise son, is asking specifically about the significance of the laws. What lasting value do the *Pesach* observances have? Accordingly he is enlightened about their deeper meaning, and he is warned that כְּהִלְכוֹת הַפֶּסַח, in accordance with their profound importance, אֵין מַפְטִירִין אַחַר הַפֶּסַח אֲפִיקוֹמָן, one is not permitted to eat anything after the *Pesach* sacrifice — thus the taste, the message of *Pesach,* will stay with him throughout the year *(Moadim Uzmanim).*

[According to the *Sfas Emes,* the wise son asks why the memory of the Exodus calls for such elaborate observances — after all, the Jews subsequently reached much greater spiritual heights, such as the giving of the Torah and the building of the Sanctuary. We answer him that in all of these 'the taste of *Pesach* lingers on': they are all built upon our liberation and entrance into God's service on *Pesach.* In fact, even though we are again in exile, the redemption to come also has its roots in the events of *Pesach.* Therefore, they are of such great and

Do then instruct him in the laws of Pesach, that one may not eat anything after eating the Pesach sacrifice!

T*he wicked son — what does he say? "What does this service mean to you?" "To you" (he says) — but not to him! Therefore, because he has excluded himself from the community, he has denied the foundation of our faith; consequently you must blunt his*

lasting importance to us and will always be celebrated (see p. 80).]

רָשָׁע — *The wicked son.* That the question here presented is that of a bad son is shown by the way it is introduced in the Torah: וְהָיָה כִּי יֹאמְרוּ אֲלֵיכֶם בְּנֵיכֶם, *'your sons will say to you' (Shemos* 12:26) — they are making a statement, rather than asking for enlightenment *(Chukas Hapesach).* It has also been suggested that the Torah speaks of one son, in the singular, when it refers to the חָכָם, for all truth is one and indivisible, and speaks with one voice; whereas 'sons', in the plural, would refer to evildoers, for there are as many different ways of departing from the truth as there are sinners *(Rabbi M. Lehmann).*

Moreover, the question itself carries a negative connotation: the questioner does not refer to God in connection with the service about which he talks,[1] and he excludes himself from it by speaking of 'you' rather than 'us.' Therefore it must be understood as a criticism: 'What is this burden that you impose upon us every year?' *(Yerushalmi Pesachim* 10:4). 'Would it not be enough simply to *think* about the Exodus, instead of having to perform all these rituals?' *(Rabbi Shlomo Kluger).* In fact, this question has been interpreted in the spirit of modern critics: 'What do your feasting and practical rituals have to do with religiosity and serving God?'[2]

The question of the רָשָׁע, wicked son, shows, as we said, that he is only in-

---

1. *'And I perceived that wisdom excels folly as light excels darkness' (Koheles* 2:13). In connection with the creation of light, the Torah mentions the name of God, but not so in connection with darkness *('God called the light day; and the darkness He called night' — Bereishis* 1:5). In the same way the wise son excels over the wicked son; unlike the latter, he mentions God's name in his question *(Vilna Gaon).*

2. The wicked son of the *Haggadah* is the prototype of the present day reformer: He thinks he knows the reasons for the commandments, and concludes that they no longer apply. A purpose of the *Pesach* offering was to demonstrate our disregard for the idols of the Egyptians; therefore, the *Pesach* lamb had to be roasted whole, so that everybody could see that we were eating the god of the Egyptians. Likewise, we were not permitted to break its bones, so that we had to dispose of them by throwing them to the dogs. The wicked son concludes that there is no more need to offer the *Pesach* sacrifice since there is no more idol-worship. He therefore asks: What good is this form of divine service? In reality, however, the commandments still apply today, for they have deeper reasons, that are rooted in the very foundations of the world. We do not fulfill them merely because we were taken out from Egypt; on the contrary, we were taken out from Egypt so that we should have occasion to fulfill them. This is the meaning of our answer to the wicked son: 'For the sake of the commandments God took me out of Egypt — the wicked son would not have been taken out since he rejects their eternal validity!' *(Bais Halevi).*

הַקְהֵה אֶת־שִׁנָּיו וֶאֱמֹר לוֹ °בַּעֲבוּר זֶה עָשָׂה יהוה לִי בְּצֵאתִי מִמִּצְרָיִם. לִי °וְלֹא לוֹ. אִלּוּ הָיָה שָׁם לֹא הָיָה נִגְאָל:

תָּם מַה הוּא אוֹמֵר. °מַה זֹּאת. וְאָמַרְתָּ אֵלָיו °בְּחֹזֶק יָד הוֹצִיאָנוּ יהוה מִמִּצְרָיִם מִבֵּית־עֲבָדִים:

וְשֶׁאֵינוֹ יוֹדֵעַ לִשְׁאוֹל אַתְּ פְּתַח לוֹ. שֶׁנֶּאֱמַר °וְהִגַּדְתָּ לְבִנְךָ בַּיּוֹם הַהוּא לֵאמֹר

terested in himself and excludes himself from the community that is concerned with acting out God's will. This attitude leads him necessarily to the denial of God Himself. In the first place, he denies that the commandments are Divinely ordained (Shibolei Haleket), and this, in itself, is tantamount to a rejection of God (Machzor Vitry). Moreover, by belittling the observance of Pesach he dissociates himself from the entire event of the Exodus (Sfas Emes); obviously he does not acknowledge the miracles that happened.

[It has also been suggested that the very act of separating oneself from the Jewish people is a form of separation from God; for we are linked to Him through the common unity of all Jewish souls, and through our common historical heritage. Moreover, by separating from the community a person in effect loses his chance to shake off his sins which divide him from God: the possibility of תְּשׁוּבָה, penitence, depends in largest measure on being associated with the community of Jews.]

In the Torah, the question of the רָשָׁע is answered thus: 'And you shall say, "It is a Pesach sacrifice for HASHEM, who passed over the houses of the children of Israel when He struck Egypt

and He saved our houses"' (Shemos 12:27). This passage in effect tells the רָשָׁע: you really do not belong to us and have no share in our celebration. In the first place, the Pesach sacrifice is to be brought for HASHEM, and can only be shared with Jews who accept God and His law (Ritva). Moreover, it is a reminder that God saved the homes of only those who did His bidding (Akeidas Yitzchak).

However, the Haggadah chooses to spell out the answer to the רָשָׁע in sharp and clear words, in order to silence him (הַקְהֵה אֶת שִׁנָּיו, lit.: 'blunt his teeth'). Therefore it quotes to him the reply given by the Torah to the child who does not know how to ask. This answer is introduced by the Torah with the word וְהִגַּדְתָּ, 'you shall tell' — meaning that you should 'talk sharply, with words hard כְּגִידִים, like sinews' (Rashbam). We are directed to point bluntly and sharply to the commandments so despised by the רָשָׁע and to tell him: בַּעֲבוּר זֶה, for the sake of my fulfilling these laws (Pesach, Matzah, and Maror, lying before me) God did this to me and redeemed me from Egypt. If the רָשָׁע had lived then, he would have assimilated long before the hour of redemption (Hashir Vehashevach); or, if he had still been among us at that time, he would have died in the three

teeth and reply to him: "It is because of this that HASHEM did for me when I went out from Egypt"; "for me" (you say), not for him — had he been there, he would not have been redeemed.

The simple son — what does he say? "What does this mean?" To him you shall say: "With a strong hand did HASHEM bring us out from Egypt, from the house of bondage."

As for the son who does not know what to ask, you must begin to speak to him, as it is stated: "You shall tell your son on that day saying: 'Because of

days of darkness, as did all Jews who did not deserve redemption (*Shibolei Haleket*).

The language of the *Haggadah* indicates that we talk about the רָשָׁע rather than to him, and that he is beyond saving. This is also suggested by the manner in which the Torah introduces the answer to the question of the רָשָׁע: וַאֲמַרְתֶּם, *'you should say'* — it does not say that we should speak *to him*. However, instead of *'for me — and not him'*, the *Mechilta* reads, *'for me — and not for you'*; and the fact that, according to the commentators cited before, we thank God even for the wicked child, and for the advice of the Torah on how to deal with him, would show that even he can be reached. Perhaps the *Haggadah* wants to suggest that sometimes, in dealing with a person who does not want to learn, the most drastic approach may be most helpful; it may shock him into listening. Accordingly, we talk about him — not to him — but in his presence. Perhaps this rebuff will shake him. [Some *Haggados* read וְכָפַר instead of כָּפַר; however, the meaning remains the same.]

תָּם — *The simple son.* He simply asks, 'What is this?' Our Sages point out that this question can have various mean-

ings. It can convey a challenge or a reproach (*Bereishis* 3:13, *Shemos* 14:5 and 11); but in our case it expresses a straightforward desire to be informed. The תָּם, *simple son*, asks simply but sincerely; and he receives an answer similar to the one that the Torah provides for the חָכָם, *the wise son* (in whose footsteps the תָּם follows): HASHEM took us out from Egypt with a strong hand.

This basic fact must be stressed to the תָּם because there have been periods of exile and suffering throughout our history, and one might lose hope for our people. Therefore we must remember that God intervened 'with a strong hand' in Egypt, to make us His people; and therein lies the assurance of our survival ever after (*Rabbi M. Lehmann*).

וְשֶׁאֵינוֹ יוֹדֵעַ לִשְׁאֹל — *The son who does not know how to ask.* The child who is as yet too immature to search for the truth himself must be guided firmly. This is shown by the expression וְהִגַּדְתָּ, meaning that *'you shall tell'* firmly (as was explained before), though with gentle concern (לֵאמֹר, *saying softly*). His education is best started by pointing out to him the concrete visual objects before him — Pesach, Matzah, Maror.

בַּעֲבוּר זֶה עָשָׂה יהוה לִי בְּצֵאתִי מִמִּצְרָיִם:

° שמות
יג:ח

יָכוֹל מֵרֹאשׁ חֹדֶשׁ. תַּלְמוּד לוֹמַר °בַּיּוֹם
הַהוּא. אִי בַּיּוֹם הַהוּא יָכוֹל מִבְּעוֹד
יוֹם. תַּלְמוּד לוֹמַר בַּעֲבוּר זֶה. בַּעֲבוּר זֶה לֹא
אָמַרְתִּי אֶלָּא בְּשָׁעָה שֶׁיֵּשׁ מַצָּה וּמָרוֹר מֻנָּחִים
לְפָנֶיךָ:

Moreover, if this child is one who does not really care to learn and may grow up to be a רָשָׁע — as suggested above — the words addressed to him contain a warning. If he wants to have a share in the joy of our redemption, he must join in the observance of God's commandments (Orchos Chayim); otherwise the ominous words לִי וְלֹא לוֹ would apply in his case also: to me God renders help — but not to him.

The four sons represent prototypes of attitudes clearly seen in our days. The חָכָם is characterized by his eagerness to learn about God's commandments; he accepts the authority of the Torah and wants to be taught by the earlier generations, the guardians of our tradition. He is the תַּלְמִיד חָכָם, the Torah scholar, who sustains the spirit of our people; it is from him that the תָּם, the simple but unlearned believer, seeks guidance and instruction.

The רָשָׁע rebels against the authority of the law, the teachers of the law, and the divine Lawgiver; he sets himself up as the judge of what is right or wrong, and for what he should exert himself. His loyal followers, represented by the אֵינוֹ יוֹדֵעַ לִשְׁאוֹל, do not ask for guidance, for they are moved by the spirit of self-centered indulgence and non-caring permissiveness.

By accepting the authority of the Torah, the good sons are truly עַבְדֵי ה', servants of God, and belong with the Jews that left Egypt as God's people. In contrast, the wicked serve only their own man-made idols: self-designed religions of convenience or glorified selfish enjoyment; thus they obviously have no link to the redemption from Egypt — 'if they had been there, they would not have been redeemed' (based on Malbim; see footnote, p. 85).

יָכוֹל — One might think. This passage elaborates on the verse which had just been quoted in response to the son who does not ask; it is therefore viewed by the Abarbanel as merely the conclusion of the discussion of the Four Sons. It may, however, be included here for a special reason: after explaining how the story of the Exodus is to be told, the Haggadah now tells us when it is to be recounted (Rashbam).

We might think that we should start at the beginning of the month of Nissan. After all, the climax of the redemption began on the first day of the month, with God's instructions to Moses (Shemos 12:1-20; Rashbam). Moreover, on that day Moses started instructing the Jews about the laws of Pesach, and we are therefore enjoined, every year, to study them from this date on (Tosefta, Megillah 3:2). Lastly, the Torah itself states in one passage וְעָבַדְתָּ אֶת הָעֲבוֹדָה הַזֹּאת בַּחֹדֶשׁ הַזֶּה, 'you shall do this service in this month' (Shemos 13:5) — apparently we should start at the very beginning of the month (Machzor Vitry).

However, the Torah here specifies that one should tell his child 'on that day'. In that case, should we perhaps recount the Haggadah in daytime, on the afternoon of עֶרֶב פֶּסַח, the day before Pesach? After all, at that time

this, HASHEM did for me when I went out from Egypt'."

One might think that the obligation to talk about the Exodus from Egypt applies from the first day of the month of Nissan; therefore the Torah says: "on that day." The expression "that day" might be understood to refer to daytime; therefore, the Torah adds that the father should say: "because of this"; that expression can only be used at a time when Matzah and Maror actually lie before you.

the Pesach offering was sacrificed (*Kolbo*).

Actually, however, the term '*day*' can also refer to nighttime. For instance, when the Torah talks of the first day of creation, it refers to the first night as well as the first day. The Torah also speaks of '*the day on which I struck every firstborn ...*' (*Bamidbor* 3:13), even though this event happened at night. Here, in our case, the Torah specifically indicates that the time for telling the *Haggadah* is in the evening, when *Pesach*, *Matzah*, and *Maror* lie before us; it is only then that we can point to them and declare that we were redeemed בַּעֲבוּר זֶה, *on their account*.

In the time of the Temple, the text of this passage actually read, '*at the time when Pesach, Matzah, and Maror are lying before you*' (*Shibolei Haleket*); today, in the absence of the sacrifice, we omit the word. *Pesach*. This does not mean that today we are not obliged by the Torah to recite the *Haggadah*. The presence of *Matzah* alone — as one of the three commandments — may be sufficient for the recitation of the *Haggadah* (hence the introductory passage, הָא לַחְמָא עַנְיָא, which draws attention to it). More likely, the obligation to recite the *Haggadah* does not depend on the actual *presence* of any of the three; the Torah merely tells us that it should be recited at the *time* when they would ordinarily be in front of us (*Trumas*

Hadeshen). Nevertheless, it is best to have all or any of them before us when we recite the *Haggadah* (*Meiri*).

Why does the Torah want us to tell the *Haggadah* on *Pesach* night rather than on *Rosh Chodesh Nissan* or on the afternoon before *Pesach*, the time when the *Pesach* sacrifice was offered?

Perhaps we are meant to understand a fundamental principle which applies to all our sacrifices, and sets them apart from the rites of pagans: most important for us is not the selection of the sacrifice, which was ordained on *Rosh Chodesh*, or its slaughtering, which took place on the day before *Pesach*, but the use of the sacrifice for its divinely willed purpose — in this case the *Pesach* meal. It has also been suggested that the *Haggadah* should be recited at night because the most important moment of our redemption was God's self-revelation when He struck the firstborn and redeemed us, on *Pesach* night, rather than the preparations we were instructed to make toward that end.

It has also been suggested that the spirit of מְסִירוּת נֶפֶשׁ, self-sacrifice, led the Jews to risk their lives on the day before *Pesach* and to slaughter the sheep which were the idols of the Egyptians; however, a momentary emotional upsurge of the spirit does not mean much by itself; it must lead to the sober and careful performance of the commandments — the observances of

מִתְּחִלָּה עוֹבְדֵי עֲבוֹדָה זָרָה הָיוּ אֲבוֹתֵינוּ. וְעַכְשָׁו קֵרְבָנוּ הַמָּקוֹם לַעֲבוֹדָתוֹ. שֶׁנֶּאֱמַר °וַיֹּאמֶר יְהוֹשֻׁעַ אֶל־כָּל־הָעָם כֹּה־אָמַר יהוה אֱלֹהֵי יִשְׂרָאֵל בְּעֵבֶר הַנָּהָר יָשְׁבוּ אֲבוֹתֵיכֶם

° יהושע
כד:ב-ד

Pesach night were therefore ordained to serve as a test of our readiness for such service of God (□ *Rabbi Yaakov Kamenetzky*).

Moreover, the three commandments that make up the meal of *Pesach* night represent the ideas to which the *Haggadah* seeks to give expression. Therefore they are needed to form the basis for the entire *Seder* and, in particular, for the recitation of the *Haggadah* (see *Overview*, p. 24); the *Haggadah* must be told when they are in front of us — and, in fact, it is an essential part of the *Haggadah* that we enumerate and explain these commandments (see later, רַבָּן גַּמְלִיאֵל), pointing to them and explaining that we were only redeemed for the sake of performing them.

Since the passage before us indicates that the time for telling the *Haggadah* is on *Pesach* evening, the *Vilna Gaon* opposed the common custom of reciting from the *Haggadah* (עֲבָדִים הָיִינוּ to the end of דַּיֵּנוּ) on שַׁבָּת הַגָּדוֹל, the *Shabbos* before *Pesach*. However, the custom has generally prevailed, as a form of preparation for *Pesach*. It is in line with the פִּיוּטִים, special prayers for this *Shabbos*, which enumerate the main laws of *Pesach*, and the customary lecture on the subject of *Pesach* given on this *Shabbos* by the Rabbis to their congregations. In any case, it would appear that our passage does not prohibit talking about the Exodus before *Pesach* evening; it merely teaches us that the *Mitzvah* of recounting it can only be fulfilled on that evening.

מִתְּחִלָּה — *In the beginning*. Here the *Haggadah* starts once more with the account of our bondage and liberation. Moreover, this time it reaches back to the earliest beginnings of our history. Why is this necessary?

The reason has been given that up to this point, the father presented a concise account, suitable as a reply to the children, and containing all the essential elements of סִפּוּר יְצִיאַת מִצְרַיִם, telling about the Exodus: (a) the initial lowliness of our people (עֲבָדִים הָיִינוּ), (b) its triumphant liberation (וַיּוֹצִיאֵנוּ ה') or, according to the Abarbanel, the answers to the four sons), (c) the obligation to see ourselves as having gone out (... חַרָי אָנוּ וּבָנֵינוּ), and even (d) the mention of *Pesach*, *Matzah* and *Maror*(...בְּשָׁעָה שֶׁיֵּשׁ). Now we fulfill the obligation of מַרְבֶּה לְסַפֵּר, of enlarging upon our brief account (*Mishibud Lige'ulah*).

There is, however, a more basic reason for the *Haggadah* starting its account anew. We mentioned in the Overview (p. 31) that the *Talmud* records a controversy between Rav and Shemuel about the starting point of סִפּוּר יְצִיאַת מִצְרַיִם, telling about the Exodus (*Pesachim* 116a). In the light of this controversy, we can see the *Haggadah* up to this point as following the opinion of *Shemuel* that we are obliged to talk about our physical bondage and liberation, starting with עֲבָדִים הָיִינוּ, 'we were slaves'. Now we proceed to retell the story according to *Rav's* opinion that we should start with מִתְּחִלָּה, the early pagan beginnings of our ancestors — thus providing background and deeper understanding of the meaning of the Exodus.

The *Haggadah* first follows *Shemuel* and begins עֲבָדִים הָיִינוּ, 'We were slaves', for the *Talmud* appears to favor this opinion (thus, Rabbi Nachman acted according to it). Also, since *Mah Nishtanah* is based on the question of the wise son, it is logical for the father

*I*n the beginning our fathers were worshipers of idols, but now the Ever-Present has brought us to His service, as it is said: "And Joshua spoke to the whole people: Thus has HASHEM, God of Israel, spoken: 'Your fathers dwelt in olden times beyond

to respond with עֲבָדִים הָיִינוּ (which is the Torah's answer to the wise son). However, we also want to comply with the opinion of *Rav (Rif)*, to help us grasp the wider significance of the events *(Avudraham)*; therefore we now recite מִתְּחִלָּה, *'In the beginning.'*

The words with which *Shemuel* wants us to start the story of the Exodus are obviously very appropriate, for they form the Torah's answer to the wise son, as we just pointed out. What prompts *Rav* to offer a divergent opinion? According to *Rabbeinu Manoach*, he also bases himself on the Torah's reply to the wise son; it concludes by stressing that the purpose of the *Pesach* observances is לְיִרְאָה אֶת ה' אֱלֹקֵינוּ, *'to fear HASHEM, our God'* — therefore we should not talk just about our physical bondage and redemption but about our spiritual elevation from idolatry.

The *Ritva* (quoted in the *Overview*, p. 31) is actually of the opinion that both *Rav* and *Shemuel* sought the recitation of עֲבָדִים הָיִינוּ as well as מִתְּחִלָּה. Perhaps, however, they disagreed on the order in which they were to be said: according to the chronological sequence (מִתְּחִלָּה first) or as story and interpretation (עֲבָדִים first). In effect, we answer the wise son's questions, in the *Mah Nishtanah*, by telling the actual account of bondage and liberation; and then we add מִתְּחִלָּה, to clarify our lowly spiritual beginnings that made the Egyptian bondage necessary and that were redressed by our liberation. It has been suggested, in fact, that עֲבָדִים הָיִינוּ

might have been a sufficient answer to the wise son; מִתְּחִלָּה is added for the benefit of the wicked son who is blind to spiritual matters and sees no need to be grateful for liberation from a bondage into which God put us Himself *(Yalkut Tov;* this would explain why מִתְּחִלָּה follows immediately upon the passage of the four sons).

Why, indeed, should we be grateful for deliverance from a bondage which God had planned, as He told Abraham, and which He then brought about so carefully? We pointed out previously (p. 73) that the demonstration of Egyptian power during the years of slavery, and its subsequent overthrow by God, served to show to all of mankind that God rules the world. Thus these events proved an immeasurable blessing. However, this is not the complete answer — as we stressed in the *Overview* (p.31), we have to look even deeper in order to understand the meaning of our bondage in Egypt.

At the very beginning of history, man was created to be God's partner, so to speak, in perfecting God's world according to His plan. However, the forces of קִנְאָה תַּאֲוָה וְכָבוֹד, human jealousy, lust, and self-assertion *(Avos* 4:28) led to catastrophic failures — the first of them by Adam and Eve, when they took it upon themselves to transgress God's command and to eat from the 'tree of knowledge.'[1] Cain, the generation of the flood, and the builders of the Tower of Babylon, marked further failures. Each of them

1. The duty to eat *Matzah* and abstain from *Chametz* on *Pesach* can be viewed as a way of redressing the sin of Adam and Eve. According to some Rabbinic opinions, the fruit of the 'tree of knowledge', from which they ate, was wheat. By eating only flat and tasteless *Matzah*, לֶחֶם עֹנִי, we turn our back upon the pride and desire which prompted Adam and Eve and which is symbolized by the leaven in the bread.

מֵעוֹלָם תֶּרַח אֲבִי אַבְרָהָם וַאֲבִי נָחוֹר וַיַּעַבְדוּ
אֱלֹהִים אֲחֵרִים: וָאֶקַּח אֶת־אֲבִיכֶם אֶת־
אַבְרָהָם מֵעֵבֶר הַנָּהָר וָאוֹלֵךְ אוֹתוֹ בְּכָל־אֶרֶץ
כְּנַעַן וָאַרְבֶּה אֶת זַרְעוֹ וָאֶתֶּן לוֹ אֶת־יִצְחָק:
וָאֶתֵּן לְיִצְחָק אֶת־יַעֲקֹב וְאֶת עֵשָׂו וָאֶתֵּן לְעֵשָׂו
אֶת־הַר שֵׂעִיר לָרֶשֶׁת אוֹתוֹ וְיַעֲקֹב וּבָנָיו יָרְדוּ
מִצְרָיִם:

brought the need for a new beginning, under changed conditions. The last of these events, the Building of the Tower, did not lead to the destruction of the generation, but to its breakup into a multitude of nations. Among them, one nation was to arise which would keep alive within mankind the knowledge of God and His will *(Rabbi S.R. Hirsch)*. In order for such a people to exist in the pagan world, it had to be taught the dangers of man's overreaching himself. This is the story told in מַתְחִלָה: how the Jewish people arose from among the pagans to serve God.

תֶּרַח אֲבִי אַבְרָהָם — *Terach, the father of Abraham and Nachor*. We are here reminded that we came from pagan stock. At the same time, we see how very differently children of one father can develop. Abraham had the profound insight to recognize the Creator when still a child, and the strength of character to resist his entire environment at the price of his life. In this way, Abraham became worthy to be the father of our people and to lay the foundation for our closeness to God. He started a process that led to the redemption from Egypt, the receiving of the Torah and the building of God's sanctuary.

The beginning of this process is described in מַתְחִלָה which tells about the גְּנוּת, the shame, of our pagan origins. The *Haggadah* then traces it to its triumphant ending, the שֶׁבַח, which is described at the end of דַּיֵּנוּ (p.138); ...

and He built for us the Temple, to atone for all our sins' *(Meiri; others, however, see the joyful ending to the story of* מַתְחִלָה *in the blessing at the end of* Maggid, *when we thank God for our physical and spiritual deliverance —* Shibolei Haleket). But this process of becoming God's people had to unfold in a number of stages, which we shall find delineated by the *Haggadah*.

וָאַרְבֶּה אֶת זַרְעוֹ — *And I multiplied his seed*. In fact, Abraham had only one son who carried out his heritage, Isaac; the Biblical verse may therefore refer to the increase of the Jewish people in subsequent generations. The *Yerushalmi*, however, interprets the term וָאֶרֶב (which lacks a concluding ה' in the Biblical text) to mean רַבְתִּי: 'I contended with him in many ways*, putting him to so many tests, *before I gave him Isaac' (Pesachim* 10:5).

Abraham had to prove himself worthy before he and Sarah were granted Isaac. Both of them were physically unable to produce offspring until God miraculously gave them a child. The same was true of Isaac and Rebeccah, as well as Rachel and Leah. It is most significant that Divine intervention was required for them to have children. It underlined the truly miraculous way in which our people came into existence *(Overview* p. 28). It made manifest that the Patriarchs and Matriarchs represented a totally new beginning, with no hereditary indebtedness to their forefathers whom

the River (Euphrates), Terach, the father of Abraham and the father of Nachor, and they served other gods. And I took your father Abraham from beyond the River and led him throughout all the land of Canaan, and I multiplied his seed and gave him Isaac. And I gave to Isaac Jacob and Esau; and I gave to Esau Mount Seir, to possess it, and Jacob and his sons went down to Egypt'."

they repudiated. It demonstrated their outstanding merit which gained them God's favor. And, finally, it was an indication of the outstanding nature of the children thus born — great in stature if not in numbers.

Esau, however, was to have no share in Abraham's legacy, but rather to be the eternal antagonist of his twin-brother Jacob. Thus he and his descendants easily made their way in the world, inheriting the mountain of *Se'ir* — for it is the fate of the evildoer to gather his reward in this world, and to have to face judgment in the end — as predicted by the prophet: וְעָלוּ מוֹשִׁעִים בְּהַר צִיּוֹן לִשְׁפֹּט אֶת הַר עֵשָׂו, *'The rescuers will ascend Mount Zion in order to judge the mountain of Esau' (Ovadiah, 1:21)*. Jacob's lot was not destined to be so easy, as the Biblical verse points out.

וַיַּעֲקֹב וּבָנָיו יָרְדוּ — *Jacob and his sons went down to Egypt*. Three generations of Patriarchs laid the foundations of the Jewish people, each making his particular contribution. Yet, before their descendants could assume their crucial place in world history, they had to go through the harsh school of exile — wrenching and purifying — to be cleansed of the last residue of their pagan origins. The need for this cleansing process could be traced back to the very beginnings of mankind.

True, Abraham resolutely turned his back on the pagan world and was chosen father of our people on account of his אֱמוּנָה, his loyal faith. In the end it was in his merit that the Jews were

redeemed from Egypt *(Mechilta)*, and the ten plagues have been explained as a reward for the ten tests which he passed. Yet there were still traces of weakness, which made the bondage in Egypt necessary in the first place.

Abraham went to Egypt during a famine, without waiting for a specific command *(Ramban,* based on *Zohar);* he used his disciples in the war against the four kings; he asked, *'how will I know?'* when promised *Eretz Yisrael;* and he forewent the chance to gain גֵּרִים, proselytes, when he defeated the four kings *(Nedarim* 32a). All these were not mistakes in the ordinary sense of the word; there were, in fact excellent reasons for Abraham to act the way he did — and if *we* had acted similarly, no blame would have been attached to us. However, in the case of Abraham, these were further opportunities to implant absolute faith and trust in God in his descendants and when these opportunities were not utilized, it became necessary that this lesson should be taught through the suffering and miracles of the Egyptian bondage *(Michtav M'Eliyahu)*. There the Jewish people was made to realize to the fullest that they had nobody to rely on but God, and gained their freedom when they put their trust in Him, שֶׁלֹּא נִגְאֲלוּ יִשְׂרָאֵל מִמִּצְרַיִם אֶלָּא בִּשְׂכַר הָאֱמוּנָה שֶׁנֶּאֱמַר וַיַּאֲמֵן הָעָם *'for the Jews were not redeemed from Egypt except in the merit of their faith...' (Mechilta)*.

Again, the need for the hard lesson of exile was demonstrated by the way sons of Leah dealt with the sons of the

בָּרוּךְ שׁוֹמֵר הַבְטָחָתוֹ לְיִשְׂרָאֵל. בָּרוּךְ
הוּא. שֶׁהַקָּדוֹשׁ בָּרוּךְ הוּא חִשַּׁב אֶת
הַקֵּץ לַעֲשׂוֹת כְּמָה שֶׁאָמַר לְאַבְרָהָם אָבִינוּ

maidservants, and by the sale of Joseph. However good the reasons for this action — and the commentators have much to say on this score — Joseph's brothers themselves later sensed that there was a lack of brotherliness and feeling for each other, traits that were vital for the creation of God's people (Bereishis 42:21). Therefore, the bondage in Egypt came to develop feelings of self-effacing humility and understanding for strangers and slaves, that upon their liberation were turned into a cornerstone of their existence: "You sold Joseph for a slave — now you shall have to recite every year that 'we were slaves' " (Midrash Tehillim)[1].

This consciousness of their slave past was to guide them in their treatment of the poor and the unfree; in fact, while still in Egypt, they were commanded to free any slaves that they themselves owned (Yerushalmi, Rosh Hashanah 3:5). At the giving of the Torah, the laws governing their dealings with each other (מִשְׁפָּטִים) opened with the rules about freeing slaves (Lekach Tov). It is therefore not surprising that, at a later, traumatic moment in Jewish history, Jeremiah had to convey God's message to the Jews that they would lose their own freedom because they had robbed their slaves of the freedom to which they were entitled, thereby violating the covenant concluded in Egypt (Jeremiah 34:8-22). Hence, also, our ultimate redemption will depend on our treatment of our fellow-beings (see הָא לַחְמָא p. 68).

The process of education that the Jews had to undergo, had to be endured in — of all places — Egypt. This country was then not only the most powerful

nation of the time but also the most highly developed center of civilization, famous for its attainments in law, engineering, science, and medicine, and yet, at the same time, totally bereft of moral standards. In its emphasis on the comforts of so-called civilization and disregard for morality, Egypt represented the ultimate in human pride and lust, and the total antithesis to all that the Torah teaches (Vayikrah 18:3) — and for this very reason the Jews had to be in exile in this country (Maharal).

They were first to be exposed to the attractions of a flourishing society and culture; then to discover that behind them hid a corrupt and brutal regime; and finally, in the miraculous overthrow of this regime, to recognize that only God and His teachings merit loyal devotion.

That is why the exile in Egypt was such a necessary stage in the emergence of the Jewish people. It was the completion of a process of selection by which, first, Abraham was chosen, then Isaac, Jacob, and the twelve sons of Jacob from among all of Abraham's descendants, and finally those Jews who emerged from the Egyptian exile purified and strong in their dedication: מִי יִתֵּן טָהוֹר מִטָּמֵא לֹא אֶחָד, כְּגוֹן אַבְרָהָם מִתֶּרַח וכו' יִשְׂרָאֵל מֵאוּמוֹת מִי עָשָׂה כֵן מִי גָּזַר כֵן לֹא יְחִידוֹ שֶׁל עוֹלָם, 'Who draws pure from impure?' (Job 14:4), 'like Abraham from Terach ... Israel from the nations; who did so, ordained so — was it not the One and Only One?' (Midrash Rabbah).

Thus the exile which God imposed upon us was not just a prelude to a liberation for which we thank God, but was itself a favor bestowed upon us

1. The sale of Joseph into slavery was a cause for the bondage of the Jews in Egypt. But just as Joseph gained his freedom to become a ruler, so we too were redeemed to attain greatness (Rashbatz).

B lessed be He who keeps His assurance to Israel, blessed be He! For the Holy One, blessed be He, planned the end of their bondage, in order to do as He had said to our father Abraham at the Covenant

which also merits our gratitude. We said previously (p. 30) that we start the Haggadah by speaking of our bondage, because it gives us a greater appreciation of the liberty which we attained. But, there is another deeper reason why it should be mentioned tonight: our redemption, with all its blessings, had its roots in the suffering that preceeded it — and grew out of these very depths (Chever Maamorim) — just as the new wheat grows out of the seed-kernel that rots in the ground (see p. 73).[1]

That is why King David could exclaim (Tehillim 101:1): 'For kindness and justice I sing; unto You, HASHEM I give praise,' — for acts of kindness, but equally for acts of judgment; and for the same reason we are instructed to praise God for the bad that befalls us, just as we have to praise Him for the good. In fact, there are blessings that can be attained only by a prelude of suffering (our Sages enumerate Torah, Eretz Yisrael, and the World to Come). The Egyptian bondage with all its pain and misery, provided the soil from which there grew God's people.

Perhaps this thought is expressed in the Matzah, which represents both bondage and freedom. At a later point in the Seder (p. 142) we speak about the Matzah as a symbol of our redemption — and underline our remarks by lifting up the broken Matzah which, strictly speaking, represents the bread of bondage (see p. 67). Actually, slavery and deliverance merge to become one — manifestations of God's providence, for our benefit, and deserving our gratitude. If we had not gone through the crucible of Egypt, we might have enjoyed physical freedom but we would

not have attained our spiritual liberation, from the bondage of paganism and materialism. That is the basis for our gratitude to God on Seder night.

בָּרוּךְ שׁוֹמֵר הַבְטָחָתוֹ — Blessed be He who keeps His assurance to Israel. This passage (as well as וְהִיא שֶׁעָמְדָה which follows it) does not occur in Midrash or Talmud. It was inserted at the final editing of the Haggadah (at the end of the Talmudic era and the beginning of the Gaonic period), to express our gratitude to God for His direction of our destinies. As explained, we are even grateful for the exile that He announced to Abraham — but we also appreciate that limits were set to its severity: הקב"ה חִשַּׁב אֶת הַקֵּץ, 'God planned the end' and arranged a proper outcome of the bondage. The truth is that Egyptian bondage not only involved vast suffering but also profound spiritual danger.

For the Jews to reject all that Egypt stood for, when they attained their miraculous liberation, it was necessary that they first be immersed in the Egyptian world. Thus they were overawed by its culture and power, and were influenced by its way of life; and in due course, they sank to the very lowest level short of actual disappearance in the Egyptian morass. This is the nature of a melting pot; a substance thrown into it necessarily loses its form and consistency — and sometimes it can totally dissolve and disappear.

To forestall this, and to make sure that the Jews would survive their bondage, its scope was carefully limited by Divine wisdom. This was made very clear when God announced the impending exile to Abraham. In the

1. The word גָּלוּת (exile) derives from the word גִּלּוּי (revelation): under the conditions of exile the innermost self becomes revealed (Sfas Emes).

[95]   The Haggadah

בִּבְרִית בֵּין הַבְּתָרִים. שֶׁנֶּאֱמַר °וַיֹּאמֶר לְאַבְרָם
יָדֹעַ תֵּדַע כִּי־גֵר יִהְיֶה זַרְעֲךָ בְּאֶרֶץ לֹא לָהֶם
וַעֲבָדוּם וְעִנּוּ אֹתָם אַרְבַּע מֵאוֹת שָׁנָה: וְגַם אֶת־

first place, the Biblical account, which is here quoted by the *Haggadah*, stresses that their exile was to last *four hundred years*; it was not meant to go on until such time as the Jews would earn their redemption by their own merits. After all, that moment might never have come — for they had not yet been assured the revelation of God's power, which was to change the outlook of the entire world, nor the revelation of His will, in the Torah, as a means of improving themselves and bringing about their redemption. [The *Midrash* suggests that the four hundred years of exile equalled the time from the Flood to the days of Abraham. During that period, mankind piled iniquity upon iniquity, and God was, so to speak, in 'exile'; now the Jews were to attain purification by spending the same amount of time in exile.]

Furthermore, the exile was to start only with Abraham's descendants — and the time span fixed for it was not to be spent entirely under the harshest conditions *(Tosfos)*; their descent into exile was to be in stages. Three distinct periods are described in God's announcement to Abraham: (1) גֵרוּת, '*your descendants shall be strangers in a land not their own*'; (2) עֲבָדוּם, '*they shall serve them*'; and (3) עִנּוּ, '*they shall treat them harshly.*'

The first stage, גֵרוּת, began with the birth of Isaac: he and his descendants lived in the Holy Land, but they did not own it as yet (this is reflected in the name by which it was called: כְּנַעַן, *Canaan*, rather than אֶרֶץ יִשְׂרָאֵל, *the Land of Israel*). In fact, some historians suggest that at this time the Jews were already living under the overlordship of the Egyptian empire, which had pushed its boundaries northward to Syria and had taken control of *Eretz Yisrael*. Thus, Jacob saw the land as אֶרֶץ מְגוּרֵי

אָבִיו, '*where his father had only so-journed as a stranger*' (Bereishis 37:1); and he himself did not enjoy a peaceful life in it.

Yet this period was, of course, much more endurable than the later years in Egypt, and served as a precious time of preparation for them. It saw the three Patriarchs at their lifework of implanting in their descendants the crucial virtues of תּוֹרָה עֲבוֹדָה וּגְמִילוּת חֲסָדִים, Torah, Divine service, and deeds of kindness. In the course of three generations they wove '*the threefold chord* [which] *is not easily broken*' (Koheles 4:12) and built a family of seventy souls — representing the budding nation *(Maharal;* see p.104). It was only at this point that Jacob and his sons were ready for the descent to Egypt, to be strangers in an alien land in the fullest sense of these words. It has been suggested, however, that this harsher stage of their גֵרוּת existence would have started later, and would therefore have been shorter, if the quarrel between Joseph and his brothers had not brought the family to Egypt at this moment *(Hashir Vehashevach).*

The pace of exile quickened further with Jacob's death, when '*the eyes of the Jews were dulled by the burden of the bondage*' (Rashi to Bereishis 47:28). This refers to the pressure of assimilation to the Egyptian world, to the spiritual bondage; עֲבָדוּם, the actual physical enslavement, only began with the death of the last of Jacob's sons, Levi, 116 years before the Exodus. Thirty years later, when Miriam was born, the harshest mistreatment, torture and murder, were added, bringing 86 bitter years of עִנּוּי, oppression.

[The interpretation of the three stages follows *Rabbi S.R. Hirsch*. The *Maharal* sees in עֲבָדוּם, servitude, the enslave-

between the Portions, as it states: "And He said to Abram:'You should know for certain that your descendants shall be strangers in a land that is not theirs, and they shall serve them, and they shall treat them harshly, for four hundred years; but I will also judge

ment of the body, which ended when God took *'one nation from the midst of another' (Devarim 4:34), 'when Israel went out from Egypt' (Tehillim 114:1).* In עִנּוּי, oppression, he sees the enslavement of the spirit, which ended when the Jews were *'taken out of the melting pot' (Devarim 4:20), 'the house of Jacob from among a pagan people,' (Tehillim 114:1).*]

In effect, the onset of the Egyptian exile was gradual, and its harshest stages were relatively short. Considering that at the time of redemption the Jews had already fallen to the lowest level, and only one-fifth was redeemed (the others dying during the Plague of Darkness), we can perceive the kindness of God in setting such limits to their bondage, and liberating them in time, as He promised to Abraham. The phrase חִשֵּׁב אֶת הַקֵּץ, that God 'planned the end', can be interpreted, in the sense that He 'counted 190' years spent in *Eretz Yisrael* as part of the preordained 400 years of exile (the numerical value of קֵץ is 190).

There is, however, a view that God hastened to bring the redemption prematurely. It is based on the *Yalkut* to *Shir Hashirim* (2:8), *'The voice of my beloved — behold, he comes, jumping over the mountains, skipping over the hills.'* The Jews should really have spent 400 years in actual slavery. This would have been a complete fulfillment of the announcement to Abraham, and it would have purified the Jews to the point where no future exiles would have been necessary any more. The Jews, however, had to be liberated earlier because they were about to drown totally in Egyptian corruption, and therefore God speeded up their liberation. To

that end He made the years of עֲבְדוּת and עִנּוּי particularly harsh, so that they made up for the 190 years not spent in Egypt, that otherwise would have been missing from the 400 years needed for completion of the Egyptian exile.

Yet through this shortened exile the Jews were not really adequately purified; as a result, they were required to endure later exiles, to make up the years they had been spared in Egypt. In line with this view, the verse in *Eichah* (3:15), *'He sated me with Maror, he fed me wormwood'*, in which our Sages see a connection between *Pesach* and *Tisha B'Av*, can be interpreted thus: because God shortened the Egyptian exile by making it particularly bitter, we have had to endure the later destructions and exiles commemorated by *Tisha B'Av* (Bais Halevi).

It is important to note at this point that, ever since the Torah has been given, the Jews can no longer count on a fixed end to exile, or on any hastening of their redemption; now they are responsible to bring about the end of their exile through their loyal adherence to the Torah. This is indicated by *Isaiah's* statement about the redemption to come (52:12): כִּי לֹא בְחִפָּזוֹן תֵּצֵאוּ, וּבִמְנוּסָה לֹא תֵלֵכוּן, *'For you will not go out in a hurry and you will not proceed in flight.'* In Egypt, there was no need for flight (מְנוּסָה) from the enemies, but there was חִפָּזוֹן, hurry, as God hastened the redemption in order to save the Jews from spiritual destruction — at the future redemption, however, there will be neither *(Rabbi Elazar Fleckeles; Michtav M'Eliyahu).* That is why, in הָא לַחְמָא עַנְיָא, we base our prayer for speedy redemption upon the good deeds which we are doing (see p. 68).

הַגּוֹי אֲשֶׁר יַעֲבֹדוּ דָּן אָנֹכִי וְאַחֲרֵי כֵן יֵצְאוּ
בִּרְכֻשׁ גָּדוֹל:

מכסים המצות ומגביהים הכוסות ואומרים:

וְהִיא שֶׁעָמְדָה לַאֲבוֹתֵינוּ וְלָנוּ. שֶׁלֹּא אֶחָד
בִּלְבָד עָמַד עָלֵינוּ לְכַלּוֹתֵנוּ. אֶלָּא
שֶׁבְּכָל דּוֹר וָדוֹר עוֹמְדִים עָלֵינוּ לְכַלּוֹתֵנוּ.
וְהַקָּדוֹשׁ בָּרוּךְ הוּא מַצִּילֵנוּ מִיָּדָם:

True, there is a Talmudic opinion that even if we do not prove ourselves worthy, *Mashiach* will come in due course; but this is explained to mean that God will first send an evil regime that will bring us to תְּשׁוּבָה, penitence — in this way, we will merit deliverance (*Sanhedrin* 97b, *Maharsha*). Certainly, Divine Providence will not let the Jewish people be lost forever. This, itself, was part of the assurance given to Abraham at the בְּרִית בֵּין הַבְּתָרִים, the Covenant Between the Portions. He was told about the Egyptian exile and the deliverance from it — but at the same time he was also shown all later oppressive regimes under which the Jews would suffer (represented by the animals that were cut up), and the survival of the Jews (represented by the dove that was not divided).

In fact, all future exiles would follow the pattern of the Egyptian exile, whether in their pressure for Jewish assimilation or their ill-treatment of the Jews. Anyone familiar with the history of the Nazi regime, for instance, knows how Jews were first condemned to גֵּרוּת, second-class citizenship, then עַבְדוּת, special taxes and slave labor, and finally עִנּוּי, extermination. The very name of Egypt, מִצְרַיִם, has been taken as an allusion to the long row of oppressors

(מֵצָרִים) who were foreshadowed by the Egyptian exile.[1]

Likewise, the redemption from Egypt laid the foundation for the deliverance of the Jewish people from all later exiles and suffering. We explained before (p. 26) that God's self-revelation, when He Himself freed the Jewish people, became a turning-point in the history of mankind and of the Jews in particular. They would draw from it the strength to shake off all forms of spiritual servitude, and thus merit salvation from exile. The collapse of all the idols of Egypt, and of the power and pride of Pharaoh, would be echoed throughout history, as oppressors would fall; and God would, always again, stand revealed as the master of human destinies.

וְגַם אֶת הַגּוֹי ... בִּרְכוּשׁ גָּדוֹל — *I will also judge the nation that they will serve, and then they shall come out with great wealth.* The Egyptians provided a home for the Jewish people, for which they became entitled to a reward (*Brachos* 63b); the Jews are enjoined not to abominate them (*Devarim* 23:8). Moreover, even when they turned against the Jews, and enslaved them, they were carrying out the will of God. However, they were punished because

1. '*And also the nation which they shall serve, will I judge*' (*Bereishis* 15:14). What is the meaning of '*also*'? It is an allusion to all other nations which will enslave the Jews — they too will be judged and punished by God (*Midrash*).
'... *And after this they shall go out*' (*Bereishis* 15:14). '*After*' אַחֲרֵי, a combination of אַחַר, after, and י, ten) can be understood as '*after the ten plagues*' (*Daas Zekenim*).

the nation that they shall serve, and afterwards they shall come out with great wealth'."

The *Matzos* are covered, and the cups are lifted:

And it is this that has stood by our fathers and us; for not only one has risen up against us to destroy us, but in all ages they rise up against us to destroy us; and the Holy One, blessed be He, rescues us from their hands.

they did it altogether too gladly and were overzealous in their mission (*Nechemiah* 9:10: כִּי יָדַעְתָּ כִּי הֵזִידוּ עֲלֵיהֶם. 'For You knew that they wanted to do bad to them').

The Jews, on the other hand, received great reward. This can be taken to refer to both spiritual and physical rewards. Spiritually, even though they sank to such a low level during their exile, those Jews who preserved their identity and heritage lived to witness God's miraculous deliverance and rose to undreamt of heights — in the night that turned to day, at the splitting of the Sea, at the giving of the Torah, and at the dedication of the Sanctuary. Therefore the *'great wealth'* can be understood to refer to the Torah or the Sanctuary (which was the ultimate purpose of their deliverance from Egypt: אֲשֶׁר הוֹצֵאתִי אֹתָם מֵאֶרֶץ מִצְרַיִם לְשָׁכְנִי בְתוֹכָם, *'I took them out from the land of Egypt to dwell in their midst,' Shemos* 29:46).

However, the Jews also received worldly treasures — those that they obtained from their Egyptian neighbors and those that they got at the Splitting of the Sea (*Rashi, Shir Hashirim* 1:10-11). Perhaps they were given these riches because God's word comes true in every conceivable sense — or because they might not have seen in spiritual riches the fulfillment of the promise given to Abraham. It has also been suggested that they received this great wealth as a tool for the discharge of their mission on earth, in the same way as all material blessings are given to man

to be used in serving God. However, the Jewish people failed in their noble goal and misused this wealth for the making of the Golden Calf — whereupon it turned into a source of suffering (*Avos deRabbi Noson*). This is the fate of all gifts that we do not know how to use properly.

The *Zohar* points out that Moses occupied himself with the search for Joseph's coffin during the time that the other Jews were busy collecting treasures from the Egyptians. It concludes that, faced with a choice between two commandments, a person should always choose the one from which he will *not* gain material benefits. The reason may be that it is easier to fulfill this commandment without ulterior motives of gain — or it may be that we can so easily be tempted to misuse material gains, as did indeed happen with the treasures from Egypt.

Another reason for Moses' concentration on Joseph's coffin may be found in the statement of the *Meshech Chochmah* that he was the only human being able and permitted to live a purely spiritual life; thus, for instance, he separated from his wife (*Shabbos* 87a). Hence, the riches of Egypt were not meant for him.

וְהִיא שֶׁעָמְדָה — *And it is this that has stood by our fathers and us.* What is 'this' that is here referred to? The text permits various explanations, all valid. The simplest explanation is that the covenant concluded with Abraham has

צֵא וּלְמַד. מַה בִּקֵּשׁ לָבָן הָאֲרַמִּי לַעֲשׂוֹת לְיַעֲקֹב אָבִינוּ. שֶׁפַּרְעֹה לֹא גָזַר אֶלָּא עַל הַזְּכָרִים וְלָבָן בִּקֵּשׁ לַעֲקוֹר אֶת הַכֹּל. שֶׁנֶּאֱמַר. . .

always stood by us. Even though enemies have risen against us in all ages — not just Pharaoh in Egypt — we can rely on God to stand by us.

Others explain that we receive God's help *because* enemies rise against us in all ages; it is their inveterate enmity that has helped us, by gaining us God's protection. Their hostility may, in fact, be a blessing in disguise — and מַצִּילֵנוּ מִיָּדָם, may be translated to mean that God *'saves us through* (not: from) *their hands.'* Thus, Pharaoh's oppression cleansed the Jews and brought their redemption; and Moses actually grew up in his palace. In the same way, Haman unwittingly cleared Esther's road to the throne by having Vashti killed, and even built the very gallows on which he was hanged; and Ahasverus, in giving his ring to Haman, brought the Jews to penitence and salvation.

What was the nature of the promise that God made to Abraham? That His Divine Presence would always be with us *(Iyun Tefilah)* and help us against attacks *(Kolbo)*; that He would keep our enemies from uniting against us *(Sfas Emes)*, and would not let them do more than oppress us *(Ohr Yesharim)*; and that He would judge those that rise against us *(Machzor Vitry)*, not just in Egypt but during all later exiles *(Shibolei Haleket)*. Our liberation from Egypt was an act in which we all still share today; therefore any latter-day oppressors (specifically the four great empires, as stressed by our Sages) must inevitably share the fate of Pharaoh *(Avudraham)*.

It has been suggested that the word אֶחָד, *one*, in our passage can be taken as

a reference to God: we are saved by the fact that the only truly One never turned against us, even though innumerable enemies rise against us (see *Tehillim* 20:8-9).

Another explanation suggests that וְהִיא שֶׁעָמְדָה, can be translated, '*The Torah has stood by us*, וְהִיא being an allusion to Torah (the ו refers to the *six* sections of the Oral Law; the ה, to the *five* books of the חוּמָשׁ; the י, to the *ten* commandments; and the א, to the *One* and Only Lawgiver). Therefore, God always saves us, even though many enemies threaten us.

Basically, we here acknowledge that we have enemies in every age and that God saves us from them all. Abraham, who had the courage to be different from everybody else, was promised that in Egypt God would create a very different people, God's people. This event was then buttressed by the giving of the Torah at Mount Sinai, *'whence hatred descended into the world'*: the nations hate the people of the Torah for being different (the words סִינַי, *Mount Sinai*, and שִׂנְאָה, *hatred*, are here juxtaposed by our Sages; *Iyun Yaakov, Shabbos* 89a). Our unique, so-to-speak abnormal, origin and singular spiritual nature brought us enemies then — and in every generation since. There has never been enmity that was אֶחָד, unique; rather we have always endured a continuous replay of the events of Egypt — and therefore we can also count on deliverance in every generation, truly reliving the experience of the Exodus *(Rabbi A. Wolf)*.

צֵא וּלְמַד — *Go and learn.* This passage,

The cups are put down, and the *Matzos* are uncovered.

Go and learn what Laban the Aramean planned to do to our father Jacob; for Pharaoh decreed only that the male (children) should be put to death, but Laban had planned to uproot all, as it is said:

read by itself, seems out of place in the *Haggadah:* it appears to play down Pharaoh's persecution of the Jews, stressing the evil designs of Laban, who would appear to have no connection with the events of *Pesach.* It must, however, be read in conjunction with the statement that precedes it: '*In every generation they rise up to destroy us and God saves us from their hand.*' The story of Laban illustrates this fact *(Shibolei Haleket),* and shows that God's protection is extended to us when we are not even aware of our danger: when Jacob fled from Laban, he did not know that he was being pursued — but God appeared to Laban and, by His warning, stopped Laban from carrying out his evil plans *(Bereishis 31:24; Vilna Gaon).*

This salvation was even more remarkable because the danger from Laban had indeed been greater than that from Pharaoh; Laban was apparently ready to murder Jacob and his family, whereas Pharaoh merely wanted to enslave the Jews — he sought to kill the males only to do away with a possible redeemer of the Jews.

Other commentators suggest that Laban did not necessarily plan to kill Jacob and his family, but to force them to return with him to his house. His desire was to keep Jacob and his family under his control and influence — and *this* was the real threat posed by him.[1] Laban stood for such crude, materialistic and selfish trickery that Jacob found it necessary, after his es-

cape, to stress that עִם לָבָן גַּרְתִּי, *I dwelt with Laban (Bereshis 32:5),* but תרי"ג מִצְוֹת שָׁמַרְתִּי, *I managed to observe the 613 Commandments (Rashi,* from *Psikta Zuta;* [גַּרְתִּי has the same letters and numerical value as תַּרְיַ"ג, 613, and our Sages tell us that the Patriarchs indeed observed all the Torah commandments even though they had not yet been commanded]). Jacob was able to resist the spirit of Laban's house but his children would surely have succumbed and assimilated, preventing the emergence of a Jewish people. Pharaoh's killing of the boys, however tragic and cruel, posed a much lesser peril. In fact, our Sages, in the *Sifri,* state a general rule that קָשֶׁה הַמַחֲטִיאוֹ יוֹתֵר מִן הַהוֹרְגוֹ, *he who makes somebody sin is worse than he who kills him,* for the latter only robs him of his earthly life, while the former deprives him also of life in the World to Come.

It must be remembered, morever, that spiritual threats, as in Laban's case, are usually hidden behind a facade of kindness; therefore they are much more effective in undermining our resistance than outright oppression *(Vilna Gaon).* That is why Jacob felt it necessary to flee from Laban, in the first place; and God's warning, which prevented Laban from forcing him to return to his house, was indeed an outstanding example of God's constant concern for us.

But there is another, very simple reason why Laban's scheming is discussed here: it introduces the next part of the *Haggadah.* The *Haggadah* is about

1. Why was Laban called by this name, which means 'white'? Because he was a whitewashed sinner! Until his time everybody knew that sin is black and dirty; he, however, dressed it up to appear white and clean. As a descendant of Shem, he knew how to give respectability to the evilness that he had learnt from Nimrod, descendant and spiritual heir of Cain. That is why he posed such a great danger *(Yalkut Tov,* based on *Midrash).*

°אֲרַמִּי אֹבֵד אָבִי וַיֵּרֶד מִצְרַיְמָה וַיָּגָר שָׁם
בִּמְתֵי מְעָט וַיְהִי שָׁם לְגוֹי גָּדוֹל עָצוּם וָרָב:
וַיֵּרֶד מִצְרַיְמָה. אָנוּס עַל פִּי הַדִּבּוּר:

to describe in detail the Egyptian exile and our redemption from it. To this end it quotes and explains several verses from the Torah — and the first of these verses is understood by our Sages to begin with a reference to Laban: 'The Aramean sought to destroy my father ...' Therefore the *Haggadah* explains this statement before turning to the rest of the Biblical passage.

This passage is taken from *Devarim* (chapter 26), where the Torah directs farmers to bring their בִּכּוּרִים, the first fruits of their land, to the Temple. They are instructed to acknowledge God's kindness in creating our nation and bringing it to the promised land, in a declaration that contains four verses. The first verse mentions Laban's persecution of Jacob, and then describes the latter's descent into Egypt and the growth of the Jewish people whilst in Egypt. The second verse speaks about the ill-treatment of the Jews by the Egyptians; the third one shows God listening to the plight of the Jews; and the fourth, finally, describes their miraculous liberation. These four verses (Devarim 26:5-8) are explained in detail, word by word, in the *Midrash*; and it is these verses, with their *Midrashic* interpretation, that form the next part of the *Haggadah*.

(In the Torah a fifth verse follows, 26:9, which speaks of the Jews inheriting *Eretz Yisrael*; in the time of the Temple, according to *Rabbi David Zvi Hoffmann*, this verse, too, was recited and interpreted at the *Seder* — but it was dropped from the *Haggadah* when we went into Exile.)

As mentioned before (see כָּל הַמַּרְבֶּה לְסַפֵּר), *Rambam* views the Biblical verses quoted here, and their *Midrashic* interpretation, as the central part of the *Haggadah*. He stresses that it is just in

connection with this passage that lengthy explanation and elaboration is so praiseworthy. This stands to reason, for obviously the *Seder* should primarily focus on explaining to the fullest the suffering of our forefathers and the Divine miracles of our redemption.

(The emphasis of *Rambam* on this part of the *Haggadah* may also be in response to the Karaites, a sect which rejected Rabbinic interpretations of the Written Law and therefore would object to the *Midrashic* elaboration of these verses. Apparently Karaite sympathizers omitted these passages, leading Rabbi Natronai Gaon to declare that anybody eliminating them from the *Haggadah* was a heretic.)

Why did the Rabbis base the discussion of the events in Egypt just on the Biblical verses in *Devarim*? There are other Biblical passages that could have been chosen. The explanation has been offered that these verses were selected because the Torah introduces them with the words, וְעָנִיתָ וְאָמַרְתָּ, *you shall recite and say* (26:5). We know that the same expression, *reciting*, is used in connection with the commandment of talking about the Exodus; thus the *Matzah* is called לֶחֶם שֶׁעוֹנִין עָלָיו דְּבָרִים הַרְבֵּה, *the bread over which many words* (concerning the Exodus) *are recited*. This suggests that recitation of the *Haggadah* should include recitation of the verses from *Devarim* (Ohr Some'ach). It is noteworthy that *Rashi*, on the passage in *Devarim*, explains וְעָנִיתָ as 'reciting with a loud voice' — and there is a corresponding requirement that the *Haggadah* be read audibly. It has also been suggested that the link between the verses in *Devarim* and the *Haggadah* is shown by the opening words of the farmer's declaration — הִגַּדְתִּי הַיּוֹם, *I declare* (or: thank) *today* (Devarim 26:3) — which are related to the word *Haggadah* (Avudraham).

אֲרַמִּי אוֹבֵד אָבִי — *The Aramean sought to destroy my father*. These words are the beginning of the Biblical passage that is now to be discussed. From a

"The Aramean sought to destroy my father, and the latter went down to Egypt and sojourned there, with a family few in number; and he became there a nation, great, mighty and numerous."

"And he went down to Egypt" — *compelled by Divine decree.*

strictly grammatical viewpoint the three words could be, and have been, translated in different ways. Thus, the word אֹבֵד usually means *'straying'* or *'wandering'*, and the verse has therefore been taken as a reference to Jacob: *'My father was a wandering Aramean'* (*Ibn Ezra*). However, our Sages understood אֹבֵד as *'destroying'*, and the whole phrase as a reference to Laban: *'The Aramean sought to destroy my father'*; this interpretation was based on tradition (*Mizrachi*) and can be supported on grammatical grounds (*Haksav Vehakabalah*). But why does the Torah start the account of Jacob's descent to Egypt by referring to Laban's evil deeds? What connection did they have with Jacob's journey to Egypt? This can be understood in various ways:

In the first place, Jacob's stay with Laban helped prepare the Jews for the tribulations and temptations of exile. At the same time the evil designs of Laban, and his dangerous influence, described before, made it necessary that the exile announced to Abraham could not be in Aram, Laban's home; therefore Jacob, when faced with famine, turned to Egypt rather than to Aram, even though food was available there.

Secondly, Laban's trickery in exchanging Leah for Rachel, as Jacob's first wife, set off the feud between Jacob's sons which led to the sale of Joseph and ultimately brought the entire family to Egypt (*Chukas Hapesach*).

אֹבֵד means *'he destroys'*; the use of the present instead of the past ('he destroyed') has been explained on the grounds that Laban was always seeking to destroy Jacob — and that, in fact, the forces which he represented, today are

still seeking our undoing (*Hashir Vehashevach*).

But why does the Torah speak of Laban as actually 'destroying' rather than as 'trying, or wanting, to destroy'? The *Ritva*, based on the *Talmud Yerushalmi*, explains that the evil intentions of the nations are considered as though they had actually been carried out; the reason may be, as the *Avudraham* points out, that only God's intervention prevents their execution — therefore the evildoers cannot be excused for not having carried out their foul plans.

In fact, says the *Sfas Emes*, if Laban had not 'wanted to uproot all', he might have been able to do us some harm; however, because he wanted to destroy us totally, God did not let him do anything (this was also the fate of Haman when he overreached himself, centuries later).

In the simplest way, the term אֹבֵד can be understood as the *Zohar* explains it: 'the destroyer.' Just as a doctor is called a רוֹפֵא, a healer, whether he actually succeeds in healing his patients or not, so Laban can be described as the 'destroyer' of Jacob even though he did not succeed in his scheming.

אָנוּס עַל פִּי הַדִּבּוּר — *Compelled by Divine decree.* Jacob deserved no blame for leaving *Eretz Yisrael*, for his move to Egypt was not by his free choice. The Divine decree which was announced to Abraham, *'Your seed shall be strangers in an alien land'* (*Bereishis* 15:13), set in motion an irresistible chain of events (*Lekach Tov*). Jacob was, indeed, so apprehensive that he had to be reassured by God, *'Do not be afraid to go down to*

וַיָּגָר שָׁם. מְלַמֵּד שֶׁלֹּא יָרַד יַעֲקֹב אָבִינוּ
לְהִשְׁתַּקֵּעַ בְּמִצְרַיִם אֶלָּא לָגוּר שָׁם. שֶׁנֶּאֱמַר
°וַיֹּאמְרוּ אֶל פַּרְעֹה לָגוּר בָּאָרֶץ בָּאנוּ כִּי אֵין
מִרְעֶה לַצֹּאן אֲשֶׁר לַעֲבָדֶיךָ כִּי־כָבֵד הָרָעָב
בְּאֶרֶץ כְּנָעַן וְעַתָּה יֵשְׁבוּ נָא עֲבָדֶיךָ בְּאֶרֶץ גֹּשֶׁן:

° בראשית
מ"ז:ד

בִּמְתֵי מְעָט. כְּמָה שֶׁנֶּאֱמַר °בְּשִׁבְעִים נֶפֶשׁ
יָרְדוּ אֲבֹתֶיךָ מִצְרָיְמָה וְעַתָּה שָׂמְךָ יְהוָה
אֱלֹהֶיךָ כְּכוֹכְבֵי הַשָּׁמַיִם לָרֹב:

° דברים
י':כב

וַיְהִי שָׁם לְגוֹי. מְלַמֵּד שֶׁהָיוּ יִשְׂרָאֵל מְצֻיָּנִים
שָׁם:

Egypt, for I shall make you there into a
great people. I will go down with you to
Egypt, and I will also surely bring you
up' (Bereishis 46:3-4; Shibolei Haleket,
Rashbam).

The Sfas Emes suggests that דִּבּוּר
refers to the word Joseph sent to Jacob,
which brought about his journey to
Egypt (Joseph referred to himself as the
מְדַבֵּר, speaker — Bereshis 45:12). Our
Sages state that, according to the Divine
edict of Exile, Jacob was really destined
to be dragged to Egypt in iron chains —
but his great merits caused him to be
pulled there by the bonds of his love for
Joseph (Shabbos 89b).

לָגוּר שָׁם — To stay there for a time. וַיָּגָר
could be taken to mean that the Jews'
stay in Egypt was of a temporary nature
(גור means to sojourn for a while).
Therefore the verse quoted in explanation of וַיָּגָר makes it clear that this expression does not refer to the stay as
such — which turned out to be quite
lengthy — but to the intentions of the
Jews in descending to Egypt: they only
meant to stay for the duration of the
famine (Abarbanel). We see here that,
even though Jacob and his sons could
expect the best treatment in Egypt —
and did indeed receive it until the time
of Joseph's death — they did not want to
leave Eretz Yisrael and did so most

reluctantly, seeing their departure as a
form of Exile, גֵּרוּת (Chidah).

Also, they did not want לְהִשְׁתַּקֵּעַ, to
settle in Egypt permanently, because
they saw the danger of assimilation —
the Hebrew term here used literally
means 'to submerge oneself' in the new
home (YalkutTov). In fact, Jacob was
afraid that his descendants would
become Egyptianized, and his dying re-
quest to be buried in Eretz Yisrael was
meant to remind them that Eretz Yisrael
was their real home (Rabbi S. R.
Hirsch).

אֵין מִרְעֶה — There is no pasture. Why
would the sons of Jacob expect to find
pasture in Egypt? After all, was there
not famine there too? It is possible that
grass grew despite the famine; in Canaan, however, the starving inhabitants
would eat it, whereas in Egypt they
could buy food. It is also possible that
Egypt had some grass because the land
was irrigated from the Nile, whilst Canaan was dependent on rain (Ramban;
see Devarim 11:10).

בְּשִׁבְעִים נֶפֶשׁ — With seventy persons.
They formed a small family clan — but
it was the nucleus of a nation that
would in due course play a crucial role
among the seventy nations of the world,
'a sheep among seventy wolves.' Their

"And he sojourned there" — *which teaches that our father Jacob did not go to Egypt to settle there permanently, but merely to stay there for a time, as it says:*

"And they (the sons of Jacob) said to Pharaoh: 'We have come to sojourn in this land for there is no pasture for the flocks that belong to your servants, for the famine is severe in the land of Canaan; and now please let your servants dwell in the land of Goshen'."

"With few in number" — *as it is said: "Your fathers went down to Egypt with seventy persons; and now HASHEM, your God, has made you as numerous as the stars of heaven."*

"And he became there a nation" — *which teaches that the Jews were distinctive there.*

number, at this stage, foreshadowed their future role as a counterpart to the rest of the nations — God *'set the boundaries of the nations according to the number of the children of Israel'* (*Devarim* 32:8). Each of the seventy nations has its own historical role to play; in the same way, within the ranks of the Jewish people, each of the seventy souls of Jacob's family was destined to make a unique contribution to the future course of history. (We also find that 'there are seventy aspects to the Torah.' Correspondingly, the Jewish people, as guardian of the Torah, began with seventy souls.)

The word נֶפֶשׁ, person, or soul, is here used in the singular — while in the case of Esau's children, it is used in the plural (נַפְשׁוֹת בֵּיתוֹ, *the persons in his family*, *Bereishis* 36:6). The souls of the Jewish people are joined in their collective closeness to God. Whenever Jews affirm their bond with God, they form one organism. Thus, their faith in God's help united them in Egypt, to the point where there were no traitors or informers among them, and this made

possible their deliverance; likewise, when they came to Mount Sinai, they were united *'like one man, with one heart'* (*Shemos* 17:2, *Rashi*), and thus were ready to receive the Torah. However, if men follow their own inclinations, and separate themselves from God, they become a crowd of disparate individuals (see above, discussion of the Wicked Son).

כְּכוֹכְבֵי הַשָּׁמַיִם — *As the stars of heaven.* The Jews are compared to the stars in their multitude; but they are also like the stars in other respects. Within the larger harmony of the galaxies, God *'calls each star by name'* (*Isaiah* 40:26), assigning to each its own specific function in the universe; in the same way, each Jew has to be aware that 'for my sake the world was created' and that he has his own individual role to play for which he must accept the full responsibility.

מְצֻיָּנִים — *They were distinctive.* The appelation גּוֹי, nation, implies that the Jews preserved their own identity. (Some *Haggados*, however, read גּוֹי גָּדוֹל,

גָּדוֹל עָצוּם. כְּמָה שֶׁנֶּאֱמַר °וּבְנֵי יִשְׂרָאֵל פָּרוּ

'a great nation', omitting the word גָּדוֹל in the next entry; according to them the distinctiveness of the Jewish people is reflected in their being called a 'great nation').

In which way were the Jews distinguishable? *Kolbo* suggests that they lived together in a close-knit community, which helped them stand by each other; *Machzor Vitry* points to their extraordinary fruitfulness, which was reflected in the official Egyptian population register. Most commentators, however, point to the tradition preserved in the *Mechilta* — that the Jews remained different from the Egyptians in their language and names, did not adopt Egyptian immorality, and harbored no informers in their midst. Other sources add that they also remained distinct in their attire.[1]

Moreover, in the worst moments of their bondage, they clung to each other. The *Tanna d'bey Eliyahu* explains that 'the Jews in Egypt assembled and concluded a covenant that they would render kindness to each other; would remember the covenant of Abraham, Isaac, and Jacob, and serve their Father in Heaven alone; and would remember the language of Jacob's house and not learn the language of Egypt.' (See also *Pesikta* quoted by *Chafetz Chaim* to *Shemos* 15:13.)

The Jews' refusal to give up their identity, and their determination to stand by each other and by the traditions of their fathers, seem to conflict with the statement of our Sages that the Jewish people in Egypt sank to the forty-ninth stage of impurity, and was in imminent danger of falling to the fiftieth stage and total extinction. There is, however, really no contradiction.

The Jews lived for many generations under the full impact of Egyptian civilization, at the mercy of their Egyptian overlords, and without the protection of Torah and commandments that saved us from total assimilation in later exiles. They were able to survive as a people, until the time of their liberation, only because they remained 'different': loyal to the traditional ways of life and standards of morality inherited from the patriarchs. But at the same time their way of thinking was inevitably becoming colored and distorted by their environment (□*Rabbi Aaron Kotler*).

If the combination of traditional ways and pagan thinking seems strange, we only have to look around today and note how often Jewish observance is combined with non-Jewish ways of thought and the worship of power, success or money. This is a problem which is bound to arise as a result of living in exile. Our Sages declare that Jews living among the nations are 'serving idols in purity': they live in purity, because they abide by the laws of the Torah and, yet, they become involved in the ways of their neighbors, and are exposed to the ideas and values of their non-Jewish environment (*Avodah Zarah* 8a). In Egypt, where the Jews were held in subjugation, at the mercy of their masters, the impact of Egyptian society was inevitably overpowering.

The spiritual decline was gradual. The pervasive influence of Egyptian society could be felt as soon as Jacob had died, but became more obvious when Joseph passed away. The *Midrash* tells that 'when Joseph died, ... the Jews said, Let us be like the Egyptians, ... and when they did so, God turned the Egyptian liking for them into hatred,' and sent a new king who imposed new edicts upon them. The *Bais Halevi* ex-

1. Our Sages emphasize that the Jews remained distinct in their clothes, their names, and their language. This may not necessarily mean that they wore specific Jewish garb or only spoke Hebrew. Perhaps their distinctiveness lay in the fact that, unlike the Egyptians, they only wore modest attire; when they talked, 'the name of God was regularly on their lips'; and they did not give their children the names of Egyptian deities.

plains God's intervention as an act of mercy. The Jews were not really intent on giving up their identity; but when Joseph died, they realized that the bitter exile that had been predicted to Abraham was about to begin. Therefore, they intended to soften its impact by currying favor with the Egyptians. There was, of course, the grave danger that, as a result, they would very speedily become assimilated; it was therefore an act of kindness on God's part that He influenced the Egyptians against them: *'He turned their hearts to hate His people'* (*Tehillim* 105:25) and thereby slowed down the process of assimilation. Time and again we find this pattern repeated in later exiles: when Jews try hardest to disappear among their neighbors, they find themselves most strongly rebuffed by them. The Egyptian exile demonstrated this function of antisemitism for the first time in Jewish history.

As the Jews grew more and more numerous, the Egyptians actually *'became sick of the children of Israel'* (*Shemos* 1:12); they saw the Jews as thorns in their side (*Sotah 11a*), and felt their entire life spoilt by the ubiquitous presence of the Jews (*Rabbi S.R. Hirsch*; see below, וַתִּמָּלֵא). Therefore they started scheming to hold down their numbers. Neither forced labor and torture nor child-murder achieved this goal. On the contrary, the Jews continued increasing. Moreover, they preserved their own way of life, and even their hope for redemption. Yet, at the same time, more and more of them were infected by the spirit of idolworship that ruled the Egyptians. The spiritual decline intensified during the last 86 years of bondage, when Egyptian oppression was at its height. The prophet Ezekiel recounts how, at that time, God sent Aaron to *'say to them: Let every man throw away the abomina-*

tions before his eyes; do not defile yourselves with the idols of Egypt ...' (20:7-8). Four-fifths of the Jews were too deeply mired in the idolatrous world of Egypt to heed the call — and they subsequently perished during the Plague of Darkness.

Rambam stresses that the Patriarchs had taught their children the knowledge of God but, 'as time passed, the Jews in Egypt learned the ways of the Egyptians and worshiped idols as they did, except for the tribe of Levi which never served idols. ... And the root that Abraham had planted was about to be uprooted, when God, out of His love for us, carrying out His promise to Abraham, sent Moses. ...' The coming of Moses and the miraculous events that followed, awakened those Jews who were not yet lost, and they rallied to God's call. Our Sages tell us that if the redemption had not come at that moment, even this remnant of Israel would have been lost. Their distinctiveness alone would have been insufficient to save the Jews.

גָּדוֹל עָצוּם — *Great, mighty.* 'Great' here refers to the distinctive qualities of the people, whilst 'mighty' refers to their remarkable fertility — each woman bearing six children every time she gave birth (*Shibolei Haleket*).

[Some versions mentioned before consider the word 'great' out of place at this point (and rather read, above, גוֹי גָּדוֹל 'great people') because here the *Midrash* is concerned with stressing the fecundity of the Jews, and not their greatness as a people. The *Abarbanel*, however, disagrees and suggests that 'great' refers to the unusual number of births, and 'mighty' to the fact that all the children were healthy even though children of multiple births are weaker as a rule.]

פָּרוּ וַיִּשְׁרְצוּ — *They were fruitful and increased.* The multiplicity of words in the

וַיִּשְׁרְצוּ וַיִּרְבּוּ וַיַּעַצְמוּ בִּמְאֹד מְאֹד וַתִּמָּלֵא
הָאָרֶץ אֹתָם:

° יחזקאל
טז:ז

וָרָב. כְּמָה שֶׁנֶּאֱמַר °רְבָבָה כְּצֶמַח הַשָּׂדֶה
נְתַתִּיךְ וַתִּרְבִּי וַתִּגְדְּלִי וַתָּבֹאִי בַּעֲדִי עֲדָיִים
שָׁדַיִם נָכֹנוּ וּשְׂעָרֵךְ צִמֵּחַ וְאַתְּ עֵרֹם וְעֶרְיָה:

° יחזקאל
טז:ו

°וָאֶעֱבֹר עָלַיִךְ וָאֶרְאֵךְ מִתְבּוֹסֶסֶת בְּדָמָיִךְ
וָאֹמַר לָךְ בְּדָמַיִךְ חֲיִי וָאֹמַר לָךְ בְּדָמַיִךְ חֲיִי:

verse illustrates the statement of our Sages that six children were born each time a Jewish woman gave birth: the Jews (1) — פָּרוּ — were fruitful, (2) וַיִּשְׁרְצוּ — increased, (3) וַיִּרְבּוּ — multiplied, (4) וַיַּעַצְמוּ — became mighty, (5) בִּמְאֹד — very, (6) מְאֹד — very much. A sceptic once questioned this contention of the Rabbis; Rabbi Eliezer Gordon pointed out to him that the Torah counts only 22,000 firstborn males among the Jews in the desert, and presumably there were approximately the same number of firstborn females. Since the Jews at the time of the Exodus included 600,000 men of military age (20-60 years old), they must have numbered in total about three million men, women, and children. This meant that only one of every 65 people was a firstborn, and that families were of extraordinary size. If we assume that mothers gave birth ten or eleven times, they had to bear six children each time.

The Torah's statements about the fertility of the Jews serve to introduce the account of Egyptian oppression and Jewish suffering: every child born stimulated the hatred of the Egyptians and, in the case of a boy, his parents had to worry about hiding him from the Egyptians, who had ordered all males drowned in the Nile (Hashir Vehashevach).

וַתִּמָּלֵא הָאָרֶץ אֹתָם — And the land was filled with them. This statement, too, is meant to explain the Egyptian oppression of the Jews. Jacob had told Pharaoh that his family consisted of sheepherders in order to obtain the land of Goshen as a separate dwelling place for the Jews; after Joseph's death, however, they spread throughout Egypt, making their presence overly felt (Binah L'Itim). Our Sages point out that the Jews crowded into the theatres and other public places of entertainment, thereby further stimulating the hatred of their hosts. It should be noted that the Levites, who kept themselves aloof from the Egyptians, escaped the enslavement which became the fate of the other Jews.

וָרָב — And numerous. The verse quoted in explanation of this word shows that וָרָב here means 'growing numerous,' just as the grass grows in proliferation (Shibolei Haleket). The comparison with the grass is enlightening; the grass of the field grows without any effort on our part; also, the more it is cut, the more it grows. In the same way, through Divine Providence, the Jewish people responded to Egyptian oppression by becoming even more numerous (Ritva). The Levites were exempt from slave labor — and by the same token they were the least numerous of the tribes.

וְאַתְּ עֵרֹם וְעֶרְיָה — And you were naked and bare. In this parable of the Prophet Ezekiel the Jewish people is described as bare of commandments. The Mechilta explains that the time had come for the Jewish people to be redeemed, ac-

multiplied and became very, very mighty; and the land was filled with them."

"And numerous" — as it says: "I made you thrive like the plants of the field, and you grew big and tall, and you came to be of great charm, beautiful of form, and your hair was grown long; but you were naked and bare. And I passed over you and I saw you downtrodden in your blood and I said to you: 'through your blood you shall live'; and I said to you: 'through your blood you shall live'."

cording to the promise made to Abraham[1]; but the Jews were without commandments to make them deserving of redemption. The fact that they preserved their identity, helped in particular by their virtuous wives, enabled them to survive the long bondage until the time of their deliverance. The merit of the Patriarchs, זְכוּת אָבוֹת, and the promise made to them, meant that G-d in due course, would listen to their supplications and send them a redeemer. But they still needed Mitzvos through which they would, at that time, prove their readiness for redemption.

Therefore God gave them two Mitzvos: דַּם פֶּסַח וְדַם מִילָה, to offer the Pesach sacrifice, and to undergo circumcision. The two commandments are hinted at in the words בְּדָמַיִךְ חֲיִי which, literally mean 'through your two bloods you shall live.'

These Mitzvos were given after nine of the Plagues had demonstrated to Jews and Egyptians alike that God is the ruler of the world. Those Jews who could not learn this lesson died during the Darkness; the others, however, came to a new understanding of the faith of their forefathers, a new dimension of אֱמוּנָה. This faith was now put to the test by the two Mitzvos given them — Pesach and Milah.

These commandments demanded a readiness to separate totally from the world of the Egyptians: Milah involved carrying the sign of the covenant on one's body; and sacrificing the Pesach lamb meant slaughtering the animal that the Egyptians worshipped as a god. These Mitzvos also involved danger: drawing blood from one's own body, and risking Egyptian retaliation for killing the Pesach lamb. To disregard all such human fears and calculations meant demonstrating true and complete faith and confidence in God. When the Jews showed their readiness to risk their very lives for these Mitzvos, they became worthy of salvation: though it may seem paradoxical, it is eminently logical that, to earn the right to live, a man has to be ready to give up his life for God.

The particular and outstanding significance of these two Mitzvos is shown by the fact that they are the only two מִצְוֹת עֲשֵׂה, positive commandments in the Torah, whose deliberate disregard is punishable by Kores, the actual elimination of the sinner from his people. Otherwise, Kores appears only as a punishment for the transgression of the most fundamental prohibitions in the Torah.

The Chidah suggests that the Jews'

1. 'And you became beautiful, בַּעֲדִי עֲדָיִים וַתָּבוֹאִי (Ezekiel 16:7).
The words used for 'beautiful', בַּעֲדִי עֲדָיִים, have the numerical value 210, corresponding to the years of exile that the Jews had to spend in Egypt proper. When these years had passed, the time of redemption had come (Alshich).

°וַיָּרֵעוּ אֹתָנוּ הַמִּצְרִים וַיְעַנּוּנוּ וַיִּתְּנוּ עָלֵינוּ עֲבֹדָה קָשָׁה:

° דברים כו:ו

וַיָּרֵעוּ אֹתָנוּ הַמִּצְרִים. כְּמָה שֶׁנֶּאֱמַר °הָבָה נִתְחַכְּמָה לוֹ פֶּן יִרְבֶּה וְהָיָה כִּי תִקְרֶאנָה מִלְחָמָה וְנוֹסַף גַּם הוּא עַל שֹׂנְאֵינוּ וְנִלְחַם בָּנוּ וְעָלָה מִן הָאָרֶץ:

° שמות א:י

preservation of their own identity was actually enough to earn them liberation from slave labor, which happened six months before the Exodus; but only through the two *Mitzvos* involving self-sacrifice did they attain the full redemption.

[It should be noted that some *Haggados* do not have the verse, וְאֶעֱבֹר עָלַיִךְ *'And I passed over you ...'* The reason may be that in the Biblical text this verse precedes, rather than follows, the one beginning *'I made you thrive ...'* which we quote first. Also, it talks about the time of redemption, whereas we are here still concerned with the beginning of the bondage. However, according to the *Ari Hakadosh*, the verse is to be included.]

וַיָּרֵעוּ אֹתָנוּ הַמִּצְרִים — *The Egyptians ill-treated us.* We now quote the second verse from *Devarim*; the first verse described the growth of the Jewish people in Egypt, and this verse stresses how the Egyptians tried to stem this increase by oppressing the Jews.

The translation of וַיָּרֵעוּ as *'ill-treated'* has been questioned, for the verse that is quoted to explain this word does not speak of ill-treatment at all, but only of Egyptian scheming, *'Let us deal cunningly with them.'* Therefore a number of other translations have been suggested — for instance, *'the Egyptians treated us worse'* than did earlier enemies, such as Esau. Pharaoh felt that Esau had made a great mistake; he had decided to wait till after Isaac's death before taking his revenge on Jacob, and by that time Jacob's family was already

too large to be exterminated by one blow. Therefore, Pharaoh started scheming as soon as he was free to do so — after the death of Levi, the last of Jacob's sons to pass away *(Midrash).* This was 116 years before the Exodus.

Others translate וַיָּרֵעוּ, *'they considered us bad'* (Abarbanel), or *'they suspected us of evil'* (Rabbi Wolf Heidenheim). This served as the explanation — and justification — for their scheming *(Bais Halevi).*[1]

הָבָה נִתְחַכְּמָה לוֹ — *Come, let us deal cunningly with them.* The *Talmud* recounts that the Egyptians used a cunning scheme to enslave the Jews. On the appointed day, Pharaoh proclaimed a national day of labor. He himself started making bricks, and the Jews, eager to prove their loyalty, responded by working along with all their might. By nightfall, Pharaoh appointed taskmasters who counted the bricks made by the Jews on that day and imposed upon them the duty to produce a like number every day thereafter.

The only ones who did not join in the first day's work were the Levites; as a result they escaped enslavement. We mentioned before that they stayed by themselves in Goshen, content to devote themselves to cultivating the sacred heritage of the Jews. Our Sages point out that they were the scholars and teachers of the Torah in Egypt. Also, they alone among the Jews continued to observe *Milah* throughout the Egyptian exile: *'they guarded Your word, and*

1. *Rabbi Shlomo Alkabetz* translates וַיָּרֵעוּ *'they made us bad.'* In that way they hoped to bring God's punishment upon us! This was their scheme.

"The Egyptians ill-treated us, oppressed us and laid heavy labors upon us."

"The Egyptians ill-treated us" — *as it is said:* "Come, let us deal cunningly with them, lest they multiply, and, if we should happen to have war, they will join our enemies, and fight against us and go out of the country."

observed 'Your covenant' (*Devarim* 33:9). The Egyptians respected the special position of the Levites as the 'priestly caste' among the Jews. This was helped in great measure by the far-sightedness of Joseph. When he reorganized Egyptian society, he accorded a special status to the priests (*Bereishis* 47:22); in this way he strengthened the veneration accorded by the Egyptians to the priesthood, and prepared the ground for the special treatment of those Jews who devoted themselves only to the service of God (*Maharal*).

For the other Jews the Egyptians had no mercy. They were convinced that they could break the vitality of the Jews, disrupt their family life, and put an end to their increase in numbers, by imposing forced labor on them. Why did the Egyptians use such an elaborate ruse, instead of rounding up the Jews for outright slave labor? It may be that they were afraid of an open confrontation, in view of the large Jewish population. The Nazis, too, tried to keep their plans for a 'final solution' of the Jewish problem a secret, and used various schemes to lull their Jewish victims into cooperating with their nefarious plans.

And why did the Egyptians not massacre the Jews outright, if they were so afraid of their growing numbers? *Ramban* suggests that the Egyptian people might not have gone along with such a drastic step; even a despot has to cloak his criminal designs in a garb of reasonable formal procedures. Obviously there were no wrongdoings of which the Jews could be accused (*Rabbi S.R. Hirsch* stresses that this was a tribute to the morality of the Jews: even at a time of weakening of their religious fiber, their social conduct was without blemish). In these circumstances, to massacre the Jews after all that Joseph had done for the country, and after they had come to live there at Pharaoh's express invitation, would have been too shocking a betrayal. Therefore, Pharaoh proceeded by steps, in the manner familiar to us from more recent tyrants.[1]

First he poisoned the minds of his people against the Jews. Then he instituted forced labor — which he could defend as a reasonable demand on foreigners in the country. The Torah quotes Pharaoh as pointing out that the Jewish people was רַב וְעָצוּם מִמֶּנּוּ, *had its size and strength from us* (according to the interpretation of the *Ohr Hachayim*), and owed the Egyptians some compensating service.

When the Jews continued to increase, Pharaoh adopted more drastic policies of repression; this stage began with the birth of Miriam, 86 years before the Exodus (the *Midrash* explains her name as

---

1. The degradation of the Jews was particularly hard on them because they had previously enjoyed all the privileges of Egyptian society. Their sudden rejection caused deep anguish, even before they had to suffer the full brunt of Egyptian oppression. This rejection, however, was the first step toward their realization that Egyptian civilization was hollow and rotten; and it therefore was the beginning of their ultimate deliverance (*Out of the Iron Furnace*).

וַיְעַנּוּנוּ. כְּמָה שֶׁנֶּאֱמַר °וַיָּשִׂימוּ עָלָיו שָׂרֵי
מִסִּים לְמַעַן עַנֹּתוֹ בְּסִבְלֹתָם וַיִּבֶן עָרֵי
מִסְכְּנוֹת לְפַרְעֹה אֶת פִּתֹם וְאֶת רַעַמְסֵס:
וַיִּתְּנוּ עָלֵינוּ עֲבֹדָה קָשָׁה. כְּמָה שֶׁנֶּאֱמַר
°וַיַּעֲבִדוּ מִצְרַיִם אֶת בְּנֵי יִשְׂרָאֵל בְּפָרֶךְ:

° שמות
א:יא

° שמות
א:יג

derived from מְרִירוּת, *bitterness*).
Pharaoh initially tried to conspire with
the Jewish midwives to have Jewish infants secretly murdered at birth. When
he failed in this effort, he encouraged
his people to drown Jewish baby boys in
the river (the Torah speaks of an edict
to throw 'all newborn males' into the
river, but the *Targum* indicates that it
was only aimed at the *Jewish* children).

When his astrologers predicted the
birth of a redeemer for the Jews,
Pharaoh broadened his order to include
even Egyptian newborns (*Sotah* 12a).
However, this stage only lasted until
after the birth of Moses, 6 years after
Miriam's birth. At that time, the
astrologers announced that the
redeemer had been born, but that he had
disappeared; this was the result of
Moses being put in the river — but they
assumed that it reflected Pharaoh's edict
having been carried out. Pharaoh then
stopped the drowning of newborn infants and instead ordered that the life of
the Jews be made as unbearable as possible; in this way he hoped to dispel any
dreams of liberation (*Pirkei deRabbi
Eliezer*).

The phrase נִתְחַכְּמָה לוֹ, strictly
translated, means '*let us deal cunningly
with it*' (the Jewish people), but it can
also be translated '*with Him*', referring
to God. Our Sages (*Sotah* 11a) point out
that the Egyptians tried to outsmart
God when they decided to drown the
Jewish infants. In oppressing the Jews
they sought to employ means that God
could not use against Egypt in retribution. Since God had promised Noah
never to bring another flood upon the
world, they felt safe in using the water
of the river as a tool of oppression.

They were mistaken, however; mankind as a whole would never again
be punished by water, but individual
nations would — and indeed, the Egyptians received their punishment at the
יַם סוּף, the Sea of Reeds.

The Torah states that all this scheming against the Jews came from a '*new
king who did not know Joseph*'
(*Shemos* 1:8). The *Talmud* (*Sotah* 11a)
records that Rav and Shemuel disagree
on whether this was actually a new ruler
(as the verse would seem to indicate).
Since the Torah does not specifically
mention the death of the old ruler, one
of the Sages holds that the old ruler
merely instituted a new, anti-Jewish
policy and acted as though he did not
remember Joseph.

It is perhaps possible to ascribe the
disagreement of the two Sages to a difference in their views as to who initiated
the oppression of the Jews — Pharaoh or
his people. There is a *Midrashic* opinion
that the Egyptians wanted Pharaoh to
persecute the Jews; when he refused,
they deposed him and only reinstated
him when he agreed to comply with
their wishes. Clearly, according to this
Midrash, he was not a *new* king. On the
other hand, if it is assumed that the
persecution of the Jews emanated from
the ruler rather than the people, we may
assume that it was a new Pharaoh who
began it. It has also been suggested that
Rav and Shemuel disagreed on how evil
a man can be — whether a ruler who had
actually known and been indebted to
Joseph could turn into such a cruel oppressor (*Rabbi Moshe Feinstein*).

But how could even a new ruler be ig-
norant of Joseph and his great services
to Egypt? The *Sfas Emes* interprets the

"They oppressed us" — *as it is said: "They placed taskmasters over them, to oppress them with their impositions, and they built store-cities for Pharaoh, Pisom and Ramses."*

"They laid heavy labors upon us" — *as it is said: "The Egyptians made the children of Israel slave rigorously."*

Biblical phrase to mean that the king no longer perceived the distinctive qualities of Joseph in the Jewish people. They had begun to assimilate and thereby had forfeited the protection given to them by the memory of Joseph.[1]

וַיְעַנּוּנוּ — *They oppressed us.* The Egyptians were not really interested in the building projects for which they used the Jews; otherwise they would have taken better care of their workmen. Their aim was to oppress and decimate the Jews by means of their conscription for forced labor (*Yalkut Me'am Loez*). This was also shown by the fact, pointed out by our Sages, that the sites chosen for the cities of Pisom and Ramses were marshy — as a result, the walls erected by the Jews promptly collapsed or sank into the ground, and the workmen had to start all over again (*Sotah* 11a).

However, the aim of the Egyptians was not achieved: The Torah tells us that, on the contrary, וְכַאֲשֶׁר יְעַנּוּ אֹתוֹ כֵּן יִרְבֶּה וְכֵן יִפְרֹץ, *the more they oppressed them, the more they increased and spread out* (*Shemos* 1:12). We pointed out that this was a special blessing for the suffering Jews; the Levites — who were exempt from slave labor — did not benefit from it.

בְּפָרֶךְ — *Rigorously.* The word בְּפָרֶךְ can be understood in different ways. Our

Sages see it as illustrating the increasing severity of the Jews' enslavement. At first they were talked into voluntary labor (בְּפֶה רַךְ, with soft talk) and ultimately they were ground under (נִפְרָךְ) by the hardships imposed on them.

The Egyptians found ever new ways of making their life unbearable. Under the pretext that the men would lose too much working time if they returned home every night, the Egyptians made them stay in the fields, separated from their families. Thus, *Rashbatz* relates בְּפָרֶךְ to פָּרֹכֶת, a separating curtain.

Also, they made the men do the work of women, and vice versa — a cruel and degrading imposition. Above all, עֲבוֹדַת פֶּרֶךְ, rigorous labor, has been interpreted as labor to which no end can be foreseen (*Midrash Hagadol*).

The details of the increasing burdens imposed on the Jews are hinted at in the Biblical verse following the one here quoted, and according to the custom of *Chabad* it, too, is recited here (*Shemos* 1:14): '*They made their lives bitter with hard labor, with mortar and brick, and through all manner of labor in the field; all their bondage at which they made them slave rigorously.*' First, when the taskmasters were imposed upon the Jews, they furnished them with the necessary materials for their construction labors. Then the Jews had to

1. '*And a new king arose, who did not know Joseph*' (*Shemos* 1:8).
  Our Sages point out that he who belies the favors received from a friend, ultimately will belie the existence of God. Pharaoh started by denying Joseph and ended by saying, '*I do not know God*' (*Shemos* 5:2). It is the way of the evildoers to be ungrateful for favors received. The Torah teaches us differently; we are forbidden to despise even the Egyptians, because we once lived in their land.

°וַנִּצְעַק אֶל יהוה אֱלֹהֵי אֲבֹתֵינוּ וַיִּשְׁמַע
יהוה אֶת־קֹלֵנוּ וַיַּרְא אֶת־עָנְיֵנוּ וְאֶת עֲמָלֵנוּ
וְאֶת־לַחֲצֵנוּ:

וַנִּצְעַק אֶל־יהוה אֱלֹהֵי אֲבֹתֵינוּ. כְּמָה

שֶׁנֶּאֱמַר °וַיְהִי בַיָּמִים הָרַבִּים הָהֵם וַיָּמָת מֶלֶךְ
מִצְרַיִם וַיֵּאָנְחוּ בְנֵי־יִשְׂרָאֵל מִן־הָעֲבֹדָה וַיִּזְעָקוּ
וַתַּעַל שַׁוְעָתָם אֶל־הָאֱלֹהִים מִן־הָעֲבֹדָה:

וַיִּשְׁמַע יהוה אֶת־קֹלֵנוּ. כְּמָה שֶׁנֶּאֱמַר

prepare the building materials them-selves.[1] Next, they were also bur-dened with all the heavy work in the fields that Pharaoh and his people re-quired. Moreover, they were mistreated and beaten, and given only the most common and simple food — fish and vegetables (Ramban).

The Tanchumah explains the verse quoted above (1:14) as a description of the day of the Jewish slave in Egypt: in the evening, after he has finished his day of construction work and would try to rest, an Egyptian would tell him to pick some vegetables or split some wood for him. Worse yet, he tells him to cook and bake, or perform other feminine tasks whilst he tells the wife to draw water or do other heavy work normally done by men.

'Labor in the field', according to the Yalkut, does not refer to agricultural work but to the previously mentioned fact that the men were required to stay in the fields rather than return home. The Yalkut adds that the women would, however, go out to the fields at night to take care of their ill-treated and utterly

exhausted husbands, bring them water for washing, and food to give them strength. Moreover, they would en-courage them and remind them that the redemption was sure to come. In this way, the women were able to preserve their family life and maintain the spirit of the people — our Sages referred to this when they declared that the deliverance of our forefathers from Egypt was due to the righteous women of that generation (Sotah 11b; see p.71).

וַנִּצְעַק — We cried. This is the third verse quoted from Devarim. Now the Jews turned to God with their prayers, and they were listened to.

וַיָּמָת מֶלֶךְ מִצְרַיִם — The king of Egypt died. Why would the Jews cry so bitter-ly upon the death of their oppressor? It has been suggested that normally they were not permitted to complain about their bitter lot; but during the period of national mourning for the king they could express their own private grief without fear (Shaar Hashomayim). Ramban suggests that they were afraid that the new Pharaoh would be even

1. '... thus said Pharaoh: I will not give you straw. You go and take straw for yourselves, from wherever you find it, because there will be no reduction in your workload' (Shemos 5:10-11).

Pharaoh could have made the life of the Jews harder by increasing the number of bricks demanded from them. Why did he choose, instead, to take away the straw that they needed? The Rebbe of Alexander explained that making more bricks would only have involved harder physical labor — whilst hunting for straw also involved worry and uncertainty about finding enough. Pharaoh was a master at mistreating his slaves; he knew that mental suffering is even worse than physical exhaustion.

"We cried to HASHEM, the God of our fathers, and HASHEM heard our voice. He saw our illtreatment, our burden and our oppression."

"We cried to HASHEM, the God of our fathers" — *as it is said: "It came to pass during that long period that the king of Egypt died, and the children of Israel groaned because of the bondage, and they cried, and their prayers rose up to God because of the servitude."*

"HASHEM heard our voice" — *as it is said: "God*

worse than the old one. Also, as long as the Pharaoh lived who had instituted the oppression of the Jews, there was a chance that he might change his mind; with his death, his decrees acquired the status of an old-established national policy (*Rabbi S.R. Hirsch*).

Our Sages, however, recount that actually Pharaoh did not die; rather, he became afflicted with צָרַעַת, a skin disease. Jewish tradition considers a person with this disease as if he were dead, for he must be excluded from all human company and normal pursuits. Pharaoh's doctors ordered that he bathe every morning and evening in the blood of children, and of course Jewish children were murdered for this purpose. Hence the great outburst of grief.

Usually, when the Torah reports the death of a ruler, it mentions his name rather than his title, for אֵין שִׁלְטוֹן בְּיוֹם הַמָּוֶת, 'there is no sovereignty on the day of death.' The Torah's reference, in our case, to the death *of the king* could support the view that he did not really die (*Vilna Gaon*).

וַיֵּאָנְחוּ — *They groaned.* Three expressions are used here to describe the prayers of the Jews: וַיֵּאָנְחוּ *they groaned*; וַיִּזְעָקוּ *they cried*; שַׁוְעָתָם *their prayer.* This repetition would indicate

that the Jews cried out with all fibers of their being. Jewish tradition sees three levels, so to speak, on which a person functions — נֶפֶשׁ, associated with his power to act; רוּחַ — associated with his power of speech; and נְשָׁמָה — associated with his power to think; when the Jews turned to God from their suffering, they did so with all their faculties.[1]

וַיִּשְׁמַע — *HASHEM heard.* In the passage in *Devarim*, God is always called HASHEM, while the explanatory verses quoted from *Shemos* call him *Elokim.* The latter name is used to describe God as the dispenser of justice, while the former describes Him as the source of mercy. It has been suggested that in the Book of *Shemos*, in the recital of the events as they happened, God is described as Judge, for that is how he appeared to the people at the time. The passage in *Devarim*, however, expresses the way we see God's actions in retrospect — as merciful and bestowing blessing upon us. Very often we are only able to perceive HASHEM's lovingkindness long after the event.

At first glance, the Biblical verses that are quoted here from *Shemos* seem repetitive: *God heard, God remembered, God saw, God took note. Ramban* explains that the time had

1. *'And we cried, to HASHEM, the God of our fathers ...' (Devarim 26:7).*
    The *Chovos Halevovos* points out that there are two ways to the knowledge of God: through perceiving Him when He reveals Himself in the world, and through the tradition passed down from our forefathers. The Jews in Egyptian bondage had not yet witnessed His self-revelation, but they cried to the God whom they knew through their fathers.

שמות °וַיִּשְׁמַע אֱלֹהִים אֶת־נַאֲקָתָם וַיִּזְכֹּר אֱלֹהִים
ב:כד אֶת־בְּרִיתוֹ אֶת־אַבְרָהָם אֶת־יִצְחָק וְאֶת־יַעֲקֹב:

וַיַּרְא אֶת־עָנְיֵנוּ. זוֹ פְּרִישׁוּת דֶּרֶךְ אֶרֶץ. כְּמָה

שמות שֶׁנֶּאֱמַר °וַיַּרְא אֱלֹהִים אֶת־בְּנֵי יִשְׂרָאֵל וַיֵּדַע
ב:כה אֱלֹהִים:

come for the Jews to be redeemed, but they were not worthy of redemption. The Torah therefore, found it necessary to elaborate that their heartfelt crying rose to God, and carried their prayers before Him; as a result, God — so to speak — reminded Himself of the covenant which He had concluded with the Patriarchs, and took note of their suffering. At this point their redemption was assured (Chever Ma'amarim) though they still had to show themselves ready for it through their acceptance of the Mitzvos of Pesach and Milah (see p. 109).[1] Sforno stresses that these verses refer to the prayers of those Jews who remained steadfast in their faith throughout all their suffering, and sought God with all their heart.

וַיִּזְכֹּר — God remembered. The Jews may not have earned redemption in their own merit; but their supplications evoked the memory of God's covenant with their forefathers. Ezekiel (20:5-6) explains that God had promised the Patriarchs that He would take the children of Jacob as His people; therefore He revealed Himself to them in Egypt, and He swore that He would be their God. This is the meaning of the passage in Shemos (6:3-7): 'I appeared to Abraham, Isaac, and Jacob ... but I did not reveal myself to them as HASHEM [Rashi: who carries out His

promises.] And I established My covenant with them ... And I heard the crying of the children of Israel ... and I remembered My covenant. Therefore say to the children of Israel, I am HASHEM, and I will take you out from under the impositions of Egypt ... and I shall be God for you, and you shall know that I am HASHEM, your God ...' (See also Devarim 7:8).

However, Ezekiel also explains that the Jews had sunk so deeply into the immorality of Egypt that they did not even deserve the fulfillment of God's promise to the Patriarchs. This promise was kept only to prevent a חִלוּל הַשֵׁם, the desecration of God's name among the nations (20:6-9). The Patriarchs had been promised that their descendants would be redeemed from Egypt for a higher purpose: to keep alive among the nations the knowledge of God; if the Jews had perished in Egypt, not only would this knowledge of God have been lost but, as a result, the entire purpose of creation would have remained unfulfilled (Rabbi Joseph Breuer).

The task of the Jewish people was to sanctify God before the nations; whenever this mission was endangered, there was the threat of חִלוּל הַשֵׁם (see Devarim 9:26-29, Tehillim 115:1-2). Therefore God kept his promise to the Patriarchs, even though the Jews did not deserve it.

1. Five things brought about the redemption of our forefathers from Egypt:
— the coming of the appointed time, as it says, 'It was after those many days ...';
— the suffering of the Jews, as it says, 'And the children of Israel cried ...';
— God's mercy, as it says, 'And God heard their groaning ...';
— the merit of the Patriarchs, as it says, 'And He remembered His covenant ...';
— the repentance of the Jews, as it says, 'And God saw ... and God took note' (Shemos 2:23-25) (Yerushalmi, Taanis 1:1).

*heard their moaning and God recalled His covenant
with Abraham, Isaac and Jacob."*

"He saw our illtreatment" — *this refers to the
breaking up of their family life, as it is said: "God
looked upon the children of Israel and God took
note."*

זוּ פְּרִישׁוּת דֶּרֶךְ אֶרֶץ — *This refers to the
break-up of their family life.* The disruption of the family life of the Jews
was a prime objective of the Egyptians.
As explained earlier, they therefore for-
bade the men to return home at the end
of the working day *(Midrash)*; and even
when they did join their families, they
were totally exhausted from the burdens
imposed on them *(Ritva)*.

Also, many Jews decided to separate
from their wives, to avoid having
children, for fear that they would be
drowned in the river *(Rashbam)*. In this
respect they followed the example of
Amram, the grandson of Levi and
spiritual leader of his generation, who
divorced his wife Yocheved. However,
his daughter Miriam, who was then still
a child, reproached him and argued that
his decision was more harmful than
Pharaoh's: the latter wanted to kill the
boys but Amram in effect renounced
any future for the Jewish people. Her
father bowed to her reasoning and
remarried Yocheved — and from this
union Moses was born *(Sotah 12a)*.

The word עָנְיֵנוּ is taken to refer to the disruption of family life because it has a connection with the term עוֹנָה, *marital duty*

(Shemos 21:10); the phrase, אִם תְּעַנֶּה אֶת בְּנֹתַי
— *if you will ill-treat my daughters (Bereishis*
31:50) is given the same interpretation by
our Sages.

It is difficult to see at first glance why
the supporting verse ('*God saw ...*') is
quoted; it mentions neither ill-treatment
nor interference with family life. The
Lubavitch Haggadah suggests that it is
meant merely to substantiate that God
saw and took note of it. Others suggest
that the dual expression in the supporting verse, *God saw ... and God took
note*, refers to two kinds of Egyptian
oppression: 'visible' measures obvious
to everybody, and interference in people's private lives, of which only God
could know and take note *(Ibn Ezra)*.
The latter kind of oppression would
refer to disruption of family relations
(Ritva). There is a similar reference to
two kinds of suffering in *Shemos* (3:7),
where God says to Moses: '*I have seen
the affliction of My people in Egypt,
and I have heard its crying, before its
oppressors, for I know its pains.*' Affliction — such as open repression — can be
seen; but only God can *know* the pain
that is in the heart.[1]

The *Midrash* offers various explana-

1. *'... and their crying went up to God ... And God saw ... and God took note' (Shemos*
2:23,25).
   The same three expressions are found in a later passage, where God says to Moses: '*I have
seen the affliction of my people ... and I have heard their crying ... for I know their pain'*
(Shemos 3:7). The suffering of the Jews could be noted on three levels: מַעֲשֶׂה, the actions of
the Egyptians which they had to endure (which God saw), דִּבּוּר, their crying (which God
heard), and מַחֲשָׁבָה, the pain in their heart (which God noted). Our Sages explain that through
their suffering the Jewish people attained *Eretz Yisrael* (a matter of action), the *Torah* (which
involves speaking), and the *World to Come* (which is purely a matter of the spirit).
   Generally, we must always be concerned to bend our powers of action, speech, and thought,
to the service of God, as our fathers taught us — through kindness in action (as taught by
Abraham), the study of Torah (the quality of Jacob), and immersion in prayer (the quality of
Isaac) *(Sfas Emes)*.

° שמות
א:כב

° שמות
ג:ט

° דברים
כו:ח

וְאֶת עֲמָלֵנוּ. אֵלּוּ הַבָּנִים. כְּמָה שֶׁנֶּאֱמַר °כָּל־
הַבֵּן הַיִּלּוֹד הַיְאֹרָה תַּשְׁלִיכֻהוּ וְכָל־הַבַּת תְּחַיּוּן:

וְאֶת לַחֲצֵנוּ. זוֹ הַדְּחַק. כְּמָה שֶׁנֶּאֱמַר °וְגַם־
רָאִיתִי אֶת־הַלַּחַץ אֲשֶׁר מִצְרַיִם לֹחֲצִים אֹתָם:

°וַיּוֹצִאֵנוּ יהוה מִמִּצְרַיִם בְּיָד חֲזָקָה וּבִזְרֹעַ
נְטוּיָה וּבְמֹרָא גָּדֹל וּבְאֹתוֹת וּבְמֹפְתִים:

וַיּוֹצִאֵנוּ יהוה מִמִּצְרַיִם. לֹא עַל־יְדֵי מַלְאָךְ

---

tions for God's *'seeing'* and *'knowing'*: He *saw* the penitence of the righteous — and He *knew* that there were stirrings of repentance even in the hearts of the sinners. He *saw* the suffering of the Jews and He *knew* that the time had come to redeem them.

וְאֶת עֲמָלֵנוּ אֵלּוּ הַבָּנִים — *'Our burden.' This refers to the children.* The *Midrash* here refers to the manifold ways in which the Egyptians tried to do away with the Jewish children — by ordering the Jewish midwives to kill them, by drowning the infants in the river, and even by immuring them in the walls of the buildings that the Jews were forced to construct: the *Midrash* tells us that, whenever a worker did not complete his assigned quota of bricks, infants were taken in place of the missing bricks.

The words *'our burden'* (עֲמָלֵנוּ) may refer to the harsh burden of the Egyptian edicts concerning the Jewish children. However, other commentators suggest that children themselves are called burdens; parents have to labor to raise them properly (*Ritva*). The *Kolbo* points out that in Egypt the children certainly could be termed a burden; the efforts devoted to their upbringing were wasted as long as they were likely to be thrown into the Nile.

The phrase וְכָל הַבַּת תְּחַיּוּן — *and every daughter you shall let live*, may appear unnecessary here. It has been pointed out, however, that the Egyptian order to let the girls live was by no

means meant as an act of kindness. The Egyptians were eager to secure healthy Jewish women (*Shemos* 1:19) as wives for their sons (*Rabbi Myski*).

זוֹ הַדְּחַק — *This refers to the pressure.* The pressure that is here referred to was the inhumanity with which the Egyptians treated their Jewish slaves. God noted their suffering and redeemed them — and punished the Egyptians for their excessive zeal in subjugating the Jews (*Ramban*).

According to *Ritva*, however, the *Haggadah* here refers to the pressure that the Egyptians used in order to convert the Jews to their way of life. When they saw that they could not stem the growth of the Jewish people by physical torment, they decided to pressure the Jews to assimilate. This was the policy chosen by the new king whose succession to the throne brought such mourning (see above, וַיֵּאָנְחוּ); accordingly, וַיֵּאָנְחוּ בְנֵי יִשְׂרָאֵל מִן הָעֲבוֹדָה should be translated, *'the children of Israel groaned because of the idol-worship'* (rather than *'because of the bondage'*; the word עֲבוֹדָה can have either meaning).

God saw the suffering of the Jews — and the redemption was further speeded because He took note of the spiritual pressures put on them. In the first place, this put into question their continued survival in Egypt; and it also provided some excuse for the spiritual decline of the Jewish people and justification for

"Our burden" — *this refers to the children, as it is said: "Every newborn son shall you cast into the river and every daughter you shall let live."*

"Our oppression"— *this refers to the pressure that is expressed in the words: "I have also seen the oppression with which the Egyptians oppress them."*

"HASHEM brought us out of Egypt with a mighty hand, with an outstretched arm, with great fearfulness, with signs and with wonders."

"HASHEM brought us out of Egypt" — *not*

God's mercy upon them. At the Sea of Reeds God's justice in drowning the Egyptians and saving the Jews was questioned: 'These serve idols and these serve idols'; the answer given was that the Jews only fell to such depths because of their intense enslavement.

וַיּוֹצִאֵנוּ — *HASHEM brought us out.* This is the fourth and final verse quoted from *Devarim*. It describes the miraculous deliverance of the Jews by the direct intervention of God.

The present-day Jew deeply senses the catastrophe of the Nazi era and the death of six million of our people. He feels with the suffering of Russian Jewry. Compared to these contemporary happenings, the long-ago bondage of our people in Egypt does not really touch his emotions. Yet on *Seder* night we are to realize that it subjugated our entire people, for several generations, to dehumanizing slave labor and calculated brutality, breakup of the families, murder of the children, crushing of any opposition — with no end in sight to all the suffering. When we let our mind dwell on the full dimen-

sions of the tragedy, we can begin to see the Egyptian exile as the heartwrenching archetype of all later Jewish suffering — and the miraculous redemption as an extraordinary and overwhelming revelation of God in His world.

The climax of that traumatic event came at midnight following the fourteenth day of Nissan. At that moment the Jews gained their freedom — not through a slave-uprising, nor through a spell-binding demagogue or politician, nor through any natural catastrophe or social upheaval in the Egyptian empire, but through one decisive blow given by God Himself. Usually, Divine providence works through intermediate agents and causes of different kinds: מַלְאָכִים, Divine messengers created to carry out specific tasks, שְׂרָפִים heavenly powers, carriers of the consuming Divine fire, or a שָׁלִיחַ, a Divinely appointed guiding force. On this occasion, however, God brought about the death of the Egyptian firstborn by direct *fiat*, without using any intermediaries to carry out His edict.[1]

Rabbeinu Bachya suggests that, if the

1. Four miracles took place on *Pesach* night: the killing of the Egyptian firstborn, the saving of the Jewish firstborn, the fall of the Egyptian idols, and the revelation of God's glory.

The first two of these miracles could have been brought about through natural forces guided by God's Providence. Such forces are sometimes called מַלְאָכִים, ministering angels (see *Tehillim* 104:4), if their work is beneficial, or שְׂרָפִים, angels of destruction, if their task is to punish. The *Haggadah* tells us that neither the killing of the Egyptians, nor the saving of the Jews, was the result of such natural forces.

The destruction of the idols could not have come about through natural circumstances, but

וְלֹא עַל־יְדֵי שָׂרָף וְלֹא עַל־יְדֵי שָׁלִיחַ. אֶלָּא
הַקָּדוֹשׁ בָּרוּךְ הוּא בִּכְבוֹדוֹ וּבְעַצְמוֹ. שֶׁנֶּאֱמַר
שמות °
יב:יב
°וְעָבַרְתִּי בְאֶרֶץ־מִצְרַיִם בַּלַּיְלָה הַזֶּה וְהִכֵּיתִי
כָל־בְּכוֹר בְּאֶרֶץ מִצְרַיִם מֵאָדָם וְעַד בְּהֵמָה
וּבְכָל אֱלֹהֵי מִצְרַיִם אֶעֱשֶׂה שְׁפָטִים אֲנִי יהוה:
וְעָבַרְתִּי בְאֶרֶץ־מִצְרַיִם בַּלַּיְלָה הַזֶּה. אֲנִי וְלֹא
מַלְאָךְ. וְהִכֵּיתִי כָל־בְּכוֹר בְּאֶרֶץ־מִצְרַיִם. אֲנִי
וְלֹא שָׂרָף. וּבְכָל־אֱלֹהֵי מִצְרַיִם אֶעֱשֶׂה שְׁפָטִים.

punishment of the Egyptians had been brought about through the usual agents of Divine justice, the Jews too would have suffered, because, not meriting redemption, they would have been punished for their sins just as were the Egyptians for theirs. Indeed, as mentioned, at the Splitting of the Sea of Reeds, the angels protested the preferred treatment of the Jews. But God Himself inflicted punishment upon the Egyptians — and He skipped over the houses of the Jews, moved by the covenant with the Patriarchs, and demanding only the blood on the doorposts as a sign that they acknowledged the God of their forefathers.

We can understand God's direct intervention even better if we call to mind the purpose of the Exodus (see *Overview*, p. 25, and וְאִלּוּ לֹא הוֹצִיא, p. 74). Pharaoh, and the pagan world in general, questioned God's mastery over the universe; they had to be unmistakeably shown God's power (*Ramban*). The Jews, freed from

Pharaoh's bondage, had to accept God's overlordship, to become His people, forever immune to the machinations of all enemies. To achieve these goals, the redemption from Egypt had to be brought about in a manner that clearly transcended all the bounds of normal, natural happenings.

Everything that occurs in the world is the work of Divine Providence; but it is wrought by Divine messengers within a normal framework that we call nature. Miracles — such as the first nine plagues — are breaks in this pattern and show that God is the master of nature and history. The effect of miracles, however, is still limited, when they are brought about by Divine agents, themselves limited in scope. As a result, faith based on miracles is not unshakeable (*Rambam*), for the lessons which they teach may not be absorbed adequately. The spiritual blindness and impurity of Egypt was such that only God's self-revelation could make the necessary impact.[1]

it could have been the work of a שָׁלִיחַ, a special Divine messenger, and therefore we are told that this was not so.

Finally, the revelation of God's glory could certainly not have been brought about even by a Divine messenger. But disbelievers might possibly see in it the work of some other deity; therefore the *Haggadah* stresses that אֲנִי הוּא וְלֹא אַחֵר, *it was I and none other* — God is one, and there exists no אַחֵר, no competing deity (*Ma'aseh Nissim*).

1. Wherever the term אָנֹכִי, I, is used by God, it refers to His own immediate presence, the *Shechinah*. Therefore you find the statement that אָנֹכִי, 'I will slay your son, your firstborn' (Shemos 4:23), for this plague was carried out by God Himself. In the same way we find that God promised Jacob that He would accompany him to Egypt: אָנֹכִי, 'I will go down with you

through an angel, not through a seraph and not through a messenger, but the Holy One, blessed be He, He alone, in His glory, as it is said: "I will pass through the land of Egypt in that night, and I will slay every first-born in the land of Egypt, from man to beast, and I will execute judgment against all the gods of Egypt, I, HASHEM."

"I will pass through the land of Egypt", I, and no angel; "I will slay every first-born in the land of Egypt," I, and no seraph; "and I will execute judg-

This may be meant by the *Zohar's* statement that the iniquity ruling in Egypt prevented God from sending any Divine messenger and caused Him to go בִּכְבוֹדוֹ וּבְעַצְמוֹ, in His own glory (*Michtav M'Eliyahu*). To attain the goal of the Exodus it was necessary that God Himself should stand revealed as the judge of the Egyptians and the saviour of the Jews. To make it crystal-clear that the Jews — downtrodden slaves in any case — played a purely passive role in their liberation, they were confined to their houses and not even permitted to prepare food for their journey, as mentioned before (p. 74).

Against their own will, the Egyptians thus provided the opportunity for the highest self-revelation of God in the world, and became worthy of a reward for this (*Kedushas Levi*); that may be a reason why they were not prohibited from joining the Jewish people forever, but were permitted (unlike Ammon and Moab) to marry into it after three generations (*Devarim* 23:4,8). We find, similarly, that descendants of Sanherib and Haman became not only proselytes but teachers of Torah: their ancestors, in receiving their punishment, had caused God's glory to be publicly manifested.

אֲנִי וְלֹא מַלְאָךְ — *I, and no angel* — What,

then, does the Torah mean by stating that '*God sent a messenger* (or: *angel*) *and he took us out from Egypt* (*Bamidbar* 20:16)? The verse may refer to Moses who was 'a messenger' sent to speak for God but did not actually bring about the death of the firstborn and the liberation of the Jews (*Avudraham*). Or the beginning of the verse may refer to the angel Michael, who appeared to Moses at the thornbush (*Shemos* 3:2, *Rashbatz*). The subject of the end of the verse, however, is God, and the verse should be read thus: '*And He* [God] *took us out from Egypt.'*

אֲנִי וְלֹא שָׂרָף — *I, and no seraph.* Since God Himself killed the firstborn, what is meant by 'the destroyer' (מַשְׁחִית), specifically excluded from the Jewish homes, who apparently did enter the Egyptian homes (*Shemos* 12:23)? The *Shibolei Haleket* explains that the reference is to the death itself which God dealt out to the firstborn. According to the *Bais Halevi*, however, it does not refer to the plague at all, but to the pestilence that resulted from the multitude of unburied bodies.

The *Vilna Gaon* takes it to mean the Angel of Death. On a normal night he would have claimed a number of victims among the large Jewish population; if any Jews whatsoever had died on the

and אָנֹכִי, *I will bring you up'* (*Bereishis* 46:4). That is why our Sages declared that, 'with אָנֹכִי the Jews went down, with אָנֹכִי they were redeemed, and with אָנֹכִי they will be redeemed in the future' (*Rabbeinu Bachya*).

אֲנִי וְלֹא הַשָּׁלִיחַ. אֲנִי יהוה. אֲנִי הוּא וְלֹא
אַחֵר:

° שמות
ט:ג

בְּיָד חֲזָקָה. זוֹ הַדֶּבֶר. כְּמָה שֶׁנֶּאֱמַר °הִנֵּה יַד
יהוה הוֹיָה בְּמִקְנְךָ אֲשֶׁר בַּשָּׂדֶה בַּסּוּסִים
בַּחֲמוֹרִים בַּגְּמַלִּים בַּבָּקָר וּבַצֹּאן דֶּבֶר כָּבֵד
מְאֹד:

° דברי הימים א'
כא:טז

וּבִזְרֹעַ נְטוּיָה. זוֹ הַחֶרֶב. כְּמָה שֶׁנֶּאֱמַר
°וְחַרְבּוֹ שְׁלוּפָה בְּיָדוֹ נְטוּיָה עַל-יְרוּשָׁלָיִם:

וּבְמֹרָא גָּדֹל. זוֹ גִּלּוּי שְׁכִינָה. כְּמָה שֶׁנֶּאֱמַר

night of *Pesach*, however, the Egyptians would have believed that the Jews, too, were hit by the slaying of the firstborn. Therefore, the Angel of Death was forbidden to smite even those Jews who would have died a natural death.[1]

Since God Himself carried out this plague, the blood that the Jews were commanded to put on the doorposts of their houses was not needed for identification. Rather, it was a test of the Jews' faith in God, and of their willingness to acknowledge Him in the face of Egyptian hostility. Therefore they were commanded to put the blood on the *inside* of their doorposts; it was to be לָכֶם לְאוֹת וְלֹא לַאֲחֵרִים לְאוֹת, *a sign for you and not for others* (Rashi, Shemos 12:13). When the Jews passed this test and thereby showed their devotion to the God of Abraham, Isaac and Jacob, they merited that the covenant with the Patriarchs be executed and their houses be spared.

אֲנִי הוּא וְלֹא אַחֵר — *It is I and no other.* It is I, and no other power, that struck this blow (*Rashi*). It is I who struck this blow, and no other power can contend with Me (*Ramban*).

Pharaoh was not only shown that '*I am HASHEM* in the midst of the land' (*Shemos* 8:19) but also that '*there is none like HASHEM, our God*' (*Shemos* 8:7). This was highlighted by the simultaneous destruction of the gods worshipped by the Egyptians. Our Sages explain that statues rotted if they were made of wood, or melted if they were made of metal. The reference may also be to the downfall of the deities themselves: their impotence was shown up by the collapse of Egyptian might.

[The *Haggadah* passage stressing that no angel, seraph, or messenger was involved in the slaying of the firstborn is not part of the *Mechilta* text that the *Haggadah* follows; it is a *Midrashic* addition which is not contained in all *Haggadah* versions.]

בְּיָד חֲזָקָה — *With a mighty hand.* Pestilence is one of the ten plagues. Why is it singled out at this point? According to the *Midrash*, every plague was accompanied by pestilence. This would explain why pestilence (which the Torah refers to as יַד ה', *the hand of HASHEM*) is here identified with the 'mighty hand' that brought about the

1. ... *And He will not let the destroyer enter your houses to strike*' (*Shemos* 12:23).
The commentators point out that the slaying of the firstborn was not the work of a destroying angel but of God Himself; what, then, is meant by '*the destroyer*'? However, the verse may refer to later years — by their loyal observance of the Law of *Pesach*, the Jews could survive all the dangers facing them through the years (□ *Rabbi Joseph Breuer*).

ment against all the gods of Egypt," I, and no messenger; "I, HASHEM," it is I and no other.

"With a mighty hand" — *this refers to the pestilence, as it is said: "Behold, the hand of HASHEM will be upon your cattle in the field, upon the horses, asses and camels, the oxen and the sheep, a very severe pestilence."*

"With an outstretched arm" — *that is the sword, as it is said: "His drawn sword in his hand, stretched out over Jerusalem."*

"With great fearfulness" — *this refers to the revelation of the Divine Presence, as it is said: "Or*

Exodus. It is also possible that the plague of pestilence is considered the 'mighty hand' since it completed the first series of five plagues, just as a hand has five fingers; in contrast, the slaying of the firstborn which marked the completion of all ten plagues and had a much greater impact, is referred to as 'the outstretched arm' of HASHEM.

וּבִזְרֹעַ נְטוּיָה — *And with outstretched arm.* The Biblical verse quoted here speaks of an 'outstretched sword'; the *Midrash* therefore concludes that the 'outstretched arm' of God also refers to the wielding of a sword. Yet we do not find the Torah mentioning swords or warfare in connection with the Exodus. The *Midrash* recounts, however, that the killing of the firstborn was preceded by intense fighting: when the firstborn heard the announcement of their impending fate, they took up arms to force the government to free the Jews and thereby to save their lives. The statement in *Tehillim* (136:10) that God 'struck the Egyptians through their firstborn' may well refer to this battle, in which many Egyptians were killed (*Kolbo*).

The *Akeidas Yitzchak* explains that the Torah uses the phrase, 'an outstretched arm', in connection with the slaying of the firstborn because this phrase suggests a continuing threat —

and the killing of the firstborn was correctly understood by the Egyptians as only the beginning of just such a threat. In terror, they declared that 'we all will die' (*Shemos* 12:33), and their premonition came true when the Egyptian army drowned in the Sea of Reeds.

וּבְמֹרָא גָּדֹל — *And with great fearfulness.* The word מוֹרָא has been translated as 'fearfulness' (from the root ירא, to fear (*Ritva*); or as 'vision' (from the root ראה, to see; *Targum*). In either case it refers to the awe-inspiring spectacle of God's majesty revealing itself in Egypt. This revelation came in successive stages.

The various plagues, step by step, showed God's power. The Egyptian magicians were forced to concede that the plagues were 'the finger of God' (*Shemos* 8:15), because God directed Moses to announce their coming and even, at will, to set a time for their ending (*Shemos* 8:56). Then, on the first day of Nissan, came God's announcement of the forthcoming redemption, which was heard throughout the land of Egypt (*Midrash*). Next, on the night of the fifteenth of Nissan, God Himself passed through Egypt to slay the firstborn. A week later, at the splitting of the Sea of Reeds, God's Presence revealed itself even to the lowliest, so that the Jews

°דברים
ד:לד
אוֹ הֲנִסָּה אֱלֹהִים לָבוֹא לָקַחַת לוֹ גוֹי מִקֶּרֶב
גּוֹי בְּמַסֹּת בְּאֹתֹת וּבְמוֹפְתִים וּבְמִלְחָמָה וּבְיָד
חֲזָקָה וּבִזְרוֹעַ נְטוּיָה וּבְמוֹרָאִים גְּדֹלִים כְּכֹל
אֲשֶׁר־עָשָׂה לָכֶם יהוה אֱלֹהֵיכֶם בְּמִצְרַיִם
לְעֵינֶיךָ:

°שמות
ד:יז
וּבְאֹתוֹת זֶה הַמַּטֶּה. כְּמָה שֶׁנֶּאֱמַר °וְאֶת־

were able to point with a finger, so to speak, and to exclaim, 'This is my God …' (Shemos 15:2). Finally, there was the scene at the foot of Mount Sinai, when all Jews attained to the level of prophecy and, awe-struck, heard God's voice proclaiming, 'I am HASHEM, your God …' (Shemos 20:2).

With the progressive unveiling of God's majesty, the resistance of the Egyptians crumbled. Finally, at the Sea of Reeds, even they — and indeed, all the nations — were forced reluctantly to acknowledge the greatness of God. But even more important was the gradual unfolding of אֱמוּנָה, the faith of the Jews, as they lived through these successive stages of revelation. For, it was through this faith that they attained redemption and the giving of the Torah: 'HASHEM saves the righteous' (Tehillim 31:24).

We pointed out before (see p.106), that, despite their spiritual decline, the Jews preserved their sense of identity throughout the long years of bondage, and remembered the promise of redemption which had been passed on to them by their forefather. Thus, when Moses first came to them, they believed that God had sent him to bring about their redemption (Shemos 4:31; see Overview, p. 32). But they did not all have the same firmness of faith.

There were those who had always clung with all their heart to the hope of redemption; they were the ones who had saved drums and trumpets through all these years, for use when the redeemer would finally come — these in-

struments were put to use during the Song at the Sea. But for the bulk of the people, faith in redemption was very tenuous: when Pharaoh rejected Moses' challenge, and made the life of the Jews even harder, 'they did not listen to Moses, because of lack of spirit and heavy bondage' (Shemos 6:9).

Very many did not listen to Moses' message because of their bondage to Egyptian idols and enslavement to Egyptian ways — according to the Midrash some of them also lived quite prosperously and did not want to give up the comforts they enjoyed as lackeys of the Egyptians; these were the people who died during the plague of darkness.

But even many others did not dare listen — because the pressure of the slave-drivers did not give them respite and they were held back by the fear that Pharaoh would kill them (Ramban).

It took the plagues to revive their faith in God, to the point where they were willing to sacrifice themselves to do His bidding. They accepted the commandments of circumcision and of the Pesach lamb, and thereby became worthy of redemption. When the night of liberation came, they marched forth into an uncertain future, 'into the desert, an unsown land' (Jeremiah 2:2). But even then their faith was not yet perfect; on Pesach night they had attained to the greatest heights of perception of God, but they were not yet able to stay at this peak of faith (Michtav M'Eliyahu).

As a result, there was fear and hesitation at the brink of the Sea of Reeds, so

has God ever sought to come and take unto Himself one nation from the midst of another nation, with trials, signs and wonders, with war and a mighty hand, and an outstretched arm and awesome manifestations, as HASHEM your God did for you in Egypt before your eyes?"

that the guardian angel of the Egyptians could still accuse them of being un-believers just like the Egyptians. It required their deliverance on this occasion to make them totally *'believe in HASHEM and His servant Moses'* (*Shemos* 14:31). Thus they climbed the ladder of faith, through the forty-nine stages of purity, until they stood at Mount Sinai. There they attained the ultimate אֱמוּנָה — based on the direct prophetic experience of God.[1]

Forty years later Moses reminded the Jews: *'From the day that God has created man on earth, and from one end of the heavens to the other end of the heavens has there ever been such a great thing, or has anything like it ever been heard? Has a people heard the voice of God speaking from amidst the fire, as you heard it and lived? Or has God ever sought to come and take unto Himself one nation from the midst of another nation, with trials ...'* (*Devarim* 4:32-34). The Exodus was meant to lead to the giving of the Torah (as foretold to Moses, *Shemos* 3:12); and, forever after, these two events became, the source of the world's knowledge of God.

גּוֹי מִקֶּרֶב גּוֹי — *One nation from the midst of another nation.* The *Midrash* compares the liberation from Egypt to the delivery of a young animal from its mother's womb — a painful process because the unborn animal is really part of its mother. In the same way, the Jews were closely linked to the Egyptians, through all that they had learned and

absorbed from them. The redemption from Egypt was, therefore, a difficult process: it involved a special effort, so-to-speak, on the part of God.

Some commentators suggest that such 'special efforts' — meaning an extraordinary degree of Divine self-revelation — were necessary because God was not only liberating the Jews from Egypt but laying the foundation for their liberation from all later exiles. That meant that the experience of the Exodus had to be extraordinarily powerful and lasting.

That may be a further reason why the Torah speaks of the liberation as taking place *'with strong hand and out-stretched arm'*; usually we understand this phrase as a description of how the miraculous events impressed the onlookers, Jewish and Gentile, rather than as a reference to a special Divine 'effort.'

וּבְאֹתוֹת — *'And with signs,'* this is the staff. What is the connection between these signs (the plagues) and Moses' staff? In the first place, Moses used the staff to bring the plagues. Also, the names of the plagues were engraved on it (*Ritva*), or at least their initials — דְּצַ"ךְ עַדַ"שׁ בְּאַחַ"ב (*Kolbo*).

Our Sages declare that this staff was created during the twilight that marked the end of the sixth day of creation and the beginning of the first *Shabbos*. This may mean that the staff and the miracles that it set in motion were not a part of the natural order created during the six days of creation; but were part of

1. The Exodus is mentioned in the Torah fifty times — corresponding to the fifty levels of impurity into which their descent was very nearly complete, and the fifty levels of purity which they ascended instead (*Zohar*).

הַמַּטֶּה הַזֶּה תִּקַּח בְּיָדֶךָ אֲשֶׁר תַּעֲשֶׂה בּוֹ אֶת־
הָאֹתֹת:

וּבְמֹפְתִים זֶה הַדָּם. כְּמָה שֶׁנֶּאֱמַר °וְנָתַתִּי
מוֹפְתִים בַּשָּׁמַיִם וּבָאָרֶץ

° יוֹאֵל
ג:ג

כשאומרים שלש מלים אלו נותנים אצבע בכוס ומטיפים לחוץ שלש
פעמים. וכן נוהגים עשר פעמים כשאומרים עשר מכות, וכן בדצ"ך עד"ש
באח"ב מטיפים שלש פעמים. אחרי כן ממלאים הכוסות.

דָּם וָאֵשׁ וְתִימְרוֹת עָשָׁן:

דָּבָר אַחֵר. בְּיָד חֲזָקָה שְׁתַּיִם. וּבִזְרֹעַ
נְטוּיָה שְׁתַּיִם. וּבְמֹרָא גָּדֹל

the Divine plan from the very outset, to help bring about the goal of creation.

The staff was given to Moses at the burning bush *(Ritva)*, and thus served as symbol of his mission. When Moses turned the staff into a snake, and the magicians of Egypt did likewise with their staffs, Moses' staff swallowed the others. This clearly demonstrated the difference between a Divine mission and human endeavors.

The *Zohar* explains that Moses' staff was turned into a snake to serve as a reminder of Adam's sin: the snake represents the יֵצֶר הָרַע, the constant tempter, and all evil comes from listening to it. When Moses turned the snake back into a staff, he thereby served a warning to Pharaoh that, as God's messenger, he would subdue the forces of evil.

וּבְמֹפְתִים — 'With wonders,' this is the blood. The *Midrash* takes the word מֹפְתִים, wonders (in the plural) to refer to blood because blood occurs at various points in the story of Israel's redemption. To which particular incident does the *Torah* here refer? Most commentators point to the first plague, when the Nile and all other waters turned to blood. This occurrence struck at the Egyptian belief in the Nile as a deity;

moreover, it demonstrated God's power to impose punishment, 'measure for measure.' The Nile had been used to drown Jewish children; now it was turned into an evil-smelling pool of blood, killing all fish and other forms of life in it.

According to the *Kolbo*, the *Torah* here refers to the sign of the blood, one of the three signs given to Moses *(Shemos* 4:9). In producing this sign before the Jews and before Pharaoh, he was to demonstate that God had sent him. *Tefilah Lemosheh* explains that the *Torah* refers to the blood that was shed during the *Pesach* night, in the fighting between the Egyptians and their firstborn which was mentioned before. Others point to the blood of Pesach sacrifice and circumcision, which served as an identifying sign setting the Jews apart from their gentile neighbors.

The *Lubavitch Haggadah*, taking 'blood' as a reference to the first plague, points out that the *Midrash* here singles out three plagues to demonstrate the scope of God's judgment: *pestilence*, which struck at the Egyptians' *possessions; slaying of the firstborn*, which hit at their own *lives*; and *blood*, which struck at their *deity, the Nile*. The *Haggadah* lists these plagues in the order of increasing severity, rather than in their

"With signs" — *this refers to the staff, as it is said: "Take this staff in your hand, with which you shall do the signs."*

"With wonders" — *that is the blood, as it is said: "I will show wonders in heaven and on earth,*

At each of the words *blood, fire* and *smoke* the finger is dipped into the cup, and a drop of wine is removed.

blood and fire and pillars of smoke."

Another explanation: "With a mighty hand" indicates two plagues, "with an outstretched arm", another two; "with great fearfulness", another two; "with signs", another two; "and with wonders",

chronological· sequence, for the first of these plagues was that of blood. The chronological order is explained by the *Yalkut* which points out that when God seeks to punish a community, He strikes down their idols first.

דָם וָאֵשׁ וְתִמְרוֹת עָשָׁן – *Blood and fire and pillars of smoke.* This verse, quoted from *Joel,* speaks of the Messianic redemption rather than of the Exodus. It is cited here merely to show that the word מוֹפֵת, *wonder,* is used to refer to the manifestation of blood.

It is possible, however, that blood, fire, and pillars of smoke appeared together in Egypt, too. The *Ritva* explains that at the first plague the blood of the Nile boiled like fire, and pillars of smoke rose from it. Another explanation points out that at the Exodus there was blood, the first plague, and fire and a cloud pillar when God led the Jews to the Sea of Reeds (*Shemos* 13:21).

When reciting דָם וָאֵשׁ וְתִמְרוֹת עָשָׁן, we

remove three drops of wine from our cups — either with a finger or by tilting the cup; the procedure is repeated for each of the ten plagues, and again for דְּצַ"ךְ עַדַ"שׁ בְּאַחַ"ב, for a total of 16 times. The method used for removing the wine may depend on the interpretation of the custom:

If it is meant to be a reminder of how 'the finger of God' (*Shemos* 8:15) brought the plagues, we would use our finger (*Darkei Mosheh*).

Abarbanel, however, explains that we remove the wine because '*you should not rejoice when your enemy falls*' (*Mishley* 24:17).[1] The *Maharil* explains that our wine cup stands for happiness and we want to avert from ourselves the punishment meted out to our enemies. According to these explanations, it would be appropriate to *pour* some wine from our cups.

דָּבָר אַחֵר – *Another explanation.* The *Midrash* does not dismiss the explana-

1. We should not rejoice when our enemy falls. In connection with the observance of *Pesach* the Torah therefore emphasizes the memory of our liberation from slavery rather than the downfall of the Egyptians. This explains why the Jews were already told in Egypt that the seventh day of *Pesach* was to be a holiday — even though they only observed one day of *Pesach* in that first year. If the commandment concerning the seventh day had been given only after their liberation, they would have considered that day a celebration of the drowning of the Egyptians in the Sea (*Meshech Chochmah*).

In connection with *Sukkos* the Torah directs us three times to be joyful; but in connection

שְׁתַּיִם. וּבְאֹתוֹת שְׁתַּיִם. וּבְמוֹפְתִים שְׁתַּיִם: אֵלּוּ
עֶשֶׂר מַכּוֹת שֶׁהֵבִיא הַקָּדוֹשׁ בָּרוּךְ הוּא עַל־
הַמִּצְרִים בְּמִצְרַיִם וְאֵלּוּ הֵן:
דָּם. צְפַרְדֵּעַ. כִּנִּים. עָרוֹב. דֶּבֶר. שְׁחִין. בָּרָד.
אַרְבֶּה. חֹשֶׁךְ. מַכַּת בְּכוֹרוֹת:

tions which were so far given for this verse; rather, it adds that the language of the verse can also be taken as referring to the ten plagues (*Malbim*). The two phrases *'strong hand'* and *'outstretched arm'* each mean two plagues, either because they are composed of two words, each standing for a plague, or because they suggest *repeated* striking. The phrase, *'great fearfulness'*, also consists of two words, and can be taken to mean more than just one shock. *'Signs'* and *'wonders'* clearly refer to two plagues each (*Kolbo, Shibolei Haleket*).

אֵלּוּ עֶשֶׂר מַכּוֹת — *These are the ten plagues.* The ten plagues mark the climax of the Jews' liberation. They should therefore occupy a central place in the discussion of the Exodus on *Seder* night. Obviously, God could have exerted irresistible pressure upon the Egyptians from the beginning, so that they would have freed the Jews right away. However, the Divine plan provided for a step-by-step approach, a gradual unfolding of the redemption process. What was this meant to teach?

In the first place, the gradual escalation of the plagues gave the Egyptians the opportunity to mend their ways before the full measure of Divine punishment struck them. It is true that *'God hardened Pharaoh's heart'* at the later plagues; however, it has been explained that this did not take away his freedom of choice, but rather gave him the strength to continue on his own

course, even in the face of the mounting pressure of the plagues. During the first plagues, Pharaoh showed that he would not give in of his own free will, though he might go through the motions of submission under extreme duress. Therefore, God gave him the fortitude to persevere in what he really had wanted to do — and he chose to defy God, despite his people's suffering (*Shemos* 3:19; *Meshech Chochmah*).

But if the successive plagues did not bring about a change of heart among the Egyptians, the dulling impact of blow after blow demonstrated to all onlookers, then and for ever after, that God *cannot* be defied. The impossibility of fighting God was underlined by the whole pattern of the ten plagues. A *Midrash* points out that the plagues corresponded to the strategy of a general laying siege to a city. Thus, the plague of blood corresponded to the poisoning of the drinking water; the frogs, to the trumpeters that would sow fear among the inhabitants; the lice, to the arrows shot into the city; the wild animals to the mercenaries that would be sent; and so on (*Tanchuma*).

The *Midrash* also stresses that each of the plagues represented punishment for a particular wrong that the Egyptians did to the Jews: 'They made them drawers of water — and so their river was turned to *blood*; they made them load their freight — and the *frogs* destroyed it; they had the Jews sweep the streets — and the dust turned into *lice*; they made the Jews watch their

with *Pesach*, rejoicing is not even mentioned once. Why? ... Because the Egyptians died on *Pesach*. In the same way you find that we recite *Hallel* all the seven days of *Sukkos*; but on *Pesach* we only recite it on the first *Yom Tov*, in the daytime and at night (*Yalkut*).

another two — these are the ten plagues which the Holy One, blessed be He, brought upon the Egyptians in Egypt, and they are as follows:

At each of the ten plagues, and again at each of the abbreviations דצ״ך עד״ש באח״ב, a drop of wine is removed. (Afterwards the cup must be replenished).

Blood, Frogs, Lice, Wild Beasts, Pestilence, Boils, Hail, Locusts, Darkness, Slaying of the Firstborn.

children — and God flooded the country with *wild animals* that devoured the children ...'. The Egyptians made them cattle-herders, whereupon the *pestilence* killed the herds. They used them to prepare their baths — and then they developed *boils* which made it impossible for them to wash. The Jews were made stone-cutters — and God sent *hailstones* against the Egyptians. They were forced to tend the vinyards and fields — and the *locust* consumed all that grew. The Egyptians sought to keep the Jews as prisoners — and were themselves shackled by the thick *darkness* that fell upon Egypt; their murderous designs upon the Jews brought the *killing of the firstborn* — and their drowning of Jewish children was repaid by their death in the Sea of Reeds *(Tanchuma)*.

Various other *Midrashim* also stress that the plagues struck מִדָּה כְּנֶגֶד מִדָּה, *measure for measure*, as divine retribution for the suffering of the Jews. We already pointed out how the plague of blood can be seen as a response to the shedding of Jewish blood and the drowning of the children in the Nile; but it has also been pointed out that the Egyptians were deprived of water by this plague because they had forced the Jews to labor without even a chance to wash off perspiration and dirt. As a result, the Jews also suffered from vermin, and this led to the plague of lice. The frogs and wild animals were sent against Egypt because the Jews had been sent afield to gather all kinds of animals — for the pleasure of the Egyptians and in order to disrupt the

family life of the Jews. When the Egyptians held their sumptuous banquets, Jews had to stand at attention, with torches on their heads, to light up the scene; hence the plague of darkness came to repay the Egyptians for the inhuman treatment of their slaves.

In a broader sense, the plagues have been interpreted as a sweeping assault upon all aspects of Egypt's self-seeking materialistic society *(Out of the Iron Furnace)*. The Nile formed the basis and the embodiment of Egyptian power. It was considered the god of the Egyptians and Pharaoh identified with it, claiming to be its creator *(Ezekiel 20:3)*. Therefore, the plagues not only started with it (see p.126) but centered on it — they were directed against it, emanated from it, or were announced at its banks.

The first plague, **blood,** struck at the Nile itself. Moreover, it demonstrated God's supreme power because it did not merely represent God's use of natural forces but an actual change in nature *(Midrash Hagadol; Maharal)*.

The **frogs** represented an invasion, by God's messengers, of all aspects of Egyptian life, down to bed chamber and oven. Incidentally, their readiness to die on their mission demonstrated the importance of carrying out God's will, even at the price of one's own life *(Pesachim 53b)*.

The **lice** represented the defeat of the all-powerful Egyptian priests and magicians; they could not duplicate this plague, acknowledged God's power, and are not mentioned again. Moreover, this plague struck at the earth which had heretofore provided man with the

רַבִּי יְהוּדָה הָיָה נוֹתֵן בָּהֶם סִמָּנִים:
דְּצַ"ךְ עֲדַ"שׁ בְּאַחַ"ב:

clay and bricks needed for his mis-guided adventures, such as the Tower of Babylon (Bereishis 11:3) and, later, Pharaoh's store-cities. This would ex-plain why, according to some Midrashic opinions, the Jews at this point were no longer forced to continue their slave-labor.

The **wild beasts** robbed the Egyptians of the use of their lands; greed and deceit were dominant forces in Egyptian society, but now the fruits of their im-moral practices would no longer be en-joyed by the Egyptians. At the same time, this plague reminded them that, as a result of their conduct, they could not expect the animals to fear them as they were supposed to (Bereishis 9:2; Tehil-lim 49:13).

The **pestilence** struck yet another blow at Egyptian pride, for it showed the Egyptians that they were no longer masters even of their own rightful pos-sessions.

The **boils** demonstrated a further tightening of the noose: even the bodies of the Egyptians were now struck. In this way, this plague also brought retribution for the immoral ways in which they misused their bodies (Vayikrah 18:3).

The plagues of **hail** and **locusts** can be seen as a punishment for the failure of the Egyptians properly to use their God-given faculties. They had refused to see God's hand in the world, or to hear His warnings; now they were forced to hear and see unmistakeable demonstrations of His power and will:

the thunder that accompanied the hailstorm, and the heavy layer of locusts that hid the entire land. The proper use of our senses is of crucial im-portance to man. All human failings began with Eve's seeing and Adam's listening to the wrong thing (Bereishis 3:6); now the plagues prepared the Jews, and all of mankind, to see and hear God's revelation on Mount Sinai.

The plague of **darkness** put an end to all constructive human activity and, in particular, isolated every individual from his fellow-beings; in this way the Egyptians were shown the effect of a total breakdown of the social order, which they had been courting by their unrestrained self-seeking and disrespect for other human beings. Whilst they were made to realize that the rule of evil is bound to bring darkness upon the world, the Jews who looked to God for their salvation enjoyed the use of light to prepare for their redemption in accor-dance with God's instructions.

The **killing of the firstborn**, finally, represented the climax of the retribution visited upon Egypt. It had been an-nounced before all the plagues (Shemos 4:22-23): 'So speaks HASHEM: Israel is my firstborn ... and you refuse to let him go; behold, I will kill your firstborn son.' This was carried out by God alone, but the Jews had to deserve it by dedicating themselves to God.[1]

Thus, the plagues can be seen not simply as a fitting punishment of the Egyptians, but as the destruction of a decadent civilization that had misused

---

1. On Pesach night, all those died who were firstborn from either their father's or their mother's side. As a result, many instances of adultery and immorality were revealed.

Even the firstborn of slaves and prisoners died. Their parents had no hand in the oppres-sion of the Jews but they rejoiced over their suffering. Moreover, if their firstborn had sur-vived, they would have ascribed this to the protection of the idols which they worshipped.

Even firstborn animals died. Otherwise, they might have been worshipped as idols. Furthermore, the Egyptians were to be shown that their conduct had put them on the same level as animals.

In houses where there were no firstborn, the head of the household was slain (Midrash).

Rabbi Yehuda grouped them by their initials:
Dezach, Adash, Beachab.

its God-given powers. At the same time, these same plagues educated the Jews to the moral perils of Egypt and to the need for dedicating to God all that they received from His hands. This lesson was driven home by the commandment to give over to God all their first-born sons, since they had been spared the fate of the Egyptians (*Shemos* 13:2).

The commentators point out a further aspect of the ten plagues. They can be perceived as a parallel to — or echo of — the עֲשָׂרָה מַאֲמָרוֹת, the ten Divine pronouncements which brought the world into existence (*Avos* 5:1). The redemption of the Jews from Egypt would, thus, appear to be a counterpart to the creation of the world. The process of creation showed God as the master of nature; the Exodus showed him as the ruler of history, bending the laws of nature to His purposes.

From a different vantage point, we can view Creation as a process of building, and the plagues as acts of destruction (*Noam Elimelech*; the plagues in this respect, were more remarkable than Creation, for they required God to restrain His quality of mercy). The *Maharal* points out that the ten pronouncements created the world, whilst the ten plagues brought about the creation of the Jewish people (see *Overview*, p. 28).

The *Midrash Rabbah* stresses the parallel between Creation and Exodus: '*God said to Moses to warn the Jews: just as I created the world, and commanded Israel to remember the Shabbos as a reminder of the creation ..., so should you be reminded of the miracles I did for you in Egypt, by remembering the day on which you went out from there; as it says, "remember the day on which you went out ..."*' (This is, indeed, one of the Biblical verses from

which *Rambam* derives the commandment to tell about the Exodus).

Our Sages ask why the world was created by ten pronouncements rather than one; they reply that this was done so that evildoers would be punished for ruining a world created by ten pronouncements, and the righteous would be rewarded for sustaining such a world (*Avos* 5:1). God knew that man, given the power of free choice, would do harm to the world. He, therefore, created it in ten stages — and the downfall of the evildoers through the ten plagues would serve to redress the harm done to every stage. Moreover, there would be men eager to do right — and they would be given the ten commandments to sanctify the world, in every respect. The revelation of God's Kingship, as a result of the ten plagues, thus opened the way for the further disclosure of God's will, through the ten commandments (*Chidushei haRim*).[1]

The punishment of the Egyptians lasted one year — exactly as long as that of Noah's generation that perished in the Flood, and as long as the punishment of evildoers in *Gehinom*. On the fifteenth of *Nissan*, exactly one year before the Exodus, Moses had the vision at the thornbush (*Shemos* 2:2), and then returned to Egypt to appear before Pharaoh. The plagues followed — each lasted seven days, and was preceded by twenty-four days of warning, or (according to another opinion) the warning lasted seven days and the plague twenty-four (*Tanchuma*). By *Rosh Hashanah* the Jews no longer had to work, and in *Nissan* they were redeemed.

רַבִּי יְהוּדָה — *Rabbi Yehudah*. Why did Rabbi Yehudah find it necessary to coin the abbreviation דְּצַ״ךְ

1. 'The ten plagues turned the ten pronouncements with which the world was created, into the ten commandments': God's sovereignty over the world, which He had created with ten

רַבִּי יוֹסֵי הַגְּלִילִי אוֹמֵר. מִנַּיִן אַתָּה אוֹמֵר
שֶׁלָּקוּ הַמִּצְרִים בְּמִצְרַיִם עֶשֶׂר מַכּוֹת
וְעַל הַיָּם לָקוּ חֲמִשִּׁים מַכּוֹת. בְּמִצְרַיִם מָה הוּא
אוֹמֵר. °וַיֹּאמְרוּ הַחַרְטֻמִּם אֶל־פַּרְעֹה אֶצְבַּע
אֱלֹהִים הוּא. וְעַל־הַיָּם מָה הוּא אוֹמֵר. °וַיַּרְא
יִשְׂרָאֵל אֶת־הַיָּד הַגְּדוֹלָה אֲשֶׁר עָשָׂה יהוה
בְּמִצְרַיִם וַיִּירְאוּ הָעָם אֶת־יהוה וַיַּאֲמִינוּ בַּיהוה

° שמות
ח:טו
° שמות
יד:לא

עֶרֶשׁ בְּאַחַ"ב? Rabbi Yehudah may have wanted to tell us that the plagues were engraved on Moses' staff in this manner (see above); in contrast, the other Rabbis held that they were engraved in full (Vilna Gaon). The Machzor Vitry suggests that Rabbi Yehudah sought to teach the plagues in a concise form that is easily remembered; and we do find in various Talmudic passages that this was Rabbi Yehudah's way (see Menachos 96a).

There is, indeed, a special need to be reminded of the ten plagues in their proper order, as given in the Torah. They are also mentioned in two places in Tehillim (in Psalms 78 and 105:28-36); but in each case they are listed in a different order. Moreover, in Psalm 78 lice, boils, and darkness are omitted, and in Psalm 105, pestilence and boils. Therefore, it is important to stress the order given by the Torah.

[An explanation has been suggested why the listing of the plagues is dif-ferent in Tehillim. Psalm 78 omits those three plagues which posed no danger to human beings (Ramban), and groups the other seven according to their direct impact on man, plants, and animals respectively.[1] Psalm 105 lists only those eight plagues which the Torah mentions as hitting אֶרֶץ מִצְרַיִם, the land of Egypt; for this Psalm stresses the mastery of God over all lands (Rabbi H. Biberfeld).]

Rabbi Yehudah arranged the initials of the plagues in three groups. It has been suggested that each group came to teach Pharaoh — and the world in general — one of the three principles which, according to Rabbi Joseph Albo, form the fundamentals of our faith. The first three plagues were designed to es-tablish the existence of God; they were introduced by the warning: 'you shall know that I am HASHEM', (Shemos, 7:17). The second group was to demonstrate God's providence; here the introduction is: 'you shall know that I

pronouncements, became evident to all as a result of His inflicting the ten plagues upon the Egyptians. It was then that He could announce to the world His law, in the form of the Ten Commandments (Chidushei haRim).

Each of the ten plagues corresponded to one of the pronouncements by which the world was created. For instance, 'Let there be light' had its counterpart in the Plague of Darkness.

1. The three plagues omitted in Tehillim 78 (lice, boils, and darkness) have several features in common. They were the third, sixth and ninth plague, respectively, and each completed a group of plagues; they came without warning; and the magicians could not imitate them. Their Hebrew names, as given in the Torah, can be fitted into a cube which can be read downwards as well as to the left:

חשך
שחן
כנם

Based on Haga'os Maimuni.

R abbi Yose the Galilean said: How can you come to say that the Egyptians were struck by ten plagues in Egypt, but by fifty plagues at the Sea? Of the plagues in Egypt it says: "And the magicians said to Pharaoh, it is the finger of God". Of those by the sea, however, it says: "When Israel saw the great hand which HASHEM laid upon the Egyptians, the people feared HASHEM, and believed in HASHEM and in His

am God in the midst of the land' (8:18). The third group, finally, was to show the *truth of prophecy;* in connection with this group the Torah speaks of those *'who would not listen to God's word'* (9:21; *Ritva).*

There is also another pattern that can be discerned in the grouping of the plagues. The first three were initiated by Aaron, with the use of Moses' staff; and they involved water and land. The next three were initiated by Moses without use of the staff, and involved those dwelling upon the land, man and beasts. The next three, finally, were initiated by Moses, with the use of his staff, and revealed God's power to strike from the air (*Ravon, Rashbam).*The slaying of the firstborn had, of course, a totally unique character.

The first two plagues in each group were always preceded by a warning; the third plague came without warning. *Rabbi S.R. Hirsch* points out that the first plague in each group (blood, wild animals, and hail) reduced the Egyptians in their own land to the insecure existence of strangers (גֵרוּת). The second plague in each group (frogs, pestilence, and locusts) robbed them of their pride, their possessions, and their sense of superiority, reducing them to lowly submission (עַבְדוּת). The third plague in each group (lice, boils, and darkness) imposed upon them actual physical suffering (עִנּוּי). This was the retribution for their oppression of the Jews which had taken these same three forms (see above, p. 96); their punishment then

reached its climax in the slaying of the firstborn.

רַבִּי יוֹסֵי הַגְּלִילִי — *Rabbi Yose the Galilean.* Rabbi Yose compares the expressions used to describe the punishment of the Egyptians in Egypt and their fate at the Sea of Reeds. The ten plagues that hit them in Egypt are called the *'finger of God';* their afflictions at the sea are called God's *'great hand.'* A hand has five fingers; it follows that the Egyptians suffered at the sea five times what they endured in Egypt — fifty plagues.

This would seem to contradict the statement of the *Mishnah (Avos* 5:1) that there were *ten* plagues at the Sea (they are all listed in *Avos de Rabbi Nosson).* It is likely, however, that the fifty plagues at the Sea of which Rabbi Yose speaks, were offshoots and different aspects of ten main afflictions that befell the Egyptians, those that are enumerated in the *Mishnah (Abarbanel).*

The statements about the finger of God in Egypt, and His whole hand at the Sea, must of course be understood in a deeper sense too. Rabbi Yose may have wanted to tell us that in Egypt the Jews only saw a limited impact of the plagues, whereas they were able to perceive the total annihilation of Egyptian power at the Sea.

חֲמִשִּׁים מַכּוֹת — *Fifty plagues.* The *Midrash* points out that Pharaoh said, מִי ה', *who is God (Shemos* 5:2); he received his answer at the Sea when he and his army were hit by fifty plagues (מִי = 50).

וּבְמֹשֶׁה עַבְדּוֹ. כַּמָּה לָקוּ בְּאֶצְבַּע עֶשֶׂר מַכּוֹת. אֱמוֹר מֵעַתָּה בְּמִצְרַיִם לָקוּ עֶשֶׂר מַכּוֹת וְעַל־הַיָּם לָקוּ חֲמִשִּׁים מַכּוֹת:

רַבִּי אֱלִיעֶזֶר אוֹמֵר. מִנַּיִן שֶׁכָּל מַכָּה וּמַכָּה שֶׁהֵבִיא הַקָּדוֹשׁ בָּרוּךְ הוּא עַל־הַמִּצְרִים בְּמִצְרַיִם הָיְתָה שֶׁל אַרְבַּע מַכּוֹת. שֶׁנֶּאֱמַר °יְשַׁלַּח־בָּם חֲרוֹן אַפּוֹ עֶבְרָה וָזַעַם וְצָרָה מִשְׁלַחַת מַלְאֲכֵי רָעִים. עֶבְרָה אַחַת. וָזַעַם שְׁתַּיִם. וְצָרָה שָׁלֹשׁ. מִשְׁלַחַת מַלְאֲכֵי רָעִים אַרְבַּע. אֱמוֹר מֵעַתָּה בְּמִצְרַיִם לָקוּ אַרְבָּעִים מַכּוֹת וְעַל־הַיָּם לָקוּ מָאתַיִם מַכּוֹת:

° תהלים
עח:מט

רַבִּי עֲקִיבָא אוֹמֵר. מִנַּיִן שֶׁכָּל־מַכָּה וּמַכָּה שֶׁהֵבִיא הַקָּדוֹשׁ בָּרוּךְ הוּא עַל הַמִּצְרִים בְּמִצְרַיִם הָיְתָה שֶׁל חָמֵשׁ מַכּוֹת. שֶׁנֶּאֱמַר °יְשַׁלַּח־בָּם חֲרוֹן אַפּוֹ עֶבְרָה וָזַעַם וְצָרָה מִשְׁלַחַת מַלְאֲכֵי רָעִים. חֲרוֹן אַפּוֹ אַחַת. עֶבְרָה שְׁתַּיִם. וָזַעַם שָׁלֹשׁ. וְצָרָה אַרְבַּע. מִשְׁלַחַת מַלְאֲכֵי רָעִים חָמֵשׁ: אֱמוֹר מֵעַתָּה בְּמִצְרַיִם לָקוּ חֲמִשִּׁים מַכּוֹת וְעַל הַיָּם לָקוּ חֲמִשִּׁים וּמָאתַיִם מַכּוֹת:

° תהלים
עח:מט

רַבִּי אֱלִיעֶזֶר — *Rabbi Eliezer*. Rabbi Eliezer considers אַף חֲרוֹן, *burning anger*, a summary description of the plagues, whereas עֶבְרָה, *wrath*, זַעַם, *indignation*, צָרָה, *trouble*, and מִשְׁלַחַת מַלְאֲכֵי רָעִים, *messengers of evil* are four ramifications of each plague. Rabbi Akiva, on the other hand, counts *burning anger* as a fifth aspect of each plague. Various explanations are offered for their disagreement.

The plagues involved the four elements that make up our world: air, water, fire, earth. Rabbi Akiva, however, also counts their composite nature itself, as involved in the punishment of the Egyptians *(Akeidas Yitzchak).* Another explanation points out that the plagues are called by the *Torah* the *finger of God.* A finger has four sides with which to strike; however, Rabbi Akiva also counts the

servant Moses." How many plagues did they receive with the finger? Ten! Then it follows that since there were ten plagues in Egypt, there were fifty at the sea (where they were hit with the whole hand).

Rabbi Eliezer said: How do we know that each plague that the Holy One, blessed be He, brought upon the Egyptians in Egypt, consisted of four plagues? For it is stated: "He sent forth upon them His burning anger: wrath, indignation and trouble, troops of messengers of evil", 'Wrath' was one plague, 'indignation' a second, 'trouble' a third, and 'troops of messengers of evil' a fourth; consequently they were struck by forty plagues in Egypt, and two hundred at the sea.

Rabbi Akiva said: How do we know that each plague that the Holy One, blessed be He, brought upon the Egyptians in Egypt, consisted of five plagues? For it is said: "He sent forth upon them His burning anger, wrath, indignation and trouble, troops of messengers of evil." 'His burning anger' was one plague, 'wrath' a second, 'indignation' a third, 'trouble' a fourth, and 'troops of messengers of evil' a fifth; consequently they were struck by fifty plagues in Egypt, and two hundred and fifty at the sea.

tip of the finger (Midrash Shocher Tov).

The deeper meaning of the controversy between Rabbi Eliezer and Rabbi Akiva can perhaps be found in the significance of the numbers four and five; they stand for יהו־ה (God exercising the quality of mercy) and אלהי־ם (God exercising the quality of justice), as these two names of God have four and five letters respectively. The plagues had a dual aspect: they punished the Egyptians and they liberated the Jews. Rabbi Eliezer saw in them primarily an act of Divine kindness to the Jews, whereas Rabbi Akiva considered them, above all, an exercise of God's judgment upon the Egyptians (Yad Chasakah).

The dual character of the plagues is stressed by King David: 'At midnight I rise to thank you for the judgments of your lovingkindness' (Tehillim 119:62); this statement is paraphrased by the Midrash:' ... to thank you for the judgments you visited on the Egyptians and the lovingkindness which you rendered us.' In accordance with this thought, the Mishnah that speaks of the ten plagues inflicted upon the Egyptians in Egypt

כַּמָּה מַעֲלוֹת טוֹבוֹת לַמָּקוֹם עָלֵינוּ:

אִלּוּ הוֹצִיאָנוּ מִמִּצְרַיִם וְלֹא־עָשָׂה בָהֶם שְׁפָטִים דַּיֵּנוּ:

אִלּוּ עָשָׂה בָהֶם שְׁפָטִים וְלֹא־עָשָׂה בֵאלֹהֵיהֶם דַּיֵּנוּ:

אִלּוּ עָשָׂה בֵאלֹהֵיהֶם וְלֹא־הָרַג אֶת־בְּכוֹרֵיהֶם דַּיֵּנוּ:

אִלּוּ הָרַג אֶת־בְּכוֹרֵיהֶם וְלֹא־נָתַן לָנוּ אֶת־מָמוֹנָם דַּיֵּנוּ:

אִלּוּ נָתַן לָנוּ אֶת־מָמוֹנָם וְלֹא־קָרַע לָנוּ אֶת־הַיָּם דַּיֵּנוּ:

אִלּוּ קָרַע לָנוּ אֶת־הַיָּם וְלֹא־הֶעֱבִירָנוּ בְּתוֹכוֹ בֶּחָרָבָה דַּיֵּנוּ:

אִלּוּ הֶעֱבִירָנוּ בְּתוֹכוֹ בֶּחָרָבָה וְלֹא־שִׁקַּע צָרֵינוּ בְּתוֹכוֹ דַּיֵּנוּ:

אִלּוּ שִׁקַּע צָרֵינוּ בְּתוֹכוֹ וְלֹא־סִפֵּק צָרְכֵּנוּ בַּמִּדְבָּר אַרְבָּעִים שָׁנָה דַּיֵּנוּ:

and at the Sea, also states that God at the same time wrought ten miracles *for our forefathers* in Egypt and at the Sea.

Why did the Sages find it important to point out how many plagues took place? In the first place, they wanted to show the full range of the miracles that marked the redemption from Egypt. Beyond that, they sought to clarify the full meaning of God's promise, 'No affliction which I put upon Egypt, will I put upon you' (Shemos 15:26); In pointing out how many disasters befell Egypt, they also made clear from how many afflictions the Jewish people will be protected if it listens to God's word (Vilna Gaon).

כַּמָּה מַעֲלוֹת — *For how many favors.* This poem as well as the just-recited statements of Rabbi Yose, Rabbi Eliezer, and Rabbi Akiva (which are taken from the *Mechilta*) are not included in the *Haggadah* text given by the *Rambam* in his *Yad Hachazakah.* According to his son, he recited them at his own *Seder* but omitted them in the *Yad Hachazakah* because they are not a necessary part of the *Haggadah.* The *Abarbanel* points out that they could be omitted because they deal primarily with miracles that happened after the Jews left Egypt. However, we do include them in the *Haggadah,* for the splitting of the Sea, the giving of the

F or how many favors do we owe thanks to the Ever-Present!

If He had brought us out of Egypt, but had not executed judgments upon the Egyptians, it would have sufficed for us!

If He had executed judgments upon them, but not upon their gods, it would have sufficed for us!

If He had destroyed their gods, but not at the same time slain their first-born, it would have sufficed for us!

If He had slain their first-born but not given us their wealth, it would have sufficed for us!

If He had given us their wealth but not also divided the sea for us, it would have sufficed for us!

If He had divided the sea without taking us through it on dry land, it would have sufficed for us!

If He had led us through it on dry land, but not drowned our oppressors in it, it would have sufficed for us!

If He had drowned our oppressors in it, but had not provided for our needs in the wilderness for forty years, it would have sufficed for us!

Torah, and the building of the Temple are the conclusion and ultimate fulfillment of the Exodus from Egypt: '... I took them out from the land of Egypt in order to dwell in their midst; I am HASHEM, their God' (Shemos 29:46).

We previously pointed out that the bondage of our forefathers was twofold — physical and spiritual — and so was their redemption (see Overview, p. 32, and מַתְחָלָה, p.91). The physical bondage came to an end on Pesach night, but the spiritual redemption reached its climax only with the building of the Temple and God's self-revelation in His sanctuary. There, appearing before the Divine Presence, we would find constant spiritual rejuvenation and Divine

inspiration; וְשָׁם נַעֲבָדְךָ בְּיִרְאָה, and there, alone, we would be able to serve HASHEM in the highest possible manner.

Every step on the road to this ultimate goal was a further act of Divine kindness to us, and a further revelation of God's majesty. That is why we give thanks for each of the מַעֲלוֹת — this word means, 'step', as well as 'favor' (or advantage) bestowed upon us. For every single step here enumerated we say דַּיֵּנוּ, 'it would have sufficed by itself to require our thanks' (Malbim).

We do not mean to say that any one step would have sufficed by itself to bring us to our goal. Obviously, for instance, the Jews required not only the

אִלּוּ סִפֵּק צָרְכֵּנוּ בַּמִּדְבָּר אַרְבָּעִים שָׁנָה וְלֹא־
הֶאֱכִילָנוּ אֶת־הַמָּן דַּיֵּנוּ:

אִלּוּ הֶאֱכִילָנוּ אֶת הַמָּן וְלֹא־נָתַן לָנוּ אֶת־
הַשַּׁבָּת דַּיֵּנוּ:

אִלּוּ נָתַן לָנוּ אֶת־הַשַּׁבָּת וְלֹא־קֵרְבָנוּ לִפְנֵי הַר־
סִינַי דַּיֵּנוּ:

אִלּוּ קֵרְבָנוּ לִפְנֵי הַר־סִינַי וְלֹא־נָתַן לָנוּ אֶת־
הַתּוֹרָה דַּיֵּנוּ:

אִלּוּ נָתַן לָנוּ אֶת הַתּוֹרָה וְלֹא הִכְנִיסָנוּ לְאֶרֶץ
יִשְׂרָאֵל דַּיֵּנוּ:

אִלּוּ הִכְנִיסָנוּ לְאֶרֶץ יִשְׂרָאֵל וְלֹא בָנָה לָנוּ אֶת
בֵּית הַבְּחִירָה דַּיֵּנוּ:

עַל אַחַת כַּמָּה וְכַמָּה טוֹבָה כְפוּלָה וּמְכֻפֶּלֶת
לַמָּקוֹם עָלֵינוּ. שֶׁהוֹצִיאָנוּ מִמִּצְרָיִם.
וְעָשָׂה בָהֶם שְׁפָטִים. וְעָשָׂה בֵאלֹהֵיהֶם. וְהָרַג
אֶת־בְּכוֹרֵיהֶם. וְנָתַן לָנוּ אֶת־מָמוֹנָם. וְקָרַע לָנוּ
אֶת־הַיָּם. וְהֶעֱבִירָנוּ בְתוֹכוֹ בֶּחָרָבָה. וְשִׁקַּע
צָרֵינוּ בְּתוֹכוֹ. וְסִפֵּק צָרְכֵּנוּ בַּמִּדְבָּר אַרְבָּעִים
שָׁנָה. וְהֶאֱכִילָנוּ אֶת הַמָּן. וְנָתַן לָנוּ אֶת
הַשַּׁבָּת.וְקֵרְבָנוּ לִפְנֵי הַר־סִינַי. וְנָתַן לָנוּ אֶת־
הַתּוֹרָה. וְהִכְנִיסָנוּ לְאֶרֶץ יִשְׂרָאֵל. וּבָנָה לָנוּ
אֶת בֵּית הַבְּחִירָה לְכַפֵּר עַל־כָּל־עֲוֹנוֹתֵינוּ:

splitting of the Sea but the possibility of crossing it on dry land. However, every one of the happenings mentioned represented a new remarkable miracle — and it is also clear that God need not have performed these miracles if He had not seen a particular purpose in each. For instance, the splitting of the Sea, and the miracles connected with it, could have been avoided if God had forestalled the Egyptian pursuit of the Jews — and instead of the Revelation at Mount Sinai the Jews could have been given the Torah through the teachings of Moses alone. Instead, however, God favored us with the splitting of the Sea and the Revelation at Mount Sinai; and through them we were lifted to new

If He had provided for our needs in the wilderness for forty years but not fed us with Manna, it would have sufficed for us!

If He had fed us with Manna, but not also given us the Shabbos, it would have sufficed for us!

If He had given us the Shabbos, but not led us to Mount Sinai, it would have sufficed for us!

If He had brought us before Mount Sinai, but not given us the Torah, it would have sufficed for us!

If He had given us the Torah, but not led us into the land of Israel, it would have sufficed for us!

If He had led us into the land of Israel and not built a Temple for us, it would have sufficed for us!

Thus, how much more so do we owe thanks to the Ever-Present for all His manifold favors! He brought us forth from Egypt, executed judgments upon them and upon their gods, slew their first-born, gave us wealth, divided the sea for us, led us through it on dry land and drowned our oppressors in it, supplied our needs in the wilderness for forty years and fed us with Manna, gave us the Shabbos, led us before Mount Sinai, gave us the Torah, brought us into the Promised Land and built us a Temple to atone for all our sins.

spiritual heights (this, too, is a meaning of the term מַעֲלוֹת; it can be translated *ascents* — see *Ezekiel* 11:5).

This climb is described here in fifteen steps. They represent fifteen acts of Divine kindness, corresponding to God's name יָה (whose letters total 15). The number 15 appears, indeed, to reflect in many different ways, the link between God and us.

In connection with the fifteen stages mentioned in the *Haggadah*, the *Abarbanel* points to *Ezekiel* (16:9-13) who enumerates a like number of favors done by God for the Jews in Egypt; the *Midrash* explains that, because of these

favors, the Jews were commanded to contribute the same number of materials to the construction of the Sanctuary (they are enumerated in *Terumah* 25:3-7; note our previous observation that the building of the sanctuary was the goal of the redemption from Egypt).

It has also been pointed out that there were fifteen generations from Abraham, the father of our people, to King Solomon who built the Holy Temple, the embodiment of our national aspirations. There were fifteen steps that led from the forecourt of the Temple up to the inner court; it was on these steps that the Levites sang their hymns in

רַבָּן גַּמְלִיאֵל הָיָה אוֹמֵר. כָּל־שֶׁלֹא־אָמַר
שְׁלֹשָׁה דְבָרִים אֵלּוּ בַּפֶּסַח לֹא־יָצָא יְדֵי
חוֹבָתוֹ. וְאֵלּוּ הֵן. פֶּסַח. מַצָּה. וּמָרוֹר:

praise of God, and King David composed *his fifteen* שִׁירֵי הַמַּעֲלוֹת, *Songs of Ascent,* for them *(Ritva).*

Finally, we have at our *Seder* fifteen stages, from the moment we prepare for קדוש till we have attained נִרְצָה, God's acceptance of our *Seder* service (see the list on p. 53).

רַבָּן גַּמְלִיאֵל — *Rabban Gamliel.* About which duty does Rabban Gamliel speak here? Does he mean the duty of *Haggadah,* and tells us that this includes listing and explaining the three principal commandments of the evening? Or does he mean the duty of eating *Pesach, Matzah,* and *Maror,* and stresses that we are required to spell out these commandments and the reasons for them? We find both views among the commentators; but this is certain according to all of them: there is a close bond between talking about the Exodus, and the fulfillment of the practical commandments which have been given in connection with it. This bond we already saw reflected in the rule that the *Haggadah* should be recited when *Matzah* and *Maror* are in front of us (pp. 24, 88).

According to most commentators, Rabban Gamliel talks about the obligation to tell about the Exodus, the account of which we just completed. He tells us that, in order to fulfill this duty properly *(Ran),* we must also *talk* about

Pesach, Matzah, and *Maror.* Our passage is thus the conclusion of *Maggid,* in preparation for the praise we are now about to offer God, in the first chapters of *Hallel* and the concluding blessing of *Maggid.*

It has been pointed out that the telling of the *Pesach* story is triggered by *actions,* notably by the breaking of the *Matzah, the bread over which many things are recited,* and by the Four Questions which also deal with concrete and practical actions. Now that the whole story has been told, the cycle closes as these actions are tied in and explained in terms of the story. The need for this is actually indicated by the Torah: the duty to have *Pesach, Matzah* and *Maror* before us during the *Haggadah,* is conveyed to us by the verse בַּעֲבוּר זֶה עָשָׂה ה' לִי, *'Because of this, HASHEM did for me' (Shemos* 13:8), and the expression בַּעֲבוּר זֶה, 'because of *this',* would indicate that we have to point at *Pesach, Matzah* and *Maror* and explain them *(Malbim).*[1]

Beyond this, Rabban Gamliel would appear to teach us that it is not enough to *retell* historical reminiscences — they must lead to *definite and concrete actions.* In the first place, it is only through such actions that we are really influenced to absorb the lessons which we are taught *(Sefer Hachinuch,* see p. 22). Conversely it is also true that any lessons to be learnt need to be put to

1. The wicked son had questioned the value of our *Pesach* observances, and we had answered that we were redeemed on their account. Here this is explained in more detail:
— the *Pesach* sacrifice was to protect our houses; this protection was necessary because in our houses there were some who did not deserve to be spared;
— the *Matzah* was a result of the hurry in which we had to leave; this was necessary because we had almost succumbed to Egytian impurity;
— the *Maror* reflected our suffering in Egypt; this, too, was a necessary consequence of our spiritual decline and assimilation (see p. 107).
Therefore, these observances serve today as a warning not to follow the path of the sinners in Egypt, but to go in the way of the Torah *(Yalkut Tov).*

R abban Gamliel used to say: Whoever does not explain the following three things at the Pesach festival, has not fulfilled his duty, namely: the Pesach sacrifice, Matzah, and Maror.

concrete and practical use. It is fundamental to Judaism that *'great is study, for it brings to action'*, and Judaism has in fact been defined as a faith that expresses itself in action. The failure to perceive this was the tragedy of the Reform movement.

According to other commentators, however, Rabban Gamliel wants to stress that the proper performance of the commandments of Pesach, Matzah, and Maror requires calling to mind the reasons for them *(Kolbo)*. Generally speaking, when we fulfill a commandment, it is enough to want to obey God's word; we do not have to think about the purpose of the commandment (in fact, in connection with most commandments we cannot really be sure what their deeper purposes are, and we can only *try* to understand what lessons the Divine Lawgiver wants to teach us through them). However, where the Torah itself spells out the reasons for a law, it is desirable — and, according to some Rabbis, essential — that we keep in mind the purpose given (for instance, in the case of *Sukkah*).

With reference to the commandment to offer the Pesach sacrifice, the Torah specifically stresses, *'And you shall say: This is the Pesach sacrifice for HASHEM who passed over the houses...'* (Shemos 12:27); and since the Torah links Matzah and Maror to the Pesach offering (Shemos 12:8), the reasons for all three have to be enumerated.

Apparently, it is not even enough to *think* of these reasons; they must be put into words and have to be elaborated upon. This is very unusual; generally, all we have to say before fulfilling a commandment is the appropriate blessing. The *Maharsha* explains that the laws of Pesach are in a special category:

they were designed to lift the Jews out of the impurity of Egypt into the sphere of Divine holiness (compare Overview p. 29). To bring about this drastic transformation, it is not enough to eat Pesach, Matzah, and Maror; their purpose has to be clearly verbalized. In the case of the Pesach offering, the verse quoted here makes this clear. The *Maharsha* also finds a specific Biblical basis for the duty to talk about Matzah and Maror. In the case of Maror, there is the Torah's statement, *'you should remember that you were a slave in Egypt ...'* (Devarim 5:15 ; generally, when the Torah orders us to remember, this requires putting it into words). The duty to talk about Matzah can similarly be found in the verse, *'you shall eat Matzos ... so that you will remember the day of your going out from Egypt...'* (Devarim 16:3).

פֶּסַח מַצָּה וּמָרוֹר — *The Pesach sacrifice, Matzah and Maror.* The order in which the three commandments are listed here deserves our attention. Historically, the events commemorated by Maror occurred before the offering of the Pesach sacrifice. Moreover, on Seder night the Pesach lamb was eaten last. Why, then, is it mentioned first?

The *Abarbanel* explains that Rabban Gamliel follows the order of the Torah (Shemos 12:8); the verse mentions all three commandments but reflects the primary role of the Pesach sacrifice. Its special significance is also shown by the fact that it is one of only two מִצְוֹת עֲשֵׂה, positive commandments, whose transgression carries the punishment of כָּרֵת, elimination from the ranks of the Jewish people at God's hands (the other such commandment is circumcision, see above, p. 109).

אֵין לְהַרְאוֹת בָּאֶצְבַּע עַל הַזְּרוֹעַ שֶׁעַל הַקְּעָרָה כְּשֶׁאוֹמְרִים זֶה.

פֶּסַח שֶׁהָיוּ אֲבוֹתֵינוּ אוֹכְלִים בִּזְמַן שֶׁבֵּית־
הַמִּקְדָּשׁ הָיָה קַיָּם עַל־שׁוּם מָה. עַל־
שׁוּם שֶׁפֶּסַח הַקָּדוֹשׁ בָּרוּךְ הוּא עַל בָּתֵּי
אֲבוֹתֵינוּ בְּמִצְרָיִם. שֶׁנֶּאֱמַר °וַאֲמַרְתֶּם זֶבַח־
פֶּסַח הוּא לַיהוה אֲשֶׁר פָּסַח עַל־בָּתֵּי בְנֵי־
יִשְׂרָאֵל בְּמִצְרַיִם בְּנָגְפּוֹ אֶת־מִצְרַיִם וְאֶת־
בָּתֵּינוּ הִצִּיל וַיִּקֹּד הָעָם וַיִּשְׁתַּחֲווּ:

° שְׁמוֹת
יב:כז

מַגְבִּיהִים הַמַּצָּה הָאֶמְצָעִית לְהַרְאוֹתָהּ לַמְסוּבִּים וְאוֹמְרִים:

מַצָּה זוֹ שֶׁאָנוּ אוֹכְלִים עַל־שׁוּם מָה. עַל־
שׁוּם שֶׁלֹּא הִסְפִּיק בְּצֵקָם שֶׁל אֲבוֹתֵינוּ

The *Pesach* is, indeed, eaten last; but that is only so that its taste (read: impact) should remain with us, and not because it is the least important of these three commandments.

Maror is mentioned last because, in the absence of a *Pesach* sacrifice, as today, it is not Biblically commanded. However, the *Rambam*, following the *Talmud Yerushalmi*, lists *Maror* before *Matzah* — this was apparently the order in the times of the Temple, when there was a *Pesach* sacrifice which required *Maror* with it (*Maharil*).

The primary and central role of the *Pesach* sacrifice is explained by the *Sfas Emes*. *Matzah* reminds us of the redemption of the Jews: they had to depart quickly before their dough could rise. *Maror* reflects the *wickedness of the Egyptians*, which led to their well-deserved punishment. But both these thoughts should be subordinate to the message of the *Pesach* sacrifice: the self-revelation of God when He passed over the Jewish homes and killed the Egyptian firstborn.

In a similar vein, it has been stressed that we should not see our redemption as due to our own actions (symbolized by the *Matzah* we baked), or to the wickedness of Pharaoh (reflected in the *Maror*) but to the mercy of God, of which we are reminded by the *Pesach* sacrifice (*Rabbi Avrohom Wolf*).

Others have suggested that *Pesach*, *Matzah*, and *Maror* teach us the three basic principles to which *Rabbi Joseph Albo* reduced the thirteen articles of faith of the *Rambam*: the *Pesach* lamb (involving the rejection of idol worship) symbolizes faith in *God's existence*; *Matzah* (involving obedience to the divine prohibition of *Chametz*) expresses acceptance of the *Torah*; and *Maror* (with its emphasis on suffering) reflects the belief in *reward and punishment*.

Rabbi Mosheh Chayim Luzzatto sees in these three commandments the steps by which the Jews rose from pagan ways to the pure worship of God: first they withdrew from idol-worship (as shown by their sacrifice of the lamb, the idol of the Egyptians); then they drew on sustenance completely free of human imperfection (the *Matzah*, devoid of all *Chametz*, which stands for the Evil Instinct); and finally they had to scour and cleanse themselves of all impurities previously acquired (with *Maror* as the cleansing agent).

*T*he Pesach sacrifice that our fathers ate at the time when the Holy Temple was still standing — for what reason? Because the Holy One, blessed be He, passed over the houses of our fathers in Egypt, for so it is said in the Torah: "You shall say, it is a Pesach sacrifice for HASHEM, because He passed over the houses of the children of Israel in Egypt, when He struck the Egyptians, and He saved our houses; and the people bowed down and prostrated themselves."

The middle *Matzah* is held up for all to see, and the following passage is recited:

*T*his matzah that we eat — for what reason? Because the dough of our fathers did not have time to

It has also been suggested that *Pesach*, *Matzah* and *Maror* all are symbols of redemption. This is obvious in the case of the *Pesach* sacrifice; and the *Matzah*, too, though also eaten during bondage, became the symbol of the hurried deliverance. But what about the *Maror*? The *Lubavitch Haggadah* explains that it was the suffering of the Jews which earned them their liberation. In fact, the name חֲזֶרֶת, for *Maror*, has been explained as a reminder that הקב"ה הֶחֱזִירָנוּ לַעֲבוֹדָתוֹ, *God brought us back to His service through the bitterness of Egypt* (Hamanhig).

According to this explanation, however, why is the *Maror* not listed first, in the proper historical order? It has been said that you cannot really appreciate the depth of suffering (represented by the *Maror*) until after you have attained release from it (*Rabbi Bunim of Parshischa*); also it is important to remember former suffering even after one's deliverance from it (*Vayagidu Lemordechai*). The *Maror* may also be mentioned last because it points to later exiles that followed the redemption from Egypt.

פֶּסַח — *The Pesach Sacrifice.* It represented a twofold freedom: spiritual freedom, from the paganism of Egyptian society, and physical freedom — as the *Pesach* blood on the doorposts saved the Jews while the Egyptian firstborn died. The new freedom of the Jews was reflected in the fact that they were not permitted to eat the Pesach sacrifice in the manner of poor, starving slaves who would break the bones or boil the meat to get every last ounce of taste out of it, save it up for another day, or take it with them wherever they went (*Sefer Hachinuch*). Others, however, see in the prohibition of these practices not a reflection of freedom and dignity, but of the haste with which the Jews had to eat the *Seder* meal in Egypt (*Rambam*).

וְאֶת בָּתֵּינוּ הִצִּיל — *and He saved our houses.* Why this special emphasis? And why did the Jews owe thanks to God for the fact that He passed over their houses? After all, they were not the target of the plague! Our Sages point out, however, that God reached into the homes of the Jews to kill those Egyptian firstborn who tried to hide there; yet, at the same time, no Jews were struck — even though they had not yet totally shaken off the influence of

לְהַחֲמִיץ עַד שֶׁנִּגְלָה עֲלֵיהֶם מֶלֶךְ מַלְכֵי
הַמְּלָכִים הַקָּדוֹשׁ בָּרוּךְ הוּא וּגְאָלָם. שֶׁנֶּאֱמַר
°וַיֹּאפוּ אֶת־הַבָּצֵק אֲשֶׁר הוֹצִיאוּ מִמִּצְרַיִם °שמות
עֻגֹת מַצּוֹת כִּי לֹא חָמֵץ כִּי גֹרְשׁוּ מִמִּצְרַיִם וְלֹא יב:לט
יָכְלוּ לְהִתְמַהְמֵהַּ וְגַם־צֵדָה לֹא־עָשׂוּ לָהֶם:

מגביהים המרור להראותו למסובים ואומרים:

מָרוֹר זֶה שֶׁאָנוּ אוֹכְלִים עַל־שׁוּם מָה. עַל־
שׁוּם שֶׁמֵּרְרוּ הַמִּצְרִים אֶת־חַיֵּי

Egyptian ideas (see above p. 124).

מַצָּה — Matzah. The Haggadah would seem, at first glance, to tell us that the Jews ate Matzos on Seder night because they had no time to wait for their dough to rise. But actually they were commanded well in advance to have Matzos with the Pesach offering (Shemos 12:8). It is therefore clear that they ate Matzah because of the Divine commandment. The Haggadah, however, explains why this commandment was given — God knew, of course, that the redemption would be so hurried and therefore told the Jews in advance to eat Matzah on Pesach night (Shibolei Haleket); in fact, in the verse here quoted, the Torah tells us that in the end the moment of freedom came so suddenly that they did not even have enough time to bake Matzos for the journey, and simply took their raw dough on their backs.

According to the Talmud (Pesachim 28b), the prohibition of eating Chametz for seven days, announced at the time of the Exodus (Shemos 12:15), did not apply on that first Pesach — then the Jews were only forbidden Chametz for one night. However, because they did not have time to take along Chametz for the trip either, they were forbidden to eat Chametz in later years for seven days. Ramban, however, appears to reflect the existence of a dissenting Talmudic opinion, according to which Chametz was forbidden for seven days even in the first year; he therefore interprets our passage as telling us that the

Jews had no time to bake Matzos for the journey, and therefore hurried to do so on their trip, before the dough could become sour. In fact, it was an act of Divine providence that it did not start rising — to serve as a reminder of the speediness of their departure (Yalkut Me'am Loez).

Since the prohibition to eat Chametz for seven days only applied in later years, according to the Talmud, why was it announced in Egypt? The Meshech Chochmah suggests that the Torah thereby teaches us not to rejoice over the destruction of our enemies but over our own deliverance. We celebrate Purim on the day on which the Jews rested, not on the day of battle; on Chanukah we commemorate the miracle of the oil, which marked the dedication of the Temple, rather than the victory in war. In the same way, the seven days of Pesach mark our departure from Egypt, whereas Seder night is the time when the Egyptian might was overthrown. Therefore the Torah emphasized from the outset the observance of the entire seven days — even though it only applied to later years (see footnote, p. 127).

The question remains: why did God tell the Jews to eat Matzah — because of the sudden redemption — rather than ordering them to prepare food in advance, at their leisure? We previously pointed out that, perhaps, the Jews were not supposed to prepare for their departure, so as to demonstrate the purely passive role that they played in the unfolding of their deliverance. Moreover, they were to be impressed with the speed of the Divine redemption; in fact,

become leavened before the King of Kings, the Holy One, blessed be He, revealed Himself to them and redeemed them; as the Torah states: "And they baked unleavened bread from the dough which they had taken with them from Egypt, for it was not leavened, because they were driven out of Egypt and could not delay there; nor had they prepared for themselves any provisions for the way."

The *Maror* is held up for all to see, while the following passage is recited:

This maror that we eat — for what reason? Because the Egyptians embittered the lives of our fathers

if they had not been taken out of Egypt so precipitately, they might have been lost there forever (see above, p.97). This suddenness of the redemption finds expression in the *Matzah* — the bread that did not have time to rise.

But why did they not prepare *Matzah* in advance? After all, *Matzah* was their regular food in Egypt! The answer can be found by reflecting on the nature of *Matzah*. *Matzah* is the bread of humility. Whereas normal dough is left to rest till it sours and rises, and is then turned into a fluffy and tasty food, *Matzah* dough is kneaded without interruption, to keep it flat, and is then baked as a heavy and tasteless wafer. The *Matzah* thus represents the absence of pleasure-seeking and arrogant haughtiness, a fitting food for Pharaoh's slaves: לֶחֶם עוֹנִי, *bread of affliction*. This aspect of the *Matzah*, as the bread of poverty, we have in mind when we tell the *Haggadah* over it. *Matzah* that is meant to express this theme could have been baked in advance of liberation. But there is also another aspect to the *Matzah:* it is the bread of freedom that we eat because God redeemed us speedily *(Mishnah*

Pesachim 10:5). The *Matzah* of freedom could only be baked by free men — when the hour of freedom struck.

Of course, the *Matzah*, in this new role, is still without taste and height, still expresses avoidance of indulgence and arrogance. But this is because, instead of slaves of Pharaoh, we are now the servants of God. Where previously Pharaoh did not let us indulge, we must now foreswear the human weakness of תַּאֲוָה וְגַאֲוָה, indulgence and pride, because they deflect us from our service of God (see *Overview*, p. 23; and p. 91, for the role of these weaknesses in the history of mankind). They are products of the יֵצֶר הָרֵע, our evil inclination which plays the same role in human nature as does the leaven in the dough *(Brachos* 17a). By eating unleavened bread, we dedicate ourselves to the simple and unspoiled life of a servant of God.

For this reason, the *Zohar* calls *Matzah* the bread of health — it heals the imperfections of our nature.[1] In fact, once the lesson of the *Matzah* has been taken to heart, on *Pesach*, we can then eat *Chametz* for the rest of the year, because we will, hopefully, remember to

1. The *Matzah* is called מֵיכְלָא דְּאַסְוָתָא, the *'food of healing'* by the *Zohar*. The Hebrew word for bread (לֶחֶם) is connected with that for war (מִלְחָמָה): bread is a subject of contention and conflicts, and reflects self-assertion. The *Matzah* is different; it serves as an antidote, because it conveys humility and subordination to God.

חַיֵּיהֶם בַּעֲבֹדָה קָשָׁה בְּחֹמֶר וּבִלְבֵנִים וּבְכָל־
עֲבֹדָה בַּשָּׂדֶה אֵת כָּל־עֲבֹדָתָם אֲשֶׁר עָבְדוּ בָהֶם
בְּפָרֶךְ:

בְּכָל־דּוֹר וָדוֹר חַיָּב אָדָם לִרְאוֹת אֶת־
עַצְמוֹ כְּאִלּוּ הוּא יָצָא מִמִּצְרָיִם.
שֶׁנֶּאֱמַר °וְהִגַּדְתָּ לְבִנְךָ בַּיּוֹם הַהוּא לֵאמֹר שמות°
יג:ח
בַּעֲבוּר זֶה עָשָׂה יהוה לִי בְּצֵאתִי מִמִּצְרָיִם.לא

use all our inclinations according to
God's will — even those tendencies that
might ordinarily be used for selfish and
wrong ends. Our Sages emphasize that
the *Torah* wants us to serve God בְּכָל
לְבָבְךָ־בִּשְׁנֵי יְצָרֶיךָ, *'with all your heart'*
(Devarim 6:5), with both your inclina-
tions (Brochos 54a). The *Zohar* gives
the example of a doctor who prescribes
a health-giving medicine — once it has
achieved its purpose, the patient can eat
a normal diet (see also *Overview*, p. 38).

מָרוֹר — *Maror*. Why do we have a
reminder of the bitterness of the Egyptian exile, but not of the riches that we
gathered at the time of liberation? The
Bais Halevi points out that the riches
disappeared in due course — whereas
the suffering remained with the Jews
through later exiles. Moreover, the
riches of Egypt became a source of trouble for the Jews, as they were used for
the making of the Golden Calf.

The bitterness of the Egyptian bondage had many facets, and our Sages
found allusions to them in the names
of the various plants that can be used as
Maror: חֲזֶרֶת, for instance, is a reminder
that the Jews had to go from door to
door (חֹזֵר), or that their suffering
brought them back to God (see above);
similarly, חַסָּא indicates that God had
mercy (חָס) on us.

בְּכָל דּוֹר וָדוֹר — *In every generation*. So

far, on the *Seder* evening, we have
talked about the Exodus and discussed
the commandments connected with it.
Now the *Haggadah* explains the purpose of the observances — namely, that
we should actually see *ourselves* as having gone out from Egypt.

We discussed before whether Rabban
Gamliel's statement, that we must explain *Pesach, Matzah,* and *Maror,* in
order to do our duty (חוֹבָה) tonight,
refers to the duty of *talking about the
Exodus,* or to the duty of *eating Pesach,
Matzah and Maror;* actually, however,
it may instead refer *to the duty of making ourselves experience the Exodus:* 'A
person is obliged literally to transform
himself into one of those that left Egypt.
This state can only be achieved through
performing the commandments ... only
in the way that the *Haggadah* provides,
through the observances of the *Seder,*
can this goal be achieved, for they have
the power to change the person'
(Chever Ma'amarim).

The *Haggadah* stated previously (p. 74)
that we would still be enslaved in
Egypt if God had not taken out our
forefathers. We therefore owe thanks
for their redemption from Egypt; like all
the Jews, we are the beneficiaries of an
event that happened many years ago.
Now the *Haggadah* elaborates and
further explains this point, telling us
that we should not view the Exodus

in Egypt; as it says in the Torah: "They made their lives bitter with hard labor, with mortar and brick, and through all manner of labor in the field; all their bondage at which they made them slave rigorously."

In every generation, one is obliged to regard himself as though he himself had actually gone out from Egypt, for the Torah says: "You shall tell your son on that day, saying: 'For the sake of this, HASHEM did for me when I went out from Egypt'. " Not only

merely as a historical event that happened long ago. Rather, we have to see it as a personal experience in which we are directly involved; only then can we tell our children בַּיּוֹם הַהוּא, *on that day* (presumably long after the Exodus), that עָשָׂה ה׳ לִי, *God did for me*, not only for my ancestors (*Maharshah*).

Rambam sees this message in the injunction of the *Torah* to remember ' "*that you were a slave in Egypt*" (*Devarim* 5:15), *meaning that you yourself were a slave and you went out and were redeemed.*'

On *Seder* night '*everybody should occupy himself with his own Exodus from Egypt* ... *he should experience the bondage in his own body and soul, and he should feel that he himself is going out from Egypt* ... *As a result, the very same benefit and goal that was attained at the Exodus by that generation will also be ours*' (*Chever Ma'amarim*). The goal of the Exodus was that God would be our God, and that we would be His people — leaving behind the authority of Pharaoh, to submit to that of God. Our people was not only taught to recognize God's kingship — a matter of intellectual understanding — but actually to become His servants. This, then, is also the objective of our *Seder*. '*Just as the generation of the Exodus came to accept the yoke of the kingdom of*

Heaven, so must we, through the retelling and remembrance of the Exodus ... [The Seder] *is not concerned with the redemption of one's forefathers, but with his own redemption*' (*Chever Ma'amarim*).[1]

On *Pesach* night, every year, the spirit of redemption bestirs itself anew (see *Overview* p. 20). It is our task to make ourselves worthy of it by throwing off the spiritual and physical shackles of our society, and to sanctify our lives as servants of God. This is the personal redemption which everyone — in every generation — must strive for (*Maaseh Nissim*).

We may ask: how can we feel like those redeemed from Egypt, since we are again in exile? Our exile, however, cannot be compared to the Egyptian bondage. The deliverance from Pharaoh's servitude was final, and we attained חֵרוּת עוֹלָם, an everlasting freedom, sealed by the giving of the *Torah*. Unlike the Jew in Egypt, we have the *Torah* with us in our exile, and through it we can indeed recapture the lessons of the Exodus (*Abarbanel*). In fact, as we do so, we also prepare the ultimate redemption through the coming of *Mashiach*.

It is noteworthy that the *Haggadah* here quotes two verses to prove that we should see ourselves as having gone out

1. '*And you shall know that I am God who takes you out* ...' (*Shemos* 6:7).
'Who takes you out' (הַמּוֹצִיא) is present tense: the redemption from Egypt is still going on!

אֶת־אֲבוֹתֵינוּ בִּלְבָד גָּאַל הַקָּדוֹשׁ בָּרוּךְ הוּא
אֶלָּא אַף אוֹתָנוּ גָּאַל עִמָּהֶם. שֶׁנֶּאֱמַר °וְאוֹתָנוּ °דברים
הוֹצִיא מִשָּׁם. לְמַעַן הָבִיא אֹתָנוּ לָתֶת לָנוּ אֶת ו:כג
הָאָרֶץ אֲשֶׁר נִשְׁבַּע לַאֲבוֹתֵינוּ:

מכסים המצות ומגביהים הכוס עד לאחר גמר ברכת **אֲשֶׁר גְּאָלָנוּ** (יש
שמגלים המצות ומניחים הכוס קודם שאומרים **הַלְלוּיָהּ הַלְלוּ**
וכו' וכשמגיעים לברכת **אֲשֶׁר גְּאָלָנוּ** מכסים המצות ומגביהים הכוס).

לְפִיכָךְ אֲנַחְנוּ חַיָּבִים לְהוֹדוֹת לְהַלֵּל
לְשַׁבֵּחַ לְפָאֵר לְרוֹמֵם לְהַדֵּר לְבָרֵךְ
לְעַלֵּה וּלְקַלֵּס לְמִי שֶׁעָשָׂה לַאֲבוֹתֵינוּ וְלָנוּ אֶת־
כָּל הַנִּסִּים הָאֵלּוּ הוֹצִיאָנוּ מֵעַבְדוּת לְחֵרוּת

of Egypt. The first of these verses stresses that *we* went out from there; the second verse adds that the purpose of the
Exodus was our settlement in the Holy
Land, under the wings of the Divine
Presence in the Temple. This goal has
not yet been achieved, and so we are
literally still on the road out of Egypt.

Because we are still caught in the
same web of human weaknesses that
marked Egyptian society, our enemies
still rise against us in every generation.
At the same time, however, we are chal-
lenged in every generation to seek our
deliverance. The observances of the
Seder are able to lift us to those levels of
קַבָּלַת עוֹל מַלְכוּת שָׁמַיִם, acceptance of
God's kingship, which will bring the
Messianic redemption to which the second part of the *Seder* is devoted (*Rabbi
M. Ch. Luzzatto*).[1]

It should be noted that *Rambam* has the
version: '... חַיָּב אָדָם לְהַרְאוֹת, *one is obliged
to show himself as if he had gone out from
Egypt.* 'This implies that we should not only
see ourselves as having been redeemed but
should demonstrate the fact to others
through our observances on this night: '*It is

*not enough to think so in his heart; one must
show it through his enthusiasm, so that all
those sitting in his house perceive it from his
joyful movements and manner*' (*Chidah*).

לְפִיכָךְ — *Therefore.* When the Jews were
redeemed from Egypt, they marched out
בְּיָד רָמָה, '*with upraised hand*' (*Shemos*
14:8), praising God who had saved
them (*Tanchumah*). In the same way, if
we realize that we ourselves were also
redeemed from Pharoah's hands, by the
grace of God, we should truly feel the
obligation to pay homage to Him for
what He has done for us (*Kolbo*). Even
though our people has not yet attained
the final national redemption, every Jew
who truly relives the experience of the
deliverance from Egypt attains his own
personal גְּאֻלָּה, salvation: an overwhelming closeness to God. That is
why our Sages have ordained that our
daily prayer be preceded by the recollection of our deliverance from Egypt
(סוֹמֵךְ גְּאֻלָּה לִתְפִילָּה); this enables us to
offer our prayer in the right manner,
and make it worthy of acceptance
(□ *Rabbi Joseph Breuer*). In the same

1. '*In the middle of the night I will rise to thank you for the judgments of your kindness*'
(*Tehillim* 119:62).
     Even in the midst of the nights of exile we rise again — thanks to the lessons taught to us by
the *Pesach* observances, ordained by God's kindness.

*our fathers did the Holy One, blessed be He, redeem,
but He also redeemed us with them, for so it says:
"And He brought us out from there, so that He might
bring us and give us the land which He had promised
to our fathers."*

The *Matzos* are now covered and the cup is lifted till after the *Brachah* אֲשֶׁר
גְּאָלָנוּ (some put the cup down and uncover the *Matzos* before they start הַלְלוּ,
הַלְלוּ, and pick it up again, covering the *Matzos*, when they reach the *Brachah*
אֲשֶׁר גְּאָלָנוּ).

T*herefore it is our duty to thank, to praise, to laud,
to glorify, to exalt, to honor, to bless, to extol and
give respect to Him who performed all these miracles
for our fathers and for us. He has brought us forth
from slavery to freedom, from sorrow to joy, from*

way, our experience of the Exodus, on
Seder night, leads us logically to praise
God by reciting *Hallel.*

The *Haggadah* here uses nine expressions of praise followed at the end of the
passage, by a tenth one, *'let us recite a
new song before Him, Hallelujah!'*
These ten expressions follow the example of the book of *Tehillim* which also
makes use of ten terms of praise to the
Almighty; this tenfold praise is offered
for the ten emanations (סְפִירוֹת),
through which God governs the world,
according to the teachings of the *Kabbalah.* Such elaborate homage to God is
usually frowned upon as presumptuous,
but it is in place on *Seder* night because
on this night we see ourselves as
the direct recipients of His miraculous
help (see p. 75).

The *Vilna Gaon* explains that the first
nine expressions of praise represent our
response to the first nine plagues, and
the last expression, which introduces
Hallel, corresponds to the tenth plague.
Hallel can only be said for a deliverance
that is complete and final; the Jews attained such salvation only with the last
plague. They ceased being slaves of
Pharoah and instead became servants of
God.

The *Haggadah* here enumerates five
stages of deliverance: the emergence
from slavery to freedom, from sorrow to
joy, from mourning to festivity, from
darkness to a great light, and from
enslavement to redemption. The *Vilna
Gaon* sees these five stages as describing
the progress from Egyptian bondage to
the time of King Solomon who built the
Temple. Some commentators, however,
have taken these five stages as descrip-
tions of our deliverance from the five
exiles imposed upon the Jews: we were
brought from the slavery of Egypt to
the freedom of the Exodus; from the
sorrow of the Babylonian destruction of
the First Temple to the joy of building
the Second Temple; from the mourning
under the Persians (as mentioned in
Megillas Esther) to the festivity of
Purim; from the darkness of Greek rule,
which sought to stamp out Torah observance, to the light of *Chanukah;* and we
will advance from the enslavement of
our present exile to the final redemption
(*Ma'aseh Nissim*). In keeping with this
interpretation it has been suggested that
the Four Cups ordained by our sages for
the *Seder* may correspond to the four
exiles from which we have already been
redeemed; the fifth cup, that of Elijah, is

מִיָּגוֹן לְשִׂמְחָה וּמֵאֵבֶל לְיוֹם טוֹב וּמֵאֲפֵלָה לְאוֹר גָּדוֹל וּמִשִּׁעְבּוּד לִגְאֻלָּה וְנֹאמַר לְפָנָיו שִׁירָה חֲדָשָׁה הַלְלוּיָהּ:

תהלים
קיג

°הַלְלוּיָהּ הַלְלוּ עַבְדֵי יהוה הַלְלוּ אֶת שֵׁם יהוה: יְהִי שֵׁם יהוה מְבֹרָךְ. מֵעַתָּה וְעַד־עוֹלָם: מִמִּזְרַח שֶׁמֶשׁ עַד־מְבוֹאוֹ מְהֻלָּל שֵׁם יהוה: רָם עַל־כָּל־גּוֹיִם יהוה. עַל הַשָּׁמַיִם כְּבוֹדוֹ: מִי כַּיהוה אֱלֹהֵינוּ. הַמַּגְבִּיהִי

not drunk, however, for we still await redemption from our present exile.

שִׁירָה חֲדָשָׁה — *A new song.* The song that will be sung at the Messianic redemption is called שִׁיר (*song,* in the masculine form; see, for instance, the blessing on p.154). Until that time all songs are called שִׁירָה, in the feminine form — they cannot be sung with full force, for our joy is not yet complete, and new troubles still follow the periods of deliverance (*Tosfos*).[1] The שִׁירָה חֲדָשָׁה 'new song' of our passage is feminine and therefore obviously does not refer to Messianic times but to the praise offered to God at the Exodus. According to some opinions, we should therefore read וְנֶאֱמַר, *it was recited,* rather than וְנֹאמַר, *we shall recite* (*Mishnah Berurah*); others read, *we shall recite,* but omit the words, *a new song* (*Lubavitch Haggadah*). However, our version is generally accepted; it means to say that *we shall sing the new song of the time of the Exodus,* never sung before, namely *Hallel.* (Some commentators explain the phrase '*new song*' differently: it was indeed sung at the Exodus but it should be like new for us since we have to view

ourselves as having just gone out of Egypt.)

Since לְפִיכָךְ introduces *Hallel,* we lift our cup for it, and keep it in our hand till we drink it after the final blessing over the *Haggadah,* for אֵין אוֹמְרִים שִׁירָה אֶלָּא עַל הַיַּיִן, *a song must be recited over wine* (*Brachos* 35a), and so must the final blessing over the *Haggadah* be said with cup in hand. As explained earlier, we must cover the *Matzah* whenever we hold the cup, and it therefore has to be covered from לְפִיכָךְ till we drink. (However, according to some opinions, the psalms of *Hallel* should be recited over the *Matzah;* according to them we would therefore put down the cup after לְפִיכָךְ, and uncover the *Matzah,* till we reach the final blessing over the *Haggadah.*)

הַלְלוּיָהּ הַלְלוּ עַבְדֵי ה' — *Hallelujah! Praise, you servants of HASHEM.* According to the *Talmud Yerushalmi (Pesachim* 5:5), when the firstborn were slain in the night of *Pesach,* Pharaoh tried to get the Jews to leave at once by declaring them free: 'Until now you were servants of Pharaoh, now you are servants of HASHEM!' The Jews responded by ex-

---

1. The song sung upon the redemption from Egypt is called שִׁירָה, in the feminine form of this word, whereas the song of the future redemption is called שִׁיר, in the masculine form. The redemption from Egypt was in the merit of the righteous women of the time; but the Messianic redemption will be due to the men (*Ahavas Jonathan*).

mourning to festivity, from darkness to bright light, and from bondage to redemption! Therefore let us recite a new song before Him. Hallelujah!

Hallelujah! *Praise, you servants of HASHEM, praise the name of HASHEM! Blessed be the name of HASHEM from this time forth and forever. From the rising of the sun unto its setting HASHEM's name is praised. HASHEM is high above all nations, His glory is above the heavens. Who is like HASHEM, our God*

claiming, 'Hallelujah! Praise, you servants of HASHEM ... '

This account is the basis for the view of *Rashbam* that the Jews recited הָא לַחְמָא עַנְיָא at the time of the Exodus, concluding with the words, 'yesterday we were slaves, today we are free; today we are here, next year in the land of Israel' — see above, p. 69.

On *Seder* night we now reiterate the praise of God that the Jews voiced at the Exodus, since we do view ourselves as also having been redeemed. That explains why we recite psalms of *Hallel* even though *Hallel* is normally not said at night. Daylight is the time when we can see God's kindness in action and sing His praises; night usually stands for trepidation and calls for faith rather than jubilation (see above, p. 79). The night of *Pesach*, however, is different from all other nights of the year. God *'lit up the night like day'* (Tehillim 139:12) through His great self-revelation, and so it is appropriate that we should say *Hallel*. In fact, according to one view, it is through the recitation of *Hallel* that we fulfill the obligation לְסַיֵם בְּשֶׁבַח, to end the story of the Exodus with praise.

There are other unusual aspects to the recitation of *Hallel* at the *Seder*. In contrast to the normal practice, we sit while reciting it — a sign of our dignity as free men (*Maharam Rothenburg*). We divide it into two parts, of which the first is said before the meal and the se-

cond one afterwards. By bracketing the *Seder* meal between hymns of praise to God, we mark it as an act of Divine service rather than an ordinary supper (*Netziv*).

Also, the first section of *Hallel* deals with the deliverance from Egypt, and therefore belongs to the part of the *Seder* preceding the meal; the second section looks ahead to the Messianic redemption, which is the theme of the *Seder* after the meal (*Overview*, p. 34).

Usually we preface *Hallel* with a blessing to God who commanded us לִקְרֹא אֶת הַהַלֵּל, to read the *Hallel*. Since we divide it on *Pesach* night, there exists a view that the second section should be introduced by a separate blessing to God for having commanded us לִגְמוֹר אֶת הַהַלֵּל, to complete the *Hallel* (*Shibolei Haleket*). However, our practice is not to say any blessing at all — because *Hallel* is divided (*Rav Zemach Gaon*); or because the recitation of *Hallel* on *Pesach* night is not in the nature of a scriptural reading but a hymn of praise (*Rav Hai Gaon*); or because in general, *Hallel*, as a formal commandment rather than our personal expression of joy, is only found in daytime (*Chidushey HaRim*). It has, however, been suggested that לְפִיכָךְ serves as an introductory blessing for *Hallel* (*Orchos Chaim*).

עַל הַשָּׁמַיִם כְּבוֹדוֹ — *His glory is above the heavens.* The first psalm of *Hallel* (Tehillim 113) is not only devoted to our praise of God — it emphasizes the difference between our concept of Him, and that held by the rest of the world.

לָשָׁבֶת. הַמַּשְׁפִּילִי לִרְאוֹת בַּשָּׁמַיִם וּבָאָרֶץ:
מְקִימִי מֵעָפָר דָּל. מֵאַשְׁפֹּת יָרִים אֶבְיוֹן:
לְהוֹשִׁיבִי עִם־נְדִיבִים. עִם נְדִיבֵי עַמּוֹ: מוֹשִׁיבִי
עֲקֶרֶת הַבַּיִת אֵם־הַבָּנִים שְׂמֵחָה הַלְלוּיָהּ:

° תהלים
קיד

°בְּצֵאת יִשְׂרָאֵל מִמִּצְרָיִם בֵּית יַעֲקֹב מֵעַם
לֹעֵז: הָיְתָה יְהוּדָה לְקָדְשׁוֹ
יִשְׂרָאֵל מַמְשְׁלוֹתָיו: הַיָּם רָאָה וַיָּנֹס. הַיַּרְדֵּן
יִסֹּב לְאָחוֹר: הֶהָרִים רָקְדוּ כְאֵילִים. גְּבָעוֹת
כִּבְנֵי צֹאן: מַה לְּךָ הַיָּם כִּי תָנוּס. הַיַּרְדֵּן תִּסֹּב
לְאָחוֹר: הֶהָרִים תִּרְקְדוּ כְאֵילִים. גְּבָעוֹת כִּבְנֵי
צֹאן: מִלְּפְנֵי אָדוֹן חוּלִי אָרֶץ. מִלְּפְנֵי אֱלוֹהַּ
יַעֲקֹב: הַהֹפְכִי הַצּוּר אֲגַם מָיִם. חַלָּמִישׁ
לְמַעְיְנוֹ מָיִם:

בָּרוּךְ אַתָּה יהוה אֱלֹהֵינוּ מֶלֶךְ הָעוֹלָם
אֲשֶׁר גְּאָלָנוּ וְגָאַל אֶת אֲבוֹתֵינוּ

The nations at best recognize God's glory as being above the heavens but they do not concede to Him any role in their earthly affairs — these they pursue in whatever way their desires and ambitions move them. We, however, understand that even though He is enthroned on high, He looks down upon the earth, governs our destinies, and demands our loyalty. Pharaoh did not understand this; he asked: 'Who is God that I should listen to His voice?' (Shemos 5:2). The fall of his mighty empire, and the triumph of a small band of slaves, provided the answer (Rabbi S.R. Hirsch).

בְּצֵאת יִשְׂרָאֵל — When Israel went out. The liberation of the Jews, as God's people, was a turning point in world history. They had dwelt in Egypt, a state that worshipped the power of nature and man, but they emerged as the people of Israel, dedicated to God's rule. Having lived amidst a people of alien culture, they emerged as the House of Jacob, in moral and spiritual purity. The entire physical universe sensed the significance of this event, and trembled before God; for at this moment He stood revealed before the world as its master. The deliverance of the Jews demonstrated God's omnipotence — and henceforth they would uphold the teachings of the God of Jacob in front of all the nations (Rabbi S.R. Hirsch).

אֲשֶׁר גְּאָלָנוּ — Who redeemed us. Before, in the passage beginning לְפִיכָךְ, we spoke of God as having performed

*who is enthroned on high, but looks down so low
upon the heavens and the earth! He raises up the
poor out of the dust, lifts up the needy from the
dunghill, in order to seat him with princes, with the
princes of His people; He turns the barren woman of
the house into a joyful mother of children! Hallelujah!*

When Israel went out of Egypt, the house of Jacob
*from a people of alien tongue, Judah became His
sanctuary, Israel His dominion. The sea saw it and
fled, the Jordan turned back. The mountains skipped
like rams, the hills like young lambs. What ails you,
O sea, that you flee, O Jordan, that you turn back,
you mountains, that you skip like rams, you hills,
like young lambs? Tremble, O earth, before the
Master, before the God of Jacob, who turns the rock
into a pool of water, the flint into a spring of water.*

*Blessed are you, HASHEM our God, King of the
universe, who redeemed us and redeemed our fathers*

miracles for our fathers and for us; here
we mention our redemption before that
of our fathers. The reason is clear:
before, we simply recounted the events,
and the miracles did happen, in the first
place, to our fathers. Here, however, we
sing of our gratitude; then it is our
redemption that must concern us most
(*Chasam Sofer*).

This blessing concludes *Maggid*.
Thus it is primarily meant to give
thanks for our redemption from Egypt,
which has been the theme of the *Seder*
up to this point, and in memory of
which we eat *Matzah* and *Maror*. That
is why the conclusion of the blessing is
couched in the past tense — thanking
God '*who has redeemed Israel*'.
However, the fact that we do not have a
Pesach sacrifice prompts us to add to
this blessing our prayers for the
ultimate redemption which is still to

come, when we will be able once again
to offer sacrifices.

It has also been suggested that the
mention of the deliverance from Egypt
leads us to look ahead to the final
redemption — for *Pesach* is זְמַן חֵרוּתֵנוּ,
the season of our liberation, and all later
redemptions are foreshadowed in the
redemption from Egypt. In the times of
the Temple, the entire second part of
this blessing, referring to the future
redemption, was not said; it ended with
the words, ' ... to eat on it *Pesach*, *Matzoh* and *Maror*. Blessed are You,
HASHEM who has redeemed Israel.'

On *Chanukah* and *Purim* we recite the
blessing שֶׁעָשָׂה נִסִּים לַאֲבוֹתֵינוּ, to thank God
for the miracles that He did for our
forefather at this time; the miracles of the Exodus were certainly even greater, and we
should therefore recite this blessing on
Pesach too. The *Rokeach* explains, however,

מִמִּצְרַיִם וְהִגִּיעָנוּ הַלַּיְלָה הַזֶּה לֶאֱכָל־בּוֹ מַצָּה
וּמָרוֹר. כֵּן יהוה אֱלֹהֵינוּ וֵאלֹהֵי אֲבוֹתֵינוּ יַגִּיעֵנוּ
לְמוֹעֲדִים וְלִרְגָלִים אֲחֵרִים הַבָּאִים לִקְרָאתֵנוּ
לְשָׁלוֹם שְׂמֵחִים בְּבִנְיַן עִירֶךָ וְשָׂשִׂים בַּעֲבוֹדָתֶךָ
וְנֹאכַל שָׁם מִן הַזְּבָחִים וּמִן הַפְּסָחִים (יש אומרים
במוצאי שבת: מִן הַפְּסָחִים וּמִן הַזְּבָחִים) אֲשֶׁר יַגִּיעַ
דָּמָם עַל קִיר מִזְבַּחֲךָ לְרָצוֹן וְנוֹדֶה לְךָ שִׁיר
חָדָשׁ עַל גְּאֻלָּתֵנוּ וְעַל פְּדוּת נַפְשֵׁנוּ. בָּרוּךְ אַתָּה
יהוה גָּאַל יִשְׂרָאֵל:

כָּל הַמְסֻבִּים מְסִבִּים עַל שְׂמֹאלָם וְשׁוֹתִים כָּל הַכּוֹס אוֹ לְכָל הַפָּחוֹת רֻבּוֹ
שֶׁל כּוֹס שֵׁנִי מֵאַרְבַּע כּוֹסוֹת אַחַר אֲמִירַת בְּרָכָה זוֹ:

בָּרוּךְ אַתָּה יהוה אֱלֹהֵינוּ מֶלֶךְ הָעוֹלָם
בּוֹרֵא פְּרִי הַגָּפֶן:

that the blessing which concludes — מַגִּיד אֲשֶׁר גְּאָלָנוּ — has the purpose of thanking God for the redemption from Egypt, and therefore no additional blessing is required. The *Maharil* takes the view that the blessing שֶׁעָשָׂה נִסִּים was only introduced for holidays of Rabbinic origin. The reason may be that on the Biblically ordained *Yomim Tovim* we have instead the *Kiddush*, as a way of acknowledging God's sanctification of the day; or it may be that the Biblical holidays, though related to certain historical experiences, have a sanctity that was ordained by God even before the world's creation, and is therefore not due to events 'in those days at this time' (*Sfas Emes*).

הַלַּיְלָה הַזֶּה—*On this night.* Some versions of the *Haggadah* have לַלַּיְלָה הַזֶּה, 'to this night;' also, some *Haggados*, have הַגִּיעָנוּ, 'bring us,' instead of יַגִּיעֵנוּ, 'may He bring us.'

It is noteworthy that we thank God for giving us the opportunity to eat *Matzah* and *Maror* tonight; it is not the pleasures of the *Yomtov* for which we are grateful but the chance to fulfill God's commandments (*Malbim*).

לְמוֹעֲדִים וְלִרְגָלִים אֲחֵרִים — *To other festivals and holidays.* מוֹעֲדִים, 'festivals' here refers to *Rosh Hashanah* and *Yom Kippur*, while רְגָלִים 'holidays' refers to the pilgrim festivals, *Pesach, Shavuos* and *Sukkos* (*Abarbanel*).

מִן הַזְּבָחִים וּמִן הַפְּסָחִים — *Of the sacrifices and Pesach offerings.* The term 'sacrifices' here refers to the חֲגִיגָה, *festival offering,* that was required on *Pesach* as on the other *pilgrim festivals, Shavuos* and *Sukkos.* It is mentioned before the *Pesach offering* because the latter was eaten last (*Pesachim* 119b), so that its taste would remain in our mouths — or so, that our appetite would already be sated, and we would not come to break its bones, to extract the

from Egypt and brought us, on this night, to eat Mat-
zah and Maror. Thus may HASHEM, our God and
God of our fathers, bring us to future festivals and
holidays that may come to us in peace, when we shall
rejoice in the rebuilding of Your city and shall be
joyful in Your Temple service; and there we shall
partake of the sacrifices and Pesach offerings (on
Saturday nights some say: *of the Pesach offerings and*
sacrifices) *whose blood will be sprinkled upon the sides*
of Your altar for gracious acceptance. Then we shall
thank You with a new song for our redemption and
for the deliverance of our souls. Blessed are You,
HASHEM, who has redeemed Israel.

All participants now lean on their left side and drink all, or at least most, of the
second cup, after reciting this *Brachah:*

B *lessed are You, HASHEM our God, King of the*
universe, who creates the fruit of the vine.

marrow, out of hunger (*Yerushalmi
Pesachim* 6:4; see p. 163).

The *Maharil* points out that the
festival offering was only slaughtered
on the day before *Pesach* if this was a
weekday; if it was a *Shabbos*, however,
the festival sacrifice was offered on the
first day of *Pesach*, rather than on the
eve of the festival. Therefore the
Maharil suggests that, whenever the
day before *Pesach* is a *Shabbos*, we
should reverse the order and say מִן
הַפְּסָחִים וּמִן הַזְּבָחִים because in such a
case the *Pesach* would be eaten before
the festival sacrifice which would only
be offered the next day. However,
others disagree with the *Maharil* and
make no change, for the blessing does
not refer to *this* year's *Pesach* at all but
to next year when *Pesach* eve is not going to be on a *Shabbos*. Moreover, even
if next year's *Pesach* would start on
Sunday, according to our calendar, this
might still be changed if the Temple is
rebuilt, for then our calendar will no
longer be valid. Instead, the recon-
stituted Sanhedrin will have to deter-
mine how the holidays fall, one month
at a time.

עַל גְּאֻלָתֵנוּ וְעַל פְּדוּת נַפְשֵׁנוּ — *For our
redemption and for the deliverance of
our souls* — The term 'redemption' here
refers to the physical liberation of the
Jewish people, and 'the deliverance of
our souls' refers to the spiritual liberation. We mentioned previously that the
Exodus marked a twofold redemption
(see *Overview* p. 32), for which we here
give thanks.

[155]   *The Haggadah*

רָחְצָה

הכל נוטלים ידיהם (מביאים מים לאב ליטול מהם) ומברכים:

בָּרוּךְ אַתָּה יהוה אֱלֹהֵינוּ מֶלֶךְ הָעוֹלָם
אֲשֶׁר קִדְּשָׁנוּ בְּמִצְוֹתָיו וְצִוָּנוּ עַל־
נְטִילַת יָדָיִם:

כמו בכל סעודה אין להפסיק בין ברכת **עַל נְטִילַת יָדַיִם** לאכילת המצה. אין
להפסיק שלא לצורך עד לאחר אכילת הכורך מכיון שהברכה **עַל אֲכִילַת**
מַצָּה שייכת גם למצה שבכורך.

מוֹצִיא

האב לוקח כל המצות (שתי השלימות והפרוסה שביניהן) ומברך ברכת
הַמּוֹצִיא ויכוון להוציא בזה כל המסובים.

בָּרוּךְ אַתָּה יהוה אֱלֹהֵינוּ מֶלֶךְ הָעוֹלָם
הַמּוֹצִיא לֶחֶם מִן־הָאָרֶץ:

מַצָּה

יניח מצה השלישית להשמט מידו ויברך **עַל אֲכִילַת מַצָּה.** יכוון לפטור
בברכה זו גם המצה שבכורך והאפיקומן. טוב גם כאן להוציא כל המסובין
בברכתו. יבצע מהשלימה העליונה ומהפרוסה ונותן לכל המסובים שיעור
מספיק מהן. אוכלים בהסיבה תוך זמן הקצוב.

בָּרוּךְ אַתָּה יהוה אֱלֹהֵינוּ מֶלֶךְ הָעוֹלָם
אֲשֶׁר קִדְּשָׁנוּ בְּמִצְוֹתָיו וְצִוָּנוּ עַל־
אֲכִילַת מַצָּה:

* *Blessing for bread* — On *Shabbos* and *Yom Tov* this blessing is always recited over 'Lechem Mishneh', two whole loaves. We therefore have two unbroken *Matzos* before us on the *Seder* plate, over which to recite the *Motzi*. The broken *Matzah*, on the other hand, represents the 'bread of poverty' and is the subject of the next blessing. There is an opinion, however, that on *Seder* night a broken *Matzah* is most appropriate and should be used as one of the 'Lechem Mishneh' loaves. To satisfy all opinions we therefore recite the *Motzi* over all three *Matzos* — two whole and one broken.

* *Blessing for Matzah* — According to most authorities, this blessing refers specifically to the broken *Matzah*. There exists an opinion, however, that it should be recited over a whole *Matzah*. Therefore we pronounce it over the broken *Matzah* as well as the top *Matzah* which is whole.

We do not recite the blessing שֶׁהֶחֱיָנוּ, *that God has kept us alive*, which we usually pronounce when fulfilling a commandment that is performed seasonally. The reason is that we already recited the blessing as part of the *Kiddush*, and had in mind that it would refer to all observances of the

Rachtzah / Wash the Hands

All participants wash their hands (the father has the washbasin brought to him);
then the following blessing is said.

Blessed are You, HASHEM our God, King of the universe, who has sanctified us by His commandments and has commanded us concerning the washing of the hands.

As at every meal, it is not permitted to interrupt, by talking or otherwise, between the washing of the hands and the eating of the *Matzah*. Moreover, the blessing which we say over the *Matzah* also refers to the *Matzah* that we shall eat together with *Maror*, as a 'sandwich'; therefore one should wait until after the eating of the 'sandwich' before saying or doing anything not required for the observances that are being carried out.

Motzi / Say Blessing for Bread*...

The father takes into his hands the two whole *Matzos* and the broken *Matzah* that lies between them; and he pronounces the following blessing for himself and all participants.

Blessed are You, HASHEM our God, King of the universe, who brings forth bread from the earth.

Matzah / Say Blessing for Matzah and eat*

The father now lets the lowest *Matzah* slip from his hands and pronounces the following blessing — for himself and, preferably, also for the other participants — over the two other *Matzos* (in reciting it, he should also have in mind the *Matzah* of the 'sandwich' and the *Afikoman*).

Blessed are You, HASHEM our God, King of the universe, who has sanctified us by His commandments and has commanded us concerning the eating of *Matzah*.

Then he breaks both *Matzos* and takes for himself — and gives to all participants — appropriate portions from both *Matzos*.* He eats them together, while

evening. Moreover, *Avudraham* also points out that, at the conclusion of *Maggid* (p.154), we specifically thanked God that He had brought us, this night, to eat *Matzah* and *Maror*. This is the same as the thought expressed by שֶׁהֶחֱיָנוּ, that *'He has kept us alive.'* There is therefore no need to recite such a blessing at this point.

* *Appropriate portions from both Matzos* — The two *Matzos* have different functions, as noted above. One represents לֶחֶם מִשְׁנֶה, the required double loaves, over which we recited the blessing for bread; the other *Matzah*, over which the second blessing was recited, is meant for the fulfillment of the obligation to eat *Matzah*. We should

מָרוֹר

האב לוקח כְּזַיִת מָרוֹר וטובלו בַחֲרוֹסֶת ומנער החרוסת ממנו. וכן יעשה עבור כל המסובים. אחר הברכה אוכלים מרור בלי הסיבה ואין לשהות באכילתו. בברכה יש לכוון לפטור גם אכילת מרור שבכורך.

בָּרוּךְ אַתָּה יהוה אֱלֹהֵינוּ מֶלֶךְ הָעוֹלָם אֲשֶׁר קִדְּשָׁנוּ בְּמִצְוֹתָיו וְצִוָּנוּ עַל־אֲכִילַת מָרוֹר:

therefore eat from both *Matzos* at the same time.

The Torah commands us to 'eat' *Matzah*. Generally, the obligation to 'eat' requires that at least the equivalent of one olive be consumed. It is recommended, therefore, that this amount be eaten from each *Matzah* — a total of *two* olives. One has fulfilled his minimum obligation, however, if he ate the equivalent of one olive from both *Matzos* together.

We explained previously (p. 47) that there are different opinions concerning the size of a piece of *Matzah* that would be equal to an olive. If a person wants to eat the equivalent of only one olive, he is well advised to follow a more stringent opinion, in order to be sure that he adequately fulfilled the Biblical commandment of eating *Matzah*. However, if he wants to eat the equivalent of two olives, he may rely on a more lenient opinion concerning the size of an olive: since he eats twice this minimum amount, he is sure to fulfill the Biblical commandment, because his 'two olives' will be a greater amount than even the most stringent interpretaton of the amount required for a single olive. (This is the basis for the ruling of Rabbi Moshe Feinstein quoted on p. 48.)

* *Within the allotted time-span* — The duty of eating *Matzah*, rather than just nibbling, requires that we consume it promptly, without delay or interruption. There are different views of how much time is allowed for eating a כְּזַיִת, the equivalent of an olive. In the case of the Biblical commandment of *Matzah*, it should be eaten within two, three, or four minutes (these are the respective opinions of the *Chasam Sofer*, *Rabbi Moshe Feinstein*, the *Aruch Hashulchan*, and the *Chazon Ish*). For eating more than one כְּזַיִת, proportionately more time may, of course, be allowed.

The father cannot eat his *Matzah* and at the same time give the other participants their portions. Therefore he usually distributes their portions after reciting the blessings but before starting to eat.

[It is noteworthy that the *Chasam Sofer* used to give the participants their portions after the first blessing but before the second one (which was recited by every participant for himself). This was the procedure of *Rav Saadiah Gaon*.]

Because the *Matzos* on the *Seder* plate do not normally suffice for all participants, the father gives every participant a small piece from each of the two *Matzos* and completes the required amount with other *Matzos*. This process can be speeded up by preparing before the *Seder* measured portions of *Matzah* for each participant; at the

reclining, within the allotted time-span,* and so do the other participants.

According to most opinions, the *Matzah* is not dipped in salt* before it is eaten.

Maror / Say Blessing for Maror and eat

The father takes a quantity of *Maror* equivalent to an olive, dips it into the *Charoses*,* then shakes off any *Charoses* that remained on it. He does the same for the other participants. The following blessing is recited (having in mind also the *Maror* that will be eaten as part of the 'sandwich'). Then the *Maror* is eaten without reclining. It should be chewed before swallowing, and should be eaten without delay or interruption.

B*lessed are You, HASHEM our God, King of the universe, who has sanctified us by His commandments and has commanded us concerning the eating of Maror.*

Seder, the father only needs to add small pieces from his *Matzos* to everybody's portion (see *Moadim Uzmanim*).

* *Not dipped in salt* — Matzah, like any bread baked from pure white flour, does not require dipping in salt (*Remah*). Moreover, the *Maharal* suggests that we do not want to take away from the taste of the *Matzah*, out of love for the commandment. The *Levush* stresses that *Matzah* is the 'bread of affliction,' and it would therefore be inappropriate to indulge by eating it with salt.

[It should be noted, however, that the *Ari Hakadosh* used to dip the *Matzah* in salt; and the *Rambam* states that the *Matzah* should be dipped in *Charoses* — an opinion stemming from the *Gaonim* but not adopted by the *Halachah*.]

* *Dips it into the Charoses* — According to one Talmudic opinion, (*Pesachim* 114a) the *Charoses* is merely used as an antidote for the poisonous bitterness of the *Maror*. It should not, however, remove the bitter taste of the *Maror* altogether, and therefore we shake off the *Charoses* before we eat the *Maror*. The Talmud also emphasizes that the *Maror* should not be swallowed without first being chewed (*Pesachim* 115b).

Another Talmudic opinion holds that the dipping into *Charoses* does not only have health reasons but is a religious obligation: the *Charoses*, symbolic of mortar, is to remind us of the brickmaking in Egypt. We take the second view; but we do not pronounce a blessing over *Charoses* because it is not a separate duty but part of the obligation to eat *Maror* (*Avudraham*).

[Since the dipping of the *Maror* in *Charoses* is part of the obligation to eat *Maror*, the *Maharil* recited the blessing over the *Maror* before he dipped it into the *Charoses*. Similarly, he recited the blessing for the *Karpas* before he dipped it into saltwater; in this case, too, he considered the dipping a part of the custom of eating *Karpas*.]

Before eating *Maror* we do not recite בּוֹרֵא פְּרִי הָאֲדָמָה, the blessing usually pronounced before eating produce of the field. The reason is that we recited it before eating *Karpas* and, at that time, had the *Maror* in mind. However, even if we forgot to think of *Maror* then, we need not repeat this blessing now. We can rely on the opinion of the *Vilna Gaon* that the *Maror* does not require such a blessing at all because it is eaten after the *Matzah*, and therefore is exempt from a blessing, like all foods that are eaten as part of a meal.

כּוֹרֵךְ

האב לוקח כזית ממצה השלישית שנשארה שלימה עם כזית מרור וטובל המרור בחרוסת ומנערו ונותן לכל אחד מהמסובים. כורכים המרור במצה ואוכלים בהסיבה בלי שהייה אחר שאומרים:

זֵכֶר לְמִקְדָּשׁ כְּהִלֵּל. כֵּן עָשָׂה הִלֵּל בִּזְמַן שֶׁבֵּית הַמִּקְדָּשׁ הָיָה קַיָם. הָיָה כּוֹרֵךְ פֶּסַח מַצָּה וּמָרוֹר וְאוֹכֵל בְּיַחַד. לְקַיֵם מַה שֶּׁנֶּאֱמַר° עַל־מַצּוֹת וּמְרֹרִים יֹאכְלֻהוּ:

° במדבר
ט:יא

שֻׁלְחָן עוֹרֵךְ

אוכלים הסעודה בשמחה ובכובד ראש. יש מדקדקים להסב בשעת אכילה. נוהגים להתחיל בביצה מבושלת. אין לאכול בשר צלי בליל הסדר. יש נוהגים שלא לאכול דבר הטבול. אין להאריך בסעודה כדי שיאכלו האפיקומן לפני חצות הלילה. גם מדקדקים שלא לאכול יותר מדאי כדי שלא יאכלו האפיקומן אכילה גסה, או שירדמו קודם גמר הסדר.

* *Third Matzah* — This *Matzah* is the only one of the father's three *Matzos* which was not yet broken for any of the observances of the *Seder*. We therefore utilize it for the 'sandwich', so that it too should be used for a *Mitzvah*. It will usually not be sufficient by itself, however, to provide adequate portions for all *Seder* participants. Therefore additional *Matzos* should be used to supplement the pieces of the third *Matzah* that they receive.

* *Eaten together* — In contrast to the other Sages, *Hillel* took the view that the *Pesach* offering, *Matzah* and *Maror* must be eaten in one sandwich rather than separately.

Since the destruction of the Temple, we do not have a *Pesach* offering, and the eating of *Maror* (in the absence of a *Pesach* offering) is no longer Biblically required but only by the Rabbis; *Matzah*, on the other hand, has remained a Biblical duty ('*In the evening you shall eat Matzos*', *Shemos* 12:18). Therefore even Hillel would agree that nowadays *Matzah* and *Maror* should be eaten separately.

However, we want to preserve a reminder of Hillel's practice during the time of the Temple, since the Talmud does not give a decision as to whether Hillel was to be followed, or the other Sages. Therefore, we now eat *Matzah* and *Maror* together, even though we already ate them separately and recited the required blessings over them. Since the 'sandwich' is only a reminder, however, one does not have to pronounce a blessing over it — even if he forgot to have it in mind when he recited the blessings over *Matzah* and *Maror*.

According to the *Shulchan Aruch Harav*, the 'sandwich' is not merely a reminder of Temple times, but (according to Hillel) is required today too. Hillel would agree that *Matzah*, as a Biblical commandment, has to be eaten separately nowadays — but not so *Maror*. *Maror* was ordained by the Rabbis to perpetuate the practice of Temple times; and in those days, according to Hillel, *Matzah* was eaten with it. Therefore we should first

Korech / Eat Matzah and Maror Combined

The father takes a portion of *Maror* equivalent to an olive, together with a like portion of *Matzah* (from the so far unbroken third *Matzah** before him), and he also gives to all participants. The *Maror* is dipped into *Charoses*, then shaken off, and eaten together* with the *Matzah*, whilst reclining,* after the following has been recited. This 'sandwich', too, should be eaten promptly, without delay or interruption.

> **I** n remembrance of the Temple, according to the custom of Hillel. Thus did Hillel do at the time when the Temple was still standing. He would combine Pesach and Matzah, and Maror, and eat them together in order to fulfill what is written: "They shall eat it with unleavened bread and bitter herbs."

Shulchan Orech / Eat the Meal

*See comment- ary on next page

The meal should be eaten in joyous solemnity,* in keeping with the spirit of the *Seder*; it is desirable to recline while eating.
The common custom is to start with a hard-boiled egg.* The food should be festive; but roast meat must not be served on *Seder* night. There is a custom not to eat dipped food.
The meal should end in time for the *Afikoman* to be eaten before midnight.
Also, one should not eat so heavily that he will not have any appetite left for the *Afikoman*, or that he will be drowsy for the rest of the *Seder*.

eat *Matzah* by itself; and then *Matzah* together with *Maror*, to fulfill the Rabbinic ordinance.

* *Whilst reclining* — In the time of the Temple, Hillel did not eat *Matzah* and *Maror* separately at all but only together, as a 'sandwich'; therefore, he must have applied all the provisions connected with the eating of *Matzah* (like reclining) and of *Maror* (like dipping into *Charoses*) to the eating of the sandwich.

According to some opinions, however, the 'sandwich' should *not* be dipped into *Charoses*. The poison of the *Maror* is neutralized by the *Matzah*, and we already discharged the duty of dipping in *Charoses* when we ate the *Maror* alone; in fact, if we now dipped the 'sandwich', too, our *Seder* would feature three dippings, whereas we always only speak of two (*Ravioh*; see p. 70). However, the *Taz* rejects this argument: the dipping of the *Maror* and of the 'sandwich' must be counted as one for we only dip both

of them because we are in doubt as to which is *the* right way of eating *Maror*.

It should be noted that in the days of the Temple Hillel ate the 'sandwich' at the end of the meal, for it included the *Pesach* offering and this had to be eaten עַל הַשּׂוֹבַע, to make the person sated (*Mordechai*).

Since we do not have a *Pesach* sacrifice, we prefer to eat the 'sandwich' immediately after we ate *Matzah* and *Maror* separately. At the end of the meal we only eat the *Afikoman Matzah*, without requiring *Maror* with it (see p. 163).

פֶּסַח מַצָּה וּמָרוֹר — *Pesach offering, Matzah, and Maror*. This version reflects Hillel's practice (*Taz*). However, some authorities suggest that we should not mention the *Pesach* offering, since we are unable to follow Hillel's example and to include the *Pesach* sacrifice in our sandwich (*Chok Yakov*).

מהמצה המוצנעה נותנים לכל הפחות כזית (ולכתחילה שני זיתים) לכל
אחד מהמסובים ואוכלים בהסיבה בלי שהייה. רוב הפוסקים סוברים
שצריכים לאכול האפיקומן קודם חצות הלילה. לא יאכל שום דבר אחרי
אכילת אפיקומן ולא ישתה כי אם שתי כוסות הנשארות מארבע כוסות.
מותר לשתות תה, מים, וכדומה.

Actually, the verse that is here quoted as
the basis for Hillel's practice does not speak
about the regular *Pesach* offering, but about
פֶּסַח שֵׁנִי, the 'Second Pesach' observed thirty
days later, by people that did not bring the
Pesach offering at the proper time. Hillel may
have quoted this verse because it is clearer
than a similar passage that speaks of the
regular *Pesach* offering (*Shemos* 12:8):
'They shall eat the meat in this night, *roasted
on fire, and Matzos; with Maror they shall
eat it.*' This verse makes a distinction
between *Matzos* and *Maror*, to teach us that
on the regular *Pesach* we have to eat *Matzah*
even if we have no *Pesach* sacrifice, whilst
Maror does not have to be eaten without a
Pesach offering (*Reshash*). As a result, this
verse does not show clearly that, when we do
have *Pesach*, *Matzah*, and *Maror*, we have to
eat all of them combined. Hence, Hillel
quoted a verse that makes this quite clear (in
connection with the Second *Pesach* the
Torah did not have to differentiate between
Matzah and *Maror*, for on that day neither
had to be eaten if there was no *Pesach*
sacrifice).

* *In joyous solemnity* — The *Seder* meal
should not be viewed as an ordinary
repast; with its various observances it
constitutes a form of Divine service. We
quoted before (p. 151) the view of the
Netziv that this is why our Sages
divided the *Hallel* and bracketed the
meal between its two parts. In keeping
with the special character of the occasion, one should discuss the Exodus at
the table, sing זְמִירוֹת, hymns of praise
to God, and avoid idle talk (*Shloh*).

(Some authorities give a further reason
why we should not talk about matters un-
connected with the theme of the evening.
They hold that the blessing recited over the
Matzah at the beginning of the meal, is also
meant for the *Afikoman*; therefore we
should avoid unnecessary interruptions
between this blessing and the eating of the
Afikoman).

Since we do not have a *Pesach* offering,
many have the custom of at least
reading the details of the eating of the
Pesach sacrifice from the *Mishnah*.

* *A hard-boiled egg* — A number of
reasons have been offered for this
custom. At the first meal after a funeral,
the bereaved are usually offered an egg,
for it is a symbol of mourning. It has no
opening or mouth, just as a mourner is
struck dumb by his fate; at the same
time, however, it offers encouragement:
it signifies the turning of the wheel of
destiny which hopefully will bring joy
instead of sadness. There is a need for
this message on *Seder* night: the
absence of the *Pesach* offering evokes a
sense of mourning for the destroyed
Temple, particularly since the first
night of *Pesach* always falls on the same
day of the week as *Tishah Be'av*.
Moreover, it was on the fifteenth day of
Nissan that our father Abraham died
(*Pri Megadim*).

It has also been pointed out that it
was a pagan custom in Egypt not to eat
animal foods, and the eating of the egg
therefore symbolizes liberation from
Egypt (*Ibn Ezra*). Eggs, unlike other
food, get harder the longer they are
boiled, and thus can be taken as a symbol of how the Jews kept increasing the
more they were oppressed (*Chasam
Sofer*). Also, eggs signify the dawn of
life — just as the Exodus represented the
first beginnings of the Jewish people
(*Toras Emes*). The *Vilna Gaon* suggested that one should eat the egg from
the *Seder* plate (which represents the
Chagigah offering), as a reminder of the
Chagigah that was eaten at the *Seder*
meal.

* *Eat the Afikoman* — The name

Tzafun / Eat the Afikoman*

From the *Matzah* that he had hidden away the father takes the equivalent of one or, desirably, two olives,and also gives equal portions to the other *Seder* participants; they all eat while reclining, promptly and without delay or interruption. According to most authorities the *Afikoman* must be consumed before midnight. No food or drink may be taken after it except for the two cups of wine that must still be drunk (water, tea, or the like, are also permitted).

Afikoman was used for the dessert usually eaten at the end of a meal. Since the *Seder* meal must conclude with *Matzah*, no dessert can be eaten after it, and thus the *Matzah* itself came to be called *Afikoman*.

We are required to eat one כְּזַיִת, the equivalent of one olive, representing the *Pesach* sacrifice which had to be consumed at the end of the meal. It is recommended, however, to eat a second כְּזַיִת. According to most commentators, this is in memory of the *Matzah* that was consumed with the *Pesach* sacrifice; others suggest that it is in memory of the *Chagigah*, the festival offering, which was eaten prior to the *Pesach* sacrifice.

There are two opinions as to why our Sages ordained the eating of the *Afikoman*. The *Rosh* explains that it was instituted as a memorial to the *Pesach* offering. This had to be eaten at the end of the meal; one was not permitted to partake of it in more than one house; and nothing could be eaten after it. The reason for these rules, according to the *Yerushalmi*, was that otherwise one might eat the *Pesach* early in the meal, when he is still hungry, and might come to break the bones in order to suck the marrow — a violation of the Biblical law. Even though this reason does not apply to the *Matzah* that we eat in place of the *Pesach* offering, we must eat it under the same conditions, as a reminder of the *Pesach*. The Babylonian Talmud, however, gives another reason for these rules, which applies to *Matzah* too: we must eat the *Pesach* offering (or the *Matzah* that takes its place) at the end of the meal so that its taste should stay in our mouths. The *Rashbam* does not consider the *Afikoman* a reminder of the *Pesach* sacrifice but of the *Matzah* that was eaten with it. According to the *Rashbam*, in fact, the eating of this *Matzah*, as *Afikoman*, is the real fulfillment of our obligation to eat *Matzah*; hence,

it is particularly appropriate that we eat the *Afikoman* from the broken *Matzah* which was put aside, since this represents the לֶחֶם עוֹנִי. Of course, this *Matzah*, eaten together with the *Pesach*, had to be consumed under the same conditions — not only because the eating of the *Pesach* required these rules, but because the taste of the *Matzah* itself should stay in our mouths.

To satisfy both the view of the *Rosh* and the *Rambam*, it is therefore recommended to eat two portions of *Matzah* — one for the *Pesach* and one for the *Matzah* with it. Why, then, do we not also eat *Maror* with the *Matzah*? Since *Maror* is only rabbinically ordained, it was not considered necessary to impose this further requirement.

We should eat the *Afikoman* from that half of the broken *Matzah* that had been put aside — this represents the 'bread of affliction'. At the same time, however, our eating of the *Afikoman* completes the consumption of *this entire Matzah* and therefore serves as a symbol of our ultimate redemption from all affliction and oppression. Thus, the eating of the *Afikoman* in effect, introduces the second part of the *Seder* which is dedicated to the redemption to come.

It has, in fact, been suggested that the key to the future redemption lies in our keeping in our mouths the taste of the *Matzah*', the experience of the exile and redemption from Egypt. All the weaknesses of Egyptian society are still with us, and the lesson of the Ten Plagues has to be taken to heart, to prepare us for the Messianic age.

It should be noted that if the broken *Matzah* has been misplaced or mixed up with others, the *Afikoman* can be eaten from any *Matzah Shemurah* (see page 47). It should be eaten before midnight, as the *Pesach* sacrifice had to be eaten

מוזגים כוס שלישי. שרים **שיר המעלות** ומברכים ברכת המזון. כשיש
שלשה מברכים בזימון. נוהגים שהאב מברך.

° תהלים
קכו

°**שִׁיר** הַמַּעֲלוֹת בְּשׁוּב יהוה אֶת שִׁיבַת צִיּוֹן
הָיִינוּ כְּחֹלְמִים: אָז יִמָּלֵא שְׂחוֹק פִּינוּ
וּלְשׁוֹנֵנוּ רִנָּה אָז יֹאמְרוּ בַגּוֹיִם הִגְדִּיל יהוה
לַעֲשׂוֹת עִם אֵלֶּה: הִגְדִּיל יהוה לַעֲשׂוֹת עִמָּנוּ
הָיִינוּ שְׂמֵחִים: שׁוּבָה יהוה אֶת שְׁבִיתֵנוּ
כַּאֲפִיקִים בַּנֶּגֶב: הַזֹּרְעִים בְּדִמְעָה בְּרִנָּה יִקְצֹרוּ:
הָלוֹךְ יֵלֵךְ וּבָכֹה נֹשֵׂא מֶשֶׁךְ הַזָּרַע בֹּא־יָבֹא
בְרִנָּה נֹשֵׂא אֲלֻמֹּתָיו:

האב מתחיל:

רַבּוֹתַי נְבָרֵךְ:

האחרים עונים:

°יְהִי שֵׁם יהוה מְבֹרָךְ מֵעַתָּה וְעַד עוֹלָם:

תהלים
קיג:ב

האב עונה יהי שם וכו' וממשיך:
(אם נמצאים עשרה אנשים או יותר אומרים מה שמוקף בחצי עיגולים.)

בִּרְשׁוּת מָרָנָן וְרַבָּנָן וְרַבּוֹתַי נְבָרֵךְ (אֱלֹהֵינוּ) שֶׁאָכַלְנוּ מִשֶּׁלּוֹ:

האחרים עונים:

בָּרוּךְ (אֱלֹהֵינוּ) שֶׁאָכַלְנוּ מִשֶּׁלּוֹ וּבְטוּבוֹ חָיִינוּ:

האב:

בָּרוּךְ (אֱלֹהֵינוּ) שֶׁאָכַלְנוּ מִשֶּׁלּוֹ וּבְטוּבוֹ חָיִינוּ:

by that time (p. 78). However, if the
Seder runs late, it is absolutely essential
to make sure that at least the first Matzah is eaten before midnight.

* Recite Birchas Hamazon — It is a
Biblical commandment to give thanks to
God after we eat a meal: 'Even in the
midst of everyday circumstances, after
an ordinary meal, we are to preserve and
nurture in our hearts the conviction
which the miracle of the heavenly Manna
instilled in us in the wilderness; namely,
that each and every home and soul on
earth is favored by God's direct, immediate care and concern. Hence, we are
to look even upon a plain piece of bread
as no less a direct gift of God than the

Barech / Recite the Birchas Hamazon*

The third cup is poured, *Shir Hama'alos* is sung, and the father leads the recitation of *Birchas Hamazon*.

A Song of Ascents. When HASHEM brings back those returning to Zion, we will have been like dreamers. Then our mouth will be filled with laughter and our tongue with glad song. Then they will say among the nations: Great things has HASHEM done for these! Great things has HASHEM done for us, at which we rejoiced. Bring back, HASHEM, our prisoners, like brooks in the dry land. They that sow in tears, shall reap with glad song. The bearer of the measure of seed goes on his way weeping, but he will return with glad song, bearing his sheaves.

If at least three males, thirteen years or older, are present at the *Seder*, the father begins here:

Gentlemen, let us say Grace!

The others respond:

Blessed be the name of HASHEM from this time forth and for evermore!

The father repeats this, and then continues (including the words in parentheses if ten males, thirteen years or older, are present):

With your permission, let us praise (our God,) Him of whose store we have eaten!

The others respond:

Blessed be (our God,) He of whose store we have eaten and through whose goodness we live.

The father repeats:

Blessed be (our God,) He of whose store we have eaten and through whose goodness we live.

Manna ...' (Rabbi S.R. Hirsch).

Obviously, this everyday duty is of particular significance at the *Seder*.

During the year, it is left to us whether we will recite grace after meals over a cup of wine, giving it special impor-

אִם אֵין מְבָרְכִים בַּזִּימוּן מַתְחִילִים כָּאן:

בָּרוּךְ אַתָּה יהוה אֱלֹהֵינוּ מֶלֶךְ הָעוֹלָם הַזָּן אֶת־הָעוֹלָם כֻּלּוֹ בְּטוּבוֹ בְּחֵן בְּחֶסֶד וּבְרַחֲמִים הוּא °נוֹתֵן לֶחֶם לְכָל־בָּשָׂר כִּי לְעוֹלָם חַסְדּוֹ. וּבְטוּבוֹ הַגָּדוֹל תָּמִיד לֹא־חָסַר לָנוּ וְאַל־יֶחְסַר לָנוּ מָזוֹן לְעוֹלָם וָעֶד. בַּעֲבוּר שְׁמוֹ הַגָּדוֹל כִּי הוּא אֵל זָן וּמְפַרְנֵס לַכֹּל וּמֵטִיב לַכֹּל וּמֵכִין מָזוֹן לְכָל־בְּרִיּוֹתָיו אֲשֶׁר בָּרָא. בָּרוּךְ אַתָּה יהוה הַזָּן אֶת־הַכֹּל:

°תהלים
קלו:כה

נוֹדֶה לְךָ יהוה אֱלֹהֵינוּ עַל שֶׁהִנְחַלְתָּ לַאֲבוֹתֵינוּ אֶרֶץ חֶמְדָּה טוֹבָה וּרְחָבָה. וְעַל שֶׁהוֹצֵאתָנוּ יהוה אֱלֹהֵינוּ מֵאֶרֶץ מִצְרַיִם וּפְדִיתָנוּ מִבֵּית עֲבָדִים וְעַל בְּרִיתְךָ שֶׁחָתַמְתָּ בִּבְשָׂרֵנוּ וְעַל תּוֹרָתְךָ שֶׁלִּמַּדְתָּנוּ וְעַל חֻקֶּיךָ שֶׁהוֹדַעְתָּנוּ וְעַל חַיִּים חֵן וָחֶסֶד שֶׁחוֹנַנְתָּנוּ וְעַל אֲכִילַת מָזוֹן שָׁאַתָּה זָן וּמְפַרְנֵס אוֹתָנוּ תָּמִיד בְּכָל־יוֹם וּבְכָל עֵת וּבְכָל שָׁעָה:

tance. On *Seder* night, on the other hand, we are required to drink the third cup in connection with *Birchas Hamazon*. For the same reason, every effort should be made to have three males present, so that we can preface it with the special praise to God that is reserved for זמון, a group joining together to thank God for their meal.

The *Zohar* emphasizes the importance of guests at the *Seder* table. We should therefore make every effort, particularly on this night, to extend hospitality to those that need it (p. 68).

At the same time, this will provide the opportunity for זמון, the group recitation of grace, and also for reciting *Hallel* in the most meritorious manner (see p. 184).

Birchas Hamazon consists of several blessings: the first, הַזָּן אֶת הַכֹּל, offers thanks to God who gives food to all; the second, עַל הָאָרֶץ וְעַל הַמָּזוֹן, is a blessing for the gift of the land; and the third blessing, בּוֹנֶה בְרַחֲמָיו יְרוּשָׁלַיִם, alludes to Jerusalem and Zion, which give the land its special goodness. These three blessings are all indicated in the Biblical

Blessed be He, and blessed be His name:

If there are no three males, thirteen years or older, the father begins here:

Blessed are You, HASHEM our God, King of the universe, who feeds the whole world with His goodness, with grace, lovingkindness and mercy. He gives food to all flesh, for His lovingkindness endures for ever! Through His great goodness we have never lacked food, and may we never lack it, for ever and ever, for the sake of His great name; for He feeds and sustains all, does good to all, and prepares food for all His creatures which He has created. Blessed are You, HASHEM, who gives food to all.

We give thanks unto You, HASHEM our God, that You gave our fathers a desirable, good and spacious land as an inheritance; that You, HASHEM our God, brought us out from Egypt and delivered us from the house of bondage; that You sealed Your covenant in our flesh; that You taught us Your Torah and that You made Your statutes known to us; and for the life, grace and lovingkindness which You have bestowed upon us, and for the food with which You constantly feed and sustain us, every day, at all times and at every hour.

verse, 'When you have eaten and are satisfied, you shall praise God for the good land ...' (Devarim 8:10). However, the actual text of the blessings was fixed only after the Jews received the various benefits to which the Torah alludes. When the Manna descended, Moses recited the first blessing; when Israel entered the Holy Land, Joshua recited the second; David and Solomon composed the third blessing, whose text was changed after the destruction of the Temple, to fit the new circumstances. A fourth blessing was added after the

failure of the rebellion of Bar Kochba (Brachos 48b).

נוֹדֶה לְךְ — *We give thanks.* It should be noted that this blessing for the land also contains a reference to circumcision; the possession of the land is contingent upon the observance of the *Milah*-covenant. Likewise, we refer to the Torah, for the ultimate purpose of our ownership of the land is the realization of Torah in the Jewish State; when we fail to live up to the Torah, *'we are exiled for our sins.'*

וְעַל הַכֹּל יהוה אֱלֹהֵינוּ אֲנַחְנוּ מוֹדִים לָךְ
וּמְבָרְכִים אוֹתָךְ יִתְבָּרַךְ שִׁמְךָ
בְּפִי כָּל־חַי תָּמִיד לְעוֹלָם וָעֶד. כַּכָּתוּב °וְאָכַלְתָּ
וְשָׂבָעְתָּ וּבֵרַכְתָּ אֶת־יהוה אֱלֹהֶיךָ עַל־הָאָרֶץ
הַטֹּבָה אֲשֶׁר נָתַן־לָךְ. בָּרוּךְ אַתָּה יהוה עַל
הָאָרֶץ וְעַל הַמָּזוֹן:

רַחֶם־נָא יהוה אֱלֹהֵינוּ עַל יִשְׂרָאֵל עַמֶּךָ
וְעַל יְרוּשָׁלַיִם עִירֶךָ וְעַל צִיּוֹן
מִשְׁכַּן כְּבוֹדֶךָ וְעַל מַלְכוּת בֵּית דָּוִד מְשִׁיחֶךָ
וְעַל הַבַּיִת הַגָּדוֹל וְהַקָּדוֹשׁ שֶׁנִּקְרָא שִׁמְךָ עָלָיו.
אֱלֹהֵינוּ אָבִינוּ רְעֵנוּ זוּנֵנוּ פַּרְנְסֵנוּ וְכַלְכְּלֵנוּ
וְהַרְוִיחֵנוּ וְהַרְוַח־לָנוּ יהוה אֱלֹהֵינוּ מְהֵרָה
מִכָּל צָרוֹתֵינוּ. וְנָא אַל־תַּצְרִיכֵנוּ יהוה אֱלֹהֵינוּ
לֹא לִידֵי מַתְּנַת בָּשָׂר וָדָם וְלֹא לִידֵי הַלְוָאָתָם
כִּי אִם לְיָדְךָ הַמְּלֵאָה הַפְּתוּחָה הַקְּדוֹשָׁה
וְהָרְחָבָה שֶׁלֹּא נֵבוֹשׁ וְלֹא נִכָּלֵם לְעוֹלָם וָעֶד:

בשבת מוסיפים:

רְצֵה וְהַחֲלִיצֵנוּ יהוה אֱלֹהֵינוּ בְּמִצְוֹתֶךָ וּבְמִצְוַת יוֹם הַשְּׁבִיעִי
הַשַּׁבָּת הַגָּדוֹל וְהַקָּדוֹשׁ הַזֶּה כִּי יוֹם זֶה גָּדוֹל וְקָדוֹשׁ הוּא לְפָנֶיךָ
לִשְׁבָּת בּוֹ וְלָנוּחַ בּוֹ בְּאַהֲבָה כְּמִצְוַת רְצוֹנֶךָ וּבִרְצוֹנְךָ הָנִיחַ לָנוּ
יהוה אֱלֹהֵינוּ שֶׁלֹּא תְהֵא צָרָה וְיָגוֹן וַאֲנָחָה בְּיוֹם מְנוּחָתֵנוּ
וְהַרְאֵנוּ יהוה אֱלֹהֵינוּ בְּנֶחָמַת צִיּוֹן עִירֶךָ וּבְבִנְיַן יְרוּשָׁלַיִם עִיר
קָדְשֶׁךָ כִּי אַתָּה הוּא בַּעַל הַיְשׁוּעוֹת וּבַעַל הַנֶּחָמוֹת:

אֱלֹהֵינוּ וֵאלֹהֵי אֲבוֹתֵינוּ יַעֲלֶה וְיָבֹא וְיַגִּיעַ
וְיֵרָאֶה וְיֵרָצֶה וְיִשָּׁמַע וְיִפָּקֵד
וְיִזָּכֵר זִכְרוֹנֵנוּ וּפִקְדוֹנֵנוּ וְזִכְרוֹן אֲבוֹתֵינוּ וְזִכְרוֹן

רַחֵם — *Have mercy.* This blessing expresses our longing for the rebuilding
of Jerusalem and the Temple; yet, at the
same time, it also pleads for Divine help

הגדה של פסח [168]

For all this, HASHEM our God, we give thanks to You and bless You; blessed be Your name through the mouth of all living things, continually and forever. As it is written: "When you have eaten and are satisfied, you shall bless HASHEM your God for the good land that He has given you." Blessed are You, HASHEM, for the land and for the food.

Have mercy, HASHEM our God, upon Your people Israel, upon Your city Jerusalem, Zion, the dwelling place of Your glory, upon the kingdom of the house of David, Your anointed, and upon the great and holy House which is called by Your name. Our God and Father, tend us and feed us, nourish and sustain us, and grant us relief, and free us soon, HASHEM our God, from all our troubles. Let us, HASHEM our God, never be in need of the gifts of men, nor of their loans, but only of Your full, open hand that is holy and generous, so that we may not be shamed nor humiliated for ever and ever.

On *Shabbos* add:

May it be Your will, HASHEM our God, to strengthen us, through Your commandments and through the commandment of the seventh day, this great and holy Sabbath. For this day is great and holy before You, that we may refrain on it from all work and rest on it, in love, as prescribed by Your will. May it be Your will, HASHEM our God, to grant us rest, that there be no trouble, grief or lamenting on the day of our rest. Let us, HASHEM our God, behold the consolation of Zion, Your city, and the rebuilding of Jerusalem, the city of Your holiness, for You are the Master of salvation and the Master of consolation.

Our God and God of our fathers, may there rise, come before You, reach You, be seen, find favor, be understood, be recalled and remembered before You — the remembrance and consideration of ourselves, the remembrance of our fathers, the

מָשִׁיחַ בֶּן דָּוִד עַבְדֶּךָ וְזִכְרוֹן יְרוּשָׁלַיִם עִיר קָדְשֶׁךָ וְזִכְרוֹן כָּל עַמְּךָ בֵּית יִשְׂרָאֵל לְפָנֶיךָ לִפְלֵיטָה לְטוֹבָה לְחֵן וּלְחֶסֶד וּלְרַחֲמִים לְחַיִּים וּלְשָׁלוֹם בְּיוֹם חַג הַמַּצוֹת הַזֶּה. זָכְרֵנוּ יהוה אֱלֹהֵינוּ בּוֹ לְטוֹבָה וּפָקְדֵנוּ בוֹ לִבְרָכָה וְהוֹשִׁיעֵנוּ בוֹ לְחַיִּים וּבִדְבַר יְשׁוּעָה וְרַחֲמִים חוּס וְחָנֵּנוּ וְרַחֵם עָלֵינוּ וְהוֹשִׁיעֵנוּ כִּי אֵלֶיךָ עֵינֵינוּ °כִּי אֵל מֶלֶךְ חַנּוּן וְרַחוּם אָתָּה:

°נחמיה
ט:לא

וּבְנֵה יְרוּשָׁלַיִם עִיר הַקֹּדֶשׁ בִּמְהֵרָה בְיָמֵינוּ. בָּרוּךְ אַתָּה יהוה בּוֹנֵה בְרַחֲמָיו יְרוּשָׁלָיִם אָמֵן:

בָּרוּךְ אַתָּה יהוה אֱלֹהֵינוּ מֶלֶךְ הָעוֹלָם הָאֵל אָבִינוּ מַלְכֵּנוּ אַדִּירֵנוּ בּוֹרְאֵנוּ גּוֹאֲלֵנוּ יוֹצְרֵנוּ קְדוֹשֵׁנוּ קְדוֹשׁ יַעֲקֹב רוֹעֵנוּ רוֹעֵה יִשְׂרָאֵל הַמֶּלֶךְ הַטּוֹב וְהַמֵּטִיב לַכֹּל שֶׁבְּכָל יוֹם וָיוֹם הוּא הֵטִיב הוּא מֵטִיב הוּא יֵיטִיב לָנוּ. הוּא גְמָלָנוּ הוּא גוֹמְלֵנוּ הוּא יִגְמְלֵנוּ לָעַד לְחֵן וּלְחֶסֶד וּלְרַחֲמִים וּלְרֶוַח הַצָּלָה וְהַצְלָחָה בְּרָכָה וִישׁוּעָה נֶחָמָה פַּרְנָסָה וְכַלְכָּלָה וְרַחֲמִים וְחַיִּים וְשָׁלוֹם וְכָל טוֹב וּמִכָּל טוֹב לְעוֹלָם אַל יְחַסְּרֵנוּ:

הַטּוֹב וְהַמֵּטִיב — *Who is kind and benefi-cent.* Our Sages relate this blessing to the gratitude of the Jewish people when the Romans permitted the burial of the victims of the Bar Kochba rebellion (*Brachos* 48a). It has been suggested that this blessing teaches us to be

for the individual. This may have the purpose of teaching us that our own welfare as individuals is linked to the spiritual aspirations of our people, and must be seen in this context — never only as a selfish materialistic goal by itself (*Rabbi E. Munk*).

remembrance of Mashiach, the son of David, Your servant, the remembrance of Jerusalem, Your holy city, and the remembrance of Your whole people, the House of Israel — for deliverance and well-being, for grace, for lovingkindness and for mercy, for life and for peace, on this festival of Matzos! Remember us, on it, HASHEM our God, for good, consider us on it for blessing, and help us on it to a good life. Favour us and be gracious to us through the promise of salvation and mercy, have mercy upon us and help us — for to You alone our eyes are turned, for You, HASHEM, are a gracious and merciful King!

Rebuild Jerusalem the Holy City, soon in our days! Blessed are You, HASHEM, who, in His mercy, rebuilds Jerusalem. Amen!

Blessed are You, HASHEM our God, King of the universe, Almighty, our Father, our King, our Sovereign, our Creator, our Redeemer, our Maker, our Holy One, the Holy One of Jacob, our Shepherd, the Shepherd of Israel, the good and beneficent King, who each day did good, does good and will do good to us! It is He who has dealt with us, deals with us, and for evermore will deal with us, with grace, lovingkindness, mercy, relief, to grant us salvation, success, blessing help, consolation, food and sustenance, mercy, life and peace, and all good; and of all manner of good things may He never deprive us!

grateful, even in bitter times, and for favors that might not evoke particular rejoicing (Rabbi E. Munk). At the same time this blessing, instituted after the failure of Bar Kochba, is to remind us that our national independence cannot be restored by our own power, and our future as a nation must be solely entrusted to Divine Providence (Rabbi S.R. Hirsch).

הָרַחֲמָן הוּא יִמְלוֹךְ עָלֵינוּ לְעוֹלָם וָעֶד. הָרַחֲמָן הוּא יִתְבָּרַךְ בַּשָּׁמַיִם וּבָאָרֶץ. הָרַחֲמָן הוּא יִשְׁתַּבַּח לְדוֹר דּוֹרִים וְיִתְפָּאַר בָּנוּ לָעַד וּלְנֵצַח נְצָחִים וְיִתְהַדַּר בָּנוּ לָעַד וּלְעוֹלְמֵי עוֹלָמִים. הָרַחֲמָן הוּא יְפַרְנְסֵנוּ בְּכָבוֹד. הָרַחֲמָן הוּא יִשְׁבּוֹר עֻלֵּנוּ מֵעַל צַוָּארֵנוּ וְהוּא יוֹלִיכֵנוּ קוֹמְמִיּוּת לְאַרְצֵנוּ. הָרַחֲמָן הוּא יִשְׁלַח לָנוּ בְּרָכָה מְרֻבָּה בַּבַּיִת הַזֶּה וְעַל שֻׁלְחָן זֶה שֶׁאָכַלְנוּ עָלָיו. הָרַחֲמָן הוּא יִשְׁלַח לָנוּ אֶת אֵלִיָּהוּ הַנָּבִיא זָכוּר לַטּוֹב וִיבַשֶּׂר לָנוּ בְּשׂוֹרוֹת טוֹבוֹת יְשׁוּעוֹת וְנֶחָמוֹת. הָרַחֲמָן הוּא יְבָרֵךְ

אורחים מתחילים כאן
(אם הם בבית הוריהם מוסיפים המלים שבחצי עיגולים)

אֶת (אָבִי מוֹרִי) בַּעַל הַבַּיִת הַזֶּה וְאֶת (אִמִּי מוֹרָתִי) בַּעֲלַת הַבַּיִת הַזֶּה.

בעל הבית ובעלת הבית מתחילים כאן
(אם הם נשואים אומרים מה שמוקף בחצי עיגולים)

אוֹתִי (וְאֶת אִשְׁתִּי / בַּעְלִי וְאֶת זַרְעִי) וְאֶת כָּל אֲשֶׁר לִי וְאֶת כָּל הַמְסוּבִּין כָּאן. אוֹתָם וְאֶת בֵּיתָם וְאֶת זַרְעָם וְאֶת כָּל אֲשֶׁר לָהֶם אוֹתָנוּ וְאֶת כָּל אֲשֶׁר לָנוּ כְּמוֹ שֶׁנִּתְבָּרְכוּ אֲבוֹתֵינוּ אַבְרָהָם יִצְחָק וְיַעֲקֹב בַּכֹּל מִכֹּל כֹּל כֵּן יְבָרֵךְ אוֹתָנוּ כֻּלָּנוּ יַחַד בִּבְרָכָה שְׁלֵמָה וְנֹאמַר אָמֵן:

בַּמָּרוֹם יְלַמְּדוּ עֲלֵיהֶם וְעָלֵינוּ זְכוּת שֶׁתְּהֵא לְמִשְׁמֶרֶת שָׁלוֹם. וְנִשָּׂא בְרָכָה מֵאֵת יהוה וּצְדָקָה מֵאֱלֹהֵי יִשְׁעֵנוּ וְנִמְצָא חֵן וְשֵׂכֶל טוֹב בְּעֵינֵי אֱלֹהִים וְאָדָם:

May the All-Merciful reign over us for ever and ever! May the All-Merciful be praised in heaven and on earth! May the All-Merciful be lauded from generation to generation, may He be glorified through us for ever and ever, and may He be honoured through us through all eternity! May the All-Merciful sustain us in honor! May the All-Merciful break the oppressive yoke from our necks and lead us upright to our land! May the All-Merciful send abundant blessing to this house and upon this table at which we have eaten! May the All-Merciful, send us the prophet Elijah, of blessed memory, that he may proclaim to us good tidings, salvation and consolation! May the All-Merciful, bless

Guests start here (adding the words in parentheses if in their parents' home):

(my father, my teacher) the master of this house, and (my mother, my teacher) the mistress of this house,

The host and hostess start here (add the words in parentheses if married):

me, (my wife/husband and family) and all that is mine, and all that sit here, both them and their house and family, together with all that is theirs; so also us, and all that is ours. Just as our fathers Abraham, Isaac, and Jacob were blessed in all things, through all things and with all things, may He bless us all with a perfect blessing! To that let us say: Amen!

O, may their and our merits be pleaded in heaven, to assure peace; may we receive a blessing from HASHEM and kindness from the God of our salvation and find favour and understanding in the eyes of God and man!

הָרַחֲמָן הוּא יַנְחִילֵנוּ יוֹם שֶׁכֻּלּוֹ שַׁבָּת וּמְנוּחָה לְחַיֵּי
הָעוֹלָמִים:

הָרַחֲמָן הוּא יַנְחִילֵנוּ יוֹם שֶׁכֻּלּוֹ טוֹב.
יוֹם שֶׁכֻּלּוֹ אָרוּךְ. יוֹם שֶׁצַּדִּיקִים יוֹשְׁבִים וְעַטְרוֹתֵיהֶם
בְּרָאשֵׁיהֶם וְנֶהֱנִים מִזִּיו הַשְּׁכִינָה וִיהִי חֶלְקֵנוּ עִמָּהֶם:

°שמואל ב׳ כב:נא

הָרַחֲמָן הוּא יְזַכֵּנוּ לִימוֹת הַמָּשִׁיחַ וּלְחַיֵּי
הָעוֹלָם הַבָּא. °מִגְדּוֹל יְשׁוּעוֹת מַלְכּוֹ וְעוֹשֶׂה
חֶסֶד לִמְשִׁיחוֹ לְדָוִד וּלְזַרְעוֹ עַד עוֹלָם. עֹשֶׂה
שָׁלוֹם בִּמְרוֹמָיו הוּא יַעֲשֶׂה שָׁלוֹם עָלֵינוּ וְעַל
כָּל יִשְׂרָאֵל וְאִמְרוּ אָמֵן:

°תהלים לד:י-יא קיח:א קמה:טז °ירמיה יז:ז °תהלים לז:כה

°יְראוּ אֶת יְהוָה קְדֹשָׁיו כִּי אֵין מַחְסוֹר לִירֵאָיו. כְּפִירִים רָשׁוּ
וְרָעֵבוּ וְדֹרְשֵׁי יְהוָה לֹא יַחְסְרוּ כָל טוֹב. °הוֹדוּ לַיהוָה כִּי טוֹב כִּי
לְעוֹלָם חַסְדּוֹ. °פּוֹתֵחַ אֶת יָדֶךָ וּמַשְׂבִּיעַ לְכָל חַי רָצוֹן. °בָּרוּךְ
הַגֶּבֶר אֲשֶׁר יִבְטַח בַּיהוָה וְהָיָה יְהוָה מִבְטַחוֹ. °נַעַר הָיִיתִי גַּם
זָקַנְתִּי וְלֹא רָאִיתִי צַדִּיק נֶעֱזָב וְזַרְעוֹ מְבַקֶּשׁ לָחֶם.

כט:יא

°יְהוָה עֹז לְעַמּוֹ יִתֵּן יְהוָה יְבָרֵךְ אֶת עַמּוֹ
בַשָּׁלוֹם:

הכל מסובים ושותים כל הכוס ולכל הפחות רובו של כוס שלישי של ארבע
כוסות אחר אמירת הברכה:

בָּרוּךְ אַתָּה יְהוָה אֱלֹהֵינוּ מֶלֶךְ הָעוֹלָם
בּוֹרֵא פְּרִי הַגָּפֶן:

הלל

מוזגים כוס רביעי וגם כוסו של אליהו הנביא (יש נוהגים למזוג כוס של

יוֹם שֶׁכֻּלּוֹ אָרוּךְ — *That everlasting day.*
The words printed in the text in smaller
type represent a special addition for the
Seder; in some communities they are

not recited.

* *The fourth cup* — The fourth cup is
for the recitation of the second part of

May the All-Merciful cause us to inherit the day that will be wholly Shabbos and rest for eternal life!

May the All-Merciful cause us to inherit that day which is altogether good, that everlasting day, the day when the just will sit with crowns on their heads, enjoying the reflection of God's Majesty — and may our portion be with them!

May the All-Merciful make us worthy to reach the days of Mashiach and of eternal life in the world to come! He who is a tower of salvation to His king, and shows lovingkindness to David, His anointed, and his seed for evermore; He who establishes peace in His heights; may He also establish peace for us and for all Israel — and say: Amen!

Fear HASHEM, You, His holy ones, for there is no want for them that fear Him! Young lions suffer and are hungry, but they that seek the Lord lack not any good. Give thanks unto HASHEM, for He is good, His lovingkindness endures forever! You open Your hand and satisfy the desire of everything that lives. Blessed is the man that trusts in HASHEM, and to whom HASHEM has become the source of his trust! I was young and now I have grown old, yet never have I seen a righteous man abandoned nor his children begging for bread.

HASHEM will give strength to His people, HASHEM will bless His people with peace!

All recline and drink all, or at least most, of the third cup, after pronouncing this blessing:

B*lessed are You, HASHEM our God, King of the universe, who creates the fruit of the vine.*

Hallel / Recite the Hallel

The fourth cup* is poured, and also an extra cup for the Prophet Elijah (however, some pour this cup at the beginning of the *Seder*).

Hallel. For this reason some pour only the cup of Elijah at this point, and fill the fourth cup after שְׁפֹךְ חֲמָתְךָ. It does, however, make very much sense to pour

אֵלִיָּהוּ בִּתְחִלַּת הַסֵּדֶר). פּוֹתְחִים הַדֶּלֶת וְאוֹמְרִים **שְׁפוֹךְ חֲמָתְךָ** וְכוּ' וְסוֹגְרִים הַדֶּלֶת.

° תהלים
עט:ו-ז

שְׁפֹךְ° חֲמָתְךָ אֶל הַגּוֹיִם אֲשֶׁר לֹא יְדָעוּךָ וְעַל מַמְלָכוֹת אֲשֶׁר בְּשִׁמְךָ לֹא קָרָאוּ: כִּי אָכַל אֶת יַעֲקֹב וְאֶת נָוֵהוּ הֵשַׁמּוּ:

it here, for שְׁפֹךְ חֲמָתְךָ is not a separate passage standing by itself. It can be viewed as a comment on the pouring of the fourth cup, or as an introduction to *Hallel* — and in either case the cup should be poured first.

שְׁפֹךְ חֲמָתְךָ — *Pour forth Your wrath.* The four cups signify the four cups of punishment that the nations of the world will have to drain, as the Messianic redemption comes closer; they point to the overthrow of the four great empires to which the Jewish people has been subjected, in turn, since the destruction of the first Temple (Babylonia, Persia, Greece, and Rome which represents the present Exile); and they symbolize the ingathering of the Jewish people from the four corners of the earth. The pouring of the fourth cup therefore, evokes our prayer that God may punish our oppressors and bring about the ultimate redemption *(Meiri)*.

In a similar vein it has been pointed out that the four cups correspond to the four letters of the Divine Name of HASHEM. Until the coming of *Mashiach*. and the destruction of Amalek (the forces of the extremest evil in the world) God's name is incomplete — His glory is not fully revealed in the world. The Torah makes this point by using only the first two letters of God's name when it discusses the battle against Amalek *(Shemos 17:16)*. The last two letters will complete God's name at the time of *Mashiach* — the two cups which correspond to them are therefore drunk in the second half of the *Seder*, accompanied by our prayer for his early coming.

שְׁפֹךְ חֲמָתְךָ expresses this longing, and

in this way also introduces the second part of *Hallel*; The first two chapters of *Hallel* recited before the meal, dealt with the Exodus, the splitting of the sea, and the giving of the Torah ('... *the mountains jumped'*); the next chapters deal with our servitude to the nations, the pangs of the Messianic redemption, the war with Gog and Magog, and finally the Messianic era, the resurrection of the dead, and the World to Come *(Pesachim, 118a, Yalkut)*. In reciting שְׁפֹךְ חֲמָתְךָ we express our firm confidence that God will bring about these happenings — that He has not forsaken us but protects us and will redeem us:

'*If a man is in great trouble, let him put his trust in God, the source of Israel's succour in times of oppression; just as the suffering of the Egyptian exile in the end brought about our deliverance, so the tribulations of this exile will also be the cause of Israel's final redemption' (Rabbeinu Manoach).*

Seder night is the appropriate time for this affirmation of our trust, for it is לֵיל שִׁמּוּרִים, *the night for watching* *(Shemos 12:42)*. The Torah uses this expression twice, to show us that not only the Jews in Egypt were guarded by God during this night, but it remained a night for standing watch over all later generations. In the first place, the Jews were assured of protection on this night from the forces of destruction *(Rashi;* for this reason the usual prayer before retiring to bed is only recited in abbreviated form on *Pesach* night). But *Targum Jonathan* stresses a further point: on this night, in particular, God — so to speak — watches to see when the

הגדה של פסח   [176]

Pour forth Your wrath upon the nations that do not recognize You, and upon the kingdoms that do not invoke Your name. For they have devoured Jacob

time will come for our future redemption. The process that started in Egypt will find its completion in this night — and we are promised, in fact, that all the miracles that God did in Egypt, will repeat themselves at the redemption to come (Midrash).

[The Talmud (Rosh Hashanah 11b) records conflicting views on the date of the future redemption: according to Rabbi Joshua it will indeed occur in Nissan, but Rabbi Eliezer declares that it will take place in the month of Tishrei. It has been suggested, however, that they both agree that both Nissan and Tishrei will play a role in the process of redemption. They only disagree on whether the events of Tishrei will constitute the decisive turning-point or whether the events of Nissan will; the night of Pesach, however, will in any case mark a crucial moment in the redemptive process.]

Thus, we express on Pesach night our faith in the coming of Mashiach — and our trust itself helps bring him sooner (Or Zorua). That is why we throw open the door when we recite שְׁפֹךְ חֲמָתְךָ — to show that we are not afraid of our enemies, that we expect and wait for the moment of deliverance, and that we want to welcome Elijah, the messenger of the redemption. Therefore, we actually pour a special cup for him; and some have the custom of calling out בָּרוּךְ הַבָּא, welcome, when opening the door. Since Elijah is the Angel of the Covenant, attending circumcisions throughout the ages, we also view him as pleading our case for an early redemption; he is able to testify to our loyalty to the Milah covenant.

[It has also been suggested that the special cup that we call by Elijah's name is meant to represent a fifth cup that should be drunk according to some opinions (Rif to Pesachim 118a). Since we do not know whether we should follow this view, we pour the cup but leave it on the table to await the coming of Elijah who, according to tradition, will resolve all pending questions at the dawn of our redemption (Vilna Gaon). The fifth cup, awaiting our redemption, can thus be viewed as the symbol of our future deliverance (see Overview, p. 36).]

When we throw open our doors, in expectation of the redemption to come, we thereby highlight a significant difference between the deliverance from Egypt and the redemption from this exile. In Egypt the Jews had to spend the crucial Pesach night in their homes, behind closed doors; they were not worthy to see the downfall of the Egyptians (Sfas Emes). The reason may have been that they could still be accused of being 'idol-worshippers' like the Egyptians (see p. 119) and owed their deliverance to God's mercy (see p. 97). In contrast, the future redemption will have to come through the merit of our rededication to Torah; therefore, it will take place before our eyes.

כִּי אָכַל אֶת יַעֲקֹב — For they have devoured Jacob. Literally this verse is translated, 'For he has devoured Jacob, and they have destroyed his habitation.' It has therefore been suggested that the first part of this verse refers to God, and only the second part to our enemies

°שְׁפָךְ עֲלֵיהֶם זַעְמֶךָ וַחֲרוֹן אַפְּךָ יַשִׂיגֵם:

°תִּרְדֹּף בְּאַף וְתַשְׁמִידֵם מִתַּחַת שְׁמֵי יהוה:

°לֹא לָנוּ יהוה לֹא לָנוּ כִּי לְשִׁמְךָ תֵּן כָּבוֹד עַל חַסְדְּךָ עַל אֲמִתֶּךָ: לָמָּה יֹאמְרוּ הַגּוֹיִם אַיֵּה נָא אֱלֹהֵיהֶם: וֵאלֹהֵינוּ בַשָּׁמָיִם כֹּל אֲשֶׁר חָפֵץ עָשָׂה: עֲצַבֵּיהֶם כֶּסֶף וְזָהָב מַעֲשֵׂה יְדֵי אָדָם: פֶּה לָהֶם וְלֹא יְדַבֵּרוּ

(Rabbi M. Lehmann). God ordained that the Jews should suffer from the nations on account of their sins; and if the nations carried out their task as they were meant to, in order to bring the Jews back to God, they would not deserve punishment. But they have gone far beyond their assigned task, and their persecution of the Jews does not stem from a desire to do God's will. On the contrary, they do not acknowledge God, and have oppressed the Jews because they are God's people and the carriers of His word. Therefore, they deserve punishment (Rabbi Mordechai Benet).

Another explanation suggests that 'he has devoured Jacob' refers to Pharaoh. He persecuted the Jews for his own advantage — he felt threatened by them. Our later oppressors, however, destroyed our habitation (the Temple, according to some commentators) because of pure hatred and are therefore even more worthy of punishment than Pharaoh was (Rabbi Myski).

We first ask that God's anger should be poured out אֶל הַגּוֹיִם, to the nations. We seek a warning, rather than their destruction. However, if they still persist in not recognizing God, there is no room for them beneath His heaven (Rabbi Myski).

לֹא לָנוּ — Not unto us. Here starts the second part of Hallel. As noted before

(p.65), women are obliged to recite Hallel on Seder night, since they are required to drink the four cups in the proper order and sequence, and the drinking of the fourth cup is based upon the recitation of Hallel.

The second part of the Seder, which is devoted to the future redemption, centers on Hallel. What is the connection between Hallel and the coming of Mashiach? We have to remember that the Exodus from Egypt was meant to teach the world that God is its master and that we are His people. The lesson was mastered — but only up to a point. The nations of the world know about God — but they do not bow to His will. The Jewish people became the servants of God — but our sins forced us into Exile.

To prepare the coming of Mashiach, we must overcome our alienation from God. The lesson of the Exodus, that 'I am HASHEM in the midst of the land' (Shemos 8:18) must be taken to heart. At the splitting of the Sea, the Jews exclaimed, 'This is my God' (Shemos 15:2); the future redemption will be marked by our raising this same cry, 'Behold, He is our God' (Isaiah 25:9). The Psalms of praise that form Hallel are meant to awaken in us this awareness of God. At the same time, we hope and pray, our sincere acknowledgment of God's kingship will in turn evoke a heavenly response, and God will acknowledge us as His people and

and destroyed his habitation. Pour forth Your in-
dignation upon them and let Your burning wrath
overtake them. Pursue them with anger and destroy
them from beneath the heavens of HASHEM.

Not unto us, HASHEM, not unto us, but unto Your
name give glory, for the sake of Your kindness
and truth! Why should the nations say, 'Where,
now, is their God?' But our God is in heaven, what-
soever He desires, He does! But their idols are of
silver and gold, the work of men's hands. They have
a mouth and speak not; they have eyes and see not;

redeem us from Exile, in fulfillment of
His promise: *'At that time, I will seek
out Jerusalem with lights'* (Zefaniah
1:12).

The various Psalms of *Hallel* have to
be recited in their proper order. This
reflects the fact that they follow a
chronological sequence. Psalm 115
speaks about our existence among the
nations, and the conflicts that are
generated, as well as about the pangs of
the Messianic redemption.

We are to understand that we should
not be concerned with our own well-
being — relief from suffering, or reward
for whatever good deeds we may have
done. Rather, we should seek our
deliverance because it will bring about
the recognition of God. The *'Name of
God'* — meaning His works through
which He can be perceived by man —
will be honored by those who heretofore
failed to acknowledge Him.

God's works express the qualities of
justice and kindness. However, the
Psalm omits *'and'*, in speaking of *'Your
kindness, Your truth'*. *Rabbi S.R.
Hirsch* sees in this a reminder that
ultimately His kindness and truth are
one — merely different expressions of
the same Divine concern.

אַיֵּה נָא — *Where, now, is their God?* In
Tehillim 79, the same question is asked,
but without the word נָא which is a form
of entreaty: *'please.'* The *Chasam Sofer*
explains that the question concerning
God's whereabouts is all too often a
rhetorical one, meant to mock us.
However, as the nations come to realize
that their idols let them down, they will
come to us and ask in earnest that we
should tell them about God.

עֲצַבֵּיהֶם — *Their idols.* עֶצֶב literally
means grief. Idol-worship may be a
primitive veneration of material objects
or a more sophisticated attachment to
natural forces personified by the idols.
But such worship must lead to grief, for
these objects or forces are merely blind
tools in God's hands. Those that
worship them will, in fact, become like
them; they themselves will lose the
potential for free ethical choice and
moral grandeur, and will become slaves
of their own animalic impulses. In the
end, they will realize the utter futility of
their lives.

In contrast, Israel puts its trust in
God, and thereby attains God's blessing. But this blessing is not so much
from God as it is לַהֵשֵׁם, *for* God: we will
be blessed so that thereby God's purpose in the world will be advanced.
Therefore we are urged at all times to
bear in mind our responsibility as the
carriers of God's message in the world.

עֵינַיִם לָהֶם וְלֹא יִרְאוּ: אָזְנַיִם לָהֶם וְלֹא יִשְׁמָעוּ
אַף לָהֶם וְלֹא יְרִיחוּן: יְדֵיהֶם וְלֹא יְמִישׁוּן
רַגְלֵיהֶם וְלֹא יְהַלֵּכוּ לֹא יֶהְגּוּ בִּגְרוֹנָם: כְּמוֹהֶם
יִהְיוּ עֹשֵׂיהֶם כֹּל אֲשֶׁר בֹּטֵחַ בָּהֶם: יִשְׂרָאֵל
בְּטַח בַּיהוה עֶזְרָם וּמָגִנָּם הוּא: בֵּית אַהֲרֹן
בִּטְחוּ בַיהוה עֶזְרָם וּמָגִנָּם הוּא: יִרְאֵי יהוה
בִּטְחוּ בַיהוה עֶזְרָם וּמָגִנָּם הוּא:

יהוה זְכָרָנוּ יְבָרֵךְ יְבָרֵךְ אֶת בֵּית יִשְׂרָאֵל
יְבָרֵךְ אֶת בֵּית אַהֲרֹן: יְבָרֵךְ יִרְאֵי
יהוה הַקְּטַנִּים עִם הַגְּדֹלִים: יֹסֵף יהוה עֲלֵיכֶם
עֲלֵיכֶם וְעַל בְּנֵיכֶם: בְּרוּכִים אַתֶּם לַיהוה עֹשֵׂה
שָׁמַיִם וָאָרֶץ: הַשָּׁמַיִם שָׁמַיִם לַיהוה וְהָאָרֶץ
נָתַן לִבְנֵי אָדָם: לֹא הַמֵּתִים יְהַלְלוּ־יָהּ וְלֹא כָּל
יֹרְדֵי דוּמָה: וַאֲנַחְנוּ נְבָרֵךְ יָהּ מֵעַתָּה וְעַד
עוֹלָם הַלְלוּיָהּ:

° תהלים
קטז
אָהַבְתִּי° כִּי יִשְׁמַע יהוה אֶת קוֹלִי
תַּחֲנוּנָי: כִּי הִטָּה אָזְנוֹ לִי וּבְיָמַי
אֶקְרָא: אֲפָפוּנִי חֶבְלֵי מָוֶת וּמְצָרֵי שְׁאוֹל

יְבָרֵךְ אֶת בֵּית יִשְׂרָאֵל — *He will bless the House of Israel.* In the preceding verses, the call for trust in God was addressed to Israel, to the House of Aaron, and to those that fear God. The Jewish people, as a whole, has to serve God's will. However, an even greater responsibility falls upon the House of Aaron, the priests, whose life's work is to uphold the highest standards of sanctity in the service of God. And the supreme task belongs to the God-fearing Sages, the guardians of the Torah which is the soul and constitution of our people.

In these verses we are now assured that God will bestow the appropriate blessings for the discharge of our duties. The House of Israel is blessed through receiving the crown of royalty, which was entrusted to the tribe of Judah. The blessing to the House of Aaron consists in the crown of priesthood which was granted to it. And the God fearing are blessed by attaining the crown of Torah — the greatest blessing of them all, for it is accessible to every Jew *(Rabbi Myski).*

אָהַבְתִּי — *I love.* We love HASHEM for the special relationship that He has es-

they have ears and hear not; they have a nose and smell not. Their hands — they do not feel; their feet — they cannot walk; no sound comes from their throat! Those that make them should be like them, everyone that trusts in them! Israel, trust in the Lord! He is their help and their shield. House of Aaron, trust in the Lord! He is their help and their shield. You that fear HASHEM, trust in the Lord! He is their help and their shield.

HASHEM has been mindful of us; He will bless — He will bless the House of Israel, He will bless the house of Aaron. He will bless those that fear HASHEM, both small and great. May HASHEM increase you, you and your children! Be blessed by HASHEM, the maker of heaven and earth. The heaven is the heaven of HASHEM, but the earth He has given to the children of man. The dead do not praise HASHEM, nor those that go down into the silence of the grave; but we will praise HASHEM from this time forth and forever! Hallelujah!

I love HASHEM, for He hears my voice, my prayers. He has inclined His ear to me, now will I call upon Him all the days of my life. The ropes of death encompassed me, the confines of the grave took hold of

tablished with us. It entails responsibility and accountability — and if we fail in our task we suffer (*Amos* 3:2). Yet we cherish the special bond that exists.

However, other explanations of the verse have been offered. According to the *Talmud* (*Pesachim* 118b) the Jewish people declare that '*I am loved* when God hears my voice.' *Ibn Ezra* translates: 'I love it when God hears my voice as I pray.'

Rabbi S.R. Hirsch understands the verse to say: I have come to love my voice and prayers, for God will listen to

me' — even times of trouble and need can be seen as a blessing, for they challenge us to seek out God and evoke His response. Along this line, it has been said that the punishment imposed upon the snake, to live on dust, was not designed to rob the snake of better-tasting nourishment, but to furnish it with food at all times; as a result, it had no need ever to turn to God. That may well have been the worst punishment possible.

On the other hand, adversity can indeed be the greatest blessing if it directs our thoughts to God. Then, just '*when*

מְצָאֽוּנִי צָרָה וְיָגוֹן אֶמְצָא: וּבְשֵׁם יהוה אֶקְרָא
אָנָּה יהוה מַלְּטָה נַפְשִׁי: חַנּוּן יהוה וְצַדִּיק
וֵאלֹהֵֽינוּ מְרַחֵם: שֹׁמֵר פְּתָאיִם יהוה דַּלּוֹתִי
וְלִי יְהוֹשִֽׁיעַ: שׁוּבִי נַפְשִׁי לִמְנוּחָֽיְכִי כִּי יהוה
גָּמַל עָלָֽיְכִי: כִּי חִלַּצְתָּ נַפְשִׁי מִמָּֽוֶת אֶת עֵינִי מִן
דִּמְעָה אֶת רַגְלִי מִדֶּֽחִי: אֶתְהַלֵּךְ לִפְנֵי יהוה
בְּאַרְצוֹת הַחַיִּים: הֶאֱמַֽנְתִּי כִּי אֲדַבֵּר אֲנִי עָנִֽיתִי
מְאֹד: אֲנִי אָמַֽרְתִּי בְחָפְזִי כָּל הָאָדָם כֹּזֵב:

מָה אָשִׁיב לַיהוה כָּל תַּגְמוּלֽוֹהִי עָלָי: כּוֹס
יְשׁוּעוֹת אֶשָּׂא וּבְשֵׁם יהוה אֶקְרָא: נְדָרַי
לַיהוה אֲשַׁלֵּם נֶגְדָה נָּא לְכָל עַמּוֹ: יָקָר בְּעֵינֵי
יהוה הַמָּֽוְתָה לַחֲסִידָיו: אָנָּה יהוה כִּי אֲנִי
עַבְדֶּֽךָ אֲנִי עַבְדְּךָ בֶּן אֲמָתֶֽךָ פִּתַּֽחְתָּ לְמוֹסֵרָי: לְךָ
אֶזְבַּח זֶֽבַח תּוֹדָה וּבְשֵׁם יהוה אֶקְרָא: נְדָרַי
לַיהוה אֲשַׁלֵּם נֶגְדָה נָּא לְכָל עַמּוֹ: בְּחַצְרוֹת
בֵּית יהוה בְּתוֹכֵֽכִי יְרוּשָׁלָֽיִם הַלְלוּיָהּ:

°הַלְלוּ אֶת יהוה כָּל גּוֹיִם שַׁבְּחֽוּהוּ כָּל
הָאֻמִּים: כִּי גָבַר עָלֵֽינוּ חַסְדּוֹ וֶאֱמֶת
יהוה לְעוֹלָם הַלְלוּיָהּ:

° תהלים
קיז

I am brought low, God saves me.'

This Psalm stresses the certainty of
God's help — and ultimately we will
walk before God in the Land of the living, the World of Resurrection and eternal life.

כָּל הָאָדָם כֹּזֵב — *All men are deceitful.*
The Jew may sometimes hastily
(בְחָפְזִי) have begun to wonder about the
meaningfulness of life; but, his trust in
God has never truly been shaken. *Rabbi
S.R. Hirsch* explains the verse different-

ly: the trust of the Jew, despite all his
suffering and hasty flight from his
enemies (בְחָפְזִי) was always so strong
that he rejected all the false delusions of
mankind, recognizing them as deceitful.

כּוֹס יְשׁוּעוֹת — *The cup of salvation.*
The verse, literally, speaks of the cup of
salvations, in the plural. Many are
God's salvations: there are many different ways in which God delivers us. A
previous verse had spoken of our calling out to God in time of suffering; this

me, trouble and sorrow I found — therefore I called upon the name of HASHEM: 'O, HASHEM, deliver my soul!' Kind is HASHEM and righteous, our God if full of compassion. HASHEM guards the simple; I was brought low, but He saved me. Return, my soul, unto your rest; for HASHEM dealt kindly with you! You delivered my soul from death, my eyes from tears, my feet from stumbling. Thus I will walk before HASHEM in the land of the living. I trust, even when I say I am deeply suffering; even when I said in my haste that all men are deceitful.

How can I repay HASHEM for all His kindness to me? I lift up the cup of salvation and call upon the name of HASHEM. I pay my vows to HASHEM, in the presence of all His people. Precious in the sight of HASHEM is the death of His pious ones. O, HASHEM, I am Your servant — I am Your servant, the son of Your handmaid, You have loosened my bonds. I bring thank-offerings unto You, and I call upon the name of HASHEM. I pay my vows to HASHEM in the presence of all His people, in the courts of the Temple of HASHEM, in Your midst, O Jersualem. Hallelujah.

Praise HASHEM, all the nations! Laud Him, all the peoples! For His kindness was mighty over us, and the truth of HASHEM endures forever. Hallelujah!

verse speaks of our calling upon the name of God when we are saved. Whatever happens to a Jew, he must see in it God's work and respond to his fate as God's will decrees (Ibn Ezra).

יָקָר בְּעֵינֵי ה' — Precious in the sight of God. Even the generations that suffered and died during the long exile and did not live to see the final redemption did not live in vain. Even their suffering and death, passively and patiently borne, contributed to the ultimate at-

tainment of God's purpose (Rabbi S.R. Hirsch).

כָּל גוֹיִם — All the nations. Why should the nations praise God for having been kind to us? Rabbi S.R. Hirsch explains that these verses speak of the Messianic age, when all nations will be summoned by Israel to join in praising God because His kindness has been demonstrated to all of us, Jews and Gentiles.

The (Talmud (Pesachim 118b) queries: Why should the nations praise

°תהלים
קיח

	כִּי לְעוֹלָם חַסְדּוֹ:	°הוֹדוּ לַיהוה כִּי טוֹב
	כִּי לְעוֹלָם חַסְדּוֹ:	יֹאמַר נָא יִשְׂרָאֵל
	כִּי לְעוֹלָם חַסְדּוֹ:	יֹאמְרוּ נָא בֵית אַהֲרֹן
	כִּי לְעוֹלָם חַסְדּוֹ:	יֹאמְרוּ נָא יִרְאֵי יהוה

מִן הַמֵּצַר קָרָאתִי יָּהּ עָנָנִי בַמֶּרְחָב יָהּ: יהוה
לִי לֹא אִירָא מַה יַּעֲשֶׂה לִי אָדָם: יהוה לִי
בְּעוֹזְרָי וַאֲנִי אֶרְאֶה בְשֹׂנְאָי: טוֹב לַחֲסוֹת
בַּיהוה מִבְּטֹחַ בָּאָדָם: טוֹב לַחֲסוֹת בַּיהוה
מִבְּטֹחַ בִּנְדִיבִים: כָּל גוֹיִם סְבָבוּנִי בְּשֵׁם יהוה
כִּי אֲמִילַם: סַבּוּנִי גַם סְבָבוּנִי בְּשֵׁם יהוה כִּי
אֲמִילַם: סַבּוּנִי כִדְבוֹרִים דֹּעֲכוּ כְּאֵשׁ קוֹצִים
בְּשֵׁם יהוה כִּי אֲמִילַם: דָּחֹה דְחִיתַנִי לִנְפֹּל
וַיהוה עֲזָרָנִי: עָזִּי וְזִמְרָת יָהּ וַיְהִי לִי לִישׁוּעָה:

God for the favors which *we* have received? It replies that they should give thanks for what God did for *them* — and we should be even more thankful because we received so much more kindness from Him.

It has also been said that the nations should be grateful that God's kindness protected the Jewish people from their oppressors — if they had been permitted to destroy the Jews, they would thereby have destroyed their own future and the purpose of the whole creation.

הודו — *Thank God.* The commentators stress that all of *Hallel* should be recited joyfully and melodiously, in the same way as we usually recite it in the synagogue on *Yomim Tovim*. In particular, however, the four verses that start with הודו should be recited in this manner. It is desirable that there should be at least three men at the *Seder*, so that one can appeal to the other two, הודו, *praise!*, and they will respond. If, however, there are no three men present, women and children can provide the response.

According to most commentators, this chapter, like the chapter before it, is addressed to all of mankind, not only to the Jewish people. However, it again singles out the House of Israel, the House of Aaron, and the God-fearing, calling on them in particular to pay homage to God's kindness. After this introduction, the chapter continues with a survey of the historical experiences of the Jewish people, leading up to their ultimate redemption.

מִן הַמֵּצַר — *Out of narrow confines.* We may be tempted in time of need to seek help from those around us who seem to be powerful. But we are warned that

If there are at least three people at the *Seder*, the father intones each of the following four lines, and the others respond by repeating the first line each time.

Thank HASHEM, for He is good;
>His kindness endures for ever!
Let Israel say:
>His kindness endures for ever!
Let the house of Aaron say:
>His kindness endures for ever!
Let them that fear HASHEM say:
>His kindness endures for ever!

Out of narrow confines did I call upon God; God answered by giving me wide-open freedom. HASHEM is with me, I fear nothing; what can man do to me? HASHEM is for me, through my helpers; therefore I can face my enemies! It is better to trust in HASHEM than to rely on man. It is better to trust in HASHEM, than to rely on princes. Let all the nations surround me; in the name of HASHEM, I cut them down! They encircle me, they swarm about me; in the name of HASHEM I cut them down! They swarm about me like bees, but they are extinguished like a fire of thorns; in the name of HASHEM I cut them down! You struck at me, again and again, to make me fall, but HASHEM helped me. HASHEM is my strength and

טוב לַחֲסוֹת בַּה', *it is better to trust in* HASHEM. God's help seems less concrete and obvious than what we can expect from human hands; but even princes cannot help the way God does. For the constriction of our earthly existence (מֵצַר) God substitutes true breadth of freedom (מֶרְחָב). The unique nature of this freedom is stressed by the *Talmud* which reads מֶרְחַבְיָ-ה as one word: Divine breadth of freedom (*Pesachim* 117a).

סְבָבוּנִי — *Surrounded me.* This phrase is here repeated three times, but with significant changes in each verse, which

prompted *Rabbi S.R. Hirsch* to see these three verses as referring to the three main periods of our history — the time of the First Temple when only our immediate neighbors attacked us, the time of the Second Temple when enemies came from near and far, and finally the present Exile which saw hosts of enemy nations attack us.

At the end of the days, looking back upon our history, we will see clearly that we were only able to cut down our enemies when we stood against them in the name of God — efforts to save ourselves by political and military means and by diplomatic reliance on

קוֹל רִנָּה וִישׁוּעָה בְּאָהֳלֵי צַדִּיקִים יְמִין יהוה
עֹשָׂה חָיִל: יְמִין יהוה רוֹמֵמָה יְמִין יהוה עֹשָׂה
חָיִל: לֹא אָמוּת כִּי אֶחְיֶה וַאֲסַפֵּר מַעֲשֵׂי יָהּ:
יַסֹּר יִסְּרַנִּי יָּהּ וְלַמָּוֶת לֹא נְתָנָנִי: פִּתְחוּ לִי
שַׁעֲרֵי צֶדֶק אָבֹא בָם אוֹדֶה יָהּ: זֶה הַשַּׁעַר
לַיהוה צַדִּיקִים יָבֹאוּ בוֹ: אוֹדְךָ כִּי עֲנִיתָנִי וַתְּהִי
לִי לִישׁוּעָה: אודך אֶבֶן מָאֲסוּ הַבּוֹנִים הָיְתָה
לְרֹאשׁ פִּנָּה: אבן מֵאֵת יהוה הָיְתָה זֹּאת הִיא
נִפְלָאת בְּעֵינֵינוּ: מאת זֶה הַיּוֹם עָשָׂה יהוה
נָגִילָה וְנִשְׂמְחָה בוֹ:זה

כשיש שלשה, האב אומר כל שורה מארבע שורות אלו בקול רם והאחרים
עונים אחריו.

אָנָּא יהוה הוֹשִׁיעָה נָּא:

אָנָּא יהוה הוֹשִׁיעָה נָּא:

אָנָּא יהוה הַצְלִיחָה נָּא:

אָנָּא יהוה הַצְלִיחָה נָּא:

בָּרוּךְ הַבָּא בְּשֵׁם יהוה בֵּרַכְנוּכֶם מִבֵּית
יהוה: ברוך אֵל יהוה וַיָּאֶר לָנוּ אִסְרוּ
חַג בַּעֲבֹתִים עַד קַרְנוֹת הַמִּזְבֵּחַ: אֵל אֵלִי אַתָּה
וְאוֹדֶךָּ אֱלֹהַי אֲרוֹמְמֶךָּ: אלי הוֹדוּ לַיהוה כִּי
טוֹב כִּי לְעוֹלָם חַסְדּוֹ:הודו

other nations have always proven disastrous for us (*Rabbi S.R. Hirsch* translates אֵמִילַם not as 'cutting down' but as 'facing', a derivation from מוּל, opposite).

פִּתְחוּ לִי שַׁעֲרֵי צֶדֶק — *Open to me the gates of righteousness.* These are the gates of the Law which is to guide our efforts at living a righteous life. Through our suffering, we are to mature, and fulfill our duties as set out in the Torah. It is only by following the law that we can come close to God — the gates of righteousness are the same as the gates of HASHEM to which the next verse refers: 'There is no other way to God than the path taught by His Law, which leads to a righteous daily life' (*Rabbi S.R. Hirsch*).

Anybody, who seeks this path can enter God's gate — the verse states that

song, and this has been my salvation! The sound of rejoicing and of salvation echoes in the tents of the righteous: 'The right hand of HASHEM does valiantly — the right hand of HASHEM is exalted — the right hand of HASHEM does valiantly!' No, I do not yet die! I shall live and recount the deeds of God! God has surely chastened me, but He has not given me over to death. Open to me the gates of righteousness, I will enter and thank HASHEM. This is the gate of HASHEM, the righteous shall enter into it. I thank You that You have answered me and again brought salvation to me. The stone which the builders rejected has become the corner-stone! This is HASHEM's doing, it is marvellous in our eyes! This day HASHEM has made, let us rejoice and delight in Him!

If there are at least three people at the *Seder*, the father intones each of the following four lines, and the others respond by repeating them after him.

O, HASHEM, save us!
O, HASHEM, save us!
O, HASHEM, make us prosper!
O, HASHEM, make us prosper!

Blessed be he that comes, in the name of HASHEM! We bless you from the Temple of HASHEM. HASHEM is God; He causes light to shine upon us! Bind the festive sacrifice with ropes to the corners of the altar! You are my God, I will give thanks unto You, my God, I will exalt You! Thank HASHEM, for He is good, His kindness endures for ever!

'*the righteous shall enter into it,*' rather than priests, Levites, or Jews. The role of the Jew is merely to serve as a guide to all the other nations.

מֵאֵת ה׳ — *This is HASHEM's doing.* The day marking Israel's final redemption and universal recognition by the nations can only be brought about by God; it will make us rejoice in Him — and will cause the nations, too, to direct their pleas to Him: '*O, HASHEM, save us!*'

בָּרוּךְ הַבָּא — *Blessed be he that comes.* This, according to *Rabbi S.R. Hirsch,* is our answer to the nations: bless them with the Name of God. We tell them that they will prosper if they take upon themselves the Name of God, and let themselves be guided by Him — for God

יְהַלְלוּךְ יהוה אֱלֹהֵינוּ כָּל מַעֲשֶׂיךָ
וַחֲסִידֶיךָ צַדִּיקִים עוֹשֵׂי רְצוֹנֶךָ
וְכָל עַמְּךָ בֵּית יִשְׂרָאֵל בְּרִנָּה יוֹדוּ וִיבָרְכוּ
וִישַׁבְּחוּ וִיפָאֲרוּ וִירוֹמְמוּ וְיַעֲרִיצוּ וְיַקְדִּישׁוּ
וְיַמְלִיכוּ אֶת שִׁמְךָ מַלְכֵּנוּ כִּי לְךָ טוֹב לְהוֹדוֹת
וּלְשִׁמְךָ נָאֶה לְזַמֵּר כִּי מֵעוֹלָם וְעַד עוֹלָם אַתָּה
אֵל:

תהלים
קלו

הוֹדוּ לַיהוה כִּי טוֹב   כִּי לְעוֹלָם חַסְדּוֹ:
הוֹדוּ לֵאלֹהֵי הָאֱלֹהִים   כְּלְ"חַ:
הוֹדוּ לַאֲדוֹנֵי הָאֲדוֹנִים   כִּי לְעוֹלָם חַסְדּוֹ:
לְעֹשֵׂה נִפְלָאוֹת גְּדֹלוֹת לְבַדּוֹ   כְּלְ"חַ:
לְעֹשֵׂה הַשָּׁמַיִם בִּתְבוּנָה   כִּי לְעוֹלָם חַסְדּוֹ:
לְרֹקַע הָאָרֶץ עַל הַמָּיִם   כִּי לְעוֹלָם חַסְדּוֹ:

lights up the right path for all of us. That means, however, that we cannot choose our own way of life, or our own way of attaining salvation — our festive sacrifice must be kept in bonds until it reaches God's altar and is offered as a sign of our obedience and submission. None of the many ways which man has invented to express religious feelings can substitute for the acceptance of God's authority and guidance. When this is understood by all, mankind as a whole will be able to praise God for His kindness.

הוֹדוּ לַה' — *Give thanks to HASHEM.* The Talmud calls this psalm הַלֵּל הַגָּדוֹל, *the great Hallel,* because it describes God throning on high yet granting food

to every being: feeding all creatures, day in and day out, is the greatest manifestation of God's provident kindness! *(Pesachim* 118a).

The first twenty-four verses ask us to give thanks to God who is the master of the universe, created it, redeemed us from Egypt, gave us the land of Sichon and Og, and delivered us from our enemies. They all are speaking of the God throning on high. Then comes the twenty-fifth verse which stands by itself as a separate statement: *'He gives food to all creatures'* — He is close to their needs, even though he rules in supreme splendour. In fact, the Psalm teaches us that every piece of bread that comes our way is another demonstration of the lofty ways of God's

The following passage is generally recited according to נוֹסַח אַשְׁכְּנַז, the Ashkenazic rite (however, according to the Vilna Gaon it is not recited on *Seder* night). According to the Sefardic rite, נוֹסַח סְפָרַד, it is recited later (p. 198).

All Your works shall praise You, HASHEM our God; Your pious ones, the righteous who do Your will, as well as Your entire people, the house of Israel, will joyfully thank and praise, laud and honour, exalt and revere, sanctify and do homage to Your name, our King! For it is good to thank You, and fitting to sing praises unto Your name; for from eternity unto eternity You are God!

Give thanks to HASHEM for He is good,
  His kindness endures forever!
Give thanks to the God of gods,
  His kindness endures forever!
Give thanks to the Lord of lords,
  His kindness endures forever!
Who alone does great wonders,
  His kindness endures forever!
Who, with understanding, made the heavens,
  His kindness endures forever!
Who stretched out the earth above the waters,
  His kindness endures forever!

Providence: 'The mighty acts of God, in nature and history, must interact if an honest man is to receive his daily bread in an honest manner from God's loving hand' *(Rabbi S.R. Hirsch)*.

The refrain in each verse stresses the idea of God's lovingkindness — and so does the number of verses in this Psalm. There are 26, corresponding to the Divine name that expresses מִדַּת הָרַחֲמִים, God's quality of mercy. Moreover, our Sages point out that there were 26 generations of man before the Torah was given; God's kindness provided nourishment for them even though the merit of the Torah did not yet sustain them.

This Psalm is recited on *Seder* night because it points to God's kindness in saving us in such a miraculous way from Egypt. However, there is the further message that God's kindness endures. Every day and every moment we enjoy its blessings; and so we can trust that in due course it will bring the final redemption for which we long.

לְעֹשֵׂה נִפְלָאוֹת גְּדֹלוֹת לְבַדּוֹ — *Who alone does great wonders.* God does great wonders for us *by Himself,* without our

לְעֹשֵׂה אוֹרִים גְּדֹלִים   כִּי לְעוֹלָם חַסְדּוֹ:

אֶת הַשֶּׁמֶשׁ לְמֶמְשֶׁלֶת בַּיּוֹם כִּי לְעוֹלָם חַסְדּוֹ:

אֶת הַיָּרֵחַ וְכוֹכָבִים לְמֶמְשְׁלוֹת בַּלָּיְלָה כְּלֵ"חַ:

לְמַכֵּה מִצְרַיִם בִּבְכוֹרֵיהֶם   כִּי לְעוֹלָם חַסְדּוֹ:

וַיּוֹצֵא יִשְׂרָאֵל מִתּוֹכָם   כִּי לְעוֹלָם חַסְדּוֹ:

בְּיָד חֲזָקָה וּבִזְרוֹעַ נְטוּיָה   כִּי לְעוֹלָם חַסְדּוֹ:

לְגֹזֵר יַם סוּף לִגְזָרִים   כִּי לְעוֹלָם חַסְדּוֹ:

וְהֶעֱבִיר יִשְׂרָאֵל בְּתוֹכוֹ   כִּי לְעוֹלָם חַסְדּוֹ:

וְנִעֵר פַּרְעֹה וְחֵילוֹ בְיַם סוּף   כְּלֵ"חַ:

לְמוֹלִיךְ עַמּוֹ בַּמִּדְבָּר   כִּי לְעוֹלָם חַסְדּוֹ:

לְמַכֵּה מְלָכִים גְּדֹלִים   כִּי לְעוֹלָם חַסְדּוֹ:

וַיַּהֲרֹג מְלָכִים אַדִּירִים   כִּי לְעוֹלָם חַסְדּוֹ:

לְסִיחוֹן מֶלֶךְ הָאֱמֹרִי   כִּי לְעוֹלָם חַסְדּוֹ:

וּלְעוֹג מֶלֶךְ הַבָּשָׁן   כִּי לְעוֹלָם חַסְדּוֹ:

וְנָתַן אַרְצָם לְנַחֲלָה   כִּי לְעוֹלָם חַסְדּוֹ:

נַחֲלָה לְיִשְׂרָאֵל עַבְדּוֹ   כִּי לְעוֹלָם חַסְדּוֹ:

שֶׁבְּשִׁפְלֵנוּ זָכַר לָנוּ   כִּי לְעוֹלָם חַסְדּוֹ:

וַיִּפְרְקֵנוּ מִצָּרֵינוּ   כִּי לְעוֹלָם חַסְדּוֹ:

being aware of the sheltering hand which He holds over us (Yalkut).

לְגֹזֵר יַם סוּף לִגְזָרִים — Who divided the Sea of Reeds into parts. Our Sages explain that the sea was split into twelve parts so that each tribe had its own route. Why was this miracle necessary? The Sfas Emes suggests that we were to be taught that each tribe had a role of its own within the Jewish people and therefore deserved that the sea should be split for it — and in fact every individual Jew had a share in the splitting of the sea.

Who made the great lights,
  His kindness endures forever!
The sun, to rule by day,
  His kindness endures forever!
The moon and stars, to rule by night,
  His kindness endures forever!
Who smote the Egyptians through their first-born,
  His kindness endures forever!
And liberated Israel from their midst,
  His kindness endures forever!
With a strong hand and outstretched arm,
  His kindness endures forever!
Who divided the Sea of Reeds into parts,
  His kindness endures forever!
And made Israel pass through it,
  His kindness endures forever!
And threw Pharaoh and his army into the Sea of Reeds.
  His kindness endures forever!
Who led His people through the wilderness,
  His kindness endures forever!
Who smote great kings,
  His kindness endures forever!
And slew mighty rulers,
  His kindness endures forever!
Sichon, king of the Amorites,
  His kindness endures forever!
And Og, king of Bashan,
  His kindness endures forever!
And gave their land as an inheritance,
  His kindness endures forever!
As an inheritance to his servant Israel,
  His kindness endures forever!
Who remembered us in our lowliness,
  His kindness endures forever!
And delivered us from our enemies,
  His kindness endures forever!

נֹתֵן לֶחֶם לְכָל בָּשָׂר כִּי לְעוֹלָם חַסְדּוֹ:
הוֹדוּ לְאֵל הַשָּׁמַיִם כִּי לְעוֹלָם חַסְדּוֹ:

נִשְׁמַת כָּל חַי תְּבָרֵךְ אֶת שִׁמְךָ יהוה אֱלֹהֵינוּ וְרוּחַ כָּל בָּשָׂר תְּפָאֵר וּתְרוֹמֵם זִכְרְךָ מַלְכֵּנוּ תָּמִיד. מִן הָעוֹלָם וְעַד הָעוֹלָם אַתָּה אֵל וּמִבַּלְעָדֶיךָ אֵין לָנוּ מֶלֶךְ גּוֹאֵל וּמוֹשִׁיעַ פּוֹדֶה וּמַצִּיל וּמְפַרְנֵס וּמְרַחֵם בְּכָל עֵת צָרָה וְצוּקָה. אֵין לָנוּ מֶלֶךְ אֶלָּא אָתָּה. אֱלֹהֵי הָרִאשׁוֹנִים וְהָאַחֲרוֹנִים אֱלוֹהַ כָּל בְּרִיּוֹת אֲדוֹן כָּל תּוֹלָדוֹת הַמְהֻלָּל בְּרוֹב הַתִּשְׁבָּחוֹת הַמְנַהֵג עוֹלָמוֹ בְּחֶסֶד וּבְרִיּוֹתָיו בְּרַחֲמִים. וַיהוה לֹא יָנוּם וְלֹא יִישָׁן הַמְעוֹרֵר יְשֵׁנִים וְהַמֵּקִיץ נִרְדָּמִים וְהַמֵּשִׂיחַ אִלְּמִים וְהַמַּתִּיר אֲסוּרִים וְהַסּוֹמֵךְ נוֹפְלִים וְהַזּוֹקֵף כְּפוּפִים לְךָ לְבַדְּךָ אֲנַחְנוּ מוֹדִים. אִלּוּ פִינוּ מָלֵא שִׁירָה כַּיָּם וּלְשׁוֹנֵנוּ רִנָּה כַּהֲמוֹן גַּלָּיו וְשִׂפְתוֹתֵינוּ שֶׁבַח כְּמֶרְחֲבֵי רָקִיעַ וְעֵינֵינוּ מְאִירוֹת כַּשֶּׁמֶשׁ וְכַיָּרֵחַ וְיָדֵינוּ פְרוּשׂוֹת כְּנִשְׁרֵי שָׁמַיִם וְרַגְלֵינוּ קַלּוֹת כָּאַיָּלוֹת אֵין אֲנַחְנוּ מַסְפִּיקִים לְהוֹדוֹת לְךָ יהוה אֱלֹהֵינוּ וֵאלֹהֵי אֲבוֹתֵינוּ וּלְבָרֵךְ אֶת שִׁמְךָ עַל

נִשְׁמַת — *The soul of every living thing.* Here begins a lengthy blessing which ends with the passage יִשְׁתַּבַּח (p.196). Our Sages call it בִּרְכַּת הַשִּׁיר, *the blessing of the song,* either because it forms a lengthy song (*Siddur Avodas Yisroel*), or because it serves as the conclusion to the Psalms, the songs of King David, that we recite in the morning prayers. On weekdays, when we may not have sufficient time to concentrate adequately on our prayers, we conclude the reading of the Psalms by reciting only the end of the בִּרְכַּת הַשִּׁיר, the passage starting יִשְׁתַּבַּח. On *Shabbos* and *Yom Tov,* however, we recite the entire blessing, starting from נִשְׁמַת. At the *Seder* the blessing is recited in conclusion of *Hallel;* but there are differences of opinion as to whether it should end in the same way as on *Shabbos* (see p. 196).

The recitation of the entire blessing in the *Shabbos* and *Yom Tov* prayer service dates back only to the period of the

He gives food to all creatures
  His kindness endures forever!
Give thanks unto Him, the God of heaven,
  His kindness endures forever!

The soul of every living thing shall bless Your
name, HASHEM our God, and the spirit of all flesh
shall always glorify and exalt the remembrance of
You, our king. From eternity unto eternity You are
God, and beside You we have no King, Redeemer and
Helper, Saviour and Deliverer, Sustainer and Com-
forter at all times of trouble and distress; we have no
King but You! You are, God of the first and the last,
God of all creatures, Lord of all generations, who is
extolled through a multitude of praises, who guides
His world with lovingkindness and His creatures with
mercy. HASHEM neither slumbers nor sleeps. He
awakens the sleepers and arouses the slumberers,
gives speech to the mute, frees the bound, supports
the falling, raises up those that are bowed down. To
You alone we give thanks! Even if our mouths were
filled with song like the sea, and our tongues with
jubilation like the multitude of its waves, and our lips
with praise like the expanse of the heaven, and our
eyes shining like the sun and the moon, and our
hands spread out like the eagles of heaven, and our
feet swift like deer, we would still be unable to thank
Your sufficiently, HASHEM our God and God of our
fathers, and to praise Your name for even one of the

Gaonim; but it was composed much
earlier and various parts of it are quoted
in the Talmud (*Rabbeinu Jonah*). It has
been suggested that it was composed by
Shimon ben Shetach, during the
Hasmonean period (*Kolbo*); others have
ascribed it to an author *Isaac*, otherwise
unknown.

Its inclusion in the *Seder* is very un-
derstandable. Not only is the Exodus
from Egypt mentioned, but it is placed
in the context of God's lasting
Providence, as savior and protector of
His creatures. There emerges the most
eloquent description of our unlimited
indebtedness to God, and we are inspired to pile more and more expressions of praise on top of each other, in a
vain effort to do justice to our obligations.

אַחַת מֵאֶלֶף אֶלֶף אַלְפֵי אֲלָפִים וְרֻבֵּי רְבָבוֹת
פְּעָמִים הַטּוֹבוֹת שֶׁעָשִׂיתָ עִם אֲבוֹתֵינוּ וְעִמָּנוּ.
מִמִּצְרַיִם גְּאַלְתָּנוּ יהוה אֱלֹהֵינוּ וּמִבֵּית עֲבָדִים
פְּדִיתָנוּ בְּרָעָב זַנְתָּנוּ וּבְשָׂבָע כִּלְכַּלְתָּנוּ מֵחֶרֶב
הִצַּלְתָּנוּ וּמִדֶּבֶר מִלַּטְתָּנוּ וּמֵחֳלָיִם רָעִים
וְנֶאֱמָנִים דִּלִּיתָנוּ. עַד הֵנָּה עֲזָרוּנוּ רַחֲמֶיךָ וְלֹא
עֲזָבוּנוּ חֲסָדֶיךָ וְאַל תִּטְּשֵׁנוּ יהוה אֱלֹהֵינוּ
לָנֶצַח. עַל כֵּן אֵבָרִים שֶׁפִּלַּגְתָּ בָּנוּ וְרוּחַ וּנְשָׁמָה
שֶׁנָּפַחְתָּ בְּאַפֵּינוּ וְלָשׁוֹן אֲשֶׁר שַׂמְתָּ בְּפִינוּ הֵן
הֵם יוֹדוּ וִיבָרְכוּ וִישַׁבְּחוּ וִיפָאֲרוּ וִירוֹמְמוּ
וְיַעֲרִיצוּ וְיַקְדִּישׁוּ וְיַמְלִיכוּ אֶת שִׁמְךָ מַלְכֵּנוּ. כִּי
כָל פֶּה לְךָ יוֹדֶה וְכָל לָשׁוֹן לְךָ תִשָּׁבַע וְכָל בֶּרֶךְ
לְךָ תִכְרַע וְכָל קוֹמָה לְפָנֶיךָ תִשְׁתַּחֲוֶה וְכָל
לְבָבוֹת יִירָאוּךָ וְכָל קֶרֶב וּכְלָיוֹת יְזַמְּרוּ לִשְׁמֶךָ.
כַּדָּבָר שֶׁכָּתוּב °כָּל עַצְמוֹתַי תֹּאמַרְנָה יהוה מִי °תהלים
כָמוֹךָ מַצִּיל עָנִי מֵחָזָק מִמֶּנּוּ וְעָנִי וְאֶבְיוֹן לה:י
מִגֹּזְלוֹ. מִי יִדְמֶה לָּךְ וּמִי יִשְׁוֶה לָּךְ וּמִי יַעֲרָךְ
לָךְ הָאֵל הַגָּדוֹל הַגִּבּוֹר וְהַנּוֹרָא אֵל עֶלְיוֹן קוֹנֵה
שָׁמַיִם וָאָרֶץ. נְהַלֶּלְךָ וּנְשַׁבֵּחֲךָ וּנְפָאֶרְךָ וּנְבָרֵךְ
אֶת שֵׁם קָדְשֶׁךָ כָּאָמוּר °לְדָוִד °בָּרְכִי נַפְשִׁי אֶת °תהלים
יהוה וְכָל קְרָבַי אֶת שֵׁם קָדְשׁוֹ: קג:א

הָאֵל בְּתַעֲצֻמוֹת עֻזֶּךָ הַגָּדוֹל בִּכְבוֹד שְׁמֶךָ
הַגִּבּוֹר לָנֶצַח וְהַנּוֹרָא בְּנוֹרְאוֹתֶיךָ
הַמֶּלֶךְ הַיּוֹשֵׁב עַל כִּסֵּא רָם וְנִשָּׂא:

בָּרְכִי נַפְשִׁי אֶת ה' —*Praise HASHEM, O my soul.* The soul is given to us by God, and is our closest link to Him; He breathed it into us as part of His own Divine essence.

Moreover, the soul plays a similar role within the human being as God, so to speak, does in His world; the soul occupies the entire body but dwells in its innermost recesses, sees but is not seen,

*thousands and myriads of favors which You have
done for our fathers and for us. You redeemed us
from Egypt, HASHEM our God, and You delivered us
from the house of bondage; in hunger You fed us
and in plenty You sustained us; from the sword You
saved us; from pestilence You let us escape; and You
rescued us from evil and lasting diseases. Until now
Your mercy has helped us and Your lovingkindness
has not forsaken us, HASHEM our God, do not ever
abandon us. Therefore the limbs which You have
formed for us, and the spirit and soul which You
have breathed into our nostrils, and the tongue which
You have placed in our mouth, shall thank, bless and
laud, glorify and extol, revere, sanctify and do
homage to Your name, our King. For every mouth
shall thank You, every tongue shall swear loyalty
unto You, every knee shall bow down before You,
everything upstanding shall prostrate itself before
You, all hearts shall fear You, all men's innermost being shall sing praises unto Your name, as it is written:
"All my bones say: 'HASHEM, who is like unto You!'
You deliver the poor from one that is stronger than
he, the poor and needy from one that robs him!"
Who is like You, who is equal to You, who can be
compared unto You, great, mighty and awe-inspiring
God, supreme God, possessor of heaven and earth.
We shall praise You, laud You, glorify You, and bless
Your holy name, as it is said: "A Psalm Of David.
Praise HASHEM, O my soul, and all that is within me,
His holy name!"*

*You are God, in the omnipotence of Your
strength; great in the glory of Your name; mighty for
ever; awe-inspiring through Your awesome deeds;
the King, who is enthroned on a high and lofty
throne!*

---

and sustains the whole organism
(Midrash). Therefore, the soul is called
upon in the first place to give praise to
God — but so is כָּל קְרָבַי, *all that is
within me,* all the physical organs which
serve as tools of the soul for carrying

שׁוֹכֵן עַד מָרוֹם וְקָדוֹשׁ שְׁמוֹ. וְכָתוּב °רַנְּנוּ
צַדִּיקִים בַּיהוה לַיְשָׁרִים נָאוָה תְהִלָּה:
בְּפִי יְשָׁרִים תִּתְהַלָּל וּבְדִבְרֵי צַדִּיקִים תִּתְבָּרַךְ
וּבִלְשׁוֹן חֲסִידִים תִּתְרוֹמָם וּבְקֶרֶב קְדוֹשִׁים
תִּתְקַדָּשׁ:

וּבְמַקְהֲלוֹת רִבְבוֹת עַמְּךָ בֵּית יִשְׂרָאֵל
בְּרִנָּה יִתְפָּאַר שִׁמְךָ מַלְכֵּנוּ
בְּכָל דּוֹר וָדוֹר שֶׁכֵּן חוֹבַת כָּל הַיְצוּרִים לְפָנֶיךָ
יהוה אֱלֹהֵינוּ וֵאלֹהֵי אֲבוֹתֵינוּ לְהוֹדוֹת לְהַלֵּל
לְשַׁבֵּחַ לְפָאֵר לְרוֹמֵם לְהַדֵּר לְבָרֵךְ לְעַלֵּה
וּלְקַלֵּס עַל כָּל דִּבְרֵי שִׁירוֹת וְתִשְׁבָּחוֹת דָּוִד בֶּן
יִשַׁי עַבְדְּךָ מְשִׁיחֶךָ:

יִשְׁתַּבַּח שִׁמְךָ לָעַד מַלְכֵּנוּ הָאֵל הַמֶּלֶךְ
הַגָּדוֹל וְהַקָּדוֹשׁ בַּשָּׁמַיִם וּבָאָרֶץ
כִּי לְךָ נָאֶה יהוה אֱלֹהֵינוּ וֵאלֹהֵי אֲבוֹתֵינוּ שִׁיר
וּשְׁבָחָה הַלֵּל וְזִמְרָה עֹז וּמֶמְשָׁלָה נֶצַח גְּדֻלָּה
וּגְבוּרָה תְּהִלָּה וְתִפְאֶרֶת קְדֻשָּׁה וּמַלְכוּת
בְּרָכוֹת וְהוֹדָאוֹת מֵעַתָּה וְעַד־עוֹלָם.

לְפִי נֻסַּח אַשְׁכְּנַז אוֹמְרִים בְּרָכָה זוֹ (אָמְנָם יֵשׁ אוֹמְרִים **בָּא''י מֶלֶךְ מְהֻלָּל
בַּתִּשְׁבָּחוֹת**).

בָּרוּךְ אַתָּה יהוה אֵל מֶלֶךְ גָּדוֹל בַּתִּשְׁבָּחוֹת
אֵל הַהוֹדָאוֹת אֲדוֹן הַנִּפְלָאוֹת הַבּוֹחֵר בְּשִׁירֵי
זִמְרָה מֶלֶךְ אֵל חֵי הָעוֹלָמִים:

out God's will. Man's power to praise
God by word of mouth is limited; instead he is called upon to use all the
faculties of his body and soul in order to

He who dwells in eternity — supreme and holy is His name, and it is written: "Rejoice in HASHEM, you righteous; it is fitting for the upright to give songs of praise." By the mouth of the upright You shall be praised, through the word of the righteous You shall be blessed, by the tongue of the devoted You shall be exalted, and among the holy You shall be sanctified.

And in the assemblies of the myriads of Your people, the house of Israel, shall Your name be glorified with jubilation, O our King, in every generation; for such is the duty of all creatures before You, HASHEM our God and God of our fathers, to thank, praise, laud, glorify, extol, honour, bless, exalt and sing praises — even beyond all the words of song and praise by David, son of Yishai, Your servant, Your anointed!

Praised be Your name for ever, our King, the great and holy God and King in heaven and on earth; for to You, HASHEM our God and God of our fathers, belong song and praise, glorification and hymns, strength and dominion, victory, greatness and might, fame and glory, holiness and sovereignty, blessings and thanksgivings from now and for evermore.

According to the Ashkenazic rite, the following blessing is now recited (some, however, say instead בָּרוּךְ אַתָּה ה' מֶלֶךְ מְהוּלָל בַּתִּשְׁבָּחוֹת). The Sefardic rite continues instead with יְהַלְלוּךְ, on next page.

Blessed are You, HASHEM, God and King, great in renown, God of thanksgivings, Lord of wonders, who is pleased with songs of praise, King, God. Life of all worlds.

make his life a paean of praise to God.

יִשְׁתַּבַּח — Praised be Your name. The concluding passage of the בִּרְכַּת הַשִּׁיר contains 15 expressions of praise. As pointed out previously (p. 139), they reflect God's name, י־ה, as it is revealed in our world today (with the coming of Mashiach the entire Name, of four letters, will reveal itself in our world; p. 176).

יְהַלְלוּךְ יהוה אֱלֹהֵינוּ כָּל מַעֲשֶׂיךָ וַחֲסִידֶיךָ
צַדִּיקִים עוֹשֵׂי רְצוֹנֶךָ וְכָל עַמְּךָ בֵּית יִשְׂרָאֵל
בְּרִנָּה יוֹדוּ וִיבָרְכוּ וִישַׁבְּחוּ וִיפָאֲרוּ וִירוֹמְמוּ
וְיַעֲרִיצוּ וְיַקְדִּישׁוּ וְיַמְלִיכוּ אֶת שִׁמְךָ מַלְכֵּנוּ כִּי
לְךָ טוֹב לְהוֹדוֹת וּלְשִׁמְךָ נָאֶה לְזַמֵּר כִּי מֵעוֹלָם
וְעַד עוֹלָם אַתָּה אֵל: בָּרוּךְ אַתָּה יהוה מֶלֶךְ
מְהֻלָּל בַּתִּשְׁבָּחוֹת:

לפי כמה דעות שותים כוס רביעי כאן ואומרים **חסל סידור פסח**. ויש
שמאחרים השתיה ואמירת **חסל** וכו' עד אחר אמירת **ובכן** וכו'.

שותים כוס רביעי בהסיבה (ונכון לשתות כל הכוס) אחר אמירת ברכה זו:

בָּרוּךְ אַתָּה יהוה אֱלֹהֵינוּ מֶלֶךְ הָעוֹלָם
בּוֹרֵא פְּרִי הַגָּפֶן:

אחר שתיית כל הכוס אומרים ברכה זו.

בָּרוּךְ אַתָּה יהוה אֱלֹהֵינוּ מֶלֶךְ הָעוֹלָם עַל הַגֶּפֶן
וְעַל פְּרִי הַגֶּפֶן וְעַל תְּנוּבַת הַשָּׂדֶה וְעַל אֶרֶץ חֶמְדָּה
טוֹבָה וּרְחָבָה שֶׁרָצִיתָ וְהִנְחַלְתָּ לַאֲבוֹתֵינוּ לֶאֱכוֹל
מִפִּרְיָהּ וְלִשְׂבּוֹעַ מִטּוּבָהּ. רַחֵם נָא יהוה אֱלֹהֵינוּ עַל
יִשְׂרָאֵל עַמֶּךָ וְעַל יְרוּשָׁלַיִם עִירֶךָ וְעַל צִיּוֹן מִשְׁכַּן
כְּבוֹדֶךָ וְעַל מִזְבַּחֶךָ וְעַל הֵיכָלֶךָ וּבְנֵה יְרוּשָׁלַיִם עִיר
הַקֹּדֶשׁ בִּמְהֵרָה בְיָמֵינוּ וְהַעֲלֵנוּ לְתוֹכָהּ וְשַׂמְּחֵנוּ
בְּבִנְיָנָהּ וְנֹאכַל מִפִּרְיָהּ וְנִשְׂבַּע מִטּוּבָהּ וּנְבָרֶכְךָ עָלֶיהָ

* *According to many opinions* — The fourth cup was ordained to be drunk in connection with *Hallel*. According to many authorities it is therefore drunk at this point, after the concluding blessing over *Hallel (Maharshal)*. However, the *Maharam Rothenburg* delayed the drinking of the fourth cup until after כִּי לוֹ נָאֶה (which, in his days, was the end of the *Haggadah)*; since it is forbidden to drink anything substantial after the fourth cup, he wanted it drunk late, in order to keep the *Seder* company from getting thirsty. Many Ashkenazic communities follow his practice.

* *The fourth cup ... should be drained completely*. Why? To fulfill the duty of the Four Cups, it is enough to drink most of the contents of a cup which

(This paragraph is only recited by those who did not recite it before (p. 188) and who did not pronounce the blessing immediately preceding).

All your works shall praise You, HASHEM our God; Your pious ones, the righteous who do Your will, as well as Your entire people, the house of Israel, will joyfully thank and praise, laud and honour, exalt and revere, sanctify and do homage to Your name, our King! For it is good to thank You, and fitting to sing praises unto Your name; for from eternity unto eternity You are God! Blessed are You, HASHEM, King, extolled with praises.

According to many opinions* the fourth cup is drunk, and הַלֵּל is recited; however, others do so later (p. 210), and at this point continue with וּבְכֵן. The fourth cup should be drunk whilst reclining, and should be drained completely,* after recitation of the following blessing:

B*lessed are You, HASHEM our God, King of the universe, who creates the fruit of the vine.*

After drinking the fourth cup, the following blessing is recited:

Blessed are You, HASHEM our God, King of the universe, for the vine and the fruit of the vine, for the produce of the field and for the desirable, goodly and spacious land that You were pleased to give to our ancestors to inherit, to eat its fruits, and to satisfy themselves with its goodness. Have compassion, HASHEM our God, on Your people Israel, on Your city Jerusalem, on Zion the dwelling-place of Your holiness, on Your altar and on Your Temple. Rebuild Your holy city, Jerusalem, soon and in our days, bring us thereto, and let us rejoice in its rebuilding; that we may eat of its fruit, be satisfied with its goodness,

holds a *Revi'is* (see p. 50). However, if one only drinks *most of a Revi'is*, rather than *a whole Rivi'is*, he cannot recite the blessing that should be pronounced after drinking wine; this blessing may only be recited if we drank a complete *Revi'is*. Since the fourth cup is the last wine we drink at the *Seder*, and we would like to recite the concluding blessing, we are therefore advised to drink an entire *Revi'is*. The cups used at the *Seder* usually only contain a *Revi'is* and therefore must be drained completely. However, even if a cup is larger, there exists an opinion that it is desirable to drink it completely.

בִּקְדֻשָּׁה וּבְטָהֳרָה (בשבת וּרְצֵה וְהַחֲלִיצֵנוּ בְּיוֹם
הַשַּׁבָּת הַזֶּה) וְשַׂמְּחֵנוּ בְּיוֹם חַג הַמַּצּוֹת הַזֶּה כִּי אַתָּה
יהוה טוֹב וּמֵטִיב לַכֹּל וְנוֹדֶה לְּךָ עַל הָאָרֶץ וְעַל פְּרִי
הַגָּפֶן: בָּרוּךְ אַתָּה יהוה עַל הָאָרֶץ וְעַל פְּרִי הַגָּפֶן:

נִרְצָה

חֲסַל סִדּוּר פֶּסַח כְּהִלְכָתוֹ. כְּכָל מִשְׁפָּטוֹ
וְחֻקָּתוֹ. כַּאֲשֶׁר זָכִינוּ לְסַדֵּר אוֹתוֹ. כֵּן
נִזְכֶּה לַעֲשׂוֹתוֹ: זָךְ שׁוֹכֵן מְעוֹנָה. קוֹמֵם קְהַל
עֲדַת מִי מָנָה. בְּקָרוֹב נַהֵל נִטְעֵי כַנָּה. פְּדוּיִם
לְצִיּוֹן בְּרִנָּה:

לְשָׁנָה הַבָּאָה בִּירוּשָׁלָיִם:

אומרים זה בליל ראשון של פסח. בליל שני מתחילים **וּבְכֵן וַאֲמַרְתֶּם** וכו' (עמוד 204).

וּבְכֵן וַיְהִי בַּחֲצִי הַלַּיְלָה:

בַּלַּיְלָה.	אָז רוֹב נִסִּים הִפְלֵאתָ
הַלַּיְלָה.	בְּרֹאשׁ אַשְׁמוֹרֶת זֶה

נִרְצָה — *Our Observance is Accepted.* The exact meaning of this phrase is not clear. According to some *Haggados*, it marks the end of the formal part of the *Haggadah* and expresses our prayer that our Seder observance should be found acceptable by God. This is the same thought conveyed by the passage that follows, חֲסַל. *Vayaged Mosheh* suggests that it introduces the informal part of the *Seder*. We have completed all the required observances, but it is desirable and praiseworthy to continue talking about the Exodus throughout the entire night or at least until sleep overtakes us. We therefore express the hope that this next part of the *Seder* should also be

found worthy and acceptable.

חֲסַל — *The order of the Pesach service is now completed.* This passage is the concluding part of the פִּיּוּט, the liturgical poem which *Rabbi Joseph Tov Elem (Bonfils)* wrote for the *Shabbos* before *Pesach*, and in which he summarized all the laws and observances connected with *Pesach*.

The passage included in the *Haggadah* states that, just as we were found worthy to perform (לְסַדֵּר) the Pesach service, so may we be worthy to do it (לַעֲשׂוֹתוֹ) in future. The Hebrew expression לְסַדֵּר can be taken in various ways. It can be translated *'to plan'* or *'to ar-*

and praise You for it in holiness and purity. (May it
be Your will to fortify us on this Sabbath day). Let us
rejoice on this festival of Matzos, for You, HASHEM,
are good, and beneficient to all, and we thank You
for the land and the fruit of the vine. Blessed are You,
HASHEM, for the land and the fruit of the vine.

Nirtzah / Our Observance is Accepted

The order of the Pesach service is now completed in
accordance with all its laws, its ordinances and
statutes. Just as we were found worthy to perform it,
so may we be worthy to do it in future. O Pure One,
who dwells on high, raise up the congregation which
is without number! Soon, and with rejoicing, lead the
offshoots of the stock that you have planted,
redeemed, to Zion.

Next year in Jerusalem!

The following is said on the first night of *Pesach*. On the second night, continue
on p. 204.

It came to pass at midnight.
Of old, You performed many miracles by night.
At the beginning of the first watch of this night.

range'; in this sense it very well
describes what we did when we recited
the פִּיּוּט in the synagogue. It can also be
translated 'to perform in an orderly
fashion', in which case it describes our
Seder night observances. However, it
does not have the same definite meaning
as לַעֲשׂוֹתוֹ, 'to do it' — for, indeed, we
were not able 'to do' the Seder as it
should be done, since we do not have a
Pesach sacrifice. The author, in effect,
prays that in the merit of our studying
the laws of Pesach (before Pesach), or
our observance of the Seder ritual (in
this night), we should see the Temple
rebuilt, and be able to fulfill all the laws
of Pesach.

וּבְכֵן וַיְהִי — It came to pass. The night of
Pesach is לֵיל שִׁמּוּרִים, a night for
watching. It is set aside for miraculous
manifestations of God's might and His
concern for the Jewish people (Ohr
Hachaim). This poem lists some of the
outstanding happenings that took place
in various Pesach nights in the course of
our history. It was written by Jannai,
one of the first and greatest of our syn-
agogal poets, who lived in Eretz Yisrael
at the end of the Talmudic era. He chose
the form of an acrostic for this poem;
the first letters of each line are in the
order of the Alephbet.

גֵּר צֶדֶק נִצַּחְתּוֹ כְּנֶחֱלַק לוֹ   לַיְלָה.

וַיְהִי בַּחֲצִי הַלַּיְלָה:

דַּנְתָּ מֶלֶךְ גְּרָר בַּחֲלוֹם   הַלַּיְלָה.

הִפְחַדְתָּ אֲרַמִּי בְּאֶמֶשׁ   לַיְלָה.

וַיָּשַׂר יִשְׂרָאֵל לְמַלְאָךְ וַיּוּכַל לוֹ   לַיְלָה.

וַיְהִי בַּחֲצִי הַלַּיְלָה:

זֶרַע בְּכוֹרֵי פַתְרוֹס מָחַצְתָּ בַּחֲצִי   הַלַּיְלָה.

חֵילָם לֹא מָצְאוּ בְּקוּמָם   בַּלַּיְלָה.

טִיסַת נְגִיד חֲרוֹשֶׁת סִלִּיתָ בְּכוֹכְבֵי   לַיְלָה.

וַיְהִי בַּחֲצִי הַלַּיְלָה:

יָעַץ מְחָרֵף לְנוֹפֵף אִוּוּי הוֹבַשְׁתָּ פְגָרָיו   בַּלַּיְלָה.

כָּרַע בֵּל וּמַצָּבוֹ בְּאִישׁוֹן   לַיְלָה.

לְאִישׁ חֲמוּדוֹת נִגְלָה רָז חֲזוֹת   לַיְלָה.

וַיְהִי בַּחֲצִי הַלַּיְלָה:

מִשְׁתַּכֵּר בִּכְלֵי קֹדֶשׁ נֶהֱרַג בּוֹ   בַּלַּיְלָה.

Thirteen events are described here:

— Abraham's defeat of the four Canaanite kings (Bereishis 14); according to the Midrashic interpretation of the Biblical text, the night of the fifteenth of Nissan was divided into two halves: the first was dedicated to Abraham's miraculous victory over the kings, and the second half of the night was set aside for the awesome final stage of the Exodus.

— God's warning to Abimelech that he would die unless he returned Sarah to Abraham (Bereishis 20).

— God's appearance to Laban the night before his encounter with Jacob, when He warned Laban not to harm Jacob (Bereishis 31); the phrase בְּאֶמֶשׁ לַיְלָה can mean either 'the dark of night' or 'the preceding night.'

— Jacob's struggle with the angel of Esau. It was the triumphant battle with an angel that earned him the name Israel (Bereishis 32).

— The killing of the firstborn, when the Egyptian people lost 'their host,' their army (others translate חֵילָם as 'their strength' or 'their possessions').

— The defeat of Sisra's army thanks to the intervention of the stars (Shoftim 4 and 5). טִיסָה, flight, is used to describe the army, either because it moved fast, as if on wings, or because of its waving flags.

— The annihilation of Sancherib's army — which had laid siege to God's dwelling place, Jerusalem — after he had sent his envoy to blaspheme God (Melachim II 19); literally הוֹבַשְׁתָּ means that God made Sancherib's dead wither into dry

To the righteous convert (Abraham) You gave victory when there was divided for him the night.

It came to pass at midnight.

You judged the king of Gerar (Abimelech with death) in a dream by night.

You frightened the Aramean (Laban) in the dark of night.

Israel (Jacob) fought with an angel and overcame him by night.

It came to pass at midnight.

The first-born children of the Egyptians You crushed at midnight.

They did not find their host when they arose at night.

You swept away the army of the prince of Charoshes (Sisra) with the stars of night.

It came to pass at midnight.

The blasphemer (Sancherib) had planned to raise his hand against Jerusalem; You laid low his dead by night.

The idol Bel was overthrown, with its pedestal, in the darkness of the night.

To Daniel, in whom You delighted, the secret vision was revealed at night.

It came to pass at midnight.

He who caroused from the holy vessels (Belshazar) was slain on that same night.

---

bones, as seen by the prophet Ezekiel.

— The dream of Nebuchadnezzar in which he saw the collapse of a giant idol — here called *Bel*, after Babylon's national deity *(Daniel 2)*.

— The revelation to Daniel, that

Nebuchadnezzar's dream presaged the rise and fall of the four great empires of the world *(Daniel 2)*.

— The assassination of Belshazar, on the very night that he had desecrated the Temple vessels at a royal feast *(Daniel 5)*.

לַיְלָה.   נוֹשַׁע מִבּוֹר אֲרָיוֹת פּוֹתֵר בִּעֲתוּתֵי

בַּלַּיְלָה.   שִׂנְאָה נָטַר אֲגָגִי וְכָתַב סְפָרִים

וַיְהִי בַּחֲצִי הַלַּיְלָה:

לַיְלָה.   עוֹרַרְתָּ נִצְחֲךָ עָלָיו בְּנֶדֶד שְׁנַת

מִלַּיְלָה.   פּוּרָה תִדְרוֹךְ לְשׁוֹמֵר מַה

לַיְלָה.   צָרַח כַּשׁוֹמֵר וְשָׂח אָתָא בוֹקֶר וְגַם

וַיְהִי בַּחֲצִי הַלַּיְלָה:

לַיְלָה.   קָרֵב יוֹם אֲשֶׁר הוּא לֹא יוֹם וְלֹא

הַלַּיְלָה.   רָם הוֹדַע כִּי לְךָ הַיּוֹם אַף לְךָ

הַלַּיְלָה.   וְכָל הַיּוֹם כָּל לְעִירְךָ הַפְקֵד שׁוֹמְרִים

לַיְלָה.   תָּאִיר כְּאוֹר יוֹם חֶשְׁכַּת

וַיְהִי בַּחֲצִי הַלַּיְלָה:

אוֹמְרִים זֶה בְּלֵיל שֵׁנִי שֶׁל פֶּסַח. בְּלֵיל רִאשׁוֹן אוֹמְרִים **כִּי לוֹ נָאֶה**

וּבְכֵן וַאֲמַרְתֶּם זֶבַח פֶּסַח

— The deliverance from, the lions' den of Daniel, the interpreter of the 'terrors' of the night. The reference may be to the mysterious inscription that appeared on the wall to terrify Belshazar and which Daniel interpreted as predicting Belshazar's fall (*Daniel* 6).

— Haman's drafting of orders for the extermination of the Jews (*Esther* 3), and the subsequent beginning of his downfall, due to Ahasverus' sleeplessness (*Esther* 6).

— The forthcoming punishment of the nations, (symbolized by the working of the wine-press *Isaiah* 63), and the message of redemption to the Jews (*Isaiah* 21:12). אָתָא בֹקֶר וְגַם לַיְלָה may be interpreted that the 'dawn' of deliverance will follow the 'night' of Exile, or that the 'dawn' will come for the Jews, and 'night' will descend for their oppressors.

The poet concludes by imploring God to end the darkness of Exile and to bring

the day of redemption — a day which will be unlike either day or night, because the night will be as light as day (*Zecharia* 14:7).

We mentioned previously that the redemption to come will follow the pattern of the Exodus from Egypt, and God will reveal Himself as He revealed Himself in Egypt: כִּימֵי צֵאתְךָ מֵאֶרֶץ מִצְרָיִם, אַרְאֶנּוּ נִפְלָאוֹת, *like in the days of your going out from Egypt I will show them wonders* (*Michah* 7:15). When God revealed His majesty in Egypt, the night was lit up like day (*Tehillim* 139:12), so that the Torah speaks of *'this day on which you went out from Egypt'* (*Shemos* 13:3); the same miracle will happen again at the time of the future redemption.

It should, however, be remembered that, when the Torah speaks of *the day* of the Exodus, it does not necessarily refer to *Pesach* night but may mean the following day. Pharaoh did set the Jews

From the lions' den was rescued he who in-
terpreted the meaning of the terrors of the night.

Haman bore hatred in his heart and wrote
proscriptions at night.

It came to pass at midnight.

You began Your triumph over him when You
disturbed the sleep of his king at night.

You will tread the wine-press to help those who
ask the watchman, 'Ah, when will there be an end to
the long night?'

He will exclaim, like a watchman and say, 'Morn-
ing will come after this night.'

It came to pass at midnight.

Bring near the day (with the coming of Mashiach),
that is neither day nor night.

Show, Most High, that Yours is the day as well as
the night.

Appoint watchmen to Your city (Jerusalem) by
day and by night.

Illumine as with the light of day, the darkness of
the night.

It came to pass at midnight.

The following is said on the second night of *Pesach*. On the first night, continue
on p. 208.

And you shall say: This is the feast of Pesach

free at night, but they refused to leave,
like thieves, in the dark of night *(Avos
DeRabbi Nosson)*. Therefore they only
left the next day *(Brachos 9a)*.

Some texts end the poem with the
final line וַיְהִי בַּחֲצִי הַלַּיְלָה, *And it will be
in the middle of the night,* a reference to
the future redemption taking place on
Pesach night. This reflects the view of
Rabbi Joshua. As mentioned before
(p. 176), however, even Rabbi Eliezer,

who places the crucial moment of
redemption in *Tishrei*, may agree that
Nissan marks an important stage in the
redemptive process.

וּבְכֵן וַאֲמַרְתֶּם — *And you shall say: This
is the feast of Pesach.* The author of this
poem, *Rabbi Elazar Hakalir*, composed
it during the period of the *Gaonim
(Heidenheim)*, as part of the synagogue
liturgy for the second day of *Pesach.* It
follows the pattern of the preceding

אֹמֶץ גְּבוּרוֹתֶיךָ הִפְלֵאתָ   **בַּפֶּסַח.**

בְּרֹאשׁ כָּל מוֹעֲדוֹת נִשֵּׂאתָ   **פֶּסַח.**

גִּלִּיתָ לְאֶזְרָחִי חֲצוֹת לֵיל   **פֶּסַח.**

וַאֲמַרְתֶּם זֶבַח פֶּסַח:

דְּלָתָיו דָּפַקְתָּ כְּחוֹם הַיּוֹם   **בַּפֶּסַח.**

הִסְעִיד נוֹצְצִים עֻגוֹת מַצּוֹת   **בַּפֶּסַח.**

וְאֶל הַבָּקָר רָץ זֵכֶר לְשׁוֹר עֵרֶךְ   **פֶּסַח.**

וַאֲמַרְתֶּם זֶבַח פֶּסַח:

זוֹעֲמוּ סְדוֹמִים וְלוֹהֲטוּ בָּאֵשׁ   **בַּפֶּסַח.**

חֻלַּץ לוֹט מֵהֶם וּמַצּוֹת אָפָה בְּקֵץ   **פֶּסַח.**

טִאטֵאתָ אַדְמַת מוֹף וְנוֹף בְּעָבְרְךָ   **בַּפֶּסַח.**

וַאֲמַרְתֶּם זֶבַח פֶּסַח:

יָהּ רֹאשׁ כָּל אוֹן מָחַצְתָּ בְּלֵיל שִׁמּוּר   **פֶּסַח.**

כַּבִּיר עַל בֵּן בְּכוֹר פָּסַחְתָּ בְּדַם   **פֶּסַח.**

לְבִלְתִּי תֵּת מַשְׁחִית לָבֹא בִפְתָחַי   **בַּפֶּסַח.**

וַאֲמַרְתֶּם זֶבַח פֶּסַח:

מְסֻגֶּרֶת סֻגְּרָה בְּעִתּוֹתֵי   **פֶּסַח.**

נִשְׁמְדָה מִדְיָן בִּצְלִיל שְׂעוֹרֵי עֹמֶר   **פֶּסַח.**

poem but mentions several additional incidents that took place on *Pesach* night:

— God appeared to Abraham at the Covenant between the Portions (*Bereishis* 15; see *Pirkei deRabbi Eliezer*) and told him about the redemption destined for the night of *Pesach*.

— God appeared to Abraham, and the three angels came to visit him (*Bereishis* 18); Abraham served them *Matzos* and an ox. The serving of the ox has been interpreted as a symbol of the *Chagigah* sacrifice that is offered on *Pesach*, or as a reference to the Torah passage, *'An ox or a lamb ...'* (*Vayikrah* 22:26), which is read on the second day of *Pesach*.

— The people of Sodom were destroyed on *Pesach* (*Bereishis* 19), but Lot was saved after he served *Matzos* to the angels.

— Egypt was 'swept clean' of its first-born when God passed through the land on *Pesach* night; but He passed over the homes of His own 'firstborn,' the Jews because of the blood of the *Pesach* sacrifice on their doorposts, and did not permit any destroyer to enter (*Shemos* 12).

— The city of Jericho was besieged just after the beginning of *Pesach* (*Joshua* 6).

— Midian was destroyed by Gideon, who was encouraged to give battle by

The strength of Your powers You wondrously displayed on Pesach.

Therefore You raised above all festivals that of Pesach.

To the Oriental (Abraham) You revealed the wondrous midnight of Pesach.

And you shall say: This is the feast of Pesach.

You knocked at his door (Abraham) in the midday heat on Pesach;

He entertained the angels of God with unleavened cakes on Pesach,

And he ran to the cattle — a model for the sacrificial beast on Pesach.

And you shall say: This is the feast of Pesach.

The men of Sodom angered God and were consumed in flames on Pesach;

Lot was saved from among them — he had baked unleavened cakes for the angels on Pesach.

Moph and Noph (Egyptian provinces) You swept clean when You passed through them on the night of Pesach.

And you shall say: This is the feast of Pesach.

You, God, destroyed all the first-born on the night of the observance of Pesach.

But Your first-born, Master, You passed over because of the blood of the sacrifice of Pesach,

Because of it You did not let destruction enter my doors on Pesach.

And you shall say: This is the feast of Pesach.

The beleaguered city (Jericho) was besieged on Pesach.

Midian was destroyed by means of the barley cake, the offering of the Omer on Pesach.

שׂוֹרְפוּ מִשְׁמַנֵּי פוּל וְלוּד בִּיקַד יְקוֹד   פֶּסַח.

וַאֲמַרְתֶּם זֶבַח פֶּסַח:

עוֹד הַיּוֹם בְּנוֹב לַעֲמוֹד עַד גָּעָה עוֹנַת   פֶּסַח.

פַּס יַד כָּתְבָה לְקַעֲקֵעַ צוּל   בַּפֶּסַח.

צָפֹה הַצָּפִית עָרוֹךְ הַשֻּׁלְחָן   בַּפֶּסַח.

וַאֲמַרְתֶּם זֶבַח פֶּסַח:

קָהָל כִּנְּסָה הֲדַסָּה צוֹם לְשַׁלֵּשׁ   בַּפֶּסַח.

רֹאשׁ מִבֵּית רָשָׁע מָחַצְתָּ בְּעֵץ חֲמִשִּׁים   בַּפֶּסַח.

שְׁתֵּי אֵלֶּה רֶגַע תָּבִיא לְעוּצִית   בַּפֶּסַח.

תָּעֹז יָדְךָ וְתָרוּם יְמִינְךָ כְּלֵיל הִתְקַדֶּשׁ חַג פֶּסַח.

וַאֲמַרְתֶּם זֶבַח פֶּסַח:

כִּי לוֹ נָאֶה. כִּי לוֹ יָאֶה:

אַדִּיר בִּמְלוּכָה. בָּחוּר כַּהֲלָכָה. גְּדוּדָיו יֹאמְרוּ
לוֹ. לְךָ וּלְךָ. לְךָ כִּי לְךָ. לְךָ אַף לְךָ. לְךָ יהוה
הַמַּמְלָכָה. כִּי לוֹ נָאֶה. כִּי לוֹ יָאֶה:
דָּגוּל בִּמְלוּכָה. הָדוּר כַּהֲלָכָה. וָתִיקָיו יֹאמְרוּ
לוֹ. לך ולך וכו׳.

the dream about a barley cake rolling into the camp of Midian (Shoftim 7); the barley cake was a symbol of the Omer sacrifice which had to be brought on the second day of Pesach.

— The Assyrian army fell on Pesach, after Sancherib's threat to advance quickly upon Nob, in preparation for his attack on Jerusalem (Melachim II 19).

— The warning inscription on the wall appeared to Belshazar as he sat down to feast in his palace (Daniel 5); צָפֹה הַצָּפִית may mean that 'the guard was set' or that 'the covers were spread.'

— Esther proclaimed a three day fast that included the beginning of Pesach,

and Haman was hung on the last day of the fast (Esther 7).

— Edom will be doubly punished at the future redemption, by both widowhood and childlessness (Isaiah 47).

This poem, too, ends with the prayer that God may reveal His might and bring the final redemption on Pesach.

כִּי לוֹ נָאֶה — To Him praise is due. This poem was composed in the Middle Ages, by an unknown author. It was already part of the Seder observances in the time of Maharam Rothenburg, 700 years ago.

It is based on a Midrash which comments on the verse, לְךָ יוֹם אַף לְךָ לָיְלָה 'To You belongs the day, and also to

*The princes of Pul and Lud (Assyria) were con-
sumed in a mighty conflagration on Pesach.*

And you shall say: This is the feast of Pesach.

*He (Sancherib) threatened to be that day in Nob,
before the advent of Pesach.*

*An invisible hand wrote prophecying the destruc-
tion of Zul (Babylon) on Pesach,*

*Just when the watch was set, and the royal table
was decked, on Pesach.*

And you shall say: This is the feast of Pesach.

*Hadassah (Esther) gathered her people for a three-
day fast on Pesach.*

*You caused the head of the evil tribe (Haman) to be
hanged on a gallows fifty cubits high, on Pesach.*

*Double misfortune You will bring in one moment
upon Utsis (Edom) on Pesach;*

*May Your hand be strong, Your right hand ex-
alted, as on that night wherein You made holy the
festival of Pesach.*

And you shall say: This is the feast of Pesach.

To Him praise is due!
To Him praise is fitting!

*He is powerful in Kingship. He is truly
distinguished. His companies of angels say to him:*

*Yours and only Yours; Yours, yes Yours; Yours,
surely Yours; Yours, HASHEM, is the sovereignty. To
Him praise is due. To Him praise is fitting.*

*Supreme is He in kingship, truly glorious is He.
His faithful say to Him:*   *Yours etc.*

You the night' (Tehillim 74:16): 'The day praises You, and the night praises You. Just as the day is ruled by You, so also is the night. When You work miracles for us in daytime, the day is Yours; and when You work miracles for us in nighttime the night also is Yours. When You do miracles for us in the day,

זַכַּאי בִּמְלוּכָה. חָסִין כַּהֲלָכָה. טַפְסְרָיו יֹאמְרוּ
לוֹ. לְךָ וּלְךָ וְכוּ'.

יָחִיד בִּמְלוּכָה. כַּבִּיר כַּהֲלָכָה. לִמּוּדָיו יֹאמְרוּ
לוֹ. לְךָ וּלְךָ וְכוּ'.

מוֹשֵׁל בִּמְלוּכָה. נוֹרָא כַּהֲלָכָה. סְבִיבָיו יֹאמְרוּ
לוֹ. לְךָ וּלְךָ וְכוּ'.

עָנָיו בִּמְלוּכָה. פּוֹדֶה כַּהֲלָכָה. צַדִּיקָיו יֹאמְרוּ
לוֹ. לְךָ וּלְךָ וְכוּ'.

קָדוֹשׁ בִּמְלוּכָה. רַחוּם כַּהֲלָכָה. שִׁנְאַנָּיו יֹאמְרוּ
לוֹ. לְךָ וּלְךָ וְכוּ'.

תַּקִּיף בִּמְלוּכָה. תּוֹמֵךְ כַּהֲלָכָה. תְּמִימָיו יֹאמְרוּ
לוֹ. לְךָ וּלְךָ. לְךָ כִּי לְךָ. לְךָ אַף לְךָ. לְךָ יהוה
הַמַּמְלָכָה. כִּי לוֹ נָאֶה. כִּי לוֹ יָאֶה:

אֵלּוּ שֶׁלֹּא שָׁתוּ כּוֹס רְבִיעִי מִקֹּדֶם שׁוֹתִים כָּאן, וּמְבָרְכִים קֹדֶם וְלְאַחַר
שְׁתִיָּיה וְאוֹמְרִים **חֲסַל סִדּוּר פֶּסַח** (לְעֵיל עַמּוּד 198)

אַדִּיר הוּא יִבְנֶה בֵּיתוֹ בְּקָרוֹב. בִּמְהֵרָה
בִּמְהֵרָה בְּיָמֵינוּ בְּקָרוֹב. אֵל בְּנֵה אֵל
בְּנֵה. בְּנֵה בֵּיתְךָ בְּקָרוֹב:

בָּחוּר הוּא גָּדוֹל הוּא דָּגוּל הוּא יִבְנֶה בֵּיתוֹ
בְּקָרוֹב. בִּמְהֵרָה בִּמְהֵרָה בְּיָמֵינוּ בְּקָרוֹב. אֵל
בְּנֵה אֵל בְּנֵה. בְּנֵה בֵּיתְךָ בְּקָרוֹב:

we sing to You in the daytime; as it says, 'Devorah sang ... on that day' (Shoftim 5:1). When You do miracles for us at night, we sing to You at night; as it says, 'The song shall be for you as in the night when the festival is sanctified' (Isaiah 30:29). It is Your due that we recite a song to You in daytime, and also at night.'

The refrain is here loosely translated.

Actually it is a contraction of the verse on which this Midrash is based, and of two other verses. לְךָ וּלְךָ means 'To You ... and to You' and alludes to the verse, 'To You belongs praise, O God, in Zion, and to You a vow should be paid' (Tehillim 65:2). לְךָ כִּי לְךָ means 'To You ... for to You' and alludes to the verse, 'To You, HASHEM, belongs greatness, strength, ... for to You belongs all that

He is pure in kingship. He is truly mighty. His angels say unto Him: *Yours etc.*

He is one alone in kingship. He is truly omnipotent. His disciples say unto Him: *Yours etc.*

Ruler is He in kingship. Truly awesome is He. Those about Him say: *Yours etc.*

Gentle is He in Kingship. He is truly the Redeemer. His righteous ones say: *Yours etc.*

Holy is He in kingship. Truly merciful is He. His troops of angels say: *Yours etc.*

Almighty is He in kingship. He truly sustains all. His perfect ones say: *Yours etc.*

Those who did not drink the fourth cup before (p.198), do so here; they recite the blessing before and after drinking it as well as חֲסַל סִדּוּר פֶּסַח, which can be found on pp. 198-200.

*H*e *who is most mighty, may He soon rebuild His House, speedily, yes speedily, in our days, soon. Rebuild, God, rebuild God, rebuild Your House soon!*

He who is supreme, great and most exalted, may He soon, etc.

is in heaven and earth ...' (*Divrei Hayomim II* 29:11). Finally, לְךָ אַף לְךָ means 'To You ... also to You' and alludes to the verse, 'To You belongs the day, and also to You the night' (*Tehillim* 74:16). The end of the refrain, לְךָ ה' הַמַּמְלָכָה, 'To You, HASHEM, belongs sovereignty', is the conclusion of the verse in *Divrei Hayamim*.

The various expressions used for God and the angels are culled from Biblical verses and arranged in the order of the *Alephbet*. This is not merely to make it easier to remember them. Each letter of the *Alephbet* represents a different sound that we are able to produce — and we want to praise God in every way possible to us.

אַדִּיר הוּא — *He who is most mighty.* This poem and the two that follow were composed in Germany about 500 years ago. אַדִּיר הוּא expresses the fervent craving of the Jewish people for the rebuilding of the Holy Temple. It was, therefore, often sung on occasions other than the *Seder*; and it was translated into German at an early time.

By putting our heart into the prayerful words of the song, and expressing our sincerest longing for *Mashiach*, we hopefully can speed his coming and the building of the Temple. That is why it was old-established popular usage in Germany to speak of *'gut bauen'* (*'building well'*) instead of *'performing the Seder well.'* The *Seder* is a reliving

הָדוּר הוּא וָתִיק הוּא זַכַּאי הוּא חָסִיד הוּא
יִבְנֶה בֵיתוֹ בְּקָרוֹב. בִּמְהֵרָה בִּמְהֵרָה בְּיָמֵינוּ
בְּקָרוֹב. אֵל בְּנֵה אֵל בְּנֵה. בְּנֵה בֵיתְךָ בְּקָרוֹב:

טָהוֹר הוּא יָחִיד הוּא כַּבִּיר הוּא לָמוּד הוּא
מֶלֶךְ הוּא נוֹרָא הוּא שַׂגִּיב הוּא עִזּוּז הוּא פּוֹדֶה
הוּא צַדִּיק הוּא יִבְנֶה בֵיתוֹ בְּקָרוֹב. בִּמְהֵרָה
בִּמְהֵרָה בְּיָמֵינוּ בְּקָרוֹב. אֵל בְּנֵה אֵל בְּנֵה. בְּנֵה
בֵיתְךָ בְּקָרוֹב.

קָדוֹשׁ הוּא רַחוּם הוּא שַׁדַּי הוּא תַּקִּיף הוּא
יִבְנֶה בֵיתוֹ בְּקָרוֹב. בִּמְהֵרָה בִּמְהֵרָה בְּיָמֵינוּ
בְּקָרוֹב. אֵל בְּנֵה אֵל בְּנֵה. בְּנֵה בֵיתְךָ בְּקָרוֹב:

בליל שני של פסח, אלו שעדיין לא קיימו מצות ספירת העומר אומרים
כאן:

בָּרוּךְ אַתָּה יהוה אֱלֹהֵינוּ מֶלֶךְ הָעוֹלָם אֲשֶׁר
קִדְּשָׁנוּ בְּמִצְוֹתָיו וְצִוָּנוּ עַל סְפִירַת הָעוֹמֶר:
הַיּוֹם יוֹם אֶחָד לָעוֹמֶר:

יְהִי רָצוֹן מִלְּפָנֶיךָ יְיָ אֱלֹהֵינוּ וֵאלֹהֵי אֲבוֹתֵינוּ
שֶׁיִּבָּנֶה בֵּית הַמִּקְדָשׁ בִּמְהֵרָה בְּיָמֵינוּ וְתֵן חֶלְקֵנוּ
בְּתוֹרָתֶךָ. וְשָׁם נַעֲבָדְךָ בְּיִרְאָה כִּימֵי עוֹלָם וּכְשָׁנִים
קַדְמוֹנִיּוֹת:

אֶחָד מִי יוֹדֵעַ. אֶחָד אֲנִי יוֹדֵעַ. אֶחָד אֱלֹהֵינוּ
שֶׁבַּשָּׁמַיִם וּבָאָרֶץ:

of the Exodus; but at the same time it is the preparation for the future deliverance.

It should be noted that we ask God to build the Temple. The *Midrash* (*Tanchumah*; cf. *Shevu'os* 15b) stresses that the Third Temple will not be built by man but will descend from heaven when the time is ripe for the redemption.

* *Count the Omer* — In the time of the Temple, the counting of the *Omer* was a Biblical obligation. It involved counting the 49 days from the second day of *Pesach* (when an *Omer* of barley was cut and offered in the Temple) to the first day of *Shavuos* (when two loaves made of wheat were offered). Most take the view that since the destruction of the Temple the counting of the *Omer*

He who is all-honoured and all-worthy, faultless, may He soon etc.

He who is merciful, pure, the sole God, may He soon, etc.

He who is all-powerful, wise, King, may He soon, etc.

He who is most glorious, sublime, great in strength, may He soon, etc.

He who is the Redeemer, the all-righteous, the Holy One, may He soon etc.

He who is most compassionate, the Almighty, the omnipotent, may He soon, etc.

On the second night of *Pesach,* those who did not yet count the Omer,* do so now (all others continue אֶחָד מִי יוֹדֵעַ, as on the first night of *Pesach).*

Blessed are You, HASHEM, our God, King of the universe, who has sanctified us by His commandments and commanded us about the counting of the Omer.

Today is one day of the Omer.

May it be Your will, HASHEM our God and God of our fathers, that the Holy Temple be built speedily in our days, and give us our share in Your Torah. There we will serve You in awe, as in olden days and earlier years.

Who knows one? I know one; one is our God, in heaven and on earth.

is a Rabbinic duty.

During the other nights of the *Omer* period, it is recommended that one count the *Omer* at the evening prayers, and as soon as possible after nightfall; this is particularly necessary if he wants to sit down to a meal, for he might otherwise come to forget to count. *Yavetz* stresses that, for this reason, one should count the *Omer* in the synagogue on *Seder* evening too. Others, however, take the view that on *Seder* night the *Omer* should be counted at the end of the *Seder (Birkei Joseph);* they feel that, logically, the *Seder* (which marks the beginning of *Pesach)* should precede the counting of the *Omer* (which belongs to the second day of *Pesach).* Therefore, at least those who were not in the synagogue and had no opportunity to count with the congregation, should count at the end of the *Seder.*

אֶחָד מִי יוֹדֵעַ — *Who knows one?* This

שְׁנַיִם מִי יוֹדֵעַ. שְׁנַיִם אֲנִי יוֹדֵעַ. שְׁנֵי לְחוֹת הַבְּרִית.
אֶחָד אֱלֹהֵינוּ שֶׁבַּשָּׁמַיִם וּבָאָרֶץ:

שְׁלֹשָׁה מִי יוֹדֵעַ. שְׁלֹשָׁה אֲנִי יוֹדֵעַ. שְׁלֹשָׁה אָבוֹת.
שְׁנֵי לְחוֹת הַבְּרִית. אֶחָד אֱלֹהֵינוּ שֶׁבַּשָּׁמַיִם וּבָאָרֶץ:

אַרְבַּע מִי יוֹדֵעַ. אַרְבַּע אֲנִי יוֹדֵעַ. אַרְבַּע אִמָּהוֹת.
שְׁלֹשָׁה אָבוֹת. שְׁנֵי לְחוֹת הַבְּרִית. אֶחָד אֱלֹהֵינוּ
שֶׁבַּשָּׁמַיִם וּבָאָרֶץ:

חֲמִשָּׁה מִי יוֹדֵעַ. חֲמִשָּׁה אֲנִי יוֹדֵעַ. חֲמִשָּׁה חֻמְשֵׁי
תוֹרָה. אַרְבַּע אִמָּהוֹת. שְׁלֹשָׁה אָבוֹת. שְׁנֵי לְחוֹת
הַבְּרִית. אֶחָד אֱלֹהֵינוּ שֶׁבַּשָּׁמַיִם וּבָאָרֶץ:

שִׁשָּׁה מִי יוֹדֵעַ. שִׁשָּׁה אֲנִי יוֹדֵעַ. שִׁשָּׁה סִדְרֵי מִשְׁנָה.
חֲמִשָּׁה חֻמְשֵׁי תוֹרָה. אַרְבַּע אִמָּהוֹת. שְׁלֹשָׁה אָבוֹת.
שְׁנֵי לְחוֹת הַבְּרִית. אֶחָד אֱלֹהֵינוּ שֶׁבַּשָּׁמַיִם וּבָאָרֶץ.

שִׁבְעָה מִי יוֹדֵעַ. שִׁבְעָה אֲנִי יוֹדֵעַ. שִׁבְעָה יְמֵי
שַׁבַּתָּא. שִׁשָּׁה סִדְרֵי מִשְׁנָה. חֲמִשָּׁה חֻמְשֵׁי תוֹרָה.
אַרְבַּע אִמָּהוֹת. שְׁלֹשָׁה אָבוֹת. שְׁנֵי לְחוֹת הַבְּרִית.
אֶחָד אֱלֹהֵינוּ שֶׁבַּשָּׁמַיִם וּבָאָרֶץ:

שְׁמוֹנָה מִי יוֹדֵעַ. שְׁמוֹנָה אֲנִי יוֹדֵעַ. שְׁמוֹנָה יְמֵי
מִילָה. שִׁבְעָה יְמֵי שַׁבַּתָּא. שִׁשָּׁה סִדְרֵי מִשְׁנָה. חֲמִשָּׁה
חֻמְשֵׁי תוֹרָה. אַרְבַּע אִמָּהוֹת. שְׁלֹשָׁה אָבוֹת. שְׁנֵי
לְחוֹת הַבְּרִית. אֶחָד אֱלֹהֵינוּ שֶׁבַּשָּׁמַיִם וּבָאָרֶץ:

תִּשְׁעָה מִי יוֹדֵעַ. תִּשְׁעָה אֲנִי יוֹדֵעַ. תִּשְׁעָה יַרְחֵי
לֵדָה. שְׁמוֹנָה יְמֵי מִילָה. שִׁבְעָה יְמֵי שַׁבַּתָּא. שִׁשָּׁה
סִדְרֵי מִשְׁנָה. חֲמִשָּׁה חֻמְשֵׁי תוֹרָה. אַרְבַּע אִמָּהוֹת.

song does not have any obvious connection with the *Seder*. It has been suggested that the loving enumeration of
the basic elements of our faith expresses
our affection for the commandments

and observances of the Torah. Also, it
serves to keep the children awake.

However, others have found in it allusions to *Pesach*. Thus it has been suggested that we ask here: 'Who knows

Who knows two? I know two; two are the tablets of the Covenant; one is our God, in heaven and on earth.

Who knows three? I know three; three are the patriarchs; two are the tablets of the Covenant; one is our God, in heaven and on earth.

Who knows four? I know four; four are the matriarchs; three are the patriarchs; two are the tablets of the covenant; one is our God, in heaven and on earth.

Who knows five? I know five; five are the books of Torah; four are the matriarchs; three are the patriarchs; two are the tablets of the Covenant; one is our God, in heaven and on earth.

Who knows six? I know six; six are the sections of the Mishnah; five are the books of Torah; four are the matriarchs; three are the patriarchs; two are the tablets of the Covenant; one is our God, in heaven and on earth.

Who knows seven? I know seven; seven are the days of the week; six are the sections of the Mishnah; five are the books of the Torah; four are the matriarchs; three are the patriarchs; two are the tablets of the Covenant; one is our God, in heaven and on earth.

Who knows eight? I know eight; eight are the days of circumcision; seven are the days of the week; six are the sections of the Mishnah; five are the books of Torah; four are the matriarchs; three are the patriarchs; two are the tablets of the Covenant; one is our God, in heaven and on earth.

Who knows nine? I know nine; nine are the months of pregnancy; eight are the days of circumcision; seven are the days of the week; six are the sections of the Mishnah; five are the books of the

שְׁלֹשָׁה אָבוֹת. שְׁנֵי לֻחוֹת הַבְּרִית. אֶחָד אֱלֹהֵינוּ
שֶׁבַּשָּׁמַיִם וּבָאָרֶץ:

עֲשָׂרָה מִי יוֹדֵעַ. עֲשָׂרָה אֲנִי יוֹדֵעַ. עֲשָׂרָה דִבְּרַיָּא.
תִּשְׁעָה יַרְחֵי לֵדָה. שְׁמוֹנָה יְמֵי מִילָה. שִׁבְעָה יְמֵי
שַׁבַּתָּא. שִׁשָּׁה סִדְרֵי מִשְׁנָה. חֲמִשָּׁה חֻמְשֵׁי תוֹרָה.
אַרְבַּע אִמָּהוֹת. שְׁלֹשָׁה אָבוֹת. שְׁנֵי לֻחוֹת הַבְּרִית.
אֶחָד אֱלֹהֵינוּ שֶׁבַּשָּׁמַיִם וּבָאָרֶץ:

אַחַד עָשָׂר מִי יוֹדֵעַ. אַחַד עָשָׂר אֲנִי יוֹדֵעַ. אַחַד
עָשָׂר כּוֹכְבַיָּא. עֲשָׂרָה דִבְּרַיָּא. תִּשְׁעָה יַרְחֵי לֵדָה.
שְׁמוֹנָה יְמֵי מִילָה. שִׁבְעָה יְמֵי שַׁבַּתָּא. שִׁשָּׁה סִדְרֵי
מִשְׁנָה. חֲמִשָּׁה חֻמְשֵׁי תוֹרָה. אַרְבַּע אִמָּהוֹת. שְׁלֹשָׁה
אָבוֹת. שְׁנֵי לֻחוֹת הַבְּרִית. אֶחָד אֱלֹהֵינוּ שֶׁבַּשָּׁמַיִם
וּבָאָרֶץ:

שְׁנֵים עָשָׂר מִי יוֹדֵעַ. שְׁנֵים עָשָׂר אֲנִי יוֹדֵעַ. שְׁנֵים
עָשָׂר שִׁבְטַיָּא. אַחַד עָשָׂר כּוֹכְבַיָּא. עֲשָׂרָה דִבְּרַיָּא.
תִּשְׁעָה יַרְחֵי לֵדָה. שְׁמוֹנָה יְמֵי מִילָה. שִׁבְעָה יְמֵי
שַׁבַּתָּא. שִׁשָּׁה סִדְרֵי מִשְׁנָה. חֲמִשָּׁה חֻמְשֵׁי תוֹרָה.
אַרְבַּע אִמָּהוֹת. שְׁלֹשָׁה אָבוֹת. שְׁנֵי לֻחוֹת הַבְּרִית.
אֶחָד אֱלֹהֵינוּ שֶׁבַּשָּׁמַיִם וּבָאָרֶץ:

שְׁלֹשָׁה עָשָׂר מִי יוֹדֵעַ. שְׁלֹשָׁה עָשָׂר אֲנִי יוֹדֵעַ.
שְׁלֹשָׁה עָשָׂר מִדַּיָּא. שְׁנֵים עָשָׂר שִׁבְטַיָּא. אַחַד עָשָׂר
כּוֹכְבַיָּא. עֲשָׂרָה דִבְּרַיָּא. תִּשְׁעָה יַרְחֵי לֵדָה. שְׁמוֹנָה
יְמֵי מִילָה. שִׁבְעָה יְמֵי שַׁבַּתָּא. שִׁשָּׁה סִדְרֵי מִשְׁנָה.
חֲמִשָּׁה חֻמְשֵׁי תוֹרָה. אַרְבַּע אִמָּהוֹת. שְׁלֹשָׁה אָבוֹת.
שְׁנֵי לֻחוֹת הַבְּרִית. אֶחָד אֱלֹהֵינוּ שֶׁבַּשָּׁמַיִם וּבָאָרֶץ:

why we were redeemed from Egypt?'
The thirteen replies can all be seen as
answers to this question — for instance,
God Himself, our future acceptance of

the Torah, the merit of the Patriarchs
and Matriarchs, the Shabbos that our
fathers kept in Egypt, and circumcision.
The various replies given also serve

Torah; four are the matriarchs; three are the patriarchs; two are the tablets of the Covenant; one is our God, in heaven and on the earth.

Who knows ten? I know ten; ten are the Ten Commandments; nine are the months of pregnancy; eight are the days of circumcision; seven are the days of the week; six are the sections of the Mishnah; five are the books of Torah; four are the matriarchs; three are the patriarchs; two are the tablets of the Covenant; one is our God, in heaven and on earth.

Who knows eleven? I know eleven; eleven are the stars (constellations); ten are the Ten Commandments; nine are the months of pregnancy; eight are the days of circumcision; seven are the days of the week; six are the sections of the Mishnah; five are the books of Torah; four are the matriarchs; three are the patriarchs; two are the tablets of the Covenant; one is our God, in heaven and on earth.

Who knows twelve? I know twelve; twelve are the tribes; eleven are the stars; ten are the Ten Commandments; nine are the months of pregnancy; eight are the days of circumcision; seven are the days of the week; six are the sections of the Mishnah; five are the books of Torah; four are the matriarchs; three are the patriarchs; two are the tablets of the Covenant; one is our God, in heaven and on earth.

Who knows thirteen? I know thirteen; thirteen are the attributes of God; twelve are the tribes; eleven are the stars, ten are the Ten Commandments; nine are the months of pregnancy; eight are the days of circumcision; seven are the days of the week; six are the sections of the Mishnah; five are the books of Torah; four are the matriarchs; three are the patriarchs, two are the tablets of the Covenant; one is our God, in heaven and on earth.

חַד גַּדְיָא. חַד גַּדְיָא. דְּזַבִּין אַבָּא בִּתְרֵי זוּזֵי. חַד גַּדְיָא חַד גַּדְיָא:

וְאָתָא שׁוּנְרָא וְאָכְלָה לְגַדְיָא דְּזַבִּין אַבָּא בִּתְרֵי זוּזֵי חַד גַּדְיָא חַד גַּדְיָא:

וְאָתָא כַלְבָּא וְנָשַׁךְ לְשׁוּנְרָא. דְּאָכְלָא לְגַדְיָא. דְּזַבִּין אַבָּא בִּתְרֵי זוּזֵי. חַד גַּדְיָא חַד גַּדְיָא:

וְאָתָא חוּטְרָא וְהִכָּה לְכַלְבָּא. דְּנָשַׁךְ לְשׁוּנְרָא. דְּאָכְלָה לְגַדְיָא. דְּזַבִּין אַבָּא בִּתְרֵי זוּזֵי. חַד גַּדְיָא חַד גַּדְיָא:

וְאָתָא נוּרָא וְשָׂרַף לְחוּטְרָא. דְּהִכָּה לְכַלְבָּא. דְּנָשַׁךְ לְשׁוּנְרָא. דְּאָכְלָה לְגַדְיָא. דְּזַבִּין אַבָּא בִּתְרֵי זוּזֵי. חַד גַּדְיָא חַד גַּדְיָא:

וְאָתָא מַיָּא וְכָבָה לְנוּרָא. דְּשָׂרַף לְחוּטְרָא. דְּהִכָּה לְכַלְבָּא. דְּנָשַׁךְ לְשׁוּנְרָא. דְּאָכְלָה לְגַדְיָא. דְּזַבִּין אַבָּא בִּתְרֵי זוּזֵי. חַד גַּדְיָא חַד גַּדְיָא:

וְאָתָא תוֹרָא וְשָׁתָה לְמַיָּא. דְּכָבָה לְנוּרָא. דְּשָׂרַף לְחוּטְרָא. דְּהִכָּה לְכַלְבָּא. דְּנָשַׁךְ לְשׁוּנְרָא. דְּאָכְלָה לְגַדְיָא. דְּזַבִּין אַבָּא בִּתְרֵי זוּזֵי. חַד גַּדְיָא חַד גַּדְיָא:

וְאָתָא הַשּׁוֹחֵט וְשָׁחַט לְתוֹרָא. דְּשָׁתָא לְמַיָּא. דְּכָבָה לְנוּרָא. דְּשָׂרַף לְחוּטְרָא. דְּהִכָּה לְכַלְבָּא. דְּנָשַׁךְ לְשׁוּנְרָא. דְּאָכְלָה לְגַדְיָא. דְּזַבִּין אַבָּא בִּתְרֵי זוּזֵי. חַד גַּדְיָא חַד גַּדְיָא:

וְאָתָא מַלְאַךְ הַמָּוֶת וְשָׁחַט לְשׁוֹחֵט. דְּשָׁחַט לְתוֹרָא. דְּשָׁתָה לְמַיָּא. דְּכָבָה לְנוּרָא. דְּשָׂרַף לְחוּטְרָא. דְּהִכָּה לְכַלְבָּא. דְּנָשַׁךְ לְשׁוּנְרָא. דְּאָכְלָה לְגַדְיָא. דְּזַבִּין אַבָּא בִּתְרֵי זוּזֵי. חַד גַּדְיָא חַד גַּדְיָא:

as an answer to anybody who might ask what good the deliverance from Egypt did us — after all, we are in Exile again. This is true enough; but as a result of the Exodus we have acquired national treasures that will forever keep us alive as servants of God.

חַד גַּדְיָא — *A kid, a kid*. On the surface this appears to be a simple folksong.

A kid, a kid, a kid, which my father bought, for two zuzim, a kid, a kid.

Then came the cat and devoured the kid, which my father bought for two zuzim, the kid, the kid.

Then came the dog, which bit the cat, which devoured the kid, which my father bought for two zuzim, the kid, the kid.

Then came the stick, and beat the dog, which bit the cat, which devoured the kid, which my father bought for two zuzim, the kid, the kid.

Then came fire, and burnt the stick, which beat the dog, which bit the cat, which devoured the kid which my father bought for two zuzim, the kid, the kid.

Then came water, and quenched the fire, which burnt the stick, which beat the dog, which bit the cat, which devoured the kid, which my father bought for two zuzim, the kid, the kid.

Then came the ox, and drank the water, which quenched the fire, which burnt the stick, which beat the dog, which bit the cat, which devoured the kid, which my father bought for two zuzim, the kid, the kid.

Then came the slaughterer, and slaughtered the ox, which drank the water, which quenched the fire, which burnt the stick, which beat the dog, which bit the cat, which devoured the kid, which my father bought for two zuzim, the kid, the kid.

Then came the angel of death, and killed the slaughterer, who slaughtered the ox, which drank the water, which quenched the fire, which burnt the stick, which beat the dog, which bit the cat, which devoured the kid, which my father bought for two zuzim, the kid, the kid.

However, it would not have been included in the *Seder* if there were no deeper lessons to be derived from it. A number of them have been pointed out by the commentators.

The goat has been identified with the

וְאָתָא הַקָּדוֹשׁ בָּרוּךְ הוּא וְשָׁחַט לְמַלְאַךְ הַמָּוֶת. דְּשָׁחַט לְשׁוֹחֵט. דְּשָׁחַט לְתוֹרָא. דְּשָׁתָה לְמַיָּא. דְּכָבָה לְנוּרָא. דְּשָׂרַף לְחוּטְרָא. דְּהִכָּה לְכַלְבָּא. דְּנָשַׁךְ לְשׁוּנְרָא. דְּאָכְלָה לְגַדְיָא. דְּזַבִּין אַבָּא בִּתְרֵי זוּזֵי. חַד גַּדְיָא חַד גַּדְיָא:

Then came the Holy One, blessed be He, and slew the angel of death, who killed the slaughterer, who slaughtered the ox, which drank the water, which quenched the fire, which burnt the stick, which beat the dog, which bit the cat, which devoured the kid, which my father bought for two zuzim, the kid, the kid.

חייב אדם לעסוק בהלכות הפסח וביציאת מצרים ובנפלאות שעשה הקב"ה לאבותינו עד שתחטפנו שינה.

*One should continue to occupy himself with the story of the *Exodus,* and the laws of *Pesach,* until sleep overtakes him.

Jewish people, the father with God, and the two coins with Moses and Aaron, the two agents through whom He redeemed us; others have suggested that the two coins are the two tablets of the Law, or the Half-*Shekel* (consisting of two *Zuzim*) which our forefathers were asked to give in the desert. The further course of the poem shows the suffering of the Jews among the nations — 'one lamb among seventy wolves', as our Sages put it — until the final redemption.

Yaavetz suggests that the goat represents man's soul which is sent down to earth, 'sold by the father'; the poem describes the suffering of the soul as it undergoes all the tribulations of human life.

* *One should continue* — Our obligation on *Seder* night is to talk as much and deeply as possible about our deliverance from Egypt; therefore, we should not stop just because we finished reciting the *Haggadah.* It is customary to recite *Shir Hashirim* which describes the special love between God and Israel that marked the beginning of our history. Then one should continue talking about the awesome happenings of the Exodus — if possible for the rest of the night. In fact the *Abarbanel* points out that the very act of remaining awake all night is a way of showing that we consider ourselves as having gone out from Egypt; certainly the Jews did not sleep during the night of the Exodus!

The *Ibn Ezra* explains the phrase לֵיל שִׁמּוּרִים to mean that God watched over us on the night of the Exodus, and that therefore this night should remain for us, for all generations, a night on which we watch to fulfill God's commandments, *Pesach, Matzah* and *Maror* ... and we should not sleep but give thanks and tell the miracles of God in taking us out of Egypt.

In this way may we merit to see the speedy fulfillment of God's assurance that He will show us wonders as in the days of our going out from Egypt — כִּימֵי צֵאתְךָ מֵאֶרֶץ מִצְרָיִם אַרְאֶנּוּ נִפְלָאוֹת — אָמֵן כֵּן יְהִי רָצוֹן.

תם ונשלם שבח לאל בורא עולם

שיר השירים
Shir HaShirim / Song of Songs*

א

שִׁיר הַשִּׁירִים אֲשֶׁר לִשְׁלֹמֹה: יִשָּׁקֵנִי מִנְּשִׁיקוֹת פִּיהוּ כִּי־טוֹבִים דֹּדֶיךָ מִיָּיִן: לְרֵיחַ
שְׁמָנֶיךָ טוֹבִים שֶׁמֶן תּוּרַק שְׁמֶךָ עַל־כֵּן עֲלָמוֹת אֲהֵבוּךָ:   מָשְׁכֵנִי אַחֲרֶיךָ נָּרוּצָה
הֱבִיאַנִי הַמֶּלֶךְ חֲדָרָיו נָגִילָה וְנִשְׂמְחָה בָּךְ נַזְכִּירָה דֹדֶיךָ מִיַּיִן מֵישָׁרִים אֲהֵבוּךָ:
שְׁחוֹרָה אֲנִי וְנָאוָה בְּנוֹת יְרוּשָׁלָ͏ִם כְּאָהֳלֵי קֵדָר כִּירִיעוֹת שְׁלֹמֹה: אַל־
תִּרְאוּנִי שֶׁאֲנִי שְׁחַרְחֹרֶת שֶׁשֱּׁזָפַתְנִי הַשָּׁמֶשׁ בְּנֵי אִמִּי נִחֲרוּ־בִי שָׂמֻנִי נֹטֵרָה אֶת־
הַכְּרָמִים כַּרְמִי שֶׁלִּי לֹא נָטָרְתִּי: הַגִּידָה לִּי שֶׁאָהֲבָה נַפְשִׁי אֵיכָה תִרְעֶה אֵיכָה
תַּרְבִּיץ בַּצָּהֳרָיִם שַׁלָּמָה אֶהְיֶה כְּעֹטְיָה עַל עֶדְרֵי חֲבֵרֶיךָ: אִם־לֹא תֵדְעִי לָךְ הַיָּפָה
בַּנָּשִׁים צְאִי־לָךְ בְּעִקְבֵי הַצֹּאן וּרְעִי אֶת־גְּדִיֹּתַיִךְ עַל מִשְׁכְּנוֹת הָרֹעִים:
לְסֻסָתִי בְּרִכְבֵי פַרְעֹה דִּמִּיתִיךְ רַעְיָתִי: נָאווּ לְחָיַיִךְ בַּתֹּרִים צַוָּארֵךְ בַּחֲרוּזִים:
תּוֹרֵי זָהָב נַעֲשֶׂה־לָּךְ עִם נְקֻדּוֹת הַכָּסֶף: עַד־שֶׁהַמֶּלֶךְ בִּמְסִבּוֹ נִרְדִּי נָתַן רֵיחוֹ:
צְרוֹר הַמֹּר | דּוֹדִי לִי בֵּין שָׁדַי יָלִין: אֶשְׁכֹּל הַכֹּפֶר דּוֹדִי לִי בְּכַרְמֵי עֵין גֶּדִי:
הִנָּךְ יָפָה רַעְיָתִי הִנָּךְ יָפָה עֵינַיִךְ יוֹנִים: הִנְּךָ יָפֶה דוֹדִי אַף נָעִים אַף־עַרְשֵׂנוּ
רַעֲנָנָה: קֹרוֹת בָּתֵּינוּ אֲרָזִים רַהִיטֵנוּ בְּרוֹתִים:

ב

אֲנִי חֲבַצֶּלֶת הַשָּׁרוֹן שׁוֹשַׁנַּת הָעֲמָקִים: כְּשׁוֹשַׁנָּה בֵּין הַחוֹחִים כֵּן רַעְיָתִי בֵּין
הַבָּנוֹת: כְּתַפּוּחַ בַּעֲצֵי הַיַּעַר כֵּן דּוֹדִי בֵּין הַבָּנִים בְּצִלּוֹ חִמַּדְתִּי וְיָשַׁבְתִּי וּפִרְיוֹ
מָתוֹק לְחִכִּי: הֱבִיאַנִי אֶל־בֵּית הַיַּיִן וְדִגְלוֹ עָלַי אַהֲבָה: סַמְּכוּנִי בָּאֲשִׁישׁוֹת רַפְּדוּנִי
בַּתַּפּוּחִים כִּי־חוֹלַת אַהֲבָה אָנִי: שְׂמֹאלוֹ תַּחַת לְרֹאשִׁי וִימִינוֹ תְּחַבְּקֵנִי: הִשְׁבַּעְתִּי
אֶתְכֶם בְּנוֹת יְרוּשָׁלַ͏ִם בִּצְבָאוֹת אוֹ בְּאַיְלוֹת הַשָּׂדֶה אִם־תָּעִירוּ | וְאִם־תְּעוֹרְרוּ
אֶת־הָאַהֲבָה עַד שֶׁתֶּחְפָּץ: קוֹל דּוֹדִי הִנֵּה־זֶה בָּא מְדַלֵּג עַל־הֶהָרִים
מְקַפֵּץ עַל־הַגְּבָעוֹת: דּוֹמֶה דוֹדִי לִצְבִי אוֹ לְעֹפֶר הָאַיָּלִים הִנֵּה־זֶה עוֹמֵד אַחַר
כָּתְלֵנוּ מַשְׁגִּיחַ מִן־הַחַלֹּנוֹת מֵצִיץ מִן־הַחֲרַכִּים: עָנָה דוֹדִי וְאָמַר לִי קוּמִי לָךְ
רַעְיָתִי יָפָתִי וּלְכִי־לָךְ: כִּי־הִנֵּה הַסְּתָו עָבָר הַגֶּשֶׁם חָלַף הָלַךְ לוֹ: הַנִּצָּנִים נִרְאוּ
בָאָרֶץ עֵת הַזָּמִיר הִגִּיעַ וְקוֹל הַתּוֹר נִשְׁמַע בְּאַרְצֵנוּ: הַתְּאֵנָה חָנְטָה פַגֶּיהָ
וְהַגְּפָנִים | סְמָדַר נָתְנוּ רֵיחַ קוּמִי לָךְ רַעְיָתִי יָפָתִי וּלְכִי־לָךְ:   יוֹנָתִי בְּחַגְוֵי
הַסֶּלַע בְּסֵתֶר הַמַּדְרֵגָה הַרְאִינִי אֶת־מַרְאַיִךְ הַשְׁמִיעִנִי אֶת־קוֹלֵךְ כִּי־קוֹלֵךְ עָרֵב
וּמַרְאֵיךְ נָאוֶה: אֶחֱזוּ־לָנוּ שׁוּעָלִים שׁוּעָלִים קְטַנִּים מְחַבְּלִים כְּרָמִים
וּכְרָמֵינוּ סְמָדַר: דּוֹדִי לִי וַאֲנִי לוֹ הָרֹעֶה בַּשּׁוֹשַׁנִּים: עַד שֶׁיָּפוּחַ הַיּוֹם וְנָסוּ
הַצְּלָלִים סֹב דְּמֵה־לְךָ דוֹדִי לִצְבִי אוֹ לְעֹפֶר הָאַיָּלִים עַל־הָרֵי בָתֶר:

ג

עַל־מִשְׁכָּבִי בַּלֵּילוֹת בִּקַּשְׁתִּי אֵת שֶׁאָהֲבָה נַפְשִׁי בִּקַּשְׁתִּיו וְלֹא מְצָאתִיו: אָקוּמָה
נָּא וַאֲסוֹבְבָה בָעִיר בַּשְּׁוָקִים וּבָרְחֹבוֹת אֲבַקְשָׁה אֵת שֶׁאָהֲבָה נַפְשִׁי בִּקַּשְׁתִּיו וְלֹא
מְצָאתִיו: מְצָאוּנִי הַשֹּׁמְרִים הַסֹּבְבִים בָּעִיר אֵת שֶׁאָהֲבָה נַפְשִׁי רְאִיתֶם: כִּמְעַט
שֶׁעָבַרְתִּי מֵהֶם עַד שֶׁמָּצָאתִי אֵת שֶׁאָהֲבָה נַפְשִׁי אֲחַזְתִּיו וְלֹא אַרְפֶּנּוּ עַד־
שֶׁהֲבֵיאתִיו אֶל־בֵּית אִמִּי וְאֶל־חֶדֶר הוֹרָתִי: הִשְׁבַּעְתִּי אֶתְכֶם בְּנוֹת יְרוּשָׁלַ͏ִם

*For an allegorical translation and anthology of commentaries on Shir HaShirim, the reader is
directed to the ArtScroll Tanach Series edition.

בִּצְבָאוֹת אוֹ בְּאַיְלוֹת הַשָּׂדֶה אִם־תָּעִירוּ | וְאִם־תְּעוֹרְרוּ אֶת־הָאַהֲבָה עַד שֶׁתֶּחְפָּץ:
מִי זֹאת עֹלָה מִן־הַמִּדְבָּר כְּתִימֲרוֹת עָשָׁן מְקֻטֶּרֶת מוֹר וּלְבוֹנָה מִכֹּל
אַבְקַת רוֹכֵל: הִנֵּה מִטָּתוֹ שֶׁלִּשְׁלֹמֹה שִׁשִּׁים גִּבֹּרִים סָבִיב לָהּ מִגִּבֹּרֵי יִשְׂרָאֵל: כֻּלָּם
אֲחֻזֵי חֶרֶב מְלֻמְּדֵי מִלְחָמָה אִישׁ חַרְבּוֹ עַל־יְרֵכוֹ מִפַּחַד בַּלֵּילוֹת:
אַפִּרְיוֹן עָשָׂה לוֹ הַמֶּלֶךְ שְׁלֹמֹה מֵעֲצֵי הַלְּבָנוֹן: עַמּוּדָיו עָשָׂה כֶסֶף רְפִידָתוֹ זָהָב
מֶרְכָּבוֹ אַרְגָּמָן תּוֹכוֹ רָצוּף אַהֲבָה מִבְּנוֹת יְרוּשָׁלָ‍ִם: צְאֶינָה | וּרְאֶינָה בְּנוֹת צִיּוֹן
בַּמֶּלֶךְ שְׁלֹמֹה בָּעֲטָרָה שֶׁעִטְּרָה־לּוֹ אִמּוֹ בְּיוֹם חֲתֻנָּתוֹ וּבְיוֹם שִׂמְחַת לִבּוֹ:

ד

הִנָּךְ יָפָה רַעְיָתִי הִנָּךְ יָפָה עֵינַיִךְ יוֹנִים מִבַּעַד לְצַמָּתֵךְ שַׂעְרֵךְ כְּעֵדֶר הָעִזִּים
שֶׁגָּלְשׁוּ מֵהַר גִּלְעָד: שִׁנַּיִךְ כְּעֵדֶר הַקְּצוּבוֹת שֶׁעָלוּ מִן־הָרַחְצָה שֶׁכֻּלָּם מַתְאִימוֹת
וְשַׁכֻּלָה אֵין בָּהֶם: כְּחוּט הַשָּׁנִי שִׂפְתוֹתַיִךְ וּמִדְבָּרֵךְ נָאוֶה כְּפֶלַח הָרִמּוֹן רַקָּתֵךְ
מִבַּעַד לְצַמָּתֵךְ: כְּמִגְדַּל דָּוִיד צַוָּארֵךְ בָּנוּי לְתַלְפִּיּוֹת אֶלֶף הַמָּגֵן תָּלוּי עָלָיו כֹּל
שִׁלְטֵי הַגִּבֹּרִים: שְׁנֵי שָׁדַיִךְ כִּשְׁנֵי עֳפָרִים תְּאוֹמֵי צְבִיָּה הָרֹעִים בַּשּׁוֹשַׁנִּים: עַד
שֶׁיָּפוּחַ הַיּוֹם וְנָסוּ הַצְּלָלִים אֵלֶךְ לִי אֶל־הַר הַמּוֹר וְאֶל־גִּבְעַת הַלְּבוֹנָה: כֻּלָּךְ יָפָה
רַעְיָתִי וּמוּם אֵין בָּךְ:   אִתִּי מִלְּבָנוֹן כַּלָּה אִתִּי מִלְּבָנוֹן תָּבוֹאִי תָּשׁוּרִי |
מֵרֹאשׁ אֲמָנָה מֵרֹאשׁ שְׂנִיר וְחֶרְמוֹן מִמְּעֹנוֹת אֲרָיוֹת מֵהַרְרֵי נְמֵרִים: לִבַּבְתִּנִי
אֲחֹתִי כַלָּה לִבַּבְתִּנִי בְּאַחַת מֵעֵינַיִךְ בְּאַחַד עֲנָק מִצַּוְּרֹנָיִךְ: מַה־יָּפוּ דֹדַיִךְ אֲחֹתִי
כַלָּה מַה־טֹּבוּ דֹדַיִךְ מִיַּיִן וְרֵיחַ שְׁמָנַיִךְ מִכָּל־בְּשָׂמִים: נֹפֶת תִּטֹּפְנָה שִׂפְתוֹתַיִךְ
כַּלָּה דְּבַשׁ וְחָלָב תַּחַת לְשׁוֹנֵךְ וְרֵיחַ שַׂלְמֹתַיִךְ כְּרֵיחַ לְבָנוֹן: גַּן | נָעוּל
אֲחֹתִי כַלָּה גַּל נָעוּל מַעְיָן חָתוּם: שְׁלָחַיִךְ פַּרְדֵּס רִמּוֹנִים עִם פְּרִי מְגָדִים כְּפָרִים
עִם־נְרָדִים: נֵרְדְּ | וְכַרְכֹּם קָנֶה וְקִנָּמוֹן עִם כָּל־עֲצֵי לְבוֹנָה מֹר וַאֲהָלוֹת עִם כָּל־
רָאשֵׁי בְשָׂמִים: מַעְיַן גַּנִּים בְּאֵר מַיִם חַיִּים וְנֹזְלִים מִן־לְבָנוֹן: עוּרִי צָפוֹן וּבוֹאִי
תֵימָן הָפִיחִי גַנִּי יִזְּלוּ בְשָׂמָיו יָבֹא דוֹדִי לְגַנּוֹ וְיֹאכַל פְּרִי מְגָדָיו:

ה

בָּאתִי לְגַנִּי אֲחֹתִי כַלָּה אָרִיתִי מוֹרִי עִם־בְּשָׂמִי אָכַלְתִּי יַעְרִי עִם־דִּבְשִׁי שָׁתִיתִי
יֵינִי עִם־חֲלָבִי אִכְלוּ רֵעִים שְׁתוּ וְשִׁכְרוּ דּוֹדִים: אֲנִי יְשֵׁנָה וְלִבִּי עֵר קוֹל |
דּוֹדִי דוֹפֵק פִּתְחִי־לִי אֲחֹתִי רַעְיָתִי יוֹנָתִי תַמָּתִי שֶׁרֹאשִׁי נִמְלָא־טָל קְוֻּצּוֹתַי
רְסִיסֵי לָיְלָה: פָּשַׁטְתִּי אֶת־כֻּתָּנְתִּי אֵיכָכָה אֶלְבָּשֶׁנָּה רָחַצְתִּי אֶת־רַגְלַי אֵיכָכָה
אֲטַנְּפֵם: דּוֹדִי שָׁלַח יָדוֹ מִן־הַחֹר וּמֵעַי הָמוּ עָלָיו: קַמְתִּי אֲנִי לִפְתֹּחַ לְדוֹדִי וְיָדַי
נָטְפוּ־מוֹר וְאֶצְבְּעֹתַי מוֹר עֹבֵר עַל כַּפּוֹת הַמַּנְעוּל: פָּתַחְתִּי אֲנִי לְדוֹדִי וְדוֹדִי חָמַק
עָבָר נַפְשִׁי יָצְאָה בְדַבְּרוֹ בִּקַּשְׁתִּיהוּ וְלֹא מְצָאתִיהוּ קְרָאתִיו וְלֹא עָנָנִי: מְצָאֻנִי
הַשֹּׁמְרִים הַסֹּבְבִים בָּעִיר הִכּוּנִי פְצָעוּנִי נָשְׂאוּ אֶת־רְדִידִי מֵעָלַי שֹׁמְרֵי הַחֹמוֹת:
הִשְׁבַּעְתִּי אֶתְכֶם בְּנוֹת יְרוּשָׁלָ‍ִם אִם־תִּמְצְאוּ אֶת־דּוֹדִי מַה־תַּגִּידוּ לוֹ שֶׁחוֹלַת
אַהֲבָה אָנִי: מַה־דּוֹדֵךְ מִדּוֹד הַיָּפָה בַּנָּשִׁים מַה־דּוֹדֵךְ מִדּוֹד שֶׁכָּכָה הִשְׁבַּעְתָּנוּ:
דּוֹדִי צַח וְאָדוֹם דָּגוּל מֵרְבָבָה: רֹאשׁוֹ כֶּתֶם פָּז קְוֻצּוֹתָיו תַּלְתַּלִּים שְׁחֹרוֹת כָּעוֹרֵב:
עֵינָיו כְּיוֹנִים עַל־אֲפִיקֵי מָיִם רֹחֲצוֹת בֶּחָלָב יֹשְׁבוֹת עַל־מִלֵּאת: לְחָיָו כַּעֲרוּגַת
הַבֹּשֶׂם מִגְדְּלוֹת מֶרְקָחִים שִׂפְתוֹתָיו שׁוֹשַׁנִּים נֹטְפוֹת מוֹר עֹבֵר: יָדָיו גְּלִילֵי זָהָב
מְמֻלָּאִים בַּתַּרְשִׁישׁ מֵעָיו עֶשֶׁת שֵׁן מְעֻלֶּפֶת סַפִּירִים: שׁוֹקָיו עַמּוּדֵי שֵׁשׁ מְיֻסָּדִים
עַל־אַדְנֵי־פָז מַרְאֵהוּ כַּלְּבָנוֹן בָּחוּר כָּאֲרָזִים: חִכּוֹ מַמְתַקִּים וְכֻלּוֹ מַחֲמַדִּים זֶה
דוֹדִי וְזֶה רֵעִי בְּנוֹת יְרוּשָׁלָ‍ִם:

אָנָה הָלַךְ דּוֹדֵךְ הַיָּפָה בַּנָּשִׁים אָנָה פָּנָה דוֹדֵךְ וּנְבַקְשֶׁנּוּ עִמָּךְ: דּוֹדִי יָרַד לְגַנּוֹ
לַעֲרֻגוֹת הַבֹּשֶׂם לִרְעוֹת בַּגַּנִּים וְלִלְקֹט שׁוֹשַׁנִּים: אֲנִי לְדוֹדִי וְדוֹדִי לִי הָרוֹעֶה
בַּשּׁוֹשַׁנִּים: יָפָה אַתְּ רַעְיָתִי כְּתִרְצָה נָאוָה כִּירוּשָׁלָ͏ִם אֲיֻמָּה כַּנִּדְגָּלוֹת:
הָסֵבִּי עֵינַיִךְ מִנֶּגְדִּי שֶׁהֵם הִרְהִיבֻנִי שַׂעְרֵךְ כְּעֵדֶר הָעִזִּים שֶׁגָּלְשׁוּ מִן־הַגִּלְעָד: שִׁנַּיִךְ
כְּעֵדֶר הָרְחֵלִים שֶׁעָלוּ מִן־הָרַחְצָה שֶׁכֻּלָּם מַתְאִימוֹת וְשַׁכֻּלָה אֵין בָּהֶם: כְּפֶלַח
הָרִמּוֹן רַקָּתֵךְ מִבַּעַד לְצַמָּתֵךְ: שִׁשִּׁים הֵמָּה מְלָכוֹת וּשְׁמֹנִים פִּילַגְשִׁים וַעֲלָמוֹת
אֵין מִסְפָּר: אַחַת הִיא יוֹנָתִי תַמָּתִי אַחַת הִיא לְאִמָּהּ בָּרָה הִיא לְיוֹלַדְתָּהּ רָאוּהָ
בָנוֹת וַיְאַשְּׁרוּהָ מְלָכוֹת וּפִילַגְשִׁים וַיְהַלְלוּהָ: מִי־זֹאת הַנִּשְׁקָפָה כְּמוֹ־
שַׁחַר יָפָה כַלְּבָנָה בָּרָה כַּחַמָּה אֲיֻמָּה כַּנִּדְגָּלוֹת: אֶל־גִּנַּת אֱגוֹז יָרַדְתִּי לִרְאוֹת
בְּאִבֵּי הַנָּחַל לִרְאוֹת הֲפָרְחָה הַגֶּפֶן הֵנֵצוּ הָרִמֹּנִים: לֹא יָדַעְתִּי נַפְשִׁי שָׂמַתְנִי
מַרְכְּבוֹת עַמִּי נָדִיב:

שׁוּבִי שׁוּבִי הַשּׁוּלַמִּית שׁוּבִי שׁוּבִי וְנֶחֱזֶה־בָּךְ מַה־תֶּחֱזוּ בַּשּׁוּלַמִּית כִּמְחֹלַת
הַמַּחֲנָיִם: מַה־יָּפוּ פְעָמַיִךְ בַּנְּעָלִים בַּת־נָדִיב חַמּוּקֵי יְרֵכַיִךְ כְּמוֹ חֲלָאִים מַעֲשֵׂה יְדֵי
אָמָּן: שָׁרְרֵךְ אַגַּן הַסַּהַר אַל־יֶחְסַר הַמָּזֶג בִּטְנֵךְ עֲרֵמַת חִטִּים סוּגָה בַּשּׁוֹשַׁנִּים: שְׁנֵי
שָׁדַיִךְ כִּשְׁנֵי עֳפָרִים תָּאֳמֵי צְבִיָּה: צַוָּארֵךְ כְּמִגְדַּל הַשֵּׁן עֵינַיִךְ בְּרֵכוֹת בְּחֶשְׁבּוֹן עַל־
שַׁעַר בַּת־רַבִּים אַפֵּךְ כְּמִגְדַּל הַלְּבָנוֹן צוֹפֶה פְּנֵי דַמָּשֶׂק: רֹאשֵׁךְ עָלַיִךְ כַּכַּרְמֶל
וְדַלַּת רֹאשֵׁךְ כָּאַרְגָּמָן מֶלֶךְ אָסוּר בָּרְהָטִים: מַה־יָּפִית וּמַה־נָּעַמְתְּ אַהֲבָה
בַּתַּעֲנוּגִים: זֹאת קוֹמָתֵךְ דָּמְתָה לְתָמָר וְשָׁדַיִךְ לְאַשְׁכֹּלוֹת: אָמַרְתִּי אֶעֱלֶה בְתָמָר
אֹחֲזָה בְּסַנְסִנָּיו וְיִהְיוּ־נָא שָׁדַיִךְ כְּאֶשְׁכְּלוֹת הַגֶּפֶן וְרֵיחַ אַפֵּךְ כַּתַּפּוּחִים: וְחִכֵּךְ כְּיֵין
הַטּוֹב הוֹלֵךְ לְדוֹדִי לְמֵישָׁרִים דּוֹבֵב שִׂפְתֵי יְשֵׁנִים: אֲנִי לְדוֹדִי וְעָלַי תְּשׁוּקָתוֹ: לְכָה
דוֹדִי נֵצֵא הַשָּׂדֶה נָלִינָה בַּכְּפָרִים: נַשְׁכִּימָה לַכְּרָמִים נִרְאֶה אִם־פָּרְחָה הַגֶּפֶן פִּתַּח
הַסְּמָדַר הֵנֵצוּ הָרִמּוֹנִים שָׁם אֶתֵּן אֶת־דֹּדַי לָךְ: הַדּוּדָאִים נָתְנוּ־רֵיחַ וְעַל־פְּתָחֵינוּ
כָּל־מְגָדִים חֲדָשִׁים גַּם־יְשָׁנִים דּוֹדִי צָפַנְתִּי לָךְ:

מִי יִתֶּנְךָ כְּאָח לִי יוֹנֵק שְׁדֵי אִמִּי אֶמְצָאֲךָ בַחוּץ אֶשָּׁקְךָ גַּם לֹא־יָבֻזוּ לִי: אֶנְהָגְךָ
אֲבִיאֲךָ אֶל־בֵּית אִמִּי תְּלַמְּדֵנִי אַשְׁקְךָ מִיַּיִן הָרֶקַח מֵעֲסִיס רִמֹּנִי: שְׂמֹאלוֹ תַּחַת
רֹאשִׁי וִימִינוֹ תְּחַבְּקֵנִי: הִשְׁבַּעְתִּי אֶתְכֶם בְּנוֹת יְרוּשָׁלָ͏ִם מַה־תָּעִירוּ | וּמַה־תְּעֹרְרוּ
אֶת־הָאַהֲבָה עַד שֶׁתֶּחְפָּץ: מִי זֹאת עֹלָה מִן־הַמִּדְבָּר מִתְרַפֶּקֶת עַל־
דּוֹדָהּ תַּחַת הַתַּפּוּחַ עוֹרַרְתִּיךָ שָׁמָּה חִבְּלַתְךָ אִמֶּךָ שָׁמָּה חִבְּלָה יְלָדַתְךָ: שִׂימֵנִי
כַחוֹתָם עַל־לִבֶּךָ כַּחוֹתָם עַל־זְרוֹעֶךָ כִּי־עַזָּה כַמָּוֶת אַהֲבָה קָשָׁה כִשְׁאוֹל קִנְאָה
רְשָׁפֶיהָ רִשְׁפֵּי אֵשׁ שַׁלְהֶבֶתְיָה: מַיִם רַבִּים לֹא יוּכְלוּ לְכַבּוֹת אֶת־הָאַהֲבָה וּנְהָרוֹת
לֹא יִשְׁטְפוּהָ אִם־יִתֵּן אִישׁ אֶת־כָּל־הוֹן בֵּיתוֹ בָּאַהֲבָה בּוֹז יָבוּזוּ לוֹ:
אָחוֹת לָנוּ קְטַנָּה וְשָׁדַיִם אֵין לָהּ מַה־נַּעֲשֶׂה לַאֲחֹתֵנוּ בַּיּוֹם שֶׁיְּדֻבַּר־בָּהּ: אִם־
חוֹמָה הִיא נִבְנֶה עָלֶיהָ טִירַת כָּסֶף וְאִם־דֶּלֶת הִיא נָצוּר עָלֶיהָ לוּחַ אָרֶז: אֲנִי
חוֹמָה וְשָׁדַי כַּמִּגְדָּלוֹת אָז הָיִיתִי בְעֵינָיו כְּמוֹצְאֵת שָׁלוֹם: כֶּרֶם הָיָה לִשְׁלֹמֹה
בְּבַעַל הָמוֹן נָתַן אֶת־הַכֶּרֶם לַנֹּטְרִים אִישׁ יָבִא בְּפִרְיוֹ אֶלֶף כָּסֶף: כַּרְמִי שֶׁלִּי לְפָנָי
הָאֶלֶף לְךָ שְׁלֹמֹה וּמָאתַיִם לְנֹטְרִים אֶת־פִּרְיוֹ: הַיּוֹשֶׁבֶת בַּגַּנִּים חֲבֵרִים מַקְשִׁיבִים
לְקוֹלֵךְ הַשְׁמִיעִנִי: בְּרַח | דּוֹדִי וּדְמֵה־לְךָ לִצְבִי אוֹ לְעֹפֶר הָאַיָּלִים עַל הָרֵי בְשָׂמִים:

Bibliography
Books of the Bible

Bereishis / Genesis
Shemos / Exodus
Vayikrah / Leviticus
Bamidbar / Numbers
Devarim / Deuteronomy
Joshua
Shoftim / Judges
Melachim / Kings
Isaiah
Jeremiah
Ezekiel
Hoshea / Hosea
Joel
Amos
Ovadiah / Obadiah

Zefaniah
Michah
Chaggai / Haggai
Zechariah
Malachi
Tehillim / Psalms
Mishley / Proverbs
Iyov / Job
Shir Hashirim / Song of Songs
Eichah / Lamentations
Koheles / Ecclesiastes
Esther
Daniel
Nechemiah / Nehemiah
Divrey Hayamim / Chronicles

Talmudic and Midrashic Sources

Mishnayos / Brachos, Pesachim, Avos, Midos
Talmud, Babyl. / Brachos, Shabbos, Pesachim,
    Beitzah, Rosh Hashanah, Megillah, Nedarim,
    Sotah, Sanhedrin, Avodah Zarah, Menachos
Talmud, Yerush. / Pesachim, Rosh Hashanah, Taanis
Tosefta / Pesachim, Megillah
Avos de Rabbi Nosson
Pirkey de Rabbi Eliezer
Mechilta / Tannaitic Midrash to Shemos
Midrash Hagadol
Midrash Rabbah

Midrash Tehillim / (also called: **Shocher Tov**)
Midrash Shocher Tov
Sifri / Tannaitic Midrash to Bamidbar, Devarim
Tanchuma
Tanna d'Bey Eliyahu
Yalkut / Yalkut Shimoni / R. Shimon of Frankfurt /
    13th century / anthology of Talmudic and
    Midrashic comments on the Bible
Zohar
Midrash Haneelam / part of the Zohar
Targum Jonathan

Earlier Rabbinic Sources
(Until the end of the 16th Century of the common era)

Many of the dates given are approximate or are the subject of controversy. Generally, those
works of an author are mentioned from which the material quoted in the Haggadah is drawn.

In the alphabetical arrangement, Rabbi or Rav (R.) is disregarded, and so is Haggadah (H.), but
not Rabbeinu. Also, the first name is disregarded wherever there is a family or other second
name.

Abarbanel / Rabbi Yitzchak Abarbanel / H. Zevach
Pesach / 1437-1508
Rabbi Joseph Albo / Sefer Ha'ikkarim / d. 1420
Akeidas Yizchak / Rabbi Yitzchak Arama / 1420-
1494
Rabbi Shlomo Alkabetz / 1505-1584
Alshich / Rabbi Mosheh Alshich / Toras Moshe /
1508-1600
Rav Amram Gaon / Seder R. Arman / d. 875
Ari Hakadosh / Rabbi Yitzchak Luria / 1534-1572
Avudraham / Rabbi David Bar Yoseph Avudraham
/ fourteenth Cent.
Behag / Baal Halachos Gedolos / either Rabbi

Shimon of Kaira or Rabbi Yehudai Gaon /
8th Cent.
Besomim Rosh / responsa ascribed to Rosh / (see
Rosh)
Chovos Halevovos / R. Bachyah ibn Pakudah
Hadayan / 11th Cent.
Chukas Hapesach / Rabbi Mosheh Fisanti /16th
Cent.
Daas Zekeinim / Baaley Tosfos / 13th Cent.
Darkei Mosheh / See Remah
Haga'os Maimuni / Rabbi Meir Hacohen / 13th
Cent.
Rav Hai Gaon / d. 1038

SILVER PAGE

Mr. & Mrs. David Bassalali

Mr. & Mrs. Perry Greenberg

Chase Manhattan Bank

Mr. & Mrs. A. Schallamach

North Shore Hebrew Academy

Sisterhood Great Neck Synagogue

Mr. & Mrs. Howard Stackman

Mr. & Mrs. Henry Katz

Mr. & Mrs. Ben Klapper

Mr. & Mrs. Paul Weinberg

Mr. & Mrs. Samuel Goldberg

Patsy & Meyer Berman

Mr. & Mrs. Julie Berman

Mann, Judd, Landau C.P.A.

Golenbock & Barrell Foundation Inc.

Jean & Bob Batz

GOLD PAGE

Mr. & Mrs. Ezra Dabah

❧ ☙

Mr. & Mrs. Harold Domnitch

❧ ☙

Ellen & Martin Domnitch

❧ ☙

Lawrence Domnitch

❧ ☙

Mr. & Mrs. Mansour Rahmanan

Hamanhig / Rabbi Avraham bar Nosson HaYarchi / 13th Cent.

Ibn Ezra / Rabbi Avraham Ibn Ezra / 1092-1167

Rabbi Joseph Tov Elem (Bonfils) / 11th Cent.

Kolbo / either by R. Shmarya ben Simchah or R. Joseph ben Tuviah / ca. 1300

Lekach Tov (also called Pekista Zuta) / Rabbi Tuviah ben Eliezer / 11th Cent.

Levush / Rabbi Mordechai Yaffe / 1530-1612

Machzor Vitry / Rabbi Simcha of Vitry / early 12th Cent.

Maharal / Rabbi Yehuda Loew (Prague) / *Gevuros Hashem* / ca. 1520-1609

Maharam Rothenburg / Rabbi Meir of Rothenburg / 1220-1293

Maharil / Rabbi Yaakov Molin / 1365-1427

Maharsha / Rabbi Shmuel Eidelis (Ostrow) / 1555-1631

Maharshal / Rabbi Shlomo Luria / 1510-1573

Meiri / Rabbi Menachem haMeiri / *Bais Habechirah* / 1249-1315

Mizrachi / Rabbi Eliyahu Mizrachi / 1455-1526

Mordechai / Rabbi Mordechai ben Hillel / 1240-1298

Rav Natronai Gaon / d. 858

Ohr Zorua /Rabbi Yitzchak ben Mosheh (Vienna) / 1180-1260

Orchos Chayim / R. Aaron Hacohen (Lunel) / ca. 1300

Pesikta Zuta / See *Lekach Tov*

Rabbeinu Chananel / ca. 990-1056

Rabbeinu Bachya (ben Asher) / 1255-1340

Rabbeinu Jonah (Gerundi) / d. 1263

Rabbeinu Monoach / *Sefer Hamenuchah* / 13th Cent.

Rambam / Rabbi Mosheh ben Maimon / *Mishneh Torah* / 1135-1204

Ramban / Rabbi Mosheh ben Nachman / 1194-1270

Ran / Rabbenu Nissim Gerundi / 1340-1380

Rashbam / Rabbi Shmuel ben Meir / ca. 1085-1158

Rashbatz / Rabbi Shimon ben Zemach Duran / *H. Yavin Shemuah* / 1361-1444

Rashbo / Rabbi Shlomo ben Aderes / 1235-1310

Rashi / Rabbi Shlomo Yitzchaki / 1040-1105

Ravioh / Rabbi Elieser ben Joel Halevi / 1140-1225

Ravon / Rabbi Eliezer ben Nathan (Mayence) / d. after 1152

Remah / Rabbi Moshe Isserles / *Darkey Mosheh, Mappah* / 1520-1572

Rif / Rabbi Yitzchak Alfasi / 1013-1103

Rivta / Rabbi Yom Tov ben Ashbeli / early 14th Cent.

R'ma Mipanu / Rabbi Menachem Azaryah MiPanu / 1548-1620

Rokeach / Rabbi Eliezer ben Yehudah (Worms) / 1176-1238

Rosh / Rabbi Asher ben Yechiel / 1250-1327

Rav Saadiah Gaon / 892(?)-942

Rav Sherirah Gaon / 10th Cent.

Sefer Hachinuch / R. Aaron (?) Halevi of Barcelona / 13th Cent.

Sforno / Rabbi Ovadiah bar Yacov Sforno / 1470-1550

Shibolei Haleket / R. Zidkiah ben Abraham Harofeh / early 13th Cent.

Shloh / Rabbi Yeshayu Halevi Hurwitz / 1565-1630

Shulchan Aruch / Rabbi Joseph Karo / 1488-1575

Trumas Hadeshen / Rabbi Yisrael Isserlein (Neustadt) / 1390(?) 1460

Tosfos / Baaley Tosfos, Talmud Commentators / 11th to 13th Cent.

Tur / Rabbi Yaakov ben haRosh / 1270-1340

Rabbi Yehudah Halevi / *Kuzari* / 1075-1140(?)

Rav Zemach Gaon / d. 880

Later Rabbinic Sources
(From the 17th Century to our days)

Aruch Hashulchan / Rabbi Yechiel Mechel Epstein / 1830-1908

Ateres Zekeinim / Rabbi Menachem Mendl Auerbach / d. 1689

Bais Halevi / Rabbi Joseph Dov Halevi Soloveitchik (Brisk) / d. 1892

Rabbi Mordechai Benet / 1753-1829

Binah L'Itim / Rabbi Azariah Figo / 1579-1647

Birkey Yosef / see *Chidah*

B'ney Yisoschor / Rabbi Tzvi Elimelech of Dinov / d. 1841

Dr. Isacc Breuer / *Judenproblem* / 1882-1946

Brisker Rav / Rav Yitzchak Zev Halevi Soloveitchik / 1887-1959

Rabbi Bunim of Parshischa / 1765-1827

Chasam Sofer / Rabbi Mosheh Sofer / *Toras Mosheh* / 1762-1839

Chazon Ish / Rabbi Avraham Yeshaya Karelitz / 1878-1953

Chever Ma'amarim / Rabbi Yeruchem Levovitz (Mir) / d. 1936

Chidah / Rabbi Joseph Chayim David Azulai / *H. Simchas Haregel, Birkey Yosef* / 1724-1806

Chidushei haRim / Rabbi Yitzchak Meir of Gur / 1799-1866

Chochmah Im Nachalah / Rabbi H. Klein / 20th Cent.

Chok Yaakov / (see *Iyun Yaakov*)

Derech Hashem / See Rabbi Mosheh Chayim Luzzatto

Rabbi Elazar Fleckeles / H. Ma'aseh BeRabbi Eliezer / 1754-1826

Rabbi Eliezer Gordon (Telshe) / 1851-1910

Ha'amek Davar / See Netziv

Haksav Vehakabalah / Rabbi Yaacov Tzvi Mecklenburg (also: Iyun Tefillah) / 1785-1865

Hashir Vehashevach / Rabbi Zalman Sorotzkin / 1880-1966

Rabbi Wolf Heidenheim / Siddur Safah Berurah / 1757-1832

Rabbi Samson Raphael Hirsch / Nineteen Letters,Chumash and Tehillim Commentaries / 1808-1888

Rabbi David Zvi Hoffmann / Commentary to Devarim / 1843-1921

Iyun Yaakov / Rabbi Yaakov Reisher (Prague); also Chok Ya'akov / 17th Cent.

Iyun Tefillah / See Haksav Vehakabalah

Kedushas Levi / Rabbi Levi Yitzchak of Berditchev / 1740-1810

Rabbi Shlomo Kluger / Yeriyos Shlomo / 1783-1869

Rabbi Aaron Kotler / 1891-1962

Ksav Sofer / Rabbi Avraham Shmuel Binyamin Sofer / 1815-1871

Rabbi Marcus Lehmann / Hagaddah Shel Pesach / 1831-1890

Rabbi Levi Yitzchak of Berditshev / see Kedushas Levi

Rabbi Mosheh Chayim Luzzatto / Derech Hashem / 1707-1747

Ma'aseh Nissim / Rabbi Yaakov Lorberbaum (Lissa) / 1760-1832

Maggid of Dubno / R. Yaakov Kranz / 1741-1804

Malbim / Rabbi Meir Leibush Malbim / Haggadah, Chumash Commentary / 1809-1879

Mayana Shel Torah / Rabbi Alexander Zusha Friedman / 20th Cent.

Meshech Chochmah / Rabbi Meir Simcha Hacohen (Dvinsk) / (also: Ohr Someach) / 1843-1926

Michtav M'Eliyahu / Rabbi Eliyahu Eliezer Dessler / 1891-1954

Mishna Berura / Rabbi Yisroel Meir Kagan / (Chafetz Chaim) / 1838-1933

Netziv / Rabbi Naftali Zvi Yehuda Berlin (Volozhin) / Ha'amek Davar, H. Imrey Shefer / 1817-1893

Noam Elimelech / Rabbi Elimelech of Liszensk / 1717-1787

Ohr Hachayim / Rabbi Chaim ben Atar / 1696-1743

Ohr Some'ach / see Meshech Chochmah

Ohr Yesharim / Rabbi Yechiel Heller / 1814-1863

Rabbi Pinchas of Koretz / 1726-1791

Pri Megadim / Rabbi Joseph Tumim / 1727-1792

Sfas Emes / Rabbi Yehuda Aryeh Leib Alter of Gur / 1847-1905

Shaagas Aryeh / Rabbi Aryeh Leib ben Asher (Metz) / 1695-1785

Shaar Hashomayim / see Yaavetz

Rabbi Meir Shapiro / Lubliner Rav / 1887-1933

Shulchan Aruch Harav / Rabbi Schneur Zalman of Liady / 1747-1812

Siddur Avodas Israel / Seligman Baer / 1829-1897

Simchas Haregel / see Chidah

Rabbi Chayim Soloveitchik / 1853-1918

Reshash / Rabbi Shemuel Strashun / 1794-1872

Taz / Rabbi David Halevi bar Shmuel / Turei Zahav / 1586-1667

Toras Emes

H. Vayagidu LeMordechai

Vilna Gaon / Rabbi Eliyahu of Vilna / 1720-1797

Yad Chazakah / Rabbi Yaakov Piaskin / d. 1835

Yalkut Me'am Loez / Rabbi Yacov Kuli / 1689-1732

H. Yalkut Tov / Rabbi Eliyahu Kitov / 20th Cent.

Yaavetz / Rabbi Yaakov Emden / Siddur Shaar Hashamayim / 1698-1776

Contemporary Rabbinic Sources

Rabbi Dr. Joseph Breuer / Der Prophet Jecheskel

Rabbi Moshe Feinstein / Kol Rom

Rabbi Isaac Hutner / Pachad Yitzchak

Rabbi Yaakov Kamenetzky

Lubavitch Haggadah / Rabbi M. M. Schneersohn (Admur of Lubavitch)

Rabbi H. Biberfeld / Essay in Hamayan

H. Mishibud Lige'ulah / Rabbi Chayim Nussbaum

H. Moadim Uzmanim / Rabbi Mosheh Sternbuch

Rabbi E. Munk / World of Prayer

Rabbi J. Myski / Haggadah

Out of the Iron Furnace / Rabbi Eliezer Ben David

Vayaged Mosheh / Rabbi Chayim Yehudah Katz

Rabbi Avrohom Wolf / Ha'oros Lehaggadah, essay in Diglenu

CHILDREN'S PAGE

Rivka & Borach Morganstern
Adam Katsals
Jason & Andrew Magida
Jaime & Shira Mittleman
Zachary Evan
Adena Machnikoff
Daniella Machnikoff
Zehava Machnikoff
Deborah, Gabrielle, Aviva,
Efrem, Joshua & Adam Klapper

Thank You

The Great Neck Synagogue wishes to thank Dr. Ed Parver, Robert Spitalnick, Perry Greenberg, Ezra Dabah, Mansour Rahmanan, Mina Kotler, and Florence Hoffman for their untiring efforts.

DONORS

The Dime Savings Bank
Chadwick Hardware
C.L.C. Communications
L.I. Mat Company
Bestall Chemical
Jad Corp
Peerless Waterproofing
Skillman Plumbing
U.S. Inc.
Dr. & Mrs. Ronald Glaser
Smirlock & Unger
Eisenberg Sons Carpentry
Alex Coleman
Brian Corcoran
North Shore Abstract
Rabbi & Mrs. M. Scholar
Acct. Statistics
Signalert
Lou G. Siegel
Joe Eisenberger
Pearl Diskin
Evvco Ent. Inc.
Mr. & Mrs. Shelley Goren
Carlson & Carlson
Levean Int.
Nassimi
Fred Moheban
Rug Renovating Co.
Hav Int. Frght Corp.
Dr. I. Kornberg
Scobee Grill
Park Avenue Cleaners
Nassau North Funeral Chapels
Middleneck Pharmacy
Manhasset Skin Care
La Pace
Custom Mental Crafters
Millies Place
Mr. & Mrs. Harry Loewenstein

Penstral Enterprises
Kagel Furs
Crossman Cadillac
A & M Fruit
Atti Rest
House of Trimmings
Gel Kosher Meats
Gertrude Yusen
North Shore Auto
Navona Restaurant
Charles Goodman
J 2H Toys Inc.
Kings Kosher Bakery
Lifetime Photographers
Kensington Deli
Jewelers of Bond St
North Shore Hardware
Best Tire
Nu Clear Cleaners
Ren Rob Fabrics
Empire Fuel Corp.
Dr. & Mrs. Martin Ehrenberg
Sid Hall
Dr. Joseph Schein
Dr. & Mrs. L. Gordonson
Mr. & Mrs. Zachary Dicker
Mr. & Mrs. C. Zarucki
Dr. & Mrs. A. Adler
Dr. & Mrs. L. Kahn
Cecilia & David Klein
Dr. & Mrs. L. Zackheim
Mr. & Mrs. M. Henis
Mr. & Mrs. Leo Kaminer
Mr. & Mrs. M. Klapper
Royal Grimm
Mr. & Mrs. A. Pariser
Drive in Construction Inc.
M. Robert Kohler
Pearl Diskin LTD. Reality

SPONSORS

Mr. & Mrs. Danny Arbusman
Mr. & Mrs. Allan Bachman
Mr. & Mrs. Rose Baim
Mr. & Mrs. Moussa Banilevi
Mr. Anthony & Dr. Elena Berkowitz
Mr. & Mrs. David Birnbaum
Mr. & Mrs. Gershon Bodner
Mr. & Mrs. Ronald Braun
Dr. & Mrs. Martin Brownstein
Mr. & Mrs. Morris Chalfin
Mr. & Mrs. Moosa Ebrahimian
Dr. & Mrs. Martin Edelstein
Mr. & Mrs. Stanley Fischer
Mr. & Mrs. Irving Forman
Dr. & Mrs. Mark Gersten
Dr. & Mrs. Ronald Golden
Mr. & Mrs. Benny Hakimi
Mr. & Mrs. Abraham Hedaya
Mr. & Mrs. Michael Hoenig
Mr. & Mrs. Lionel Hope
Mr. & Mrs. Sidney Ingber
Mr. & Mrs. Stuart Kaufman
Mr. & Mrs. David Kordvani
Mr. & Mrs. Herman Kotler
Dr. & Mrs. Philip Lanzkowsky
Mr. & Mrs. Leo Lieberman
Mr. & Mrs. Ira Lubin
Mr. & Mrs. Kenneth Magida
Mr. & Mrs. Steven Mayer
Dr. & Mrs. Myles Mittleman
Dr. & Mrs. Samuel Movsas
Mr. & Mrs. Robert Newhouse
Dr. & Mrs. Edward Parver
Mr. & Mrs. Nasser Rahmanan
Mr. & Mrs. Nathan Rosenblatt
Dr. & Mrs. Raymond Sandler
Mr. & Mrs. Charles Sassoon
Cantor & Mrs. L. Schulman
Mr. & Mrs. Nasser Shaer
Mr. & Mrs. Abraham Sigman
Mr. & Mrs. Leon Silverman
Mr. & Mrs. Martin Sokol
Mr. & Mrs. Jonas Steigman
Dr. & Mrs. Ephraim Wolf
Republic Elevator

Mr. & Mrs. Moussa Aziz
Mr. & Mrs. Seymour Bader
Mr. & Mrs. Laftolla Banilevi
Mr. & Mrs. Hal Beretz
Mr. & Mrs. Aaron Bernstein
Mr. & Mrs. Gabriel Blau
Mr. & Mrs. Ignatz Brand
Dr. & Mrs. Melvin Breite
Mr. & Mrs. Ruby Cassel
Mr. & Mrs. William Davis
Mr. & Mrs. Herbert Eckstein
Dr. & Mrs. Martin Ehrenberg
Dr. & Mrs. Herschel Flax
Dr. & Mrs. Jeffrey Freedman & David
Mr. & Mrs. Joseph Gil
Mr. & Mrs. Martin Groob
Mr. & Mrs. Farhad Hakimian
Mr. & Mrs. Robert Heller
Mr. & Mrs. Murry Honig
Mr. & Mrs. Gedale Horowitz
Mr. & Mrs. Leslie Kahn
Mr. & Mrs. Ben Kornreich
Mr. & Mrs. Ephraim Kordvani
Mr. & Mrs. Abraham Krieger
Mr. & Mrs. Samuel Levitt
Mr. & Mrs. Jack Lipsky
Mr. & Mrs. Philip Machnikoff
Mr. & Mrs. Sidney Mauthner
Mr. & Mrs. Joshua Miller
Mr. & Mrs. Milton Mitzner
Mr. & Mrs. Yousef Nassimi
Dr. & Mrs. Seymour Olshin
Rabbi & Mrs. Dale Polakoff
Mr. & Mrs. Yosef Razon
Mr. & Mrs. Irving Roshwalb
Mr. & Mrs. Albert Safdieh
Mr. & Mrs. Arno Schallamach
Mr. & Mrs. Aaron Seligson
Mr. & Mrs. Nasser Chafieian
Mr. & Mrs. Howard Silberstein
Mr. & Mrs. Israel Slochowsky
Mr. & Mrs. Robert Spitalnick
Mr. & Mrs. David Wagner
Mr. & Mrs. Steven Zuckerman
Colonial Roofing

GUARDIAN PAGE

Mr. & Mrs. Martin Goldman

Mr. & Mrs. Irwin Hochberg

Mr. & Mrs. Michael Kon

Dr. & Mrs. George Miner

Mr. & Mrs. S. Springfield

Mr. & Mrs. Henry Schwartz

Mr. & Mrs. Howard Silberstein

Mr. & Mrs. Manny Strulovic

Mr. & Mrs. Joseph Zollo

Alley Pod Nursery

E.S.M. Construction

Panor Corporation

Mr. & Mrs. Charles Sassoon

Message from

Dr. Ephraim Wolf

Rabbi Emeritus

The Great Neck Synagogue will be honoring our First Couple Harold and Lorraine Domnitch. It is most appropiate that we read in this week's sedrah "Bo" of the first mitzvah given to the Jewish people that of sanctifying the new moon.

Fulfillment of this mitzvah was a prerequisite to their redemption. It teaches the Jewish people the importance of mastering and sanctifying time.

The moon is given the distinction of ushering in the first mitzvah because it is able to reflect the life giving properties of the sun.

So too our First Couple reflects the life sustaining light of Torah. They have Sanctified both time and environment by serving The North Shore Hebrew Academy and UJA to name a few.

Here then we have an inspiring description of the activities of Lorraine and Harold Domnitch, our guests of honor. Throughout their careers they have sought to build a home that would sanctify time and environment and radiate Jewish values. They have been involved in every phase of Synagogoue activity, Lorraine in the Sisterhood and Harold in the Congregation. They have sanctified their days by giving blocks of time to U.J.A., Bonds, North Shore Hebrew Academy, Yeshiva University, Soviet Jewry and more. They have always sought to reflect the light of Torah radiance to their surroundings. Who can forget their Succah gatherings, and the many parlor meetings in their home. They have extended themselves so many times and in so many ways to bring peace and harmony to the Congregation and to the community.

The entire community salutes them on the occasion of their being honored. This tribute is but a small measure of the appreciation and love they enjoy.

Elaine and I extend to them our prayers that they be blessed with good health and happiness, Simcha and Nachas from their children and family.

Dr. Ephraim Wolf
Rabbi Emeritus

Message from

Rabbi Dale Polakoff

Mora D'Asra of the
Great Neck Synagogue

Dear Friends:

We are very proud of our family tonight as we gather to honor two people who have worked diligently to ensure a sense of family in our Synagogue. Well known throughout the community for their acts of "ahavat Yisrael", they have given generously of their time and substance to the leadership of the Great Neck Synagogue. Committed to the idea that actions speak louder than words, they have set a standard for involvment in communal work and have encouraged others to follow that example.

Just as Moshe Rabeinu was hesitant to accept the responsibility of leading the Jewish people, so too do Lorraine and Harold evince a sense of humility and an awareness of the burden of responsibility. And just as God assured Moshe that Aharon would greet his acceptance of that responsibility with words of praise and gratitude to the Domnitch family, may we at the Synagogue be blessed with their presence and guidance for a long time to come.

Very cordially yours,

Rabbi Dale Polakoff

On this significant occasion, the annual dinner of the Great Neck Synagogue, it is most fitting that we have chosen to honor Mr. and Mrs. Harold Domnitch.

Their deep commitment to the Great Neck Synagogue, their selfless service and philanthropic spirit have constantly set an inspiring example to all.

Harold, President of the Great Neck Synagogue and Lorraine, an active member of Sisterhood have dedicated themselves to the growth and development of the Great Neck Community.

Their sons Martin and Lawrence stand as a mirror of their accomplishments. Both are active in their own Jewish affairs.

The tribute paid to Lorraine and Harold represents only a small token of affection and esteem with which they are regarded by all.